# THE CLASSICAL GUITAR

*"The guitar is a wonderful instrument which is understood by few."*

Schubert

*"The instrument most complete and richest in its harmonic and polyphonic possibilities."*

Manuel de Falla

*"I love the guitar for its harmony; it is my constant companion in all my travels."*

Nicolo Paganini

*"Nothing is more beautiful than a guitar, save perhaps two."*

Chopin

# THE CLASSICAL GUITAR

## ITS EVOLUTION

## AND

## ITS PLAYERS

## SINCE 1800

BY

MAURICE J. SUMMERFIELD

First Edition 1982

Second Edition 1991

 For information write to Ashley Mark Publishing Co., Olsover House, 43 Sackville Road, Newcastle-upon-Tyne NE6 5TA, United Kingdom.

FIRST EDITION MARCH 1982

SECOND EDITION MAY 1991

Typeset and printed in United Kingdom.

ISBN 1 872639 00 3 HARDBACK

ISBN 1 872639 01 1 PAPERBACK

# THE CLASSICAL GUITAR

## CONTENTS

*To My Wife, Tricia*

# THE CLASSICAL GUITAR

### *PREFACE TO THE FIRST EDITION*

I have long felt the need for a book dealing specifically with the classical guitar and its most important players and personalities since 1800. Those authors who have written books in past years about the history of the classical guitar have usually devoted a large section of their work to the lute, vihuela and early guitar. As a result in these books many important players and personalities, in particular contemporary classical guitarists, are not included or are given only a brief mention.

Since the publication of my first book, 'The Jazz Guitar – Its Evolution And Its Players' in 1978, it often occurred to me that the format I applied to this work would lend itself admirably to one on the classical guitar. Amongst the many enthusiastic letters I have received from guitarists all over the world about this first book, many of the writers supported this view. With their encouragement I began to write this book early in 1980. Originally I had hoped to complete the new work early in 1981 but the task proved much greater than I expected. The book was finally completed earlier this year and I am now satisfied that 'The Classical Guitar – Its Evolution and Its Players Since 1800' is currently the most complete and up-to-date work dealing with the modern classical guitar.

As with my book on the jazz guitar, one of the most important features of this new book is its very full listing of records, music and details of books and magazine articles. Most of the items detailed are still currently in production or print. Those which are not can be obtained with a little patience by using the Sources of Supply section at the back of the book. I have personally found that an advert placed in one or more of the specialist guitar magazines will often bring that elusive item. You will also be amazed, particularly if you live in a larger city, at what your local main library can offer. In regard to records you should remember that many items are available in different countries with different brands, sleeves and numbers, so be careful not to duplicate or be misled.

The collection of photographs in this book of classical guitarists, past and present, is I believe a unique one. It gives me really great pleasure to see such a collection under one cover and I wish to give special thanks to all those who have supplied them. Their contribution has been vital to the excellent illustration of this book.

I realise there is a possibility that some readers may feel that some other classical guitarists they know of and admire have been omitted. However, I have sincerely tried to include all those guitarists who I believe have made an impact on the evolution of the guitar in classical music since 1800. I have not included the many great guitarists who play the classical guitar but not classical music. Therefore Nashville stylists like Chet Atkins, Latin American virtuosos such as Baden Powell and Sebastião Tapajos, and jazz guitarists like Charlie Byrd and Lenny Breau are not included. I am aware that there are many fine classical guitarists throughout the world who may well deserve a place in future editions of this book but circumstances and events have not as yet allowed them to contribute in an effective way to the evolution of the classical guitar. Some of these guitarists that I have heard play in concert or on record, or know of, are illustrated in the appendix to the players' section of this book as a tribute to their ability and important contribution to the growth of today's classical guitar world.

*Maurice J. Summerfield, June 1982*

# THE CLASSICAL GUITAR

### *PREFACE TO THE SECOND EDITION*

The first edition of this book sold out within a few months of its publication in June 1982. My intention in 1983 was to correct the various errors in the first edition and release an updated second edition in the same year. My involvement in other matters, in particular the birth (in September 1982) and the subsequent monthly publication of Classical Guitar magazine, has meant that my original intention was delayed by about seven years. And what good job it was! In this relatively short period of time the classical guitar world has seen an explosion in the volume of world-class players emerging on the scene. Similarly the output of classical guitar scholarship and research, with its many publications and recordings, is unprecedented in the history of the instrument. As a result, this edition contains over one hundred and fifty new entries with all the original historical and other information updated on the evidence of the most recent research published by scholars all over the world. Also included in this edition is a chapter on the great flamenco guitarists of the twentieth century.

Without writing a book of encyclopaedic proportions it would be impossible for me to cover in any comprehensive way the enormous area now inhabited by the classical guitar. My selection has therefore been made according to my own feelings and beliefs, and to those who will inevitably criticise it on the grounds that certain (and no doubt numerous) names that have been omitted should have been included, I can only say that I agree wholeheartedly and wish that the book could have been big enough to encompass them all. Nevertheless I believe that it does give a clear outline of the classical guitar's development since 1800 in terms of its players, its composers, its constructors and the very many scholars and personalities who make up the history of this fascinating instrument.

My association with Classical Guitar magazine, now recognized internationally as the foremost magazine of its type, has of course helped me greatly in finalizing this second edition. In particular my special thanks must go to my friend and colleague Colin Cooper, the general editor of Classical Guitar magazine. Without his support, his many suggestions and encouragement, this new edition could not have been published in such a complete and accurate way.

The preface to my first edition of 'The Classical Guitar – Its Evolution and Its Players Since 1800', printed on the previous page, is still valid, with the exception of the last sentence in the second paragraph. It is this new, updated and enlarged edition which I now confidently believe is the most complete and up-to-date work dealing with the modern classical guitar.

*Maurice J. Summerfield, March 1991*

---

# ACKNOWLEDGEMENTS


George M. Bowden
Liz Beeson

CBS Records
Prof. Jaques Chaîné
Classical Guitar Magazine
Colin Cooper

Decca Records
John W. Duarte
Basil Douglas Ltd
Deutsche Grammophon

EMI Records
Eduardo Falu

Izydor Geffner
Gendai Guitar (Japan)
Gramofon AB BIS (Sweden)
Guitar Review

ICM Artists

Kallaway Ltd. (London)

Andrew Liepins

Mario Maccaferri
Jorge Morel
Matanya Ophee
M. Perott

Polydor Classics
Philips Records

Radio France
Thérèse Wassily Saba

Shaw Concerts
C. E. H. Smith
Richard Stover

T. Tazawa

Zen-On Music Co.

**All photographs are from the files of Classical Guitar magazine unless stated otherwise**

# THE CLASSICAL GUITAR

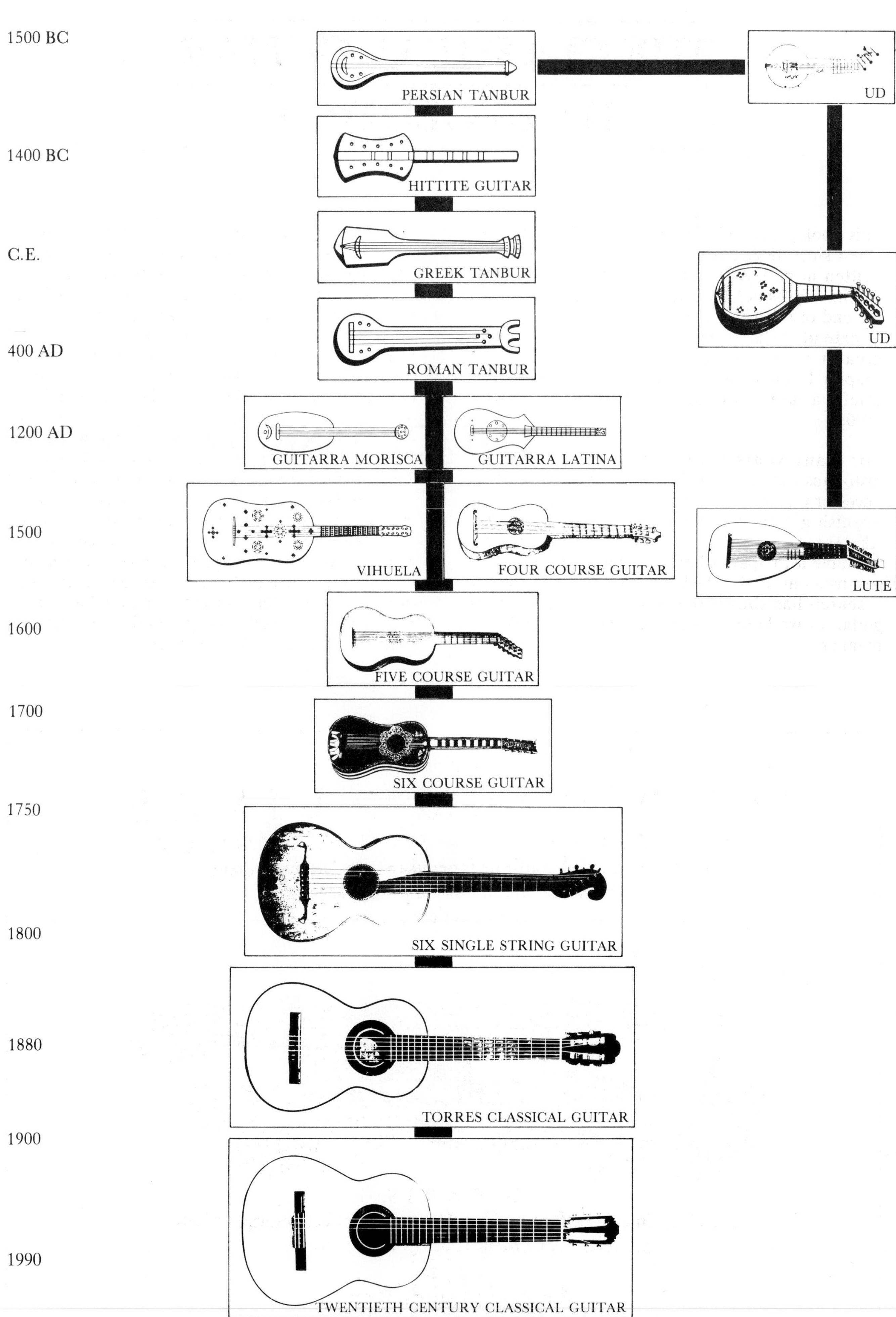


*Chart showing the evolution of the classical guitar as an instrument from 1500 BC to the present day*

# THE CLASSICAL GUITAR
# ITS EVOLUTION

This book deals with the evolution of the classical guitar since 1800. Many excellent books have been written in past years on the history of the guitar and its origins before that time. These are listed at the end of this chapter for those readers who wish to extend their research of this earlier period in greater detail. Nevertheless, as a start to this chapter I believe it necessary to make the reader briefly aware of the origins of the guitar before 1800.

For many years several guitar scholars and historians put forward the theory that the guitar's ancestor was the Persian ud. They claimed that the Spanish guitar gradually evolved from this lute-like instrument after the Moors brought the instrument to Spain when they invaded the Iberian peninsula around 711AD. However, more recent research has shown that the six-string classical guitar, as we know it today, evolved in a different manner.

The first guitar-like instrument on record is shown on a 1400BC archaeological object taken from the city gates of the new Hittite settlement at Alaja Huyuk. It shows a Hittite musician playing a long-necked guitar-shaped instrument rather than the more common tanbur. During this period of history the popular instrument of the region was the tanbur which, although having a fretted or marked neck, had a distinctive bowl-shaped body as opposed to the guitar shape of today. The word guitar itself is derived from two Persian words, tar – meaning string, and char – meaning four. Therefore char-tar stood for a four-stringed instrument. Many of these early stringed instruments originally had four strings. Over the years the name char-tar gradually evolved into the word guitarra in Spain and then into similar names throughout most of Europe. An exception was Portugal, where the word for a guitar has always been violão, derived from the Latin word fidicula (a small plucked fiddle-like instrument).

LE
TROYSIEME LIVRE
CONTENANT PLVSIEVRS DVOS, ET
Trios,auec la bataille de Ianequin a trois, nouuellement
mis en tabulature de Guiterne,par Simon
Gorlier, excellent ioueur.

A PARIS.
De l'Imprimerie de Robert GranIon & Michel Fezandat,au Mont
S. Hylaire,à l'Enſeigne des Grandz Ions.
1551.
Auec priuilege du Roy.

*Illustration of four course guitar in 1551 music book*

From these early tanburs/chartars emerged the Greek tanbur in 300BC. Later the Romans developed their own tanbur around 300AD. These instruments were both chartars, i.e. four-stringed instruments. It now seems absolutely certain that the Romans took their tanburs to the Iberian peninsula in 476AD, almost three centuries before the Moors' invasion of Spain, and it was this Roman tanbur that was later developed into the guitarra morisca and the guitarra latina. These were both guitar-like instruments, distinctly illustrated in the important historical document 'The Cantigas of Alfonso the Wise' in 1270AD. The guitarra latina had a flat back, as has the modern guitar, and the soundboard had one hole over which the strings passed. It was used for playing chords and was a forerunner of the vihuela. The guitarra morisca had a vaulted back, the fingerboard was large and the soundboard had several soundholes. It was used for the playing of melodies.

It was these instruments that later evolved into the aristocratic vihuela (a six double stringed instrument tuned GCFADG) which dominated the courts of Spain and Portugal during the sixteenth century. The four-course guitar (tuned CFAD – the same as the middle four strings of the vihuela) was used mainly by troubadours to accompany songs and dancing.

The ud, which had also evolved from early tanburs, eventually developed into the baroque lute (like the vihuela the original lutes were tuned GCFADG). This instrument became extremely popular in England, France, Italy and Germany during the seventeenth century. Although related to the early guitar, because of its similar origins, the lute really had little part in the evolution of the guitar. Nevertheless the technique required to play both fretted instruments had many similarities, with each instrument's strings laid out in courses (that is, pairs of strings tuned either in octaves or unison) and with similar tuning.

Both these instruments were fretted – fret is derived from the old French word ferreté, meaning 'banded with iron'. The frets on early instruments, unlike the metal frets of the modern guitar, were made of gut and tied around the neck. The lute and vihuela had ten or eleven frets, whereas the early guitar had between four and eight. The number was dependent on whether the guitar was to be used for melody or the strumming of chords. A great deal of the music originally written for the lute and vihuela in later years became successfully transcribed for the six-string classical guitar, and now forms a valuable part of its repertory.

The period of musical history from 1400BC to 1800AD saw a vast multitude of plucked string

COURTESY: RCA RECORDS

*Julian Bream playing a Renaissance lute*

*An interesting illustration from Pablo Minguet's "Modo de taner todos los instrumentos mejores" (Method of Playing All the Best Instruments) published in Madrid 1752*

instruments evolving first in the Middle East, Asia and the Far East. Later, in Europe, the Greeks and Romans had, as well as their tanburs, the harp-like lyra and kithara. It seems likely that the kithara, originally a four-stringed hand harp, also derived its name from the Persian words char-tar. In India the sitar, surbahar and tampura were popular stringed instruments. The Chinese had their p'i p'a and the Japanese their samisen. There is little doubt that all these early instruments are distant relatives of the guitar, sharing with it their origin in the tanbur (sometimes mistakenly called the nefer). In the sixteenth century many versions of the lute also appeared. The chittarone and theorbo lutes were two of the more popular versions of this aristocratic descendant of the Persian ud. The citterne, a mixture of the lute and four-course guitar, also appeared in the sixteenth century, as did the first mandolins in Italy. Many of these had six courses of strings, but as the eighteenth century drew to a close the four-course mandolin, as it is known today, became established. As most of these early fretted string instruments fell into disuse and became museum pieces the mandolin remained one of the few to survive in the guitar-dominated nineteenth and twentieth centuries.

In Europe both the lute and the vihuela gradually fell into disuse towards the end of the seventeenth century. The lute suffered from the addition of more and more strings so that it became virtually impossible to master (and also to tune). When the tuning of the four-course guitar changed to DGBE and a fifth course (low A) was added, the vihuela began to lose its popularity. The addition of this fifth string on the four-course guitar is often accredited to the Spanish poet and musician Vicente Espinel (1551-1624). By the time the six-string guitar came into being towards the end of the eighteenth century the vihuela was extinct.

It is not known exactly when the sixth string was added to the guitar but most historians agree it happened around 1780, and probably almost simultaneously in Italy and Germany. (Some scholars now suggest it could have developed in France (the term chitarra francesca being employed by the Italians to speak of single-string instruments, regardless of the number of strings). The German luthier Jakob August Otto has often been credited to be the first person to make a six-string guitar, adding its lower E, around 1790. But it now seems probable that the first six-single-string guitars were being made in Italy a little after the middle of the eighteenth century.

By 1800 most countries of Europe had given up the five- and six-course guitar in favour of the six single-string guitar. In Russia a seven-string guitar was developed by the guitarist Andrei Ossipovitch Sychra (1772-1850). This was tuned DGBDGBD, and was to remain very popular for many years in that part of the world. The noted Italian composer Luigi Boccherini (1743-1805) had given the 'new'

*Frontispiece of Luys Milan's "El Maestro", a collection of vihuela music, which was published in Valencia, Spain in 1535. It shows Orpheus playing a six course vihuela*

guitar its first taste of musical 'respectability' by adapting several of his finest quintets to include a part for guitar. This he did in Spain under the patronage of the Marquis de Benavente, an enthusiastic amateur guitarist, around 1790. By 1800 several virtuosos of the six-string classical guitar were beginning to emerge in various parts of Europe, and the first golden age of the classical guitar was about to begin.

This golden age of the guitar began simultaneously in Spain and Italy around 1775. The appearance of the first six-single-string guitars coincided at the beginning of the nineteenth century with another important development in the internal construction of the instrument, fan strutting. This is the term used for the strips of wood attached in a particular manner to the back of the soundboard of the guitar. These strips not only help to distribute the sound waves along the soundboard, but also reinforce the soundboard, enabling it to be thinner and so able to vibrate more freely. In time there would be many variations and extensions of fan strutting, but there is no doubt that even these early simplified versions were an important innovation. The years 1800 to 1980 were to see a gradual development of the instrument in three main areas. These were the guitarist's technique, the guitar's repertory and the construction of the instrument. These parallel developments began in Spain, and to a lesser exent in Italy, at the end of the eighteenth century. Towards the end of the nineteenth century there would be a period of decline in the progress and popularity of the guitar as it became overshadowed by orchestral and keyboard instruments. It was again in Spain at the end of the nineteenth century that the evolution of the classical guitar would be given an enormous boost by the luthier Antonio de Torres Jurado and the virtuoso guitarist Francisco Tárrega.

Torres, inspired originally by the virtuoso guitarist Julián Arcas, had developed a larger bodied guitar with advanced fan strutting and a wider fingerboard. It was with this new version of the instrument that Francisco Tárrega developed a new playing technique which would eventually make musicians aware of the enormous potential of the guitar. His work was to be extended in the first half of the twentieth century by more Spanish guitarists, in particular Andrés Segovia. It was Segovia who, against extreme opposition, would embark upon a worldwide crusade lasting for almost eighty years to promote the instrument. This crusade was eventually to be successful, and today the guitar has become one of the most popular classical instruments, with a repertory of available music that approaches in quantity and in quality that of any other instrument.

Towards the end of the eighteenth century a well-known organist, Father Basilio, a monk of the Citeaux order, turned his full attention to the guitar. He developed a fine solo technique on the

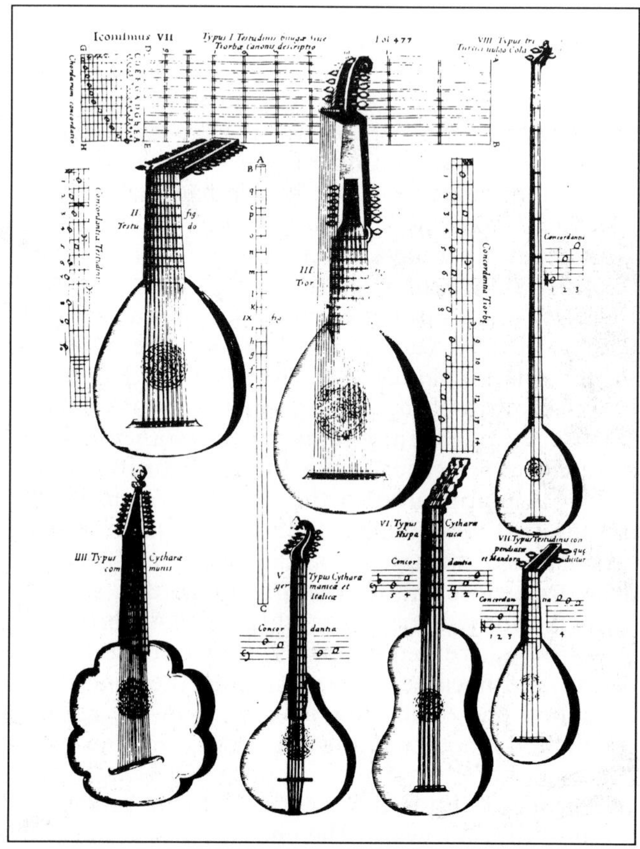

*A variety of stringed instruments, including a five course guitar (named Cythara Hispanica), from Athanasius Kircher's "Musurgia Universalis" published in Rome 1650*

instrument and his virtuosity became widely recognised in Spain. He was asked to play for Charles IV of Spain, and later he was to become tutor to Queen Marie Louise. Basilio, whose real name was Miguel Garcia, influenced two other important eighteenth century guitarists, Fernando Ferrandiere and Don Federico Moretti. In 1799 Ferrandiere published his method for the six-string guitar in modern notation, 'Arte de tocar la Guitarra Española', and Moretti published his 'Principios para tocar la guitarra de seis ordenes'. It has been suggested by some scholars that both these works drew upon an earlier work, published in 1780, 'Obra para Guitarra del sexsto orden, by the guitarist Antonio Ballesteros.

It was these men who laid the foundations in Spain for a nineteenth century revival of the guitar which would be completed by two of Spain's greatest exponents of the six-single-string guitar, Fernando Sor (1778-1839) and Dionisio Aguado (1784-1849). These two brilliant musicians led very active careers of concertizing and teaching. Both lived for a good part of their lives in Paris, then as now one of Europe's most important centres for music and the arts. Sor in fact died in Paris; Aguado returned to Spain to spend his last years in his native city Madrid. Both men were prolific composers and their music still remains an integral part of the twentieth century guitarist's repertoire. Sor was the greater and more prolific composer of the two, but Aguado's books, in particular his New Guitar Method, made an unparalleled contribution to the learning of the guitar in the nineteenth century.

Dionisio Aguado was also the inventor of the tripodison, an unusual guitar accessory devised to hold the guitar rather than resting it on the right thigh. However, this invention did not achieve any lasting success. Both Sor and Aguado published important guitar methods which, over the years, were translated into several languages and are still used to this day.

It is interesting to note the variation in these two great guitarists' right-hand technique. Whilst both agreed on the 'tirando' stroke to pluck the strings (that is, the right-hand fingers rise after plucking the string as against 'apoyando' in which the fingers continue past the string to rest on the string below), Aguado advocated the use of the fingernails whereas Sor used the pads of his right-hand fingertips. Nineteenth century guitarists were divided on this matter, and the controversy has continued to the present day. At the beginning of the twentieth century Francisco Tárrega advocated the right-hand 'no nail' technique, and this method of plucking the strings was continued by Emilio Pujol among several other important guitarists. The vast majority of twentieth century players

*Portrait of Francesco Corbetta on music "Varii Scherzi di Sonate Per La Chittara Spagnola" published Brussels, Belgium 1648*

have followed the use of the nails as advocated by Andrés Segovia (and by Miguel Llobet) from the early 1920s.

The early part of the nineteenth century saw many fine guitarists, but two are regarded as being the most outstanding: Fernando Sor from Spain and, from Italy, Mauro Giuliani (1778-1829). Little is known of Giuliani's early musical background, but on his arrival in Vienna in 1806 musicians soon became aware that he was a guitarist/composer extraordinary. He associated with and became the friend of many other fine musicians in the Austrian capital, including Beethoven, Hummel, Diabelli, Moscheles and Mayseder. Giuliani has the distinction of having had the first guitar magazine in English, 'The Giulianiad', named in his honour. It was published in London in the early 1830s by the German-born guitarist Ferdinand Pelzer. Vienna, where Giuliani made his home, was one of the great European centres for the arts, music and the guitar at the beginning of the nineteenth century. It was also the home of several other important and influential guitarists including Simon Molitor (1766-1848) and Johann Kaspar Mertz (1806-1856) as well as guitar makers like Johann Staufer.

Two other important and influential Italian guitarists were Matteo Carcassi (1792-1853) and Ferdinando Carulli (1770-1841). Although not of the stature of Giuliani, Carcassi and Carulli were prolific composers and contributed greatly to the nineteenth century repertory for the guitar. All three Italian guitarists performed widely throughout Europe. Whereas Giuliani made Vienna his home and centre of work, Carulli and Carcassi chose Paris.

Other important nineteenth century guitarists were Giulio Regondi (1822-1874) and Napoléon Coste (1806-1883) from France, Luigi Legnani (1790-1877) and Zani de Ferranti (1802-1878) from Italy, and Don A. F. Huerta (1805-1875) and Julián Arcas (1832-1882) from Spain. In Russia Andreas O. Sychra (1772-1852) and Nicolas Makarov (1810-1890) were also important figures in the development of the guitar. The Italian violinist Nicoló Paganini (1782-1840) was also a virtuoso guitarist and composed several important pieces for the instrument.

An important feature of the evolution of the instrument in the early years of the nineteenth century, and one which has continued to this day, was the co-operation between the guitarist and the guitar maker in improving the quality of sound and volume of the instrument. Fernando Sor worked closely with René François Lacôte in France and Louis Panormo in London, Luigi Legnani worked with Staufer, and towards the end of the century Julián Arcas was instrumental in developing the larger-bodied classical guitar with Antonio de Torres Jurado in Spain.

Although after 1860 the guitar continued to have a few outstanding soloists, its acceptance in most musical circles as a serious musical instrument began to decline. There were several reasons for this. Despite the large output of compositions by guitarists themselves, the instrument's repertory was limited because none of the great composers had written for it. Hector Berlioz (1803-1869) and Franz Schubert (1797-1828) were both guitarists, but with the exception of a few songs written with a guitar accompaniment by Schubert and a few simple studies by Berlioz, neither wrote for the guitar. Although Coste had begun to transcribe the baroque music of Robert de Visée in the 1830s, little of the excellent music of past centuries, written for the lute, vihuela and guitar had at that time been transcribed for the six-string instrument. With the exception of the compositions of Sor and Giuliani, the quality of most guitar music did not compare with the vast library of fine music available for other instruments. The use of the guitar in folk music, accompanying singers and dancers (as in flamenco), and in other popular forms of music lowered further the estimation of the guitar in the eyes of the vast majority of serious musicians and music teachers throughout Europe. These prejudices against the guitar lasted for many years and even today still linger on in some areas of the classical music world. The original nineteenth century small-bodied guitars also suffered from a lack of volume which hindered their use when played in company with other instruments.

*Francisco Tárrega*

It was the great Spanish guitarist Francisco Tárrega (1854-1909) who was to set the guitar back on an illustrious and firm course. Originally a talented pianist, he won first prize for harmony and composition at the Conservatory of Madrid. He began to play the guitar as a child and continued to develop his technique on the instrument throughout his conservatory career. It was Julián Arcas (1832-1882) who had originally encouraged the luthier Antonio Torres to make a wider-bodied guitar with a wider neck, and subsequently Torres developed and improved the pattern of fan strutting, also paying close attention to the type of bridge referred to by Aguado in his Escuela of 1825. Tárrega realised that to play this new guitar with its larger body and different shape, the techniques applied to the earlier and smaller guitars would have to be altered. Carulli and Molino were using footstools as early as 1810, but it was the custom to rest the instrument on the right thigh, with the right hand supported by placing the little finger on the table of the guitar between soundhole and bridge. Carulli and his fellow countryman Molino, who also lived in Paris, were advocates of this position, although we find Aguado in his Method saying that 'In no way will one rest the little finger on the table, or any other finger, because the hand must remain free and nimble'.

Guitarists of the period would also sometimes bring the thumb of their left hand over the edge of the neck to finger bass notes, and the strings seem to have been plucked more with the 'tirando' stroke than with the 'apoyando'stroke, although both strokes must be as old as the instrument itself.

Tárrega found that the larger-bodied Torres guitar needed to be rested on the left thigh, the player's leg slightly raised by the use of a footstool. The raised fingerboard made resting the little finger on the soundboard impracticable, and the abandonment of that particular technique paved the way for a closer examination of 'apoyando' technique. The wider neck meant firm rules for the placement of the fingers on the fingerboard.

Tárrega also made a significant contribution to the evolution of the modern classical guitar by extending its repertory. He not only composed a quantity of delightful original pieces and studies for the instrument, but also extended the art of transcribing for the guitar music originally written for other instruments, as Carulli, Matiegka, Giuliani, de Fossa, Heeser, Schuster and many others had done earlier in the nineteenth century. Tárrega's transcriptions of Bach, Beethoven, Mozart, Schubert, Haydn, Albéniz and Granados are a delight to hear and play. His many public performances of these transcriptions and original compositions did much to bring the guitar to prominence once again. Although he did give many concerts in several European countries,

*A Nineteenth century cartoon of an imaginary 'battle' between supporters of Carulli and Molino*

including France, Italy and England, he was not fond of travelling and preferred to stay in Spain. As a result his influence was not as great as it possibly could have been had he extended his public performances to more countries.

With the approach of the twentieth century the second and the greatest golden age of the classical guitar was beginning to dawn. As it had been Spain that had laid the foundation of the nineteenth century classical guitar, so it was Spain once again that contributed so greatly to the twentieth century guitar through the work of Tárrega, the founder of the modern guitar school, and Torres, the father of modern guitar construction.

Early in the twentieth century Emilio Pujol (1886-1980) and Miguel Llobet (1878-1938), two of Tárrega's pupils, travelled widely and gained new audiences for the guitar both in Europe and in America, yet it was to be another Spanish guitarist, Andrés Segovia (1893-1987), who would lead the classical guitar into its greatest years.

A self-taught guitarist, Andrés Segovia's great musical talent was recognized at an early age. He disregarded the advice of other Spanish classical musicians to change to a 'more serious' musical instrument and dedicated himself to establishing the guitar worldwide as an instrument equal to any other classical instrument. He decided that this could only be done by presenting the guitar in concert to as many audiences as possible and by extending its repertory. This he did with tireless energy for almost eighty years. Few would deny that his success in achieving these goals went far beyond his wildest dreams.

There are few countries in the world in which Segovia did not appear in concert. Everywhere his audiences were astounded not only by his incredible musicianship but also by the scope of the guitar in the hands of a master. It was in the early 1920s when Segovia began his campaign to encourage prominent composers to write for the guitar. His pleas were first answered by Joaquín Turina (1882-1949) and Federico Moreno Torroba (1891-1982) in 1924. In fact the first great composer of modern times to have written for the guitar was Manuel de Falla (1876-1946), who in 1920 composed Homenaje pour le tombeau de Claude Debussy, thus fulfilling an early promise to Miguel Llobet.

Segovia never let up in his campaign to enlarge the guitar's repertory. He also made many transcriptions of fine music originally written for other instruments. Within a relatively short period the guitar gained a vast library of original works. Other important composers who have written especially for the guitar as a direct result of Segovia's instigation are Joaquín Rodrigo (1902), Manuel Ponce (1886-1948), Mario Castelnuovo-Tedesco (1895-1968), Alexandre Tansman (1897-1986) and Heitor Villa-Lobos (1887-1959).

Segovia also continued the tradition of early nineteenth century guitarists by working with guitar makers to improve the quality of sound and the volume for the instrument. He worked first with the Ramirez family, and subsequently with Hauser and Fleta. He was also instrumental in the development of the nylon guitar string with the luthier Albert Augustine in 1947. This development was an enormous step forward in the evolution of the guitar.

The years from 1930 to 1990 have seen the rise of many outstanding guitarists in most countries of the world. Although there were variations in certain aspects of the technical approach, for example the 'no nail' technique versus nails, using the right-hand side of the nails or the left-hand side of the nails to pluck the strings, the great majority of guitarists have followed the technique of the instruments as developed by Tárrega and refined by Segovia.

In France, Ida Presti (1924-1967) was recognized as a child prodigy in the 1930s, and later with Alexandre Lagoya (1929) formed their guitar duo, undoubtedly one of the greatest of all time. Many great guitarists have also appeared in Spain after Pujol, Llobet and Segovia. Regino Sainz de la Maza in the 1930s was followed in more recent times by Narciso Yepes, José Tomás, Angel Romero and Pepe Romero.

In Britain two great guitarists appeared in the 1950s and 1960s. Julian Bream and John Williams both continued and extended the Segovia tradition

*Miguel Llobet with admirers. Left to right, standing: Severino Garcia Fortea, unknown, Juan del Moral Parras. Seated: A son of Tarrega, Andrés Segovia, Miguel Llobet, another of Tarrega's sons.*

COURTESY OF C. E. H. SMITH

*Andrés Segovia, 1959*

in a magnificent way, yet each has departed from it on occasion and in his own fashion: Julian Bream becoming a major figure in the revival of the Renaissance lute and its music; John Williams instigating a fusion of classical and rock music with his commercially successful group 'Sky'.

In South America during the 1920s and 1930s Agustín Barrios Mangoré was the outstanding guitar virtuoso and composer. Nevertheless Segovia still proved, after his various concert tours there, to be the most lasting influence on guitarists in more recent generations. Maria Luisa Anido, an early pupil of Miguel Llobet, has continued this tradition and has been the teacher to many of the great guitarists originating in South America in recent years. In more recent times the world has seen many more great guitarists emerge. Italy has produced Oscar Ghiglia. In the United States, Vahdah Olcott Bickford and William Foden were two of the most influential guitarists at the beginning of the twentieth century, and in more recent years Christopher Parkening, David Tanenbaum and Eliot Fisk. From Cuba Manuel Barrueco, Rey de la Torre and Leo Brouwer; from Austria Konrad Ragossnig; from Japan Akinobu Matsuda and Kazuhito Yamashita; from Czechoslovakia Vladimir Mikulka; from the Soviet Union Alexander Frauchi; from Scotland David Russell. These are only a few of the most outstanding players of the twentieth century. The chart on page 20 shows in detail the most important classical guitarists from 1800 to 1980.

Wherever he went Segovia not only encouraged prominent composers to write for the guitar but also made a point of approaching music conservatories, colleges and universities to establish a seat for the classical guitar. At the beginning of the twentieth century the guitar was not accepted in any of these institutions, although the Guildhall School of Music in London had appointed a professor of guitar as early as 1887 – Giulia Pelzer, sister of Madame Sidney Pratten. Today there are very few departments of music education which do not include the guitar in their curriculum and who do not have a professor of guitar.

Andrés Segovia was without doubt the most important classical guitar figure of the twentieth century. There is not a classical guitarist today who does not owe a direct debt to his almost superhuman efforts which, more than any others, have led to the establishment of the instrument worldwide.

The classical guitar currently rides on the crest of a wave of popularity and growth, but what of the future? Recent years have seen the development of the ten-string guitar played by Narciso Yepes, who also instigated its production. José Tomás plays and advocates an eight-string guitar, as does the Belgian guitarist Raphaëlla Smits, who has helped to promote the instrument through her recordings of music by Mertz and Coste. A seven-string guitar (with an extra string above the high E rather than a low D) has been developed. In Sweden, Göran Söllscher plays an alto guitar with eleven strings. Apart from the notable exception of Maurice Ohana, few modern composers have been tempted to write for these special instruments.

In past centuries, adding extra strings to stringed instruments usually in time spelt doom for the instrument. These current variants of the six-string guitar will no doubt linger on, but it seems certain that the standard six-string classical guitar will be dominant for many years to come. The number of talented players of the instrument, its general acceptance in all musical circles throughout the world, and the size of its repertory, all continue to grow at a staggering rate.

*Narcisco Yepes with his ten-string guitar*

# Selected Reading


*The Evolution of the Classical Guitar – Wilfrid M. Appleby (I.C.G.A. 1966).*
*La Guitare et les Guitaristes – José de Azpiazu (Editions Symphonia-Verlag AG, Bâle 1959).*
*The Illustrated History of the Guitar – Alexander Bellow (Franco-Colombo 1970).*
*The Segovia Technique – Vladimir Bobri (Macmillan 1972).*
*The Guitar and the Mandolin – Philip J. Bone (Schott 1914 and 1954)*
*Die Gitarre und Ihre Meister – Fritz Buek (Robert Lienan Normals Schlesinger 1926).*
*The Guitar in England 1800-1924 – Stuart Button (Garland Publishing Inc., New York 1989).*
*The Orphée Data base of Guitar Records. Compiled by Jacques Chaîné. Editions Orphée, Columbus, Ohio, 1990).*
*La Chitarra a cura di Ruggero Chiesa (EDT, Torino 1990).*
*Classical Guitar Magazine 1982 through 1991 (Newcastle upon Tyne).*
*Classical Guitar Music in Print – Mijndert Jape (Musicdata Inc., Philadelphia, 1989).*
*Guitars from Renaissance to Rock – Tom and Mary Evans (Paddington 1977).*
*La Guitarra: Sus Antecedentes Históricos y Biografías de Ejecutantes Celebres – Segundo N. Contreras (Buenos Aires 1927).*
*Den Klassika Gitarren – Martin Giertz (Norstedt & Söners, Stockholm, 1979).*
*Manuale di Storia della Chitarra – Vol.I, Mario Dell'Ara; Vol.II, Angelo Gilardino (Bèrben, 1988).*
*Guitares – Michel Foussard (Eurydice 1980).*
*Guitar Music Index, Volumes 1 and 2 – George Gilmore and Mark Pereira (Galliard 1976).*
*The Art and Times of the Guitar – Frederick V. Grunfeld (Macmillan 1969).*
*Guitar Review Magazine – 1946 through 1991 (New York).*
*Guitar Music in the Archives of G.F.A. – Thomas F. Heck (G.F.A. 1981).*
*The Guitar – History, Music, Players – Kozinn etc. (Columbus 1984).*
*Guitar and Vihuela Bibliography – Meredith Alice McCutcheon (Pendragon 1985).*
*Die Gitarre – Peter Päffgen (Schott, Mainz 1988).*
*Diccionario de Guitarras, Guitarristas y Guitarreros – Domingo Prat (Buenos Aires 1934, reprinted Editions Orphée 1986).*
*Classical Guitar, Lute and Vihuela Discography – Ronald C. Purcell (Belwin Mills 1976).*
*Handbuch der Gitarre und Laute – Konrad Ragnossnig (B. Schott's 1978).*
*La Guitarra Espãnola – José Villar Rodríguez (Clivis, Barcelona 1985).*
*The Story of the Spanish Guitar – A.P.Sharpe (Clifford Essex 1954).*
*Guitarren-Lexicon – Josef Powrozniak (Verlag Neue Musik 1979).*
*Gitarre – Fred Seeger (Lied der Zeit Musikverlag, Berlin 1986).*
*Die Gitarre – Alexander Schmitz (Ellert & Richter Verlag, Germany 1988).*
*The Guitar From the Renaissance to the Present Day – Harvey Turnbull (Batsford 1974).*
*Traditions of the Classical Guitar – Graham Wade (John Calder 1981).*
*Handbuch des Laute und Gitarre – Josef Zuth (George Olms Verlag 1978 reprint).*

# THE GUITAR

## DEFINITIONS BY CARL SANDBURG

*A small friend weighing less than a newborn infant, ever responsive to all sincere efforts aimed at mutual respect, depth of affection or love gone off the deep end.*

*A device in the realm of harmonic creation where six silent strings have the sound potential of profound contemplation or happy go lucky whim.*

*A highly evolved contrivance whereby delicate melodic moments mingle with punctuation of silence bringing "the creative hush".*

*A vibratory implement under incessant practice and skilled cajolery giving out with serene maroon meditations, flame dancers in scarlet sashes, snow white acrobats plunging into black midnight pools, odd numbers in evening green waltzing with even numbers in dawn pink.*

*A chattel with a soul often in part owning its owner and tantalizing him with his lack of perfection.*

*An instrument of quaint form and quiet demeanor dedicated to the dulcet rather than the diapason.*

*A box of chosen wood having intimate accessories wherefrom sound may be measured and commanded to the interest of ears not lost to hammer crash or wind whisper.*

*A portable companion distinguished from the piano in that you can take it with you, neither horses nor motor truck being involved.*

COURTESY: DAVID RUSSELL

*David Russell with Andrés Segovia*

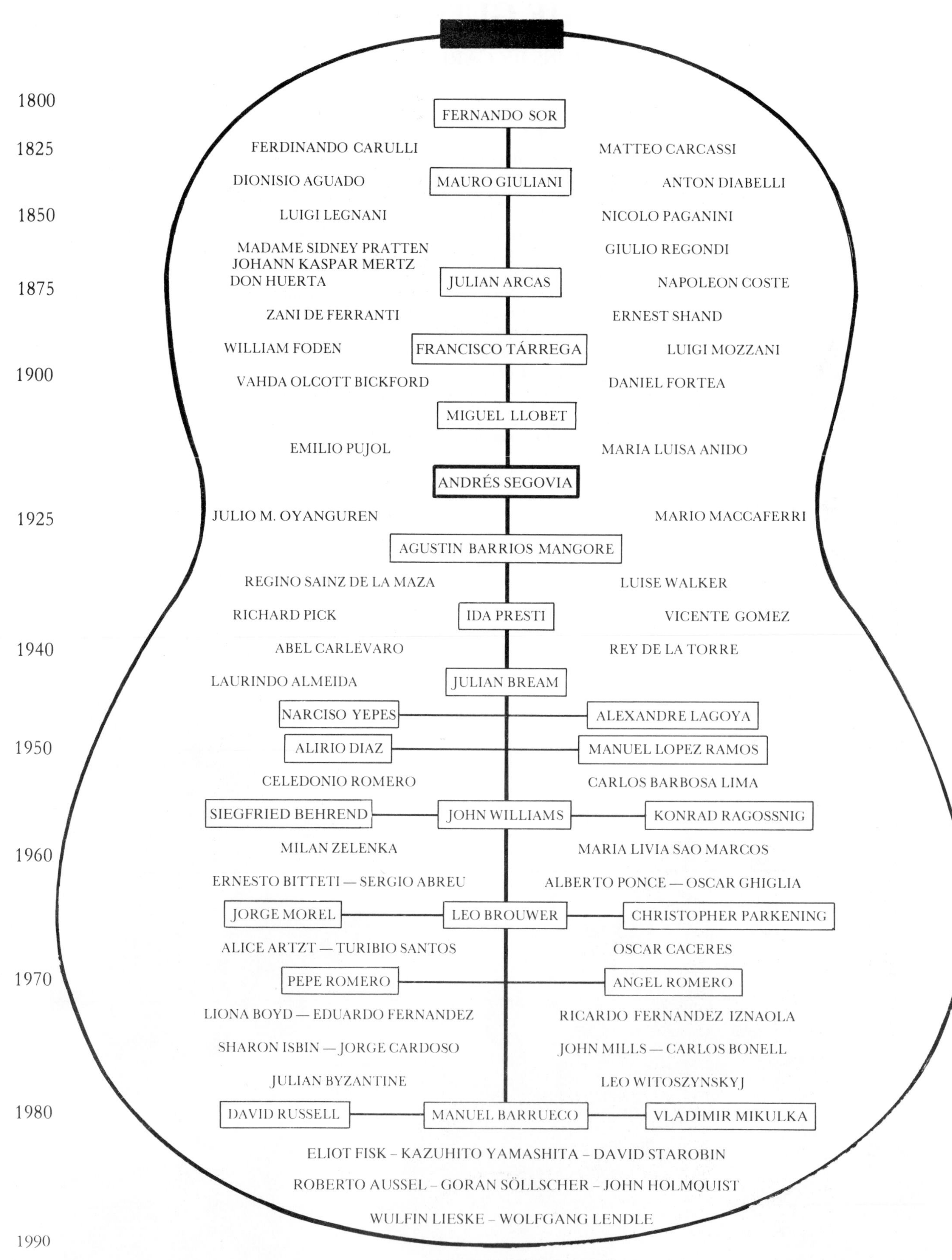


*A general chart showing the most important classical guitarists since 1800. The most outstanding soloists are highlighted*

**ERRATA** The Classical Guitar – Its Evolution, Players and Personalities Since 1800. The photographs of Jukka Savijoki (page 180) and Seppo Siirala (page 192) have been transposed. The photographs have been reproduced below to the correct size so that they can be cut out and pasted into place on these pages.

**JUKKA SAVIJOKI (page 180)**

**SEPPO SIIRALA (page 192)**

---

(Page 253) Caption of centre photograph should read Nicholas Hooper

6/91 AMPCO

# THE CLASSICAL GUITAR
# ITS PLAYERS
# AND
# ITS PERSONALITIES

# CODE TO ABBREVIATIONS OF PUBLISHERS' NAMES IN SELECTED MUSIC COLUMNS

| | |
|---|---|
| B | Broekmans en Van Poppel |
| B & B | Bote & Bock |
| B & H | Boosey & Hawkes |
| BA | Ricordi, Buenos Aires |
| BP | Brazilliance Music |
| CG | Carl Gerhmans |
| CHANT | Chanterelle |
| CO | Columbia Music Company |
| EMB | Editio Musica Budapest |
| EMM | Ediciones Musicales Madrid |
| EMT | Editions Musicales Transatlantiques |
| ESC | Editions Max Eschig |
| FC | Franco Colombo |
| GA | Guitar Archives – Schott |
| JWC | J & W Chester |
| MB | Mel Bay |
| N | C. F. Peters |
| RIC | Ricordi |
| SI | Belwin Mills |
| SY | Ricordi |
| SZ | Suvini Zerboni |
| UE | Universal Edition |
| UME | Union Musical Espanola |
| ZA | Zanibon |
| ZM | Musikverlag Zimmerman |

NB. These abbreviations appeared in the First Edition. Additions to the Second Edition such as Bèrben, Guitarre und Laute, Editions Orphée, Sikorski and Tecla Editions are recorded in full.

# MIGUEL ABLONIZ

**Born – MICHEL AVLONITIS**

**Cairo, Egypt**

**29 May 1917**

COURTESY: MIGUEL ABLONIZ

*Miguel Ablóniz*

The son of a Greek father and an Italian mother, Miguel Ablóniz now lives in Italy. He began to teach himself the guitar at the age of eight. Qualified teachers were not to be found in Cairo at that time, and for a period of five years the young guitarist used the methods of Carulli, Albert and Carcassi. Ablóniz then managed to correspond with prominent teachers in Europe who were able to send him new guitar books and music. In 1933 he made contact with the French guitarist André Verdier, a former pupil of Miguel Llobet. Verdier recommended the young guitarist to Emilio Pujol, who also began to correspond with Ablóniz.

During the second World War Miguel Ablóniz gained a lot of experience as a concert guitarist, both in recital and on the radio. Eventually he was to devote most of his time to teaching and transcribing, rather than playing in concert. In 1946 he went to the Escuela Municipal de Música in Barcelona, Spain, to study privately with Pujol. He continued his musical studies with Juan Parras del Morral. In 1945 he travelled to Great Britain to hear and meet Andrés Segovia.

In 1953 Miguel Ablóniz moved to Milan, Italy, where he established in his home a guitar school, still in existence today. He teaches at a number of Italian academies and colleges, and also spends some time each year visiting guitar courses abroad. These include one held at the Ithaca College in the USA, where he is the principal teacher.

Over the years Miguel Ablóniz has transcribed around one thousand works for the guitar. He is widely regarded as one of the instrument's foremost authorities and teachers.

**SELECTED MUSIC**

| | |
|---|---|
| Arietta Medievale. | Bérben |
| Bulería Gitana. | Ricordi |
| Capriccio Flamenco. | Bérben |
| Chorinho. | Ricordi |
| Cowboy Melody — based on 'Colorado Trail'. | Ricordi |
| Four Preludes. | Ricordi |
| Four Recreational Pieces. | Ricordi |
| Guitar Chôro. | Bèrben |
| Improvisation – Homage to Villa-Lobos. | Ricordi |
| An Incorrigible Dreamer. | Bérben |
| Moods. | Bérben |
| Partita in E. | Ricordi |
| Polo. | Ricordi |
| Prelude and Guitar Bossa. | Bérben |
| Sequential. | Bérben |
| Tango Andaluz. | Ricordi |
| Tarantella Burlesca & Bossa Nova. | Bérben |
| Three Gitanerías. | Ricordi |
| Two Ricercari Moderni. | Ricordi |
| Valsette and Marcetta. | Ricordi |
| Crab Fingering. | Bérben |
| Essential Exercises for the Left Hand. | Bérben |
| Fifty Arpeggios for the Right Hand. | Bérben |
| Ten Melodic Studies. | Ricordi |
| The Twenty-Four Diatonic Scales. | Bérben |
| Tuning and Fingerboard Rediscovered. | Bérben |

**SELECTED READING**

Miguel Ablóniz. Article – 'Guitar Player', October 1977

# SERGIO ABREU

**Born – SERGIO REBELLO ABREU**

**Rio de Janeiro, Brazil**

**5 June 1948**

*Sergio Abreu*

Sergio Abreu showed exceptional talent from early childhood. In 1961 he and his brother Eduardo (born 19 September 1949) played for the eminent Argentinian guitarist Adolfina Raitzin Tavora, a former pupil of Andrés Segovia. She was so impressed by the brothers' ability that she immediately decided to coach them in advanced technique and musical interpretation.

As a duo the Abreu brothers performed all over the world, achieving great success. In the eyes and ears of many critics they were the true successors to the throne of Ida Presti and Alexandre Lagoya. Life as a professional guitarist did not appeal to Eduardo, and Sergio turned his attention to the solo platform, achieving much success and high critical praise in his tours of the United States of America, Australia, the United Kingdom and most other European countries. He performed a duo with the violinist Yehudi Menuhin in the Windsor Festival, England, and also took part in the Guitar '81 Festival in Toronto, Canada, appearing as performer, judge and teacher.

In recent years Sergio Abreu has devoted most of his time to the construction of classical guitars of excellent quality, but he still remains a fine guitarist. He is also active in arranging, particularly in the duo field in which he and his brother had been so prominent.

**SELECTED RECORDINGS**

| | |
|---|---|
| The Guitars of Sergio and Eduardo Abreu | CBS 61262 |
| The Guitars of Sergio and Eduardo Abreu | Ace of Diamonds SDD219 |
| Two Concertos for Two Guitars | CBS 61469 |
| Sergio Abreu Interprets Paganini and Sor. | Ariola 201614 |

**SELECTED READING**

| | |
|---|---|
| Sergio Abreu | Guitar, February 1978 |
| Sergio Abreu | Guitar, January 1979 |
| Sergio Abreu | Guitar Player, July 1980 |

# MARIO ABRIL

**Born –**

**Havana, Cuba,**

**26 February 1943**

*Mario Abril*

Mario Abril spent his early years in the small city of Sagua La Grande where he studied music theory, music literature, piano, violin and the guitar under the guidance of his mother. In 1961 he took part in the ill-fated Bay of Pigs invasion of Cuba, and was captured. During his twenty-two months imprisonment he met the well-known Cuban guitarist Hector Garcia, who was also a prisoner. Garcia became Abril's teacher, and for several years after their release from prison the two musicians worked together in the United States of America.

Mario Abril earned a Bachelor's degree in guitar from the University of Albuquerque, New Mexico, and a Ph.D. degree in music theory from the Florida State University School of Music. For many years he performed extensively throughout North America as a guitar recitalist. He is currently an associate professor of guitar and music theory at the University of Tennessee, Chattanooga. He has written articles for several guitar magazines including Guitar Review, and has had many books of guitar solos and transcriptions published by Hansen House.

# DIONISIO AGUADO

**Born – DIONISIO AGUADO Y GARCIA**

**Madrid, Spain, 8 April 1784**

**Died – Madrid, 20 December 1849**

*Dionisio Aguado*

Dionisio Aguado was the son of a prominent clergyman in Madrid. He showed an early aptitude for music and was taught the rudiments by a monk called Basilio in a Madrid college. But it was the renowned singer/guitarist Manuel García to whom Aguado owed his thorough grounding in both music and the guitar.

In 1803 Aguado moved to a small estate which had been left to him by his father, in the village of Fuenlabrada, near Aranjuez. There he was able to devote all his time to an intense study of the guitar and music. The end result was several volumes of studies for the guitar and finally his 'Method for Guitar' published in Madrid in 1825. Aguado took up residence once more in Madrid after the end of the French invasion. After the death of his mother he travelled in 1826 to Paris, where his works for guitar were already well known. He returned to Madrid in 1837. In Paris he met the great guitar virtuoso Fernando Sor. They developed a strong social and musical friendship, though their technical approach to the guitar was very different. (For instance, Aguado used his right-hand nails and dazzled his audiences with an amazing technique, in direct contrast to the 'no nails' technique of Sor.)

For a time they lived in the same house in Paris. A sign of the close friendship of these two virtuoso guitarists is Sor's duet for two guitarists, Les Deux Amis, which was dedicated to their association.

In late 1838 Aguado decided to return to his native Spain, and he took up residence once again in Madrid. Here he was to remain until his death in 1849 at the age of sixty-five.

The volume of Aguado's compositions was not as great as that of his friend and fellow countryman Fernando Sor, but there is no doubt of his genius and the lasting qualities of his music. Aguado was also the inventor of an unusual accessory for the guitar, called the tripodison. This was a three-legged stand on which the guitarist could rest his guitar whilst playing. Aguado claimed that his invention increased the volume of the guitar, and also made the guitar easier to play in concert. Despite support for this contraption from several players, including Sor, the tripodison did not gain wide support, becoming extinct within a short period of time.

**SELECTED MUSIC**

| | |
|---|---|
| Allegro and Allegro Vivace. | GA301 |
| Allegro brillante. | GA302 |
| Easy Waltzes and Studies. | GA303 |
| Fandango and Variations, ed. Tarrago. | UME |
| Selected Works. | ECH 400 |
| Six Selected Pieces. | GA55 |
| Thirty-one little Guitar Works. | N3212 |
| New Guitar Method. | Tecla |

**SELECTED READING**

The Tripodison Article. Guitar Review No.39, 1974
Dionisio Aguado the Man – José Romanillos.
Guitar International, April 1984
Guitar Method of Dionisio Aguado – Erik Stentstadvold
Classical Guitar, March & April, 1990

# MIGUEL ALCAZAR

**Born –**

**Mexico City, Mexico**

**26 April 1942**

*Miguel Alcázar*

Miguel Alcázar is one of Mexico's foremost players and teachers of the classical guitar. In 1963 he was awarded the first prize in the composition contest sponsored by the Mexican Guitar Associations. In 1964 he won the Beryl Rubinstein Scholarship for Composition at the Cleveland Institute of Music. His opera La Mujer y su Sombra won first prize in the Fundación Morales Estevez Contest and was premiered at the Fine Arts Palace in 1981.

Alcázar obtained his Masters Degree with honours from the National Conservatory of Music in Mexico in 1971. Since that time he has been a faculty member there and also at the Cleveland Institute of Music and the Universidad Veracruzana. He is also a prolific recording artist and music editor. His many editions of Mexican music have been published by Universidad Veracruzana, the Liga de Compositores de Mexico, Tecla Editions and Editions Orphée. His concert career has taken him throughout the USA and Europe.

**SELECTED RECORDINGS**

| | |
|---|---|
| Tablatura Mexicana para Guitarra Barroca. | EMI-Angel SAM 35029 |
| Paganini & Gragnani Sonatas (with Rudolf Werthen, violin) | EMI-Angel SAM 35035 |
| Música Barroca para Laud | EMI-Angel SAM 35039 |
| Ponce – 24 Preludes, Sonata de Paganini etc. | EMI-Angel ASM 77042 |
| Música Mexicana para Guitarra. | EMI-Angel SAM 35065 |
| Música Latinoamericana. | EMI-Angel SAM 35066 |
| Napoléon Coste Souvenirs. | Tritonus TTS 1003 |
| Música de Guitarra Barroca. | Tritonus TTS 1005 |
| Ponce – Obras Completas Vol.1. | Tritonus TTS 1008 |
| Vargas y Guzman Sonatas para Guitarra. | Tritonus TTS 1011 |

**SELECTED READING**

| | |
|---|---|
| Interview. | Classical Guitar, December 1984 |

# LAURINDO ALMEIDA

**Born –**

**Santos, Brazil**

**2 September 1917**

*Laurindo Almeida*

Laurindo Almeida received his earliest musical training on the piano from his mother, a concert pianist. On hearing his sister Maria play the guitar, he fell in love with the instrument and decided to master it and give up the piano.

He gave his first public recital on the guitar at the age of thirteen, and made his radio debut at the age of fifteen. He gave concerts in Brazil's main cities, following which he became a staff member of one of the country's largest radio stations. He then signed on as a musician on the ocean liner Cuyaba for a trip to Europe, where he heard the legendary gypsy jazz guitarist Django Reinhardt playing in France. The sound of Reinhardt's jazz music was to affect Laurindo's future attitude towards music as a whole.

In 1947 he moved to the United States, spending some time in Hollywood working in the film studios. He then became an important member of the Stan Kenton jazz orchestra. In 1950 he left the Kenton orchestra to play a series of solo concerts, and also to devote time to composing. He has now written more than 200 compositions.

Over the years Laurindo Almeida has recorded profusely on the classical guitar for the Capitol and Decca labels. In 1966 he performed two American debut recordings of Radamés Gnattali's Concerto de Copacabana and the Villa-Lobos Guitar Concerto.

It was Laurindo Almeida who, in the 1960s, first brought Bossa Nova to the United States He led a quartet with saxophonist Bud Shank, which recorded several successful LPs of this new Brazilian jazz for the Pacific label. In the early 1980s Almeida, now a recording artist for the Concord Record company in California, reformed the group with Shank, entitling it the L.A. Four. For many years this new group achieved great success in concert and with record sales. Almeida continues to record for the Concord label, often in collaboration with fellow guitarists Carlos Barbosa-Lima, Sharon Isbin and Charlie Byrd.

Laurindo Almeida lives in Sherman Oaks, California, and remains one of the busiest and most popular classical guitarists in the United States. There is no doubt that through his enormous output of records, publications and also his concert appearances, He has been one of the most influential guitarists on the North American Scene for over thirty years.

**SELECTED RECORDINGS**

| | |
|---|---|
| Guitar Music of Spain. | Capitol P8295 |
| Guitar Music of Latin America. | Capitol P8321 |
| Vistas D'España. | Capitol P8367 |
| Danzas. | Capitol P8467 |
| Villa-Lobos. | Capitol P8497 |
| Spanish Guitars. | Capitol P8521 |
| From the Romantic Era. | Capitol DP8601 |
| Plays Radamés Gnattali. | Capitol SP8625 |
| Virtuosi (with Deltra Eamon). | Orion ORS7260 |
| Almeida Concerto for Guitar. | Concord CC2001 |

**SELECTED READING**

| | |
|---|---|
| Laurindo Almeida. | Guitar Player, August 1968 |
| Laurindo Almeida. | Guitar, July 1974 |
| Laurindo Almeida. | Guitar, November 1979 |
| Laurindo Almeida. | Frets, June 1979 |

**SELECTED MUSIC**

| | |
|---|---|
| Chôro Para Olga. | BP25 |
| English Air. | BP29 |
| Gypsy Dance. | BP44 |
| Gypsy Suite on Popular Motives, in 5 Movements. | BP26 |
| Gypsy Suite, in 5 movements. | BP27 |
| Insomnia. | BP23 |
| Lament in Tremolo Form. | BP20 |
| Mystified. | BP38 |
| The One Minute Divertimento. | BP24 |
| Pavana for Pancho. | BP28 |
| Serenata in Memoriam to Garoto. | BP501 |
| Soledad. | BP500 |
| Sueño. | BP35 |
| Two Spanish Folk Songs. | BP45 |

# MARIA LUISA ANIDO

**Born – ISABEL MARIO LUISA ANIDO**

**Moron, near Buenos Aires, Argentina**

**26 January 1907**

**SELECTED RECORDINGS**
Grande Dame de la Guitare — Erato STU70722

**SELECTED MUSIC**
Impresiones Argentinas – Nine Compositions — Ricordi

**SELECTED READING**
Interview — Classical Guitar, August 1988

*Maria Luisa Anido*

Maria Luisa Anido's father, Don Juan Carlos Anido, was the publisher of 'La Guitarra', a magazine devoted to guitarists and guitar music. Encouraged by her father, she took up the guitar at an early age and studied first with Domingo Prat and then later with Miguel Llobet.

Maria Luisa Anido showed exceptional talent at an early age and made her concert debut at the age of ten on 7 May 1918 in Buenos Aires. Since that time she has continued to give concerts throughout the world. In 1925 she gave a series of duo concerts with her renowned teacher Llobet. Over the years she has made many recordings and broadcasts, particularly in her native Argentina. She was made professor of the guitar in the National Conservatoire of Music in Buenos Aires, and over the past fifty years has taught most of Argentina's finest classical guitarists.

In her 81st year she she took up residence in Havana at the invitation of the government of Cuba, where she continues to teach. In May 1988 she was made Doctoris Honoris Causa at the National Institute of Art, Havana.

*Maria Luisa Anido as a child with her Torres guitar.*

*A selection of B. M. G. magazine, a guitar magazine of the past*

SEATTLE CLASSIC GUITAR SOCIETY

# GUITAR NEWS

The Official Organ of the

INTERNATIONAL CLASSIC GUITAR ASSOCIATION

No. 65 Single copy price 1/8 (U.S.A. 35c.) May/June, 1962

After the Concert

*The Presti-Lagoya Duo with Segovia after the Duo's recital, New York 1961*

# GUITAR NEWS

The Official Organ of the

INTERNATIONAL CLASSIC GUITAR ASSOCIATION

No. 87 Single copy price 2/- (U.S.A. 45c.) Jan./Feb., 1966

AT COMPOSTELA

Photo: Robert J. Vidal

ROBERT J. VIDAL INTERVIEWS ANDRES SEGOVIA

# GUITAR NEWS

The Official Organ of the

INTERNATIONAL CLASSIC GUITAR ASSOCIATION

No. 94 Single copy price 2/6 (U.S.A. 50c.) June/Aug., 1967

GOLDEN JUBILEE

THE PRESENTATION TO

MARIA LUISA ANIDO

# GUITAR NEWS

The Official Organ of the

INTERNATIONAL CLASSIC GUITAR ASSOCIATION

No. 112 Single copy price 15p (U.S.A. 50c.) April/June, 1971

THOMAS F. HECK

# GUITAR NEWS

The Official Organ of the

INTERNATIONAL CLASSIC GUITAR ASSOCIATION

No. 107 Single copy price 2/6 (U.S.A. 50c.) Jan./March, 1970

FREDERICK NOAD

# GUITAR NEWS

The Official Organ of the

INTERNATIONAL CLASSIC GUITAR ASSOCIATION

No. 81 Single copy price 1/8 (U.S.A. 35c.) Jan./Feb., 1965

MATHANYA OPHEE

*A selection of 'Guitar News' which ceased publication in 1973*

# WILFRID APPLEBY

**Born – WILFRID MORRISON APPLEBY**

**Brighton, England, 3 July 1892**

**Died – Cheltenham, England, 10 December 1987**

*Wilfrid Appleby*

For many years Wilfrid Appleby was one of the leading personalities on the British guitar scene. As editor of 'Guitar News' he kept British guitarists informed on international and British guitar events and personalities for over twenty years, following the end of World War II.

Together with his wife Kay, Wilfrid Appleby originally decided to take up the study of the guitar to fill the time created by the wartime curtailment of his international Esperanto activities. After a period of intense study of books from the public library, and also music obtained through friends in Spain and Argentina, he became a proficient player and teacher. As an acknowledged authority on the guitar, he was invited by A.P.Sharpe, the editor of the long-established fretted instrument magazine B.M.G., to write a monthly column on the classical guitar. In a period of over five years he wrote almost 80 articles.

Appleby then took an active part in the revived Philharmonic Society of Guitarists. He was also very much involved in his own local guitar society in Cheltenham, formed in 1946. Together with Boris M. Perott, he helped to promote the talents of the young guitar prodigy Julian Bream.

In 1951 he decided that B.M.G. ('Banjo, Mandolin, Guitar') did not cater enough for the classical guitar lover. Together with his wife Kay and a few friends he formed the International Classical Association (I.C.G.A.). He also produced the first copies of 'Guitar News', which was to provide an excellent service to its readers all over the world until it ceased publication in 1973. Wilfrid Appleby also gave occasional recitals on the guitar, and was often called upon to give lectures about the instrument. All his work for the guitar was a labour of love, both the Guitar Society and 'Guitar News' being run on a non-profit basis.

From his home in Cheltenham, Wilfrid Appleby continued a very active life until his death at the age of 95. Throughout his long life he put his many talents to various uses, becoming in addition to a guitarist a poet, a writer, an Esperanto expert, a philatelist, a herpetologist, and a painter good enough to have his work hung in the West of England Academy of Art.

**SELECTED READING**


B.M.G. — regular articles

Guitar News. — regular articles

Guitar Review. — various articles

The Evolution of the Classical Guitar – Wilfrid M. Appleby. I.C.G.A. (1966)

# JULIAN ARCAS

**Born – Almería, Spain – 25 October 1832**

**Died – Antequera, Málaga, Spain**

**16 February 1882**

*Julián Arcas*

Julián Arcas, a virtuoso guitarist, was one of the most important figures in Spanish music of the nineteenth century. The music he performed was based mainly on traditional Spanish folk and flamenco melodies.

During the years 1860-70 Arcas was at the height of his career as a recitalist. He made lengthy and highly successful concert tours of Spain and the rest of Europe. In 1862 he performed for the British royal family in Brighton, England.

In 1864 he made his name in Barcelona, Spain, and then appeared in several concerts throughout Spain with a young pianist called Patanas. By 1870 he was tired of travelling and settled once again in his native city of Almería. There he established a business in the Calle Granada.

He then became very interested in guitar construction, and co-operated with the famed maker Antonio Torres of Seville in developing the instrument. After ten years in business in Almería, he retired to Antequera, Málaga, where he died soon after, at the age of fifty, in 1882.

One of Spain's great nineteenth century guitar virtuosos, Julián Arcas was also a highly respected and prolific composer and arranger for the guitar of national melodies and dances.

**SELECTED MUSIC**

| | |
|---|---|
| El Delirio – Fantasía. | UME |
| El Fagot – Waltz (Oliva). | Ricordi |
| Jota Aragonesa. | Ricordi |
| Los Panaderos – Bolero. | Ricordi |
| Soleá de Concierto. | Ricordi |
| Spanish Guitar Music, ed. Benkö. | EMB |

# ALICE ARTZT

**Born –**

**New York, USA**

**16 March 1943**

*Alice Artzt*

Alice Artzt showed exceptional musical talent from an early age. After studying the piano and flute, she turned to the classical guitar at the age of thirteen. Her first important teacher was Alexander Bellow in New York. She later studied with Ida Presti and Alexandre Lagoya in France, and with Julian Bream in England. She also studied composition with Darius Milhaud at Aspen, Colorado, and has done graduate work in composition and musicology at Barnard College, Columbia University, earning her B.A. there in 1965.

Alice Artzt made her European debut in London in 1969. Since then she has toured Europe extensively and performed throughout North and South America and most other parts of the world. She has had works dedicated to her by several well-known composers, including John W. Duarte and Guido Santórsola. She has been featured on many television and radio programmes, including a special recital produced and broadcast by the BBC in London in honour of the 75th birthday of Sir Lennox Berkeley. The author of a popular guitar technique book, The Art of Practising, she is also a prominent member of the Board of Directors of the Guitar Foundation of America, and also an authority on the comedian Charlie Chaplin.

**SELECTED RECORDINGS**

| | |
|---|---|
| Classic Guitar | Gemini. GME 1018 |
| Original Works. | Gemini GME 1019 |
| Bach & his Friends. | Klavier KS 555 |
| Music by Fernando Sor. | Meridian E77 066 |
| Music by Tárrega. | Meridian E77 026 |
| English Guitar Music. | Meridian E77 037 |
| Romantic Virtuoso Guitar Music. | Hyperion A66040 |
| Glory of the Guitar. | AVM1007 (Reissue of Gemini GME 1018) |
| Musical Tributes. | Hyperion A66146 |
| Variations and Chaconnes. | Hyperion Helios CDH 88026 |

**SELECTED READING**

| | |
|---|---|
| Interview. | Guitar, August 1973 |
| Interview. | Guitar, November 1977 |
| Article. | Guitar Player, May 1979 |
| Interview. | Classical Guitar, Jan/Feb 1984 |

# ROBERTO AUSSEL

**Born –**

**Buenos Aires, Argentina**

**13 July 1954**

*Roberto Aussel*

Roberto Aussel began his guitar studies at the age of seven and gave his first recital at the age of thirteen. His principal teacher was Jorge Martínez Zarate. In 1975 and 1976 he was awarded first prize in three of the most important international guitar competitions, the Radio France Competition in Paris, the Alirio Diaz Prize in Caracas, Venezuela, and the International Competition in Porto Alegre, Brazil.

Since that time Roberto Aussel has established himself as one of the world's finest classical guitarists, giving concerts throughout Europe and the Americas. Several composers have dedicated works to him, including Marius Constant, Francis Kleynjans, Astor Piazzolla, Francis Schwartz, Jose Luis Campana and Raúl Maldonado. In 1980 he was made a Master of the Bordeaux International Guitar Seminary. He has been editor of guitar music for the publishers Henri Lemoine, Paris, since 1983.

Roberto Aussel lives in Paris.

**SELECTED RECORDINGS**

| | |
|---|---|
| Recital de Guitare | Vol.1. Adda CIR 822 |
| Recital de Guitare | Vol.2. AddaCIR 825 |
| Bondon Guitar Concerto. | Cybelia CY 655 |
| Roberto Aussel. | GHA 5256002 |
| Latin American Music | Circe 87 101 LD CD |

**SELECTED READING**

| | |
|---|---|
| Interview. | Classical Guitar, March/April 1984 |
| Roberto Aussel. | Classical Guitar, April 1985 |

# JOSE DE AZPIAZU

**Born – Onante, Spain – 26 May 1912**

**Died – Geneva, Switzerland**

**28 December 1986**

Born in the Basque region of Spain, José de Azpiazu began to study the guitar at the age of thirteen. His first teacher was his uncle. When still a teenager, Azpiazu was asked to give recitals at the festivals in San Sebastián. He met with considerable success as a guitarist at these recitals, but still decided to devote most of his spare time to his other talent, painting. He won the first prize for designing and painting at the School of Modern Arts in San Sebastián in 1929. He was also active in the Basque Folklore Society.

It was not until, at the age of twenty-four years, Azpiazu made his debut on Radio Bilbao that he started his professional career as a guitarist. He soon gave up his other activities, devoting all his time to his career as a concert guitarist. He toured Spain extensively for many years but, owing to to World War II, it was not until 1950 that he performed abroad. He had a very successful concert tour of Switzerland which included several radio broadcasts.

While in Geneva he became friendly with painter Andrés Segovia junior, who introduced the guitarist to his father. Segovia was so impressed that on his recommendation the professorship of guitar at the College of Music in Geneva was bestowed upon José de Azpiazu.

*José de Azpiazu*

Azpiazu was a prolific arranger and composer of guitar music. His Suite in C won first prize in the 1954 International Competition held in Modena, Italy.

**SELECTED MUSIC**

| | |
|---|---|
| Cachucha. | Ricordi |
| Cubana. | Ricordi |
| Fandanguillo de Huelva. | Ricordi |
| Five Iberian Miniatures for Guitar. | Ricordi |
| Jota on popular themes. | Ricordi |
| Minué del Baztán Errimina – Nostalgie. | Ricordi |
| Six Children's Stories. | Ricordi |
| Theme with Variations – Homage to Sor. | Ricordi |
| Tonadilla – Homage to Granados. | Ricordi |

**SELECTED READING**

La Guitare et les Guitaristes des origines aux temps modernes. Edition Symphonia-Verlag AG. Bâle, 1959.

# CARLOS BARBOSA-LIMA

**Born –**

**São Paulo, Brazil**

**17 December 1944**

*Antonio Carlos Barbosa-Lima*

Antonio Carlos Barbosa-Lima began to play the guitar at the age of nine. His teachers were Isaias Savio and B. Moreira. By the time he was thirteen years old he was regarded as a child prodigy, and had already made a successful recording in Brazil.

At the age of twelve Carlos Barbosa-Lima had made his concert debuts in São Paulo and Rio de Janeiro. He then went to the USA, making his New York concert debut at the Alice Tully Hall in March 1972. Following this success the young guitarist made extensive concert tours of the North and South Americas and Europe. In March 1974 he made his debut in Paris at the International Week of the Guitar, and in June 1979 he was the first guitarist to participate in the 'Festival Casal' in Puerto Rico.

In recent years Barbosa-Lima has lived in New York, leading a busy life as an international concert guitarist and recording artist. He is active as a transcriber, and his work has resulted in many excellent transcriptions for the guitar of music by Scarlatti, Bach, Handel and modern South American composers. He has had works written for and dedicated to him by many well-known composers including Francisco Mignone, Leonardo Balada, Guido Santórsola, Albert Harris and John W. Duarte. In 1976 he commissioned Alberto Ginastera to write a work; the resulting Sonata Op.47, dedicated to Barbosa-Lima, is now regarded as one of the outstanding twentieth-century compositions for guitar.

**SELECTED RECORDINGS**

Dez Dedos Magicos Num Violão de Ouro. Chant CLP-1001
O Menino e o Violão. Chantecler CMG 1004
Musicas de J.O. Queiroz. Chantecler CMG-2434
Album de Modinhas. Chantecler 2 08 404 079
Imortal Catullo. Continental LP 1-35-404-020
Brasil e Violão. Chantecler 2-10 407-250
Scarlatti Guitar Recital. ABC Dunhill ABC/ATS 20005
Mignone – 12 Guitar Studies. Philips (Brazil) 6598-312
Scott Joplin Works. Concord Concerto CC-2006
Jobim & Gershwin. Concord Concerto CC-2005
Music of Cole Porter. Concord Concerto CC-2008
Impressions. Concord Concerto CC-2009
Brazil, With Love (Duet with Sharon Isbin). Concord Picante CJP-320
Rhapsody in Blue; West Side Story (Duo). Concord Concerto CC-2012

**SELECTED READING**

Interview. Guitar, July 1983
Interview. Guitar International, May 1984
Interview. Guitar Player, April 1983
Gentle Genius of the Guitar. Americas Magazine, July/August 1987
Interview. Classical Guitar, May/June 1983

COURTESY: JORGE MOREL

*Augustín Barrios Mangoré*

## AGUSTÍN PIO BARRIOS MANGORÉ

**Born – San Juan Bautista de las Misiones, Paraguay**

**5 May 1885**

**Died – San Salvador, El Salvador – 7 August 1944**

*Agustín Barrios Mangoré*

Almost fifty years after his death, full recognition is finally being given to the genius of the Paraguayan guitar virtuoso Agustín Barrios Mangoré.

One of eight children, Barrios was born into a musical family. He began to play the guitar at an early age and was able to use the instrument to study harmony at his school. His first formal teacher was Gustavo Sosa Escalda, who introduced the young guitarist to the music of Sor, Tárrega, Aguado and other composers of the established guitar repertoire. By the time he was thirteen years old, Barrios was recognized as a prodigy. He was awarded a scholarship to the Colegio Nacional in Asunción. There he studied calligraphy (he was a fine graphic artist) and also achieved high results in mathematics, journalism and literature.

In 1910 Barrios, already established as a guitar virtuoso, left Paraguay and went to Argentina. Over the next thirty-four years he toured the South American continent, giving concerts in the major cities and towns of Argentina, Uruguay, Brazil, Venezuela, Costa Rica and El Salvador. He also visited Chile, Mexico, Guatemala, Honduras, Panama, Columbia, Cuba and Haiti. Between 1934 and 1936 he also visited Europe, playing in Spain, Germany and Belgium.

It was in 1932 that Barrios began to call himself 'Nitsuga Mangoré – the Paganini of the guitar', Nitsuga being Agustín spelt backwards and Mangoré the name of a legendary Guarani chieftain.

By the mid-1930s Barrios was suffering from a bad heart condition and could not continue to undertake long and strenuous concert tours. He lived his last years in El Salvador, teaching, composing and giving occasional guitar recitals.

As well as being an outstanding player, Barrios was a composer of over three hundred works for the guitar, many of which are now accepted as some of the finest guitar solos ever written.

**SELECTED RECORDINGS**

| | |
|---|---|
| Agustín Barrios – Historical Recordings (3 cassettes). | Chanterelle CHR 011. 012, 013 |
| Agustín Barrios Mangoré – Original Recordings (2 LPs). | El Maestro EM8002 |
| Agustín Barrios Recordings – Vol.3. | El Maestro EM8002 V3 |
| Gentil Montana plays Barrios. | Leguiz 67-368 |
| John Williams plays Barrios. | CBS 76662 |
| Jesús Benites plays Barrios (2 LPs). | Globo 402-403 |
| La Catedral – Wulfin Lieske. | Saphir INT 830.846 |

**SELECTED READING**

| | |
|---|---|
| Agustín Barrios. | Guitar, July 1974 |
| Agustín Barrios. | Guitar Player, January 1978 |
| Agustín Barrios – Illustrated biography. (with El Maestro record set EM 8002) | Richard Stover |

**SELECTED MUSIC**

| | |
|---|---|
| 4 Volumes. | Zen-On |
| 4 Volumes ed. Stover. | Belwin Mills |
| Complete Works. | Chanterelle |

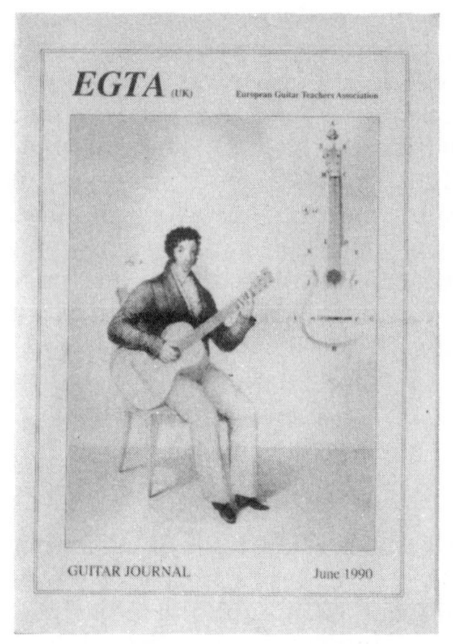


*A selection of guitar magazines*

# MANUEL BARRUECO

**Born –**

**Santiago, Cuba**

**16 December 1952**

COURTESY: THEA DISPEKER

*Manuel Barrueco*

Manuel Barrueco began his guitar studies at the age of eight in Cuba, under the tutelage of Manuel Puig. His talent showed immediately and he was enrolled in the Esteban Salas Conservatory to extend his early musical training.

In 1967 Barrueco's family moved to the United States, where the young guitarist continued his studies with Juan Mercadal in Miami and Rey de la Torre in New York. In 1971 he entered the Peabody Conservatory in Baltimore, where he was a full-scholarship student (studying under Aaron Shearer), a soloist with the Peabody Orchestra and a winner of the Peabody competition – the first guitarist to achieve these three honours.

In 1974 Barrueco won the Concert Artist Guild Award, and in the same year made his New York debut at the Carnegie Recital Hall. Success followed success, and Manuel Barrueco is now recognised as one of the finest classical guitarists of the twentieth century. He has given highly acclaimed concerts in most parts of the world and has made several outstanding recordings, first for the Vox-Turnabout label and currently with EMI.

Since 1975 Manuel Barrueco has been on the faculty of the Manhattan School of Music, where he is one of the co-founders of the guitar department. In 1990 he was appointed to the faculty of the Peabody Institute, Baltimore.

**SELECTED RECORDINGS**

| | |
|---|---|
| Villa-Lobos, Guarnieri, Chavez. | Vox Turnabout TV3467 CT 2157 (cassette) |
| Albéniz, Granados – Spanish Dances. | Vox Turnabout TV34738, CT 2247 (cassette) |
| Scarlatti, Paganini, Giuliani, Paganini. | Vox Turnabout TV34770, CT 4470 (cassette) |
| Bach Lute Suites Nos. 2, 4. | Vox Cum Laude VCL 9023 |
| Falla, Ponce, Rodrigo. | Angel/EMI CDC 7 49228 2 |
| Mozart and Sor. | Angel/EMI CDC 7 49368 2 |
| Bach, De Visée. | Angel EMI CDC 7 49980 2 |
| Villa-Lobos, Orbón, Brouwer. | Angel/EMI CDC 7 497102 |
| Flute/Guitar Duos. | EMI CDC 7 54102-2 |

**SELECTED READING**

| | |
|---|---|
| Interview. | Guitar, April 1973 |
| Interview. | Guitar, June 1979 |
| Interview. | Guitar Player, October 1980 |
| Interview. | Guitar & Lute, January 1981 |
| Interview. | Classical Guitar, May 1986 |
| Interview. | Classical Guitar, July 1989 |

## RENE BARTOLI

**Born –**

**Marseilles, France**

**1941**

*René Bartoli*

PHOTO: C. LACAN

The guitar was an established feature of the Bartoli household, and René Bartoli began his studies on the instrument at an early age. His first tutor was an uncle, and Bartoli made such progress that he decided to make the guitar his career.

In 1959 he won the Concours International de Guitare competition organized by ORTF (French radio and television). Following this success, he was able to study with Andrés Segovia, Ida Presti and Alexandre Lagoya.

In 1960 René Bartoli gave his first recital in his native town, Marseilles. Over the next few years he was to give many guitar recitals throughout France, but was rarely heard in concert in other countries. He was appointed Professor of Guitar at the Marseilles Conservatoire in 1965, a position he still holds.

Bartoli has made several recordings for the French record company Harmonia Mundi, and is one of France's most influential guitarists. In recent years he has been closely associated with the annual Festival of Arles.

**SELECTED RECORDS**

| | |
|---|---|
| René Bartoli. | RCA LSB4032 |
| Guitare 1. | Harmonia Mundi HMV572 |
| Guitare 2. | Harmonia Mundi HMV583 |
| Guitare 3. | Harmonia Mundi HMV751 |
| Music for Flute and Guitar. | Odyssey 321 60218 |

## SIEGFRIED BEHREND

**Born – Berlin, Germany – 19 November 1933**

**Died – Hausham, Bavaria, Germany**

**20 September 1990**

*Siegfried Behrend*

Siegfried Behrend's father was a guitarist who taught at a conservatory in Berlin. As a student at the age of sixteen, Behrend entered the same conservatory to study the piano, composition and conducting. While there the young musician began to take a close interest in the guitar. His father recommended him to a guitar teacher, and within a year Siegfried Behrend had given his first public concert.

He decided to gain experience and knowledge of his instrument by embarking on an extensive concert tour of Germany. At the age of twenty-one he toured throughout Italy and two years later throughout Spain. From that time Siegfried Behrend gave concerts in most countries, including the Soviet Union.

Siegfried Behrend recorded extensively for the Deutsche Grammophon label, and has had many of his original compositions and transcriptions published. He took a particular interest in avant-garde music for the classical guitar, and was regarded very highly as a teacher of his chosen instrument.

**SELECTED RECORDINGS**

Two Guitar Concertos – Rodrigo/Tedesco.
Deutsche Grammophon 139 166

Siegfriend Behrend, Guitar.
Deutsche Grammophon 139 167

| | |
|---|---|
| Deutsche Gitarren Musik. | Deutsche Grammophon 139 377 |
| Alitaliensche Gitarren Konzerte. | Deutsche Grammophon 139 417 |
| Guitar and Percussion. | Deutsche Grammophon 2530 034 |
| English Guitar Music. | Deutsche Grammophon 2530 079 |
| Chitarra Italiana. | Deutsche Grammophon 2530 561 |
| Treasures for Guitar. | Supraphon 50 780 |
| Guitarra Olé. | EMI Electrola SHZE 383 |
| Meister Werke für Zwei Gitarren (with Martin Kruger) | Acanta DC 23 098 |
| Sinfonische Folklore. | Olosseum SM 570 |

**SELECTED MUSIC**

| | |
|---|---|
| Fantasía Malagueñita. | JWC |
| Granadina de la Rambla. | JWC |
| Postkarten – Suite No.1 (7 easy pieces). | ZM 1896 |
| Six Monodien (1974) (Modern). | ZM 1907 |
| Three Spanish Dances. | ZM 1802 |
| Zorongo para Murao. | JWC |

**SELECTED READING**

| | |
|---|---|
| Interview in 'My Fifty Fretting Years' – | Ivor Mairants. Ashley Mark, 1980. |
| Interview. | Guitar International, June 1984. |

# ALEXANDER BELLOW

**Born – Moscow, Russia,1912**

**Died – Sherman, Connecticut, USA**

**12 March 1976**

*Alexander Bellow*

Alexander Bellow was a Russian-born, naturalised American citizen. A graduate of the Moscow Conservatory, he majored in composition and conducting, and was awarded the degree of Doctor of Music with honours. He also studied painting and engineering. During World War II he was imprisoned by the Germans in a concentration camp. He managed to survive, and emigrated to the United States of America in 1949 with his wife Mura and daughter Natasha.

As a classical guitarist, Bellow performed in the United States and abroad both as a solo recitalist and as part of a chamber group. On the advice of Andrés Segovia he decided to devote his musical talents to teaching. Alexander Bellow's greatest contribution to the guitar was as a teacher, and also as a transcriber of many early guitar compositions from the original tablature. Almost one hundred of his original compositions were published. He was also instrumental in forming the first USA guitar orchestra in New York.

Alexander Bellow's book 'The Illustrated History of the Guitar' is now accepted as one of the standard works for the study of the instrument, and is highly recommended reading for the guitar enthusiast.

**SELECTED MUSIC**

| | |
|---|---|
| Arpeggiato. | Kerby |
| Cavatina. | Hansen |
| Preludio e Toccata. | Kerby |
| Prelude, Scherzetto and Fugue. | Hansen |
| Scherzando. | Kerby |
| Sonata for Guitar. | FC 2794 |
| Sonata II for Guitar. | Kerby |
| Sonatina II. | Hansen |
| Suite Provençale. | Hansen |
| Tales of the Alhambra – As told by Washington Irving . | Kerby |
| Variations on a theme of Mudarra. | Kerby |

**SELECTED READING**

| | |
|---|---|
| The Illustrated History of the Guitar – Bellow. | Franco Colombo Inc.1970 |

# BALTAZAR BENITEZ

**Born –**

**Durazno, Uruguay**

**31 July 1944**

*Baltazar Benitez*

Baltazar Benitez began to play the guitar at the age of twelve, studying with Pedro Machin. He later studied with Abel Carlevaro at the National Conservatory of Montevideo. In 1968 he was chosen by the Jeunesses Musicales of Uruguay to tour his nation, since when he has won many of his country's most important musical awards. In 1970 he received a grant from the Spanish Cultural Institute to study in Santiago de Compostela with Andrés Segovia and José Tomás. In 1971 he won first prize at the International Guitar Competition held in Santiago de Compostela, and in 1973 won first prize at the Tárrega Competition in Benicasim, Spain.

Baltazar Benitez has also studied the lute and the harpsichord. Since 1972 he has led a busy life as a concert and recording artist and has held the teaching post for classical guitar in Tilburg, Holland.

**SELECTED RECORDINGS**

| | |
|---|---|
| Latin-American Music. | Nonesuch H-71349 |
| Bach & Scarlatti. | Nonesuch H-71404 |
| The Guitar Music of Astor Piazzolla. | Nonesuch 979-142-1 |

# DANIEL BENKO

**Born –**

**Budapest, Hungary**

**1947**

*Daniel Benkö*

Daniel Benkö's first instrument was the violin, which he studied from the age of six. He became interested in the guitar at the age of fifteen when he joined a pop group. His interest in classical music revived, and he joined the Bela Bartók Conservatory in Budapest to study classical guitar. After qualifying there, he went on to the Ferenc Liszt Academy of Music in Budapest, where he earned his degree in guitar at the age of twenty-four.

During his time at the Liszt Academy, Benkö became interested in the lute. He went to England to study the instrument with Diana Poulton, and also to Holland to study with Eugen M. Dombois. His interest in early music extended, and he also played in his concerts other early fretted instruments including the orpharion, the vihuela and the baroque guitar.

In 1972 Daniel Benkö founded the Bakfark Consort, and a few years later the Benkö Consort. With these groups he played music from Eastern and Western Europe, from the thirteenth to the nineteenth century.

Benkö has given concerts in many countries as a solo and ensemble artist, and is a prolific recording artist on both guitar and lute. Established as one of

Hungary's foremost guitarists, he also teaches lute at the Ferenc Liszt Academy.

**SELECTED RECORDINGS**

Romantische Ungarische Gitarrenmusik. Telefunken 6.42809 AZ
Balint Bakfark Complete Lute Music. Hungaraton SLPX 12771-75
Guitar Serenade. Hungaraton SLPX 12661
Vivaldi Lute Concertos & Trios. Hungaraton SLPX 11978
Dance Music from Hungary Telefunken 6.42782 AZ
Spanish Romance Hungaraton SLPD 12895

# HECTOR BERLIOZ

**Born – La Côte Saint André, near Grenoble, France**

**11 December 1803**

**Died – Paris, 8 March 1869**

The popularity of the music of the great nineteenth century composer and orchestrator of genius Hector Berlioz continues to grow, yet it is amazing how few musicians and music lovers, even today, realize that the guitar and the flute were the only two instruments on which he could play.

Berlioz's father encouraged him in his music studies from an early age, first on the flute and flageolet, and then the guitar. He studied, together with his elder sister, with a teacher named Dorant. At the age of eighteen Berlioz was sent by his parents to Paris to study medicine. He soon discovered that medicine was not for him, and decided to make music his life. The decision upset his father, who promptly stopped his maintenance. Berlioz was therefore forced to earn his living teaching the guitar, as well as the flute. He wrote several studies and variations for the guitar, and these were published by Aulagnier in Paris during this period.

In 1830 Berlioz won the Prix de Rome at the Conservatoire of Music, where he studied under Lesueur. This success earned him a government grant for three years' further study in Rome.

The following years saw the full development of Berlioz the composer. He became friendly with Mendelssohn and Paganini amongst many other fine musicians and composers. His very distinctive style of composition and orchestration has been attributed by some authorities to his ability to play the guitar and the flute to the exclusion of other instruments.

In his famous Treatise on Instrumentation and Orchestration, five pages are devoted to the guitar and mandolin. Berlioz's last guitar is now in the museum of the National Conservatoire of Music in Paris. Made by Grobert of Mirecourt (1794-1869), it was originally owned by Nicoló Paganini, and bears the signature of both its famous owners.

*Hector Berlioz*

**SELECTED MUSIC**

25 Romances. Chanterelle

**SELECTED READING**

Memoirs – 1865 (translated Gollancz 1969) Hector Berlioz
Treatise on Instrumentation and Orchestration Hector Berlioz
Hector Berlioz – Biography – Robert Clarson-Leach Omnibus Press, 1987

# GILBERT BIBERIAN

**Born –**

**Istanbul, Turkey**

**19 February 1944**

*Gilbert Biberian*

Gilbert Biberian was brought up and educated in England, where his family had come to live. He studied the guitar and composition at Trinity College of Music in London, graduating in 1968. In 1965 a French government grant took him to France to study with Ida Presti and Alexandre Lagoya. He continued his work with this legendary guitar duo until Ida Presti's untimely death in 1967.

After leaving Trinity College, Biberian studied interpretation with the pianist Anthony Kinsella for three years. Following a successful debut in the Wigmore Hall, he was invited to work with the London Sinfonietta and Pierre Boulez, Luciano Berio, the Nash Ensemble, the BBC Symphony Orchestra and many others. Biberian has also played at the Proms and at Covent Garden (where he played the guitar part in Tippett's King Priam) and has performed concertos and solo recitals on numerous other occasions.

While continuing his solo work, Gilbert Biberian created and directed two guitar ensembles, the Omega Players and the Omega Guitar Quartet. Both groups stimulated much original composition and made a substantial contribution to contemporary music in the 1970s and 1980s. Elisabeth Lutyens and Reginald Smith Brindle were two of the prominent composers who wrote works for these ensembles.

Gilbert Biberian has taught and lectured extensively, both in the United Kingdom and abroad. He directed the ensemble workshop in Guitar '75 and Guitar '78 at Toronto – North America's most influential guitar festival – and in Guitar '78 he was also a member of the panel of adjudicators. He is currently in charge of guitar ensemble teaching at Trinity College of Music, London.

Biberian studied composition with James Patten, Elisabeth Lutyens and Hans Keller. Since 1965 he has produced well over one hundred compositions, not only for solo and ensemble guitar but also for the voice and for various combinations of other instruments, including a concerto, two song cycles and a sonata for flute and guitar. His guitar compositions are finding their way into the standard repertoire and are being performed widely. His works have been published in England, Italy, Holland and the USA. He is currently editor of the guitar series published by J. & W. Chester.

**SELECTED MUSIC**

| | |
|---|---|
| Greek Suite | B1140 |
| Monogram. | Waterloo |
| Prelude & Fugue. | Novello |
| Sonata No.3. | G122 |

**SELECTED RECORDINGS**

Omega Guitar Quartet (Stravinsky & Biberian). President PTLS 1066

Monogram (with Ponce, J. McGuire etc.)

John Holmquist. Cavata CV 5001

Sonata No.3 – F. Henderson Musical New Services G121

**SELECTED READING**

| | |
|---|---|
| Gilbert Biberian. | Guitar, August 1972 |
| Gilbert Biberian. | Guitar, December 1976 |
| Contradicting the Unexpected – Interview. | Classical Guitar May/June 1983 |
| Gilbert Biberian's Rhythm Workshop. | Classical Guitar March/April 1983 |
| What's New about Teaching? – Biberian. | Classical Guitar |

# VAHDA OLCOTT BICKFORD

**Born – ETHEL LUCRETIA OLCOTT, Norwalk, Ohio, USA,17 October 1885**

**Died – Los Angeles, USA, 18 May 1980**

*Vahda Olcott Bickford*

As a child Vahda Olcott Bickford lived in Los Angeles, where she showed an early gift for music. She began her study of the guitar at the age of eight and became one of the last pupils of the renowned teacher Manuel Ferrer (1828-1904). She proved to be an outstanding pupil and was to give many successful concerts throughout the United States of America.

She went to New York in 1914 and soon became known through her concerts and teaching of the guitar. By invitation she lived for a time with the famous Vanderbilt family at Biltmore. There she taught Mrs Vanderbilt and her daughter Cornelia to play the guitar. It was while she was in New York that Olcott became associated with the famous astrologer Evangeline Adams, and was her only assistant for nine years, adopting her new name of Vahda.

In 1915 she married another outstanding North American musician, the guitarist/mandolinist Zarh Myron Bickford. They lived and worked together in New York, finally moving to Los Angeles in 1923. During her stay on the East Coast, Vahda Olcott Bickford established herself as an outstanding guitar soloist and teacher.

In 1923 she was instrumental in founding the American Guitar Society in Los Angeles. There is little doubt that through her promotional efforts and her transcriptions of music for the guitar, she was one of the most influential figures in the North American classical guitar scene during the first fifty years of this century.

Vahda Olcott Bickford died at the age of ninety-four in 1980. Still devoted to the guitar, she spent her last years teaching and giving her expert advice to musicologists and historians of the guitar. She continued to give concerts with her husband Zarh until his death in 1961. Bickford continued as a solo artist until her last concert at an American Guitar Society meeting in 1977. Her second husband, Robert Revere, died in 1980.

**SELECTED MUSIC**

Olcott Bickford – Method for Guitar. Oliver Ditson, Philadelphia 1921

**SELECTED READING**

Vahdah Olcott Bickford. Guitar and Lute No.14, 1980

# ERNESTO BITETTI

**Born - ERNESTO GUILLERMO BITETTI**

**Rosario, Argentina**

**20 July 1943**

*Ernesto Bitetti*

Ernesto Bitetti began his studies at the age of five in his native Argentina. He continued his musical education at the Instituto Superior de la Musica Universidad Nacional del Litoral, from which he graduated with the highest honours in 1964. In 1961 he was awarded First Prize in the 18th Concurso de la Sociedad Hebraica Argentina de Buenos Aires for stringed instrument playing, and in 1962 he reached the finals of the Coupe International de Guitare in Paris, France. In addition to the guitar, Bitetti has studied conducting, choral music, piano, flute and composition.

Since his initial and immediate success, Bitetti has continued to tour annually throughout Europe, the Soviet Union, Central and South America, the United States, Canada, Japan, Israel, New Zealand, India, the Far East and South Africa.

He has appeared as soloist with leading orchestras including the English, Israel and Munich Chamber Orchestras, and also with leading symphony orchestras throughout Europe, the Far East, North and South American, Australia and South Africa. He has given joint recitals with Teresa Berganza in Vienna, and appeared at the festivals of Edinburgh and Aix-en-Provence. During his 1980-81 United States tour, he played in concerts and recitals coast to coast, including a performance at the Kennedy Centre for the Performing Arts.

Many prominent composers have written works expressly for Bitetti, including Mario Castelnuovo-Tedesco, Joaquín Rodrigo, John W. Duarte, Federico Moreno Torroba, José Buenagu, Anton García Abril and Angelo Gilardino. With the St Louis Symphony Orchestra, Bitetti premiered the Concierto para la Guitarra Criolla by Waldove de los Rios, and in New York City's Town Hall he appeared with the violinist Ruggiero Ricci in the first performance of Duo Concerto No.2, written specifically for the occasion by the Spanish composer Tomás Marco.

Ernesto Bitetti is a major recording artist for Hispavox. Since 1989 he has been head of the Guitar Department at Indiana University School of Music, Bloomington, USA, and currently divides his time between that country and Spain, where he lives in Madrid.

**SELECTED RECORDINGS**

| | |
|---|---|
| Música Contemporanea. | Hispavox HHS 10-304 |
| Bach/Weiss Suites. | Hispavox HHS 10-331 |
| Rodrigo Concierto. | Hispavox HHS 10-335 |
| Músicos Españoles en la Guitarra. | Hispavox HHS 10-344 |
| Four Centuries of Spanish Guitar Music. | Hispavox HHS 10-365 |
| Four Centuries of Italian Guitar Music. | Hispavox HHS 10-400 |
| Halffter Concerto. | Hispavox HHS 10-420 |
| Waldove de los Rios Concerto. | Hispavox HHS 10-429 |
| Encores. | Hispavox HHS 10-450 |
| Albéniz. | Hispavox HHS 10-460 |
| Paganini Guitar/Violin Works (with R.Ricci). | Hispavox HHS 10-473 |
| Grandes Exitos. | Hispavox HHS S-60-135 |
| Rodrigo Concierto de Aranjuez. | Hispavox HHS S-60-157 |
| Manuel de Falla. | Hispavox HHS S-60-207 |
| Ernesto Bitetti plays Vivaldi. | Hispavox HHS S-60-687 |

**SELECTED READING**

Interview. Classical Guitar, May & June 1987

# DIEGO BLANCO

**Born –**

**Palma de Mallorca, Spain**

**2 June 1951**

COURTESY: GRAMMOFON AB BIS PHOTO CHRISTER VALLSTRAND

*Diego Blanco*

Diego Blanco started to learn the guitar at the age of eight with his uncle. Later he studied with the guitarist and teacher Dan Grenholm, a pupil of Emilio Pujol and Andrés Segovia.

Whilst learning the guitar Blanco was also taught the piano and the theory and history of music, by the Spanish composer and pianist Lorenso Galmes. At the age of eleven Blanco gave a series of concerts throughout Spain, but his real debut as a recitalist of importance was in Stockholm, Sweden, in 1968, where he enjoyed enormous success.

Diego Blanco has subsequently given many concerts in Scandinavia, Spain, Italy, England, Eastern Europe and the Soviet Union, and has appeared in numerous television and radio programmes in these countries. Several composers have dedicated works to him, including Koch, Karkoff, Rautavaara, Santórsola and Saeverud.

In 1979 Diego Blanco won the important Queen Sofia's International Guitar Competition in Madrid. He has made several recordings for the Swedish company BIS.

**SELECTED RECORDINGS**

Blanco Plays Ponce/Sojo/Lauro/Barrios. BIS LP33
Blanco Plays Fernando Sor. BIS LP133
Guitarra Española. RCA (Spain) LSC16359
Music for Flute & Guitar with Gunilla von Bahr Vol.1. BIS-LP 30
Music for Flute & Guitar with Gunilla von Bahr Vol.2. BIS-LP 60
Music for Flute & Guitar with Gunilla von Bahr Vol.3. BIS-LP 90

# VLADIMIR BOBRI

**Born – VLADIMIR BOBRITZKY**

**Kharkov, Ukraine, 13 May 1898**

**Died – New York, USA, 3 November 1986**

*Vladimir Bobri with Andrés Segovia*

Vladimir Bobri was brought up in a family atmosphere of culture and scholarship, and he acquired an adventurous attitude towards life and art. He was a graduate of the Imperial Art School of Kharkov, where he became interested in the theatre and in early icon painting. He studied scenic design by apprenticeship at the State Dramatic Theatre. Because of the turbulent events of the Revolution, Bobri fled from Russia in 1917, leaving his homeland for ever.

In Constantinople (Istanbul), Vladimir Bobri designed sets and costumes for the Russian ballet, produced movie posters and painted ikons in a monastery; in Anatolia (Turkey) he engaged in archaeological work. Then, in 1921, he went to the USA and settled in New York, where he became known for his imaginative murals, advertising art and book illustrations.

Although Bobri was a painter, he had a secondary, almost equal love for music, especially the music of the guitar. In 1936 he was a founding member of The Society of the Classic Guitar, an organisation that was to have far-reaching influences on the growth of interest in the guitar in this country.

From 1948 to 1986 he was the editor and art director of Guitar Review. He was the author of many essays on subjects related to the classical guitar, and composed a number of works for the instrument.

On 31 August 1972, Bobri was named 'Puntius Counselor at Large Efficientior' to 'Música en Compostela', a unique organization devoted to the study and interpretation of the music of Spain, located in Santiago de Compostela. The honour, in the form of an illustrated parchment, was given in consideration of his outstanding contribution to the appreciation of the classical guitar through his presidency of The Society of the Classic Guitar and his work as editor of Guitar Review.

On 10 January 1973, Vladimir Bobri was decorated with the Cross of Isabel la Católica with the rank of Knight-Commander (Comendador). This important decoration was bestowed in recognition of his lifelong achievements as a designer, painter, art director, composer and writer, and for his utilization of these talents to make others more keenly aware of the richness of Spanish culture. Presentation of the cross was made by H.E. Alberto Lopez Herce, Consul General of Spain in New York, at a ceremony attended by Spanish dignitaries, including Andrés Segovia.

Vladimir Bobri was without doubt one of the most important guitar personalities of the twentieth century.

**SELECTED READING**

Guitar Review – regular contributor and editor
Article. Guitar Review, Winter 1987

**SELECTED MUSIC**

| | |
|---|---|
| Very Easy Pieces. | FC |
| Complete Study of Tremolo. | FC3046 |
| Eight Melodic Exercises. | NY2604 |
| 130 Daily Studies for the Classical Guitar. | FCS2605 |
| Tango in A (1936) dedicated to Oyanguren. | Celesta Music, New York |

# PHILIP JAMES BONE

**Born –**

**Luton, England, 29 January 1873**

**Died – Luton, 17 June 1964**

*Philip J. Bone*

One of the leading personalities on the fretted instrument scene of Great Britain for many years, Philip James Bone, FRSA, MRST, was educated and trained for the scholastic profession. It was during his early days as a teacher that he became attracted to the mandolin and guitar. At first he played as a pastime, with no serious intent, but his interest in these instruments developed into a passion and he came to London to study under G.B. Marchiso, Professor of Mandolin and Guitar at Trinity College of Music. His progress was phenomenal, and he was chosen to give the first performance in England of two of Beethoven's compositions for mandolin and piano, Sonata and Adagio, at Trinity College in London.

He was awarded the Medal of the Royal Society of Arts for mandolin playing, and then followed one of the longest and most distinguished careers in the history of fretted instruments. He was founder and conductor of the Luton Mandolin Orchestra for forty years. Under his direction the orchestra gained high honours in the international sphere and was probably the first British mandolin orchestra to play on the mainland of Europe. He conducted 'The Trocadero' by request before the President of France in Paris in 1909.

His publication 'The Guitar and Mandolin – Biographies of Celebrated Composers and Players' is world renowned, and he made contributions to Cadenza, Keynotes, B.M.G. and other music journals. The numerous honours conferred on him included election to Fellowship of the Royal Society of Arts and membership of the Royal Society of Teachers.

In 1951 the British Federation of Banjoists, Mandolinist and Guitarists, then in its 22nd year, elected him its president, an office he held for thirteen years.

**SELECTED READING**

The Guitar and Mandolin
Philip J. Bone. Schott (1914, rev. 1954)

Philip J. Bone – A Bone of Contention.
Classical Guitar, May/June 1984

# CARLOS BONELL

**Born – CARLOS ANTONIO BONELL**

**London, England**

**23 July 1949**

*Carlos Bonell*

Born in London of Spanish parents, Carlos Bonell began to play the guitar at the age of five. His first interest was Spanish folk music, but by the age of seven he had already decided firmly on the classical repertoire – by studying both guitar and violin. His first teacher was his father, a keen amateur guitarist. His first public appearance was as a guitarist at the age of ten, and from the age of thirteen he dedicated himself exclusively to the guitar. He continued his studies at the Royal College of Music in London where he was invited to teach immediately upon completing his studies there in 1972.

The first major breakthrough in Bonell's career came with his nomination as a 'Young Musician '73' by the Greater London Arts Association. This led to many concerts throughout the United Kingdom, including appearances at the Camden, City of London, Brighton and Harrogate festivals. After his first concert appearance with the Royal Philharmonic Orchestra in the Royal Festival Hall came invitations from many other great orchestras, including the London Symphony, the Hallé, the Amsterdam Chamber Orchestra and the Philharmonia. In 1975 came the first of many hundreds of concerts in Europe and America, including the New York 'Mostly Mozart', the Flanders and the Israel festivals.

Apart from his recital and concerto work, Carlos Bonell's enthusiasm for chamber music has led to many memorable performances with such artists as Pinchas Zukerman, John Williams, Teresa Berganza and Lynn Harrel.

His record releases include a recital disc for Decca (with the first recording of Tárrega's unpublished 'Traviata' fantasia) and the first digital recording of Rodrigo's 'Aranjuez' concerto.

His recently-formed ensemble, which includes flute, panpipes, charango and other ethnic instruments, has been having considerable international success.

**SELECTED RECORDINGS**

| | |
|---|---|
| Guitar Music of Spain. | Enigma VAR1015 |
| Guitar Music of the Baroque. | Enigma VAR1050 |
| Guitar Showpieces. | Decca SXL6950 |
| Rodrigo's Aranjuez/Fantasia. | Decca SXDL7523 |

**SELECTED READING**

Interview. Classical Guitar, May/June 1984

# LIONA BOYD

**Born –**

**London, England**

**1950**

COURTESY: CBS RECORDS

*Liona Boyd*

Liona Boyd's father, a psychologist/sculptor, first moved to Canada in 1958. He returned to England for a short while, but finally settled in Canada in 1962. Liona Boyd is now a Canadian citizen.

The young guitarist first took a serious interest in the instrument at the age of fourteen after hearing a concert given by Julian Bream. She then began to take lessons with the noted Toronto teacher Eli Kassner and soon showed remarkable progress. At the age of seventeen she was accepted into a masterclass given by Julian Bream in Stratford, Ontario.

In 1972 Liona Boyd graduated from the University of Toronto with a Bachelor's degree in music and performance. A little later she won the Canadian National Music Competition Award for the guitar. Following this achievement, she became a pupil of Alexandre Lagoya, both in Canada and later in Paris. She stayed in Europe for a year and a half, and on her return to Canada in 1974 signed a recording contract with Boot Records. Her first release for this label was highly successful. A concert tour of Canada followed, with the popular artist Gordon Lightfoot. It exposed Boyd's classical ability to a much wider audience, and since that time she has been one of the busiest guitarists in North America.

Her popularity with the general music public has resulted in total sales of her records in the USA and Canada alone in excess of 150,000, a phenomenal achievement for a classical guitarist, and one that makes her Canada's best-selling classical artist for CBS Records. She is also a popular radio and television performer in Canada, and had her own TV show in 1978.

**SELECTED MUSIC**

| | |
|---|---|
| First Lady of the Guitar. | Hansen House |
| Miniatures for Guitar. | Hal Leonard |
| A Guitar for Christmas. | Hal Leonard |
| Folksongs for Classical Guitar. | Hal Leonard |
| Meet Liona Boyd. | Mid-Continental Music |
| Favourite Solos for Classical Guitar. | Hal Leonard |

**SELECTED RECORDINGS**

| | |
|---|---|
| The Guitar – Liona Boyd. | Boot BMC3002 |
| Miniatures for Guitar. | Boot BOS7181 |
| Classical Guitar – Liona Boyd. | London CS7015 |
| Artistry of Liona Boyd. | London CS7068 |
| First Lady of the Guitar. | CBS MW M35137 |
| Liona Boyd with the English Chamber Orchestra . | CBS MW M35853 |
| First Nashville Quartet, with Chet Atkins. | RCA HL 1-3302 |
| Spanish Fantasy. | CBS MW M36675 |
| A Guitar for Christmas. | CBS MW FM37248 |
| The Best of Liona Boyd. | CBS MV FM37788 |
| Liona Boyd – Persona. | CBS FM2120 |
| Liona Boyd – Live in Tokyo. | CBS MW IM39031 |

**SELECTED READING**

| | |
|---|---|
| Interview. | Guitar Player, October 1978 |
| Interview. | Frets, December 1980 |
| Interview. | Guitarra, March 1980 |
| 'Jet-Guitarist'. | Chatelaine, March 1982 |

# FREDERICK BRAND

**Born –**

**Regensburg, Germany, 1806**

**Died – Wùrzburg, Germany, 1874**

*Frederick Brand*

Regarded by many as one of the great guitar virtuosos of the nineteenth century, Frederick Brand was known mainly in his native Germany. He was originally a teacher in Mannheim, but after his marriage he moved to Würzburg. Here he met the guitar virtuoso Adam Darr, and together these two great guitarists obtained very many engagements as a guitar duo and also as soloists. Both guitarists received high critical acclaim wherever they went.

As well as being a highly talented player, Frederick Brand was a most respected teacher of the instrument. He wrote many original compositions for the guitar, and these were published by Pacini of Paris and Schott of Mainz.

# ARNE BRATTLAND

**Born –**

**District of Meløy, Norway**

**6 May 1955**

*Arne Brattland*

Arne Brattland began to play the guitar at the age of five and was self-taught until entering the Norwegian State Academy of Music in Oslo in 1975. He studied there with Erik Stenstadvold and Jan Danielsen.

He made his concert debut at the North Norwegian Festival in 1983. In 1985 he obtained a grant from Norwegian institutions and the British Council to study in London. During his three-year stay there, he studied with David Russell, Nigel North, Gilbert Biberian and John W. Duarte.

Arne Brattland returned to Norway in 1988 and has now established himself as one of the best young classical guitarists in Scandinavia with a busy career as a recitalist and teacher.

**SELECTED RECORDINGS**

| | |
|---|---|
| Brattland plays Grieg, Duarte and Biberian. | VEPS 013-87 |
| Guitar Favourites. | VEPS CD 028-90 |

**SELECTED MUSIC**

18 Lyric Pieces by Grieg transcribed Brattland Vols.1-3
VEPS Publishing

COURTESY: JOHN W. DUARTE

Philharmonic Society of Guitarists, London, 1947. Julian Bream in front row, 3rd from right. 4th from right: Dr Boris Perott. Also in front row, A. P. Sharpe (editor of B. M. G.), 2nd from left. On his left, Victoria Kingsley, Wilfred Appleby and centre Johanna Vollers (secretary, P. S. G.). Harry Bream, Julian's father, on the right at the end.

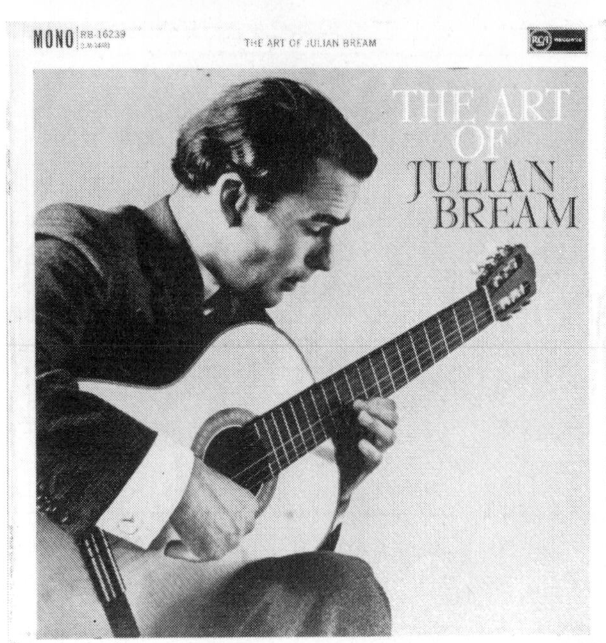

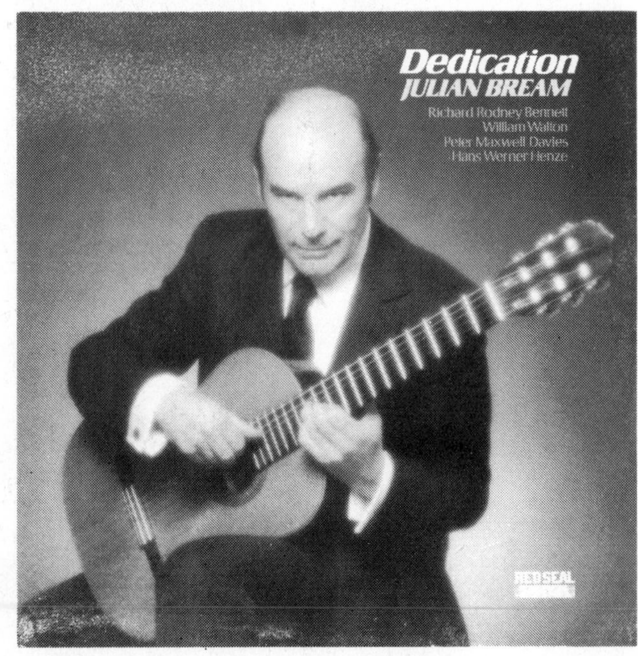


*A selection of Julian Bream records*

# JULIAN BREAM

**Born –**

**Battersea, London, England**

**15 July 1933**

*Julian Bream*

Julian Bream is one of the greatest guitarists the world has known. By the time he was seventeen, although he had not played outside Great Britain, he was already known by reputation to guitarists all over the world.

Julian Bream was brought up in a musical environment. His father, a commercial artist and book illustrator, also ran a small dance band in which he played jazz guitar. The young Bream was very attracted to the jazz guitar style of Django Reinhardt, the legendary Gypsy guitarist. Bream's father encouraged his son to play the piano, but also taught him to play the plectrum guitar. On his eleventh birthday, Julian Bream was given a classical guitar by his father.

In 1945 Julian Bream won a junior exhibition award for his piano playing. This entitled him to study the piano and the cello at the Royal College of Music, London. In the same year his father took him to play at a meeting held by the London Philharmonic Society of Guitarists, where his obvious musical talent prompted Dr Boris Perott, the Society's president, to offer to teach him the classical guitar. This he did for one year. Dr Perott, and also Wilfrid Appleby, introduced Julian Bream to Andrés Segovia, who was so impressed by what he heard that he offered to give the thirteen-year old some lessons.

Julian Bream made his professional debut in Cheltenham in 1947. Encouraged by his father, he decided to make his career in music and the guitar, abandoning an almost equally strong ambition to become a professional cricketer. At the age of fifteen he was awarded a full scholarship at the Royal College of Music, and for three years studied piano, harmony and composition there – for it was a time when no guitar tuition could be offered by the College.

Great critical acclaim greeted his debut in the Wigmore Hall, London, in 1951. Despite three years in the British Army (1952-55), he continued to appear frequently on radio and television programmes as well as at public concerts. His first European tours took place in 1954 and 1955, and were followed by extensive touring in North America (beginning in 1958), the Far East, India, Australia, the Pacific Islands and other parts of the world. In addition to masterclasses given in Canada and the USA, Bream has also conducted an international summer school in Wiltshire, England.

Julian Bream's many recordings for RCA have made him well known to a large worldwide audience and have won for him some of the highest awards in the recording industry. They include the Award of the National Academy of Recording Arts and Sciences, two Grammy awards (1963 and 1966), and an Edison award (1968). In the Queen's Birthday Honours List of 1985 he was made a Commander of the Order of the British Empire (C.B.E.).

Since 1952, when he played part of a Wigmore Hall recital on the lute, Julian Bream has also been noted for his playing of this instrument, and is responsible for bringing to light much of its music which had lain dormant for over three hundred years. He has also done much to broaden the contemporary guitar repertoire by commissioning works from such famous composers as Benjamin Britten, William Walton, Hans Werner Henze, Peter Racine Fricker, Richard Rodney Bennett, Malcolm Arnold, Alan Rawsthorne, Lennox Berkeley and Michael Tippett. It is safe to say to that no guitarist has ever done more to enrich the repertoire in this way.

Bream's association with his fellow guitarist John Williams, which resulted in three recordings and a number of concerts, has been an enormous success. BBC Television have presented a special programme about Julian Bream's life as a concert guitarist, and also a series of four masterclasses presented by Bream for guitarists. Channel 4 Television produced a series of six half-hour programmes on the classical guitar by Bream, entitled ¡Guitarra!

**SELECTED RECORDINGS**

The Art of Julian Bream. RCA RB 16239
Popular Classics for Spanish Guitar. RCA RB6593
Guitar Music of Villa-Lobos & Torroba. HMV CLP 1763
Bach Recital for Guitar. HMV CLP 1929
Julian Bream plays Bach. RCA RL 42378
Rodrigo Concerto/Vivaldi Concerto/Britten Dances. RCA SB 6635

| | |
|---|---|
| Baroque Guitar. | RCA SB 6673 |
| Twentieth Century Guitar. | RCA SB 6723 |
| Julian Bream & Friends. Boccherini Quintet/Haydn Quartet. | RCA SB 6772 |
| Classic Guitar. Giuliani/Diabelli/Mozart/Sor | RCA SB 6796 |
| Guitar Concertos Giuliani/Arnold. | RCA SB 6826 |
| Julian Bream plays Villa-Lobos. | RCA SB 6852 |
| Romantic Guitar. | RCA SB 6844 |
| Julian Bream 70s | RCA SB 6876 |
| Giuliani/Sor. | RCA ARL 1-0711 |
| Rodrigo/Berkeley Guitar Concertos. | RCA ARL 1-1181 |
| Julian Bream plays Villa-Lobos | RCA RL 12499 |
| Music of Spain.Sor/Aguado. | RCA RL 14033 |
| Live (2 LPs). | RCA SB 6862 |
| Granados & Albéniz. | RCA RS 9008 |
| Guitarra (2 LPs). | RCA RL 85417(2) |
| Brouwer/Rodrigo Concertos. | RCA RL 87718 |

*Duo with John Williams:*

| | |
|---|---|
| Together. | RCA SB 6862 |
| Together Again. | RCA ARL 1-0456 |

*Video recording:*

| | |
|---|---|
| ¡GUITARRA! The Guitar in Spain (2 videotapes) | Virgin Videos |

**SELECTED READING**

| | |
|---|---|
| Julian Bream. | Guitar, January 1973 |
| Julian Bream. | Guitar, October 1973 |
| Julian Bream. | Guitar, March 1974 |
| Julian Bream. | Guitar, August 1973 |
| Julian Bream. | Guitar, March 1977 |
| Julian Bream. | Guitar, February, 1980 |
| Julian Bream. | Frets, June 1981 |
| Julian Bream. | Guitar Player, October 1971 |
| Julian Bream. | Guitarra, July 1981 |
| Julian Bream. | Guitarra, September 1981 |
| Interview. | Classical Guitar, May/June 1983 |
| Interview. | Classical Guitar, February & March 1986 |

## *Julian Bream*

*— playing music by Mudarra on the guitar —*

Hundreds of eyes with eagerness impel
The Wizard-Medium towards his simple throne,
A crackle of applauding palms,
Welcoming, anticipating –
Then noiselessness.

From the tense silence the Six-voiced Oracle
Melodiously declaims, reincarnating
Alonso de Mudarra of Seville
Whose music was conceived
Four Spanish centuries ago.

Hundreds of ears miraculously
Hear, nay, SEE
Liquids sounds transformed into a stream
Dancing and sparkling –
And Spanish children singing.

The magic wanes, the sunlit music fades,
A silent mistiness pervades –
Or is it moistening of eyes
Brimming with wonder?

*Wilfrid M. Appleby*

# ROBERT BRIGHTMORE

**Born –**

**Leicester, England**

**25 January 1949**

*Robert Brightmore*

From the age of five Robert Brightmore studied the piano with his father, but became fascinated with the guitar. By the time he had reached his early teens, he realized that his facility was greater for the guitar than for the piano, and the instrument became something of an obsession.

After completing his studies at the Nottingham College of Art and the London Film School, he studied classical guitar with George Zarb in London, and attended masterclasses with Julian Bream and Oscar Cáceres.

He made his Wigmore Hall debut in London in 1975 and since that time has established himself as a prominent recitalist, touring extensively and giving concerts, classes and courses.

Working with composers forms a strong element in Brightmore's career, and he has given first performances of many new works by foremost composers, among them Leo Brouwer, Reginald Smith Brindle, Oliver Hunt, Stépan Rak and Carlo Domeniconi. He has recently premiered two works by the South American composer Jaime Zenamon; the guitar concerto Iguaçu, dedicated to Brightmore, and Demian, a solo work based on the book by Herman Hesse. He also initiated the stage setting of Oliver Hunt's The Barber of Baghdad at the London Collegiate Theatre for a performance of the piece set to mime.

Robert Brightmore is active as an arranger, and has made several LPs. He is currently professor of guitar at the Guildhall School of Music and Drama in London.

**SELECTED RECORDINGS**

| | |
|---|---|
| Robert Brightmore: | Vista Records VPS 1077 |
| Profile. | Barry-Musik, EMI Electrola ASD BM 8401 |
| Robert Brightmore: | Recital. Chorus Records CH 8601 |

**SELECTED READING**

| | |
|---|---|
| Interview. | Classical Guitar, July/August 1983 |
| Article. | Classical Guitar, April 1990 |

COURTESY: JORGE MOREL

*Pablo Escobar, outstanding Argentinian guitarist/composer of the past*

# LEO BROUWER

**Born –**

**Havana, Cuba**

**1 March 1939**

PHOTO: COLIN COOPER

*Leo Brouwer*

One of today's most outstanding guitarists and composers, Leo Brouwer first studied the guitar with Isaac Nicola, a pupil of Emilio Pujol. He specialized in composition, completing his studies at The Juilliard School and in Hartt College in Hartford.

In 1961 he was named Director of the Music Department of the Cinema Institute of Cuba, Professor of Composition in the Music Conservatory and musical adviser to the National Radio and Television Chain of Havana. He became Director of the experimental department of the Cuban Institute of Cinema Arts and Industry, where he continued his work as a composer.

Leo Brouwer was the first Cuban composer to use aleatory and 'open' forms, and his very many compositions include several works for guitar, percussion, prepared and non-prepared pianos, a cantata for two percussionists and piano, a contemporary ballet, a chorus of twelve members, three children and harp, and a series of orchestral works.

He has taken part as a guitarist and as a composer in the Festivals of Aldeburgh, Avignon, Edinburgh, Spoleto, Berlin (Festwochen), Toronto, Arles, Martinique and Rome, as well as in other important musical centres in Europe.

In addition to his outstanding contribution as a guitarist and composer, Leo Brouwer is also a talented conductor, and has worked with, among others, the BBC Concert Orchestra, the Langham Chamber Orchestra, the Philharmonic Orchestra of Berlin (FRG) and the National Orchestra of Scotland. He also conducted the Manson Ensemble in London and the Theatre Orchestra of Rome for the world premiere of his music for 'Julius Caesar' (1971). Brouwer was also guest composer of the Deustsche Akademische Austauschdienst in Berlin (1972) along with Morton Feldman, Earle Brown and St Bussot. He has conducted masterclasses for guitarists in France, Canada, Martinique, Cuba, Puerto Rico, Finland, Cuba and Greece, and has been a jury member in many international competitions, including those in Munich, Caracas, Esztergom, Paris and his native Havana. He founded the biennial Havana International Guitar Festival and Competition in the early 1980s, and has directed it ever since.

In recent years Leo Brouwer has concentrated more on composition than performance, producing a stream of works that reflect a moving away from his earlier experimental style towards music that contains strong elements of melody while employing certain minimalist techniques. He remains one of the most interesting figures on the contemporary guitar scene.

**SELECTED MUSIC**

| | |
|---|---|
| Canticum. | GA 424 |
| Danza Caracteristica. | GA 422 |
| Elogio de la Danza . | GA 425 |
| Fuga No.1. | ESC 7995 |
| La Espiral Eterna. | GA 423 |
| Parábola. | ESC 8198 |
| Piece Without Title. | ESC 8000 |
| Pieces Without Title Nos.2 & 3. | ESC 8452 |
| Preludio. | ESC 7996 |
| Tarantos. | ESC 8293 |
| Tres Apuntes (3 sketches). | GA 426 |
| Two Popular Cuban Airs: Guajira Criolla, Zapateada. | ESC 7999 |
| Two Popular Cuban Themes: Canción de Cuna, Ojos Brujos. | ESC 8182 |
| Etudes Simples Nos.1-20 (4 vols.). | ESC 7997, 7998, 8494, 8495 |
| Variations on a Theme of Django Reinhardt. | |
| El Decameron Negro. | EMT 1704 |
| Cuban Landscape with Rain. | DO 92 |
| Cuban Landscape with Bells. | |
| Concerto No.1 for Guitar and Orchestra. | |
| Concerto No.2 'Concierto de Lieja' for Guitar and Orchestra. | |
| Concerto No.3 'Concierto Elegiaco' for Guitar and Orchestra. | |
| Concerto No.4 'Concierto de Toronto' for Guitar and Orchestra. | |

**SELECTED RECORDINGS**

| | |
|---|---|
| Les Classiques de Cuba. | Erato STV 0669 |
| Scarlatti – Twelve Sonatas. | Erato STV 70870 |
| Leo Brouwer. | Deutsche Grammophon 2555 01 |
| Rara. | Deutsche Grammophon 2530 307 |
| Leo and Ichiro. | Camerata/Tokyo CMT-1065 |
| Guitarra. | Egrem LD 4189 |
| Leo Brouwer – Guitarrista. | Egrem LD 3876 |
| Contemporaneo 2. | Egrem LD 3653 |

**SELECTED READING**

| | |
|---|---|
| Leo Brouwer. | Guitar, June 1976 |
| Leo Brouwer. | Guitar, April 1977 |
| Leo Brouwer. | Guitar & Lute, January 1982 |
| Leo Brouwer. | Classical Guitar, September 1984 |
| Leo Brouwer – works for guitar. | Guitar Review, Spring 1989 |

# JULIAN BYZANTINE

**Born –**

**London, England**

**11 June 1945**

COURTESY: JULIAN BYZANTINE

*Julian Byzantine*

Julian Byzantine began his advanced musical studies with John Williams at the Royal College of Music, where he was awarded the first ARCM for guitar. During this period he won scholarships to further his studies with Julian Bream in England and Andrés Segovia in Siena, where he was chosen by the maestro to give a solo recital. After finishing these studies he taught on the staff of the Royal Academy of Music, London, for two years.

Besides his recital work, Byzantine makes frequent concerto appearances and has performed with some of the leading orchestras in Britain, including the Royal Philharmonic, the City of Birmingham Symphony and the Scottish Chamber Orchestras, and with many national orchestras abroad.

In the field of contemporary music he has worked with Pierre Boulez and Peter Maxwell Davies, and on numerous occasions the Arts Council of Great Britain has had works commissioned for him.

Julian Byzantine's reputation as a soloist has been extended by his broadcasts for radio and television, and these have included a television documentary on the life and guitar music of Heitor Villa-Lobos. A particular interest in the manuscripts of the early guitarists and lutenists led him to become an exponent of the baroque guitar.

One of Britain's best established concert artists, Julian Byzantine has travelled widely, making extensive concert tours of Scandinavia, Latin America, the USA and, particularly, Australasia.

**SELECTED RECORDINGS**

Julian Byzantine Plays Villa-Lobos etc. — Classics for Pleasure CFP 40209

Masterpieces for Classical Guitar — Classics for Pleasure CFP 40362

**SELECTED READING**

Julian Byzantine. — Guitar, December 1980

# OSCAR CACERES

**Born –**

**Montevideo, Uruguay**

**4 April 1928**

*Oscar Cáceres*

Oscar Cáceres began his serious study of the guitar under the guidance of the guitarists Ramon Ayestaran, Marin Sanchez and Atilio Rapat. As a child he made such good progress on the instrument that he was able to give his first public recital at the age of thirteen.

In 1957, when he was twenty-nine, Oscar Cáceres made his first European recital tour. He played with great success in Paris, Madrid, Valencia and Barcelona. On his return to South America he gave the first live performance on that continent of Rodrigo's Concierto de Aranjuez ..

Cáceres continued to make extensive concert tours of South America, at the same time devoting a large part of his work to musical research. He has a special love of Rensaissance music, but at the same time retains a keen interest in twentieth century music.

In 1967 Oscar Cáceres decided to settle in Paris. He has continued to give recitals and also to teach the guitar in most of the major cities of Europe.

**SELECTED RECORDINGS**

Les Grandes Etudes pour Guitare Vol.1. Erato STV 70614
Les Grandes Etudes pour Guitare Vol.2. Erato ATV 70904
Oscar Cáceres plays Leo Brouwer. Erato STV 70734
Musique pour Deux Guitares Vol.1 (with Turibio Santos). Erato STV 70794
Musique pour Deux Guitares Vol.2 (with Turibio Santos). Erato STV 71092
Trésors d'Amerique Latine. Erato STV 70988
Oscar Cáceres: Takemitsu/Brouwer. Pavanne ADW7097
Oscar Caleres Villa Lobos. Pavanne ADW 7097
Oscar Cáceres plays Bach/Weiss. Pavanne ADW 7040
Anthology of the Spanish Guitar (4 CD's) ADDA 484/581214/17

*An unusual 19th century guitar made by the Mauchant Brothers, Mirecourt, France. Now on display at the Gemeentemeseum – Gravenhage, The Hague, Netherlands.*

# BARTOLOME CALATAYUD

**Born – Palma de Mallorca, Spain, 1882**

**Died – Palma de Mallorca, 1973**

COURTESY: GEORGE M. BOWDEN

*Bartolome Calatayud*

Bartolome Calatayud's first teacher was Antonio Mestro, Professor and Director of the Instituto de Bachillerato and also a guitarist. To Mestro is owed the formation of an excellent group of guitarists that included Calatayud and the brothers Bernat.

Calatayud's progress with Mestro was such that he was soon giving guitar concerts in Mallorca. The eminent Catalan guitarist and composer Emilio Pujol was present at one of these concerts at the Circulo Mallorquín and invited Calatayud to give a concert in Barcelona. A great friendship between the two musicians developed after this meeting. Calatayud's first concert outside Spain was given in Toulouse, France, and soon concerts were taking place in other European countries.

Calatayud, who had had an inclination towards composition from his youth, had learned harmony from Mestro. He wrote many compositions for the guitar, including Una Lágrima, Danza Mora,Alegre Primavera, Gaviotas, and Suite Antigua. There are over fifty of his compositions listed in the catalogue of the Spanish publishers Unión Musical.

Calatayud did a great deal of work in the spreading and correct interpretation of Mallorquín folk music. In 1940 he was appointed director of Coros y Danzas of the Sección Femenina de Palma. With this organization he toured South American countries with great success and made several records which have carried Palma's folk music to all parts of the world.

Bartolome Calatayud had a special ability as a teacher, and as a result had many pupils. Such was his reputation that many guitarists came to study with him from countries other than Spain.

**SELECTED RECORDINGS**

| | |
|---|---|
| Inolvidable Guitarra. | Impacto EL 225 |
| Gabriel Estarellas interprets Bartolome Calatayud. | Maller API 86 |

**SELECTED MUSIC**

| | |
|---|---|
| Alegre, Campina, Vals. | UME 2097 |
| Alegre, Primavera. | UME 20434 |
| Boceto Andaluz. | UME 20003 |
| Cuatro Divertimientos. | UME 20557 |
| Cuatro Juguetes. | UME 21719 |
| Cuatro Piezas para Guitarra. | UME 19675 |
| Cubanita, Habañera. | UME 21718 |
| Danza Española. | UME 20212 |
| Danza Mora. | UME 21780 |
| Danza Popular de Campdevanol. | UME 21266 |
| Dos Piezas para Guitarra. | UME 19674 |
| Dos Piezas para Guitarra. | UME 20004 |
| Estampa Gitana. | UME 20217 |
| Estudio Melodico. | UME 21091 |
| Galop. | UME 21781 |

# MATTEO CARCASSI

**Born –**

**Florence, Italy, 1792**

**Died – Paris, France, 16 January 1853**

**Matteo Carcassi*

Thousands of student guitarists throughout the world today know the name Carcassi as the author of their guitar method and the composer of many attractive compositions and studies. There is no doubt he is most well known for these works, but Carcassi was also one of the great guitarists of the nineteenth century.

Matteo Carcassi studied the guitar from an early age in his native Italy. Before he was twenty he already had a reputation in Italy as a virtuoso of the guitar. In 1815 he was established in Paris as a teacher of both guitar and piano. During a concert tour of Germany in 1819 he became friendly with the French guitarist Meissonier, who in 1812 had opened a publishing house in Paris. The two guitarists became firm friends, and Meissonier published most of Carcassi's works.

In 1822 Carcassi established himself in London, after only a few concerts, as an exceptional guitar soloist and teacher. He soon returned to Paris, but was able to make an annual trip to London, where his guitar talents were much in demand.

When he first arrived in Paris, Carcassi's talents had been somewhat overshadowed by the older Italian guitar virtuoso guitarist Ferdinando Carulli, but after a few years Carcassi attained very great success. He gave annual concerts in most of the major cities of Europe, including London, but, despite a brief return to Italy in 1836, Paris was to become his permanent residence. He died there in 1853.

**SELECTED MUSIC**

| | |
|---|---|
| Andantino & Romanze, from op.60. | GA 305 |
| Fifty-four Selected Pieces: Book I (Easy). | GA 4A |
| Book II (Medium). | GA 4B |
| Book III (Difficult). | GA 4C |
| My First Carcassi, ed. Skiera | Ricordi |
| Rondoletto op.41, ed. Danner (Fac. No.8). | Belwin |
| Selected Works (facsimiles), ed. Noad. | Hansen |
| Six Caprices op.26. | GA 72 |
| Six Easy Caprices op.26, ed. Schwarz-Reiflingen. | Sik. |
| Six Easy Variations op.18. | Vieweg |
| Three Sonatinas op.1 & Six Caprices op.26. | GA 5 |
| Twelve Easy Pieces op.10. | GA 73 |
| Twenty Selected Waltzes. | GA 3 |
| Twenty-four Little Pieces op.21. | GA 6 |
| Two Waltzes from op.4. | GA 309 |
| Variations on the Dream of Rousseau op.17. | Kalmus |

**Although this portrait has been attributed to be Carcassi for many years, some authorities now doubt its authenticity.*

# JORGE CARDOSO

**Born – JORGE RUBEN CARDOSO KRIEGER**

**Posadas, Misiones Province, Argentina**

**26 January 1949**

COURTESY: JORGE CARDOSO

*Jorge Cardoso*

Originally Jorge Cardoso studied the guitar with Lucas B. Arceo and Luis J. Cassinelli. On gaining a scholarship from the National Fund in Arts in Argentina, he was able to study with Maria Hermini A. de Gomez Crespo. Later he studied harmony with Mario Perini, and composition at the National University of Córdoba in Argentina. While studying compositon at this university he also studied medicine. He eventually qualified in both, which is probably a first for any leading classical guitarist.

Since the age of fourteen, Jorge Cardoso won first prizes in several important Argentinian competitions. In 1963 he won the solo instrumental class at the Festival of Music of the Littoral, at Posadas; in 1967 the National Folklore Composition Competition at Salta, and in 1973 the International Concourse of the Classical Guitar at Morón (Buenos Aires).

Cardoso has appeared in many recitals and concerts throughout Argentina, Spain, France, Japan and Poland, but as yet has received little or no exposure in other countries. He has several records to his name, and over 100 musical works published, including two concertos for guitar and orchestra.

Jorge Cardoso lives in Madrid, where he directs the Ibero American Guitar Orchestra of Madrid. He spends most of his year in Spain, and also some time in Japan, where he is very popular. He has established himself not only as a guitarist of outstanding ability, but also as a fine composer and teacher.

**SELECTED RECORDINGS**

| | |
|---|---|
| Clásicos del Folklore SudAmericano. | DPM PM 2040 |
| Suite SudAmericana. | Dial Discos ND 5019 |
| Autores SudAmericanos. | Diapason Dial Discos 52-5038 |
| Lamento Caingua. | Diapason 52-5054 |
| Cardoso and the Niibori Guitar Orchestra. | APAC 8009 |
| Suite Litoralena. | Diapason 52-5067 |
| Jorge Cardoso. | Blue Angel BA 29005 |
| Cardoso Plays Cardoso | OPUS 9311 2123 |

**SELECTED MUSIC**

| | |
|---|---|
| Suite SudAmericana. | CASA 320 |
| Twenty-four Pieces – SudAmericana. | UME 22310, UME 22353 |
| Gavota del Crepusculo. | UME |
| Mitosis. Guitar Music, | Tokyo UT 40 |
| Suite Portena. | Guitar Music, Tokyo |
| Preludes by Bach. | UME |

**SELECTED READING**

| | |
|---|---|
| Ciencia y Método en la Tecnica Guitarristica | Capsa de los Americas (Cuba) |
| Jorge Cardoso. | Guitar International, December 1986 |

# FERDINANDO CARULLI

**Born – FERDINANDO MARIA MEINRADO PASCALE ROSARIO CARULLI**

**Naples, Italy, 9 February 1770**

**Died – Paris, France, 17 February 1841**

*Ferdinando Carulli*

Ferdinando Carulli was the son of a distinguished writer, who was secretary to the Neopolitan Jurisdiction Delegate. Carulli's first musical instrument was the cello, but he became attracted to the guitar at an early age. Although the guitar was extremely popular in Italy at that time, there were very few serious teachers of the instrument.

Carulli's musical genius became evident whilst he was still a young man. He developed a series of studies and exercises, revolutionary in their concept, to help his technique on the instrument. With these studies any dedicated guitarist could achieve excellent standards of musicianship on the guitar.

In 1797, already a highly respected teacher and player, Carulli moved to Leghorn. In 1808 he again moved, this time to Paris. Here he was to remain for the rest of his life.

In 1810 he wrote his comprehensive method for guitar (Op.27). Originally published by Carli of Paris, it became one of the standard instruction books for guitar. Its success was so great that four editions were printed in a relatively short period of time. Fifth, sixth and seventh editions (Op.241) followed; these were enlarged versions of the original, containing an appendix of forty-four progressive pieces and six studies. In 1825 Carulli wrote L'Harmonie appliqué à la guitare, a skilful work on the art of accompaniment, and the first of its kind. He published more than four hundred compositions for the guitar, including studies, concerti, several trios for guitar, flute and violin, trios for three guitars, and many compositions for two guitars and guitar and piano. All these compositions are characterized by their richness of harmony and elegance of form.

Carulli's original method is still widely used by teachers and students. Increasing interest in his music, particularly the ensemble pieces, is further evidence of his musical genius.

**SELECTED MUSIC**

| | |
|---|---|
| Allegretto. | Bèrben EB 2112 |
| Best of Carulli, ed. Castle (11 selections). | MB |
| Capriccio. | GA 310 |
| Eighteen Little Pieces | |
| Op. 211, ed. Carfagna. | Bèrben EB 2180 |
| Eighteen Very Easy Pieces Op.333. | GA 67 |
| Nice und Fileno – Sonata Op.2. | ZM 1967 |
| Overture Op.6 No.1. | N 3168 |
| Preludes for Guitar Op.114, | |
| ed. Schwarz-Reiflingen. | N 3211 |
| Six Andantes Op. 320, ed. Chiesa. | GA 313 |
| Solo Op. 76 no.2. | Zerboni SZ 7732 |
| Three Sonatas. | GA 40 |
| Twenty-four Preludes Op.114, ed. Balestra. | Ricordi ER 2746 |
| Two Minuets from Op. 270. | GA 311 |
| Variations on a Theme of Beethoven. | Bèrben EB 2097 |
| Variations on the Italian | |
| Aria 'Sul Margine d'un Rio' Op. 142. | Zerboni |
| SZ 7727 | |

**SELECTED READING**

Profilo biografico-critico e catalogo tematico della opere con numero. Vols.1 & 2 – Mario Torta (dissertation). Universita degli Studi di Roma 'La Sapienza', 1989.

# ABEL CARLEVARO

**Born –**

**Montevideo, Uruguay**

**16 December 1918**

COURTESY: ABEL CARLEVARO

*Abel Carlevaro*

Abel Carlevaro began his study of musical theory under Tomas Mujica and Pablo Kimlos. He was originally self-taught on the guitar, using the printed methods that were available in Uruguay at that time. He later studied harmony, instrumentation and orchestration, applying his knowledge of these subjects to his guitar studies. His original decision was to make his career in agriculture, but his love for the guitar eventually made him choose the field of music.

In 1937 Abel Carlevaro met Andrés Segovia. Following this meeting, he was able to study with the maestro for nine years. In 1942 Segovia presented him at the official music centre of the Republic of Uruguay. This recital established Carlevaro as a concert artist. In 1939, during the World Fair in New York, USA, Carlevaro broadcast several recitals for local radio stations. He received high critical praise for his playing, following which the Uruguayan Government gave him a special grant to enable him to travel.

Since the end of World War II Abel Carlevaro has given concerts in most countries of the world. He still appears regularly at major international guitar festivals, both in a playing and in a teaching capacity.

**SELECTED RECORDINGS**

Recital de Guitarra. Antar Telefunken ALP 1002
Carlevaro plays Carlevar. Chanterelle CR 1000

**SELECTED MUSIC**

Cronomias I – Sonata for Guitar. B & C 4014
Preludios Americanos. B & C 4010, 4011, 4005, 4023, 4018
Suite of Ancient Spanish Dances (on text & themes of Sanz). B & C 4017
School of Guitar – An Exposition of Instrumental Theory. Dacisa Sa/Boosey & Hawkes, 1978
Guitar Masterclasses Vols.I-4. Chanterelle

**SELECTED READING**

Interview. Classical Guitar, February 1985

# LEIF CHRISTENSEN

**Born –**

**Aarhus, Denmark, 1 March 1950**

**Died – Near Aarhus, 12 January 1988**

*Leif Christensen*

Leif Christensen studied with Konrad Ragossnig in the Musikakademie der Stadt Basel, Switzerland. He graduated there in 1978, and from that time enjoyed an extensive and successful concert career throughout Europe and Scandinavia. From his early student days Leif Christensen was actively involved in researching original 18th and 19th century guitar music, which led to his performing the works on original instruments. He made several highly acclaimed recordings, both as a solo performer and as a guitar duo with his wife Maria Kämmerling.

At the time of his tragic and early death in a car accident, Leif Christensen was teaching as assistant professor at the Royal Danish Academy of Music in Aarhus.

**SELECTED RECORDINGS**

Guitar Works of Giulio Regondi. Paula 10
Fernando Sor – Duos with Maria Kämmerling Paula 14
Guitar Works of Miguel Llobet. Paula 20
Henze – Royal Winter Music. Paula 25
Mauro Giuliani – Guitar Duets with Maria Kämmerling. Paula 34
The Russian 7-String Guitar – W.S.Sarenko. Paula 40
Giuliani – Virtuoso Overtures for Two Guitars. Paula 44
Tárrega, Schumann & Thalberg. Paula PACD 59

**SELECTED READING**

Leif Christensen: An Appreciation. Classical Guitar, June 1989

# GEORGE CLINTON

**Born –**

**London, England**

**6 May 1931**

George Clinton is the editor of Guitar International, formerly Guitar magazine. This monthly magazine, which originally covered most styles of guitar playing, including classical guitar, began publishing in 1972.

Clinton's first instrument was the violin. His father was a professional violinist who started his son on the instrument at the age of ten. At the age of twelve, George Clinton changed to the clarinet, an instrument to which he devoted his musical studies until he finished his army service years later. It was then that he chose to study the classical guitar. He progressed on the instrument and in 1959 gave his first public performance, a lunchtime recital at Holborn Town Hall in London. Following this concert, he made several radio broadcasts for the then popular BBC programme 'Guitar Club'.

For many years George Clinton led a busy life as a guitar teacher and as a photographer for IPC. He was a regular contributor to the long-established BMG magazine. In August 1972 the first issue of Guitar magazine under his editorship was published by his company Musical New Services Ltd. Over the next fifteen years this company also produced many guitar publications, some of which have been important

*George Clinton*

additions to the growing library of guitar literature. In September 1989 Musical New Services Ltd, went into liquidation. Guitar International remains under the editorship of George Clinton and is now published by his guitar and string distribution business, Purestop Ltd, although since late 1990 it has little content of interest for classical guitarists.

**SELECTED READING**

Guitar International. Volume 1, Issue 1 to May 1990.

# OLGA COELHO

**Born –**

**Manaus, Amazonas, Brazil**

**1909**

*Olga Coelho*

Olga Coelho is one of the finest singer/guitarists the world has known. Her musical instruction began at the age of six with piano studies, which she continued for more than ten years. She then studied harmony with O. Lorenzo Fernández, and received her diploma from the National Institute of Music in Rio de Janeiro, where her family made their home. One of Coelho's voice teachers was the noted Italian contralto Gabriella Besanzoni Lage.

Olga Coelho became intensely interested in Brazilian folklore at an early age. Through her love of this folklore she was attracted to the guitar. She has given concerts in South America, the United States, Canada, Europe, Australia, New Zealand and the Far East. She has recorded in the United States, London, Sweden, Brazil, Chile and Argentina, and has written many articles on music and folklore for magazines in South America and the United States. She speaks six languages (Portuguese, Spanish, French, Italian, German, English) and sings in several more, including Russian, Swedish, Polish, Maori and Malay. Songs have been composed for her by many outstanding composers, including Villa-Lobos, Castelnuovo-Tedesco, J. Rodriguez, Andrés Segovia, O. Lorenzo Fernandez, M.Carmargo Guarnieri, John W. Duarte and Hans Haug.

She has been honoured by many Brazilian cities; and in Rio de Janeiro there is a permanent exhibition at the Museu do Teatro Municipal of her programmes, photographs and other memorabilia. In Buenos Aires she has been honoured by membership of the Republica de la Boca. She also has the distinction of being one of the few artists honoured by the New York Society of the Classic Guitar with honorary membership.

For many years Olga Coelho was a close friend of Andrés Segovia, who transcribed much music for her. She was the first singer/guitarist for whom Segovia wrote accompaniments.

**SELECTED RECORDINGS**

Chants and Folk Ballads of Latin America. Decca DL 10018

# COLIN COOPER

**Born –**

**Birkenhead, England**

**5 July 1926**

*Colin Cooper*

Colin Cooper is now recognized as one of the world's foremost writers on the classical guitar, yet he did not begin to play the guitar until the age of thirty-six. Tuition under various teachers culminated in his participation in Gilbert Biberian's advanced course at the Chiswick Music Centre.

Since 1982 he has been general and features editor of Classical Guitar magazine, widely regarded as the leading monthly publication devoted to the instrument. His perceptive interviews, thoughtful articles and sometimes provocative reviews display his wide knowledge of the guitar and music in general.

Colin Cooper is a unique figure in the music press. A professional writer since his early twenties, he is the author of five published novels, twelve performed plays (one of them a TV prizewinner) and innumerable general articles for publications great and small. He has contributed a regular column to the Tokyo magazine Gendai Guitar for fifteen consecutive years, and was the first features editor of Guitar magazine, the first four issues of which were published from his house in London.

Although Colin Cooper has not performed as a solo guitarist, he has played in ensemble in public performance, has arranged music for the guitar and has had an original composition published.

He has served as a jury member in several international guitar competitions, in Hungary, Greece, Poland and Finland. He is also a keen photographer, and has contributed very many photographs of guitarists to Classical Guitar magazine, Gendai Guitar and other guitar journals.

**SELECTED READING**
Classical Guitar Magazine. Volume 1, Issue 1 to current issue

# ERNESTO CORDERO

**Born –**

**New York, USA**

**9 August 1946**

*Ernesto Cordero*

Ernesto Cordero's parents were Puerto Rican. His family returned to Puerto Rico in 1953. There Ernesto began private studies in music with Jorge Rubiano and Ramón Molinary. In 1963 he entered the Conservatory of Music of Puerto Rico to study music theory.

In 1967 he was given a scholarship to study guitar in Spain with Regino Sainz de la Maza, Jorge Ariza and Renata Tarragó. In 1970 he graduated from the Real Conservatorio Superior in Madrid, earning the title Professor of Guitar. Following this success, Cordero went to Italy in 1972 to study with Alirio Diaz.

It was at this time that he recognized his growing ability as a composer. He studied composition with Boris Porena and Roberto Caggiaro in Italy, and with Julian Orbón in New York.

Ernesto Cordero is currently on the faculty of the Music Department at the University of Puerto Rico, and is recognized as both a fine guitarist and a composer of originality. He has appeared as a soloist with the Puerto Rico Symphony Orchestra and has performed in the USA and Europe. He has made several recordings in Puerto Rico, and in recognition of his contribution to guitar literature a concert of his work was organized in Cuba.

**SELECTED MUSIC**

| | |
|---|---|
| Fantasia Sobre Tres Cuadros de José Campecho. | |
| Concierto Evocativo. | ME 8702 |
| Concierto Antillano. | Zanibon |
| Descarga. | MB 94080 |
| Tres Cantigas Negras. | Hubertus Nogatz |
| Album para La Juventud. | Zanibon ZA 6148 |
| Proteus. | Bèrben EB 2946 |

**SELECTED READING**

| | |
|---|---|
| Interview. | Guitar International, August 1989 |
| Interview. | Guitar Review, Winter 1989 |

# IRMA COSTANZO

**Born –**

**Buenos Aires, Argentina**

**18 December 1937**

*Irma Costanzo*

Highly regarded throughout the guitar world as one of Argentina's finest classical guitarists, Irma Costanzo studied the guitar with Abel Carlevaro in Montevideo. Later she studied with Narciso Yepes in Buenos Aires and Paris. For a time she also studied chamber music with Lyenko Spiller.

At the age of sixteen Irma Costanzo won the prize for the best performance in a competition held by the Association of Chamber Music. In 1961 she won first prize in the competition 'Juventudes Musicales de Argentina', and also, in 1962, the Grand Prix of the Fondo de las Artes. Since that time she has established herself as a leading guitar soloist, appearing in concert in most countries of the world including North and South America, Europe, Britain and Japan.

**SELECTED RECORDINGS**

| | |
|---|---|
| La Maja de Goya. | EMI (Spain) J063-21010 |
| Villa-Lobos & Turina for Guitar. | EMI (VIC) 30215 |
| Plays Villa-Lobos & Carlevaro. | Qualiton Q1 4000 |

*Atahualpa Yupanqui, legendary Argentinian singer/guitarist*

*A picture taken on December 31st 1952 at the Conservatory of Pablo Escobar. In the back row, 4th from the right, is Pablo Escobar. Jorge Morel is in the middle row, 5th from the right.*

# NAPOLEON COSTE

**Born – Daubs, France**

**27 June 1805**

**Died – Paris, 17 February 1883**

*Napoléon Coste*

Napoléon Coste started to play the guitar at the age of six. By the time he was eighteen he was not only teaching the guitar but appearing regularly as a guitar soloist for the Philharmonic Society of Valencienne, France. For a period of four years, between 1824 and 1828, he took part in several concerts with the guitar virtuoso Luigi Sagrion.

Coste decided to move to Paris in 1830. Here he soon made a name for himself as a guitarist and teacher. His concert performances were attended by the élite of Parisian society, and he received high critical acclaim from the press.

Whilst living in Paris, Coste was able to meet other great masters of the guitar, and developed intimate friendships with Aguado, Carulli, Carcassi and Sor. So impressed was he by these great musicians that he decided to make an even more serious study of the guitar in music. Coste spent the next ten years studying harmony and counterpoint.

In 1840 he first published some of his original compositions for the guitar. He submitted four compositions to the international music contest in 1856 organized in Brussels by Nikolai Makarov, the Russian guitarist, officer and nobleman. His Sérénade won second prize, the first going to J.K.Mertz for his Concertino .

Following his success in the competition, Napoléon Coste was to have over sixty of his compositions published. He wrote a second guitar part, in substitution of the orchestra, to Giuliani's Concerto for Guitar op. 36 making it a guitar duet. He also revised the original edition of Fernando Sor's guitar method for the publisher Schonenberger. It was reprinted by Lemoine of Paris.

Around 1860 Coste fell after a concert and broke his right arm. After this accident he was never able to perform again in public. This was a great tragedy, for there is little doubt that he was one of the greatest guitar virtuosos and composers France has produced. His guitar was bequeathed to the Museum of the National Conservatoire in Paris. This instrument, of Coste's own design, was unique. It was of much larger dimensions than usual, and tuned a fifth lower than the ordinary guitar. It also had a fingerplate raised from the table of the guitar, not unlike those seen on twentieth century jazz guitars.

**SELECTED MUSIC**

| | |
|---|---|
| Autumn Leaves – 12 Waltzes op.41. | GA 12 |
| Barcarole, Rondoletto, Marsch. | GA 315 |
| Rêverie. | Ricordi |
| Rondeau. | EMT 1406 |
| Rondo op.51 no.11. | Bèrben EB 2184 |
| Zur Erholung (The Guitarist's Recreation) op.41 (14 pieces). | GA 13 |
| Complete works of Napoléon Coste. | Chanterelle |

**SELECTED RECORDINGS**

Napoléon Coste Music for Guitar and Oboe (Simon Wynberg) Chandos ABR 1031

Coste & Mertz : Guitar Duets (Simon Wynberg, David Hewitt) (Meridian KE 77095

Raphaëlla Smits plays Napoléon Coste Academix DOR 1

**SELECTED READING**

Napoléon Coste's Duets for Guitar and Oboe. Simon Wynberg Classical Guitar, Sept/Oct 1983.

# COSTAS COTSIOLIS

**Born – CONSTANTINE COTSIOLIS**

**Athens, Greece**

**23 July 1957**

*Costas Cotsiolis*

Now one of the foremost classical guitarists in Greece, Costas Cotsiolis began to play the guitar at the age of six, studying with Charalambos Ekmetsoglou at the Hellenic Conservatoire in Athens. He gave his first public recital in 1968 at the age of eleven in the Parnassos Room, Athens.

Between 1970 and 1973 he took part in several international competitions for guitar in France, Italy and Spain. He also studied at various international seminars with Andrés Segovia, Alirio Diaz and José Tomás. Cotsiolis eventually won a total of fifteen international prizes and diplomas for his guitar playing. In 1972 he completed his studies at the Hellenic Conservatoire. In November that year, at the age of fifteen, he performed the Concierto de Aranjuez by Joaquín Rodrigo in Athens with the State Symphony Orchestra.

Since 1972 Costas Cotsiolis has continued an active career as a classical guitarist, and has given concerts and recitals in the principal cities of Greece. He has appeared with the symphony orchestras of Athens and Thessaloniki, and has also broadcast many times on Greek radio and television. In 1976 he became head of the department for classical guitar in the Conservatoire of Athens. In the same year he was appointed the Artistic Director of the International Festival for the Classical Guitar in Volos, Greece.

Since 1978 Costas Cotsiolis has appeared all over Europe and in Russia and Cuba. He has been active in festivals in Esztergom in Hungary, Dubrovnik in Yugoslavia, and Donietsk in the USSR. His book Guitar Technique was published, in Greek, in 1978. Cotsiolis has also recorded for the record companies Electrecord in Romania, and Melodiya in the USSR.

In 1981 he was the featured soloist with the Pro Musica Orchestra of Oxford, England, at the Festival of Athens.

**SELECTED RECORDINGS**

| | |
|---|---|
| Constantine Cotsiolis. | MelodiyaS 10-16481-2 |
| Giuliani/Tedesco Concertos. | Electrecord ST-ECE 01930 |
| Concierto de Lieja. | Auvidis A4846 LP, A5846 CD |

**SELECTED READING**

| | |
|---|---|
| Costas Cotsiolis. | Guitar, May 1976 |
| Costas Cotsiolis. | Classical Guitar, November 1987 |

# BETHO DAVEZAC

**Born –**

**Rocha, Uruguay**

**3 August 1938**

*Betho Davezac*

Betho Davezac first learnt to play the guitar at the age of six. His first teacher was his father, a conservatory professor. Davezac soon showed great promise and studied harmony and counterpoint with the composer Guido Santórsola, who at the time was living in Montevideo.

Davezac later attended masterclasses by Andrés Segovia and Alirio Diaz, and led a very active musical life in Uruguay. He was one of the founders of 'Grupo Artemus', which won the Uruguayan Critics' Society prize for the best chamber ensemble in 1965. In 1966 he left Uruguay and went to live in Paris. He soon established himself as a teacher of the classical guitar. He was a prizewinner in the 8th Concours for Guitar held by Radio France in 1966, and later won first prize in both the 1967 Ville de Liège Competition and the 1969 Cittá di Alessandria Competition. His 1974 recording of Elizabethan music was awarded the Grand Prix International du Disque by the Charles Cros Academy. In 1984 he directed the audio-visual spectacle for narrator, synthesiser, guitar orchestra, 'Le Chant du Monde' by Reginald Smith Brindle.

Davezac, who has become a French citizen, performs and gives masterclasses throughout Europe, South America and Japan. He is a professor of guitar at the Conservatoire de Paris XV and also at the Ecole Nationale de Musique de Meudon. From 1981 to 1988 he was the Artistic Director of the Festival de Sablé. He is also the founder and director of the guitar ensemble 'Harmonique 12'.

**SELECTED RECORDINGS**

| | |
|---|---|
| Musique Elizabethaine. | Erato STU 70830 |
| Variations sur la Guitare. | Erato STU 70926 |
| Guitare Française du XVIe Siècle. | Erato STU 71334 |
| Guitar Recital | Nippon Columbia 05 10-114N |

# ANTON DIABELLI

**Born – Mattsee, near Salzburg, Austria**

**6 September 1781**

**7 April 1858**

*Anton Diabelli*

Anton Diabelli was not only one of the finest guitarists of the early part of the nineteenth century, but an excellent pianist and composer. He was also a highly respected publisher of music for both the piano and the guitar, as well as church music. He received his first musical education as a chorister in the Monastery of Michaelbearn, and then at the Cathedral of Salzburg. His parents originally had hoped he would enter the priesthood, and in 1800 he entered the Monastery of Reichenhaslach.

Before he was twenty years old, Diabelli's talents as a composer were already recognized through his many compositions for one or more voices. The guitar was already his main instrument, and most of his vocal arrangements had guitar accompaniment. In 1803 the young guitarist decided to make music his career, and abandoned his original idea to take holy orders. He left for Vienna, where his talents were immediately recognized by many of the musicians living there, including Joseph Haydn, whose brother Michael had supervised Diabelli's musical training.

In 1807 Diabelli struck up a friendship with the guitar virtuoso Mauro Giuliani. There is no doubt that Giuliani was technically the greater guitarist, but he found Diabelli's musicianship stimulating. The guitar had achieved enormous popularity at that time in most of Europe, especially in Vienna, and the two guitarists achieved much success.

As a notable teacher and recitalist of both the guitar and the piano, Diabelli earned a lot of money. He became a partner in the music publishing firm of Peter Cappi in 1818. Six years later, in 1824, he bought out his partner and changed the name of the company to Diabelli and Company. Diabelli became Schubert's main publisher (sometimes complaining that Schubert wrote too much), and the company prospered under his management. He also published the music of Czerny and Strauss, and became a close friend of Beethoven and Schubert. Beethoven used a Diabelli composition as the theme for his famous Variations for Piano op.120.

In 1853 Diabelli sold his copyrights (at that time he had printed over 25,000 works) and business to C. A. Spira. He died in Vienna in 1858 at the age of seventy-six. During his highly successful career as both a musician and a businessman, he had earned enormous respect from his many friends and admirers, and has gone down in history as one of the most important guitar personalities of the nineteenth century.

**SELECTED MUSIC**

| | |
|---|---|
| Sonata for Guitar op.29/1 in C Major. | UE 14472 |
| Five Easy Recital Pieces op.39. | GA 322 |
| Little Pieces for Beginners op.39. | UE 14464 |
| Präludium & Andante Cantabile from op.39, ed. Teuchert. | SY 2248 |
| Due Fughe op.46, ed. Ablóniz. | Bèrben EB 2035 |
| Two Fugues op.46: no.1 in Am, no.2 in A. | Ric. 132512 |
| Five Viennese Dances. | UE14463 |
| Four Little Rondos, ed. Schindler. | N 1516 |
| Minuetto from Sonata in C. | Bèrben EB 2177 |
| Präludium from op.103. | GA 321 |
| Sonata in A Major, ed. Bream. | Faber |
| Sonatina in A Major, ed. Nagel arr. Meunier. | Breitkopf |
| Three Sonatas. | Kalmus |
| Twenty-Four Easy Old Viennese Ländler op.121. | GA 85 |

**SELECTED RECORDINGS**

Music for Guitar and Piano. Romulo Lazarde.
Harmonia Mundi HM 435

# ALIRIO DIAZ

**Born –**

**Caserio la Candelaria, near Carora, Venezuela**

**12 November 1923**

*Alirio Díaz*

Aliro Díaz's first guitar teacher was his uncle, who taught him to play by ear. By the age of ten he had already written several interpretations of popular Venezuelan airs. When he was fifteen years old, he was taken by Cecilio Zubbilaga to Trujilla to receive his first lessons in theory and solfeggio with Laudelino Mejias.

Díaz soon achieved great success in his musical studies, but earned his living as a proof-reader. He also wrote articles for a weekly music paper, The Crescent. In 1945 he went to Caracas and advanced his guitar studies, together with Raúl Borges, at the Higher School of Music under the tuition of Clement Pimentel. Díaz was able to pay for his music education with the money he earned playing in military bands and dance orchestras. After his graduation he gave his first recital at the National Library and received high critical acclaim. Subsequent recitals were so successful that in 1958 he was given a grant by the Mnistry of Education to help him travel to Europe to further his guitar and music studies.

After studying in Spain with Regino Sainz de la Maza for one year, Díaz was awarded the first prize at the Royal Conservatory of Music in Madrid. The young guitarist left Madrid for Siena, Italy, and for four years attended special courses given by Andrés Segovia at the Musical Academy of Chigiana. He earned the high distinction of being the assistant professor of guitar on two of these courses.

Alirio Díaz then embarked on a strenuous concert tour of most countries in Europe and the Americas, achieving enormous success. He has made a particularly strong impression amongst guitarists, not only with his superlative guitar technique but also through his many interpretations of the music of his fellow Venezuelans. His renderings of compositions by Antonio Lauro (and those of other South American composers) have established him as one of the most important guitarists of the twentieth century.

**SELECTED RECORDINGS**

| | |
|---|---|
| Masters of the Guitar Volume Two. | RCA RB 6599 |
| 400 Years of Classical Guitar. | Everest 3155 |
| Virtuoso Guitar. | Vanguard HM 32SD |
| Four Centuries of Classical Guitar. | Vanguard VSD 71135 |
| The Classical Spanish Guitar (2 LPs). | Vanguard VPD 20002 |
| Guitar Music of Spain and Latin America | EMI/HMV HQS 1175 |
| Díaz Plays Bach. | EMI/HMV HQS 1145 |
| Díaz Plays Tedesco Quintet/Ponce-Sonata. | EMI/HMV HQS 1250 |

**SELECTED READING**

| | |
|---|---|
| Alirio Díaz | Guitar, August 1974 |
| Alirio Díaz. | Guitar, November 1979 |

# MICHEL DINTRICH

**Born –**

**Bar sur Aube, France**

**10 June 1933**

Michel Dintrich is one of the most influential and popular guitarists in France today. He first studied the guitar with Ida Presti at the Schola Cantorum in Paris, and later participated in Andrés Segovia's masterclasses at the Accademia Musicale Chigiana in Siena.

Dintrich has given concerts throughout Europe and North Africa. He has made many transcriptions for the guitar of baroque music. In recent years he has changed to a ten-string guitar, similar to the one developed and used by Narciso Yepes.

As well as playing and teaching the guitar, Michel Dintrich has made several recordings, and broadcasts regularly on French radio and television. He has written and played the soundtrack music of several French films, including Madagascar au Bout de Monde. He also owns a very fine collection of rare antique guitars.

*Michel Dintrich*

**SELECTED RECORDINGS**

| | |
|---|---|
| Recital de Guitarre (2 LPs). | Musidisc 16030 |
| Les Immortels | Barclay 920 104 |
| With Duo Patrice Fontanarosa. | Classic 991 025 |

# CARLO DOMENICONI

**Born –**

**Cesena, Italy**

**20 February 1947**

Carlo Domeniconi began his studies on the guitar in 1960, with Carmen Lenzi Mozzani, granddaughter of Luigi Mozzani. In 1962 and 1964 he won first prize at the Ancona International Festival of Guitar. At the age of eighteen he completed his studies in Pesaro, earning a diploma. He then went to West Berlin, where he obtained a diploma from the Hochschule für Musik in 1966. Since that time Domeniconi has established himself as a concert artist in both the classical and the jazz idioms. He has played and taught throughout Europe, and in recent times has become known as a distinctive composer for the guitar. His compositions often have a Turkish flavour, as can be heard on his recording Koyunbaba, which reflects the time he spent in Turkey. He was a professor of guitar in Istanbul and also taught solfeggio.

**SELECTED MUSIC**

| | |
|---|---|
| 24 Präludien Vols 1 & II. | Gitarren-Studio GS 50, GS 51 |
| Gli spiriti | Gitarren-Studio GS 59 |

*Carlo Domeniconi*

| | |
|---|---|
| Suite Sudamericana. | Gitarren-Studio TPM 135 |
| 7 Compositions for Guitar. | Rüssl 066 32856 |
| Moon Lights. Bote & Bock | B&B 22695 |
| 20 Turkish Folksongs. | Gitarren-Studio GS 65 |
| Koyunbaba Suite | Margaux |
| Variations on a Turkish Folk Song. | B&B 23010 |
| Fantasia di luci e tenebre | |
| Suite in modo antico. Gitarre Aktuell | TPM 137 |
| Orient Express. Gitarre Aktuell | TPM 36 |
| Homage to A. de Saint-Exupéry. | Gitarren-Studio GS 66 |
| *For two guitars:* | |
| Naturgeister. | Edition Margaux EM 2041 |

**SELECTED RECORDINGS**

| | |
|---|---|
| Luci e Tenebre. | Podium Gitarre 8402.11 |
| Koyunbaba. | Bestell-Nr EULP 1044 |

**SELECTED READING**

| | |
|---|---|
| Carlo Domeniconi. | Classical Guitar, April 1989 |

*An interesting nineteenth century music cover*

# JOHN W. DUARTE

**Born - JOHN WILLIAM DUARTE**

**Sheffield, England**

**2 October 1919**

*John W. Duarte*

John Duarte is not only one of the foremost twentieth century composers for the guitar, but is also regarded as a world authority on matters relating to the guitar and its music.

He started playing the ukulele at the age of fourteen, and a year later he was introduced to the plectrum guitar by a local dance band guitarist. Soon afterwards he began to take lessons from Terry Usher in Manchester. Six years later, in 1940, he began to take an active interest in the classical guitar, an instrument on which he was self-taught.

Deciding that the concert platform was not his métier, John Duarte embarked upon an intensive study of the classical guitar as a musical instrument and its relationship to the world of music as a whole. His understanding and panoramic view of the guitar have been invaluably assisted by friendships with many of the world's greatest players, including Andrés Segovia and Ida Presti.

As a composer and arranger, John Duarte has had more than one hundred works published in six countries. Many of these have been recorded by the major guitarists of the age. In 1958 his composition, based on the American folk song 'The Colorado Trail', won first prize in a worldwide competition arranged by the Classical Guitar Society of New York. Duarte currently lives in London, and teaches in all aspects of guitar playing, at all levels. He is the author of several didactic works, including a comprehensive book written specifically for teaching the guitar to children. He has also published a book of technical studies endorsed by Segovia.

A prolific journalist, John Duarte has published hundreds of articles in guitar magazines all over the world. He reviews for 'The Gramophone', writes sleeve notes for guitar records for most of the major record companies, and regularly adjudicates in international guitar competitions. His special talents have made him into one of the most influential guitar personalities of the twentieth century.

**SELECTED MUSIC**

| | |
|---|---|
| All in a Row, op.51 | Bèrben EB 1971 |
| Birds, op.66. Zanibon | ZA 5733 |
| English Suite, op.31. | Novello NOV 12010108 |
| Fantasia & Fugue on Torre Bermeja, op.30. | Bèrben EB 1717 |
| A Flight of Fugues, op.44. | Broek BVP 1015 |
| Meditation on a Ground Bass, op.5 | Schott 11955 |
| Miniature Suite, op.6. | Schott SCS 6 |
| Mutations on the Dies Irae, op.58. | Bèrben EB2042 |
| Night Music, op.65. | G 124 |
| Partita, op.59. | CO 215 |
| Petite Suite Française, op.60 | ESC ME 8214 |
| Simple Variations on Las Folias, op.10. | CO 152 |
| Sonatina Lirica, op.48 – Homage to Mario Castelnuovo-Tedesco | Bèrben EB 1972 |
| Sonatinette, op.35. | Novello NOV 19720 |
| Sua Cosa, op.52. | Bèrben EB 2043 |
| Suite Ancienne, op.47. | Bèrben EB 2203 |
| Suite Piemontese, op.46. | Bèrben EB 1514 |
| Three Modern Miniatures, op.9. | Schott SCS 12 |
| Tout en Ronde, op.57 – Ritual Dance, Waltz, Spring Dance. | UE 29153 |
| Variations ona Catalan Folk Song, op.25. | Novello NOV 12031108 |

**SELECTED BOOKS**

| | |
|---|---|
| The Young Person's Way to the Guitar | Novello NOV 12030100 |
| The Guitarist's Hands (with Luis Zea). | Universal UE 26926 |

**SELECTED READING**

| | |
|---|---|
| John Duarte. | Guitar, February 1974 |
| John Duarte | Guitar, March 1975 |
| John Duarte | Complete list of works Guitar & Lute, October 1979 |

**SELECTED RECORDINGS**

| | |
|---|---|
| English Suite Op.31: Segovia. | Decca DL 710140 |
| Neil Smith plays John W. Duarte. | Guitar Masters GMR 1006 |

# ARNAUD DUMOND

**Born –**

**Paris, France**

**2 June 1950**

*Arnaud Dumond*

Arnaud Dumond studied at the Ecole Normale de Musique de Paris, from which he earned a concert-level diploma. He studied with Alberto Ponce, Narciso Yepes and Emilio Pujol.

In 1971 Dumond won first prize at the 15th International Guitar Festival presented by Radio France. He was the first French guitarist to win this prestigious event. He also won the Third International Festival of Jeunesses Musicales, held in Belgrade in 1971.

Since that time Arnaud Dumond has performed as a concert guitarist throughout Europe, Scandinavia, Africa, USSR and the USA. He is also a composer of originality and daring, his compositions often reflecting an interest in the possibilities of sound in the context of electronics and prepared tape.

**SELECTED RECORDINGS**

La Guitare D'Amerique Latine — Cezame CEZ 1048
20th Century Guitar & Recorder Duos — Arc en Ciel SM301261
La Plus Belles Pages de la Guitarre — Pierre Vernay CA 803

**SELECTED READING**

Interview. — Guitar International, September 1987
Interview. — Classical Guitar, August 1985

# ROLAND DYENS

**Born –**

**Tunisia, North Africa**

**19 October 1955**

*Roland Dyens*

Roland Dyens began to study the guitar with Robert Maison at the age of nine. He later enrolled at the Ecole Normale de Musique in Paris, where he studied with Alberto Ponce. Within a short time he was awarded a diploma in concert performance, and in 1979 he was the prize winner at the Palestrina International Competition in Porto Alegre, Brazil. In the same year he won the Special Prize at the Alessandria Competition in Italy.

Roland Dyens has also proved to be an original composer; he studied with Raymond Weber and Désiré Dondeyne. He is currently Professor of Guitar at the Conservatoire de Chaville (Hauts-de-Seine).

**SELECTED MUSIC**

Eloge de Leo Brouwer. — Lemoine LEM 24975
Hommage à Villa-Lobos. — Lemoine LEM 24885
Libre Sonatine. — Lemoine LEM 24794
Tango en Skaï. — Lemoine LEM 24793

**SELECTED RECORDINGS**

Villa-Lobos & Dyens. — Arc en Ciel SM 3011.61
Hommage à Brassens with the Enesco Quartet. — Auvidis AV 4731

# HERBERT J. ELLIS

**Born – Dulwich, London, England**

**4 July 1865**

**Died – London, 13 October 1903**

*Herbert J. Ellis*

Herbert Ellis's first instrument was the piano, but he became fascinated by the banjo. Although he had no true academic music education, his natural musical talent enabled him to write a highly successful tutor, 'Through School for the Banjo'.

In 1888, with the rising popularity of the guitar and the mandolin, Ellis decided to study and master these other fretted instruments. His 'Through School for Mandolin', which soon appeared, was also highly successful, and several editions had to be printed. He then completed his trio of best-selling fretted instrument tutors with the publication of 'Through School for Guitar'. With its unique and simple manner, this became the most popular guitar method of its type for many years. It is in fact still used today, in a revised edition by Bernard Sheaff.

Herbert J. Ellis proved to be one of the most important and lasting guitar personalities on the English scene. In all, over one thousand of his original compositions for guitar and mandolin were published. Although they were very popular in the latter part of the nineteenth century, they are seldom played today.

# GABRIEL ESTARELLAS

**Born –**

**Palma de Mallorca, Spain**

**14 October 1952**

*Gabriel Estarellas*

Gabriel Estarellas is one of the finest guitarists to emerge from Spain in recent years. He began his music and guitar studies at an early age, and by the time he was twelve he had given his first public recital. This performance was received with great enthusiasm. Estarellas crossed to the mainland of Spain to study with José Tomás, and later completed his musical studies with Gerardo Perez Busquier.

In 1970 Estarellas was awarded the first prize at the 'Ramírez' International Guitar Competition in Santiago de Compostela. In the same year he also won first prize at the Viotti International Guitar Competition.

An intensive concert tour of Europe was made in 1972, during which Gabriel Estarellas gave the first performance of Tansman's concerto for guitar and orchestra, Musique de Cour. Over the next few years the young guitarist was much in demand for concerts and radio and television broadcasts throughout Europe. In 1975 he won the 'Francisco Tárrega' Competition in Benicasim, Spain. In the same year he gave the first performance of A. Blanquer's Concertino for Guitar and Orchestra. Many contemporary composers, including Richard Stoker, Angelo Gilardino and Bernardo Juliá, have dedicated works to him. In 1978 he was nominated to be the conductor of the Manacor Chamber Orchestra, and in the same year he gave the first performance of

Bernardo Juliá's Concierto Juglar for guitar and orchestra.

Gabriel Estarellas currently spends much of his year in Spain, where he holds the post of Director and Professor of Guitar at the Academia de Auditorium, Palma de Mallorca, and also teaches in Madrid.

**SELECTED RECORDINGS**

| | |
|---|---|
| Estarellas Interprets. | Fonal MM-S56 |
| Estarellas Interprets Calatayud. | Maller API-86 |

**SELECTED READING**

| | |
|---|---|
| Interview. | Classical Guitar, November 1986 |

# REINBERT EVERS

**Born –**

**Dortmund, West Germany**

**23 August 1949**

*Reinbert Evers*

Although he had been playing the guitar from the age of ten, Reinbert Evers first studied the instrument seriously at twenty-two. His first teacher was Maritta Kersting in Düsseldorf. He went on to study with Karl Scheit in Vienna. From the age of fourteen he had also studied the double bass and had become an accomplished player on this instrument, but gave it up at the age of twenty-two when he made the decision to devote his full time to the guitar.

In 1976 Evers was appointed Professor of Guitar at the Music Academy of Westfalen-Lippe, Institut Münster. In 1980 he received a Young Artist's award from the city of Dortmund.

Over the past few years Reinbert Evers has established himself as one of Germany's finest classical guitarists. He has made many radio broadcasts, several recordings, and performed extensively widely throughout Germany and other parts of Europe. Prominent contemporary composers, including Gunther Becker, Edison Denisov, Tilo Medek, Luca Lombardi and Manfred Trohjahn, have written works especially for him.

**SELECTED RECORDINGS**

| | |
|---|---|
| Classical Sonatas for Guitar. | FSM 53221 EB |
| Virtuoso Fantasias & Variations: F. Sor. | FSM 53213 EB |
| Twentieth Century Guitar Music. | EMI Electrola CD MD G3292 |
| Galante-Music for Flute and Guitar. | EMI Electrola CD MD G3061 |
| New Guitar Music. | Pro Viva ISPV 118 |
| Royal Winter Music 1 & 2: Henze. | EMI Electrola CD MD G1110 |
| Bach Lute Suites etc. | EMI Electrola MD G1119 |
| Bach Lute Suites etc. | Ambitus CD 97818 |
| Edison Denisov Sonatas. | EMI Electrola MD G1269 |
| Serenades for Flute & Guitar. | Pantheon CD D 14112 |

**SELECTED READING**

| | |
|---|---|
| Interview. | Classical Guitar, January 1989 |

# EDUARDO FALU

**Born –**

**El Galpon, Province of Salta, Argentina**

**7 July 1923**

*Eduardo Falú*

Eduardo Falú is Argentina's best-known folk guitarist/composer and singer. Although not a classical guitarist, he has a brilliant technique on the instrument, and his music over the years has influenced, and become part of, the classical guitar repertoire.

Falú was given a guitar as a child, and soon was playing many of the traditional folk airs of the Argentine. During his teens he formed a duo with Cesar Perdiguero. The partnership was successful, and they soon had many radio broadcasts to their credit. When Perdiguero decided to devote his carer to literature, journalism and poetry, Falú continued his career as a solo artist.

Falú used the classical methods of Sor and Aguado to extend his technique on the instrument to a very high level. To improve his musical knowledge he studied harmony, theory and composition privately with the composer Carlos Guastavino. At the same time he co-operated with many leading Argentinian poets, in particular Jaime Davalos, to write what have now become some of his country's best-loved folk songs. Falú possesses a beautiful natural baritone voice, and as a singer and guitarist has become an international concert performer and prolific recording artist. In recent times he has appeared in duos with his son Juan José Falú, and with the flamenco guitarist Paco Peña. His evocative solos and folk song transcriptions for guitar are played on stage and record by many of today's leading classical guitarists.

**SELECTED MUSIC**

| | |
|---|---|
| El Condor Pasa. | BA 13454 |
| Preludio del Pasto. | G + L 111 |
| La Cuartelera. | Ricordi BA 12059 |
| Suite Argentina. | Ricordi BA 13267 |
| Variaciones de Milonga | Ricordi BA 12058 |
| Preludio y Danza | Ricordi BA 12103 |

**SELECTED RECORDINGS**

| | |
|---|---|
| Lo Mejor de Falú. | Caravelle 70-02 7 |
| Señor del Folklore. | Caravelle 70-26 3 |
| Nocheando con Falú. | DM Series 70-159 |
| Eduardo Falú: Solos de Guitarra Vol.2 | DM Series 50-4548-9 |
| Simplemente Falú. | Epic 60.327 |
| Tonada del Viejo Amor. | Music Hall M-504.031 |
| Falú: A Solas con mi Guitarra. | Music Hall S-32.559 |
| Suite Argentina: Falú & Guastavino Quartet. | Philips 812 287-4 |
| Eduardo Falú: Recital | Philips 818 448-4 |
| Guitarra y Una Voz. | Philips 63 47 160 |
| Eduardo Falú: Vol.1 | Aconcagua A-3539 |
| Eduardo Falú: Vol.2 | Aconcagua A-3908 |
| Eduardo Falú: Vol.3. | Aconcagua A-4455 |
| Eduardo Falú: Vol.4. | Aconcagua |
| Resolana: Eduardo Falú | Nimbus NI 5281 |

# DIMITRI FAMPAS

**Born –**

**Melina, near Volos, Greece**

**22 December 1921**

*Dimitri Fampas*

Dimitri Fampas is one of the most important guitar personalities in Greece today. He showed that he had musical talent at an early age. When he was twenty years old he studied the guitar under Niko Ioannou, at the same time studying theory and harmony at the Athens Conservatory. He graduated in 1953, winning not only the first prize in his year but also a special award for his musical ability.

An active concert career followed for Fampas in the major recital halls of Greece. In 1955-56 he won scholarships to study with Andrés Segovia and Emilio Pujol at the Academy of Chigiana in Siena, Italy. In 1959 he again studied with Segovia, in Santiago de Compostela, Spain.

Since that time, Fampas has continued a busy career as a concert artist and teacher. He has played in nearly every major European city, and has made several radio broadcasts. He has also written several original compositions for the guitar, which he has also recorded. He has been involved in teaching, not only in Athens, where he is the Professor of Guitar at the National Conservatory, but also abroad.

**SELECTED MUSIC**

| | |
|---|---|
| Bolero. | CO 154 |
| Greek Dance No.1. | Ric. 129953 |
| Greek Suite No.4. | BR 3221 |

**SELECTED RECORDINGS**

| | |
|---|---|
| Greek Music for Guitar. | Polydor Greece 45-96 |
| Dimitri Fampas Plays. | Odeon EMI Greece OMGC 67 |

# EDUARDO FERNANDEZ

**Born –**

**Montevideo, Uruguay**

**28 July 1952**

*Eduardo Fernández*

Eduardo Fernández began his study of the guitar at the age of seven with Raúl Sanchez, a former pupil of Andrés Segovia. Further studies included work with the composer Guido Santórsola in interpretation, harmony, counterpoint and fugue. His study of the guitar continued with Abel Carlevaro, the famous Uruguayan guitarist.

Fernández began to give concerts in 1963 as part of a duo guitar team with his brother, but since 1971 he has pursued a career as a soloist. He won first prize in the Uruguayan Guitar Society Competition and in the International Competition of Porto Alegre, Brazil. In both competitions the judges were unanimous in their choice. In 1975 he was chosen as one of four finalists in the Radio France Competition in Paris, and in the same year he was a prizewinner in the 'Andrés Segovia' Competition in Palma de Mallorca, Spain.

In 1977 Eduardo Fernández gave a highly acclaimed performance at his United States debut in New York. Since that time he has maintained a very active concert career in both North and South America. He has also taught at several international guitar seminars, including those held in São Paulo and Buenos Aires.

**SELECTED RECORDINGS**

| | |
|---|---|
| Legnani, Giuliani, Sor, Diabelli, Paganini. | Decca 414 160-1 |
| Ponce, Brouwer, Savio etc. | Decca 421 816-2 CD |
| Rodrigo, Falla, Granados Albéniz, Turina, Torroba. | Decca 414 161-1 |
| Rodrigo, Tedesco Concertos. | Decca 417 199-1 |
| Albéniz, Granados, Tárrega. Turina, Segovia, Llobet. | Decca 417 618-1 |
| Villa-Lobos Preludes/Etudes, Ginastera Sonata. | Decca 414 616-1 |
| Arnold/Chappell/Brouwer Concertos. | Decca 430 233-2 |

**SELECTED READING**

Interview. Classical Guitar, October 1985

# ZANI DE FERRANTI

**Born – MARCO AURELIO MARIA LUIGI FELICE GIOVANNI BATTISTA DE FERRANTI**
**Bologna, Italy, 23 December 1801**
**Died – Pisa, Italy, 28 November 1878**

*Zani de Ferranti*

At the age of twelve Zani de Ferranti was recognised as a child prodigy, not only as a violinist but also as a poet and linguist.

In 1818 he made a highly successful concert tour of Europe on the violin. Everywhere he played, his virtuoso performances were received with high acclaim. In 1820 he went to Russia and gained the position of librarian to Senator Miatleff in St Petersburg. A little later he was appointed secretary to Count Kyrille Alexandrovich Narischkin, a cousin of the Tsar. It was during his stay in Russia that Ferranti became attracted to the guitar, and within a relatively short period of time he became a virtuoso guitarist. He gave his first public recital as a guitarist in Hamburg, Germany, in 1824. He later played in Brussels (1821), Paris (1826) and London (1827).

Ferranti toured the United States of America in 1845 with the famous violinist Camillo Sivori. On his return to Europe in 1846 he was appointed Court Guitarist to King Leopold of Belgium. In 1854 he once again made a concert tour of France and Italy. At the end of this tour he decided to remain in Bologna, his native town. Ferranti continued to devote his life to the guitar, both playing and composing, until his death in Pisa, in 1878 at the age of seventy-six.

**SELECTED MUSIC**

Trois Mélodies Nocturnes et une Etude. Leduc
Selected Works. ECH 416
Complete Works of Zani de Ferranti (14 volumes). Chanterelle

**SELECTED RECORDINGS**

Zani de Ferranti and José Ferrer Simon Wynberg. Chandos CHAN 8512 CD

**SELECTED READING**

Zani de Ferranti: Biography (Simon Wynberg) Chanterelle (1989)
Ferranti, Makaroff and the 1856 Competition: Simon Wynberg. Classical Guitar, July 1989

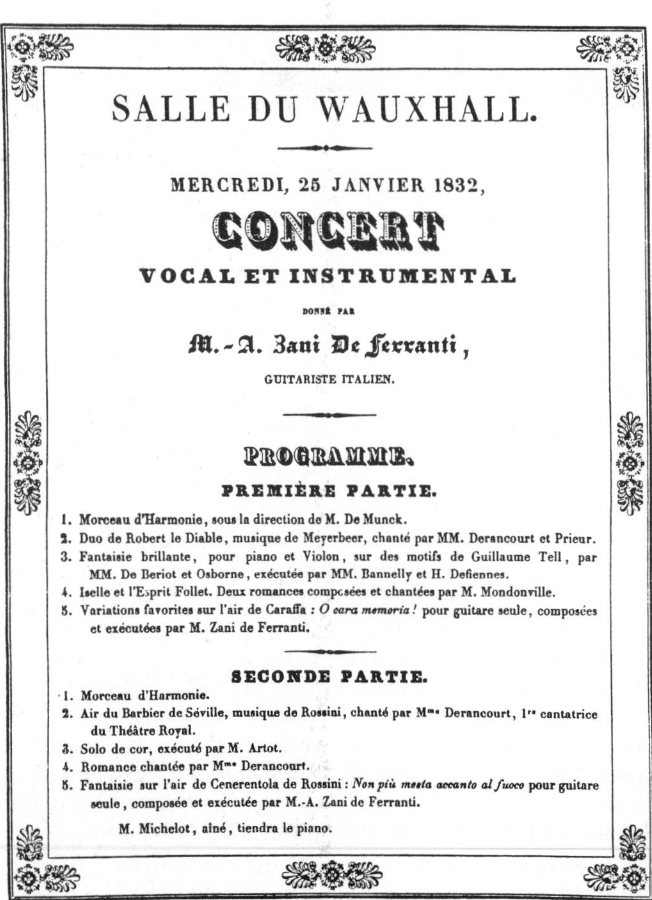

SALLE DU WAUXHALL.

MERCREDI, 25 JANVIER 1832,

CONCERT

VOCAL ET INSTRUMENTAL

DONNÉ PAR

M.-A. Zani De Ferranti,

GUITARISTE ITALIEN.

PROGRAMME.

PREMIÈRE PARTIE.

1. Morceau d'Harmonie, sous la direction de M. De Munck.
2. Duo de Robert le Diable, musique de Meyerbeer, chanté par MM. Derancourt et Prieur.
3. Fantaisie brillante, pour piano et Violon, sur des motifs de Guillaume Tell, par MM. De Beriot et Osborne, exécutée par MM. Bannelly et H. Defiennes.
4. Iselle et l'Esprit Follet. Deux romances composées et chantées par M. Mondonville.
5. Variations favorites sur l'air de Caraffa : *O cara memoria !* pour guitare seule, composées et exécutées par M. Zani de Ferranti.

SECONDE PARTIE.

1. Morceau d'Harmonie.
2. Air du Barbier de Séville, musique de Rossini, chanté par M^me^ Derancourt, 1^re^ cantatrice du Théâtre Royal.
3. Solo de cor, exécuté par M. Artot.
4. Romance chantée par M^me^ Derancourt.
5. Fantaisie sur l'air de Cenerentola de Rossini : *Non più mesta accanto al fuoco* pour guitare seule, composée et exécutée par M.-A. Zani de Ferranti.

M. Michelot, aîné, tiendra le piano.

IMPRIMERIE DE H. REMY.

*1832 Concert Programme*

# ELIOT FISK

**Born –**

**Philadelphia, USA**

**10 August 1954**

*Eliot Fisk*

Eliot Fisk began to study the guitar at the age of seven. His father was a professor of marketing at the Wharton School of the University of Pennsylvania. He studied first with William Viola in Philadelphia, and performed his first solo recital at the age of thirteen. In 1970 he won a full scholarship to the Aspen Music School, where he studied with Oscar Ghiglia before joining the Aspen faculty as Ghiglia's assistant at the age of eighteeen. In the same year he received a grant to study at the Banff School of Fine Arts with Alirio Diaz.

Eliot Fisk graduated summa cum laude from Yale College in 1976. His studies there with Ralph Kirkpatrick, the noted harpsichordist and Scarlatti scholar, inspired him to continue his interest in expanding the guitar repertoire through transcriptions of works by Scarlatti, Haydn, Mozart, Beethoven and Paganini, amongst others. In 1977 he received his MA degree from the Yale School of Music, and that autumn he founded the School's guitar department.

In addition to teaching at Yale, Eliot Fisk serves on the faculty of the Aspen School of Music and frequently gives masterclasses at universities throughout the USA. While keeping a demanding solo concert schedule, he has performed in duo recitals with the renowned soprano Victoria de los Angeles. He is also a co-founder of the Concerto Soloists of Philadelphia, with whom he has appeared as a soloist at the Wolf Trap and in the group's Carnegie Hall debut in 1979.

As his concert performances and record releases have confirmed, Eliot Fisk is without doubt one of the finest American classical guitarists to have emerged in recent years.

**SELECTED RECORDINGS**

| | |
|---|---|
| Plays Scarlatti and Bach. | MLAR C45 000 006 |
| Latin American Guitar. | Music Masters MM 20008 |
| American Virtuoso. | Music Masters MM 20032 |
| Eliot Fisk Plays Scarlatti etc. | Gitarre & Laute G & L 8201 |
| Eliot Fisk Plays Villa-Lobos, Morel, Barrios etc. | EMI 14-6757-1 |
| Guitarra Española | EMI 27-0216-1 |

**SELECTED READING**

| | |
|---|---|
| Eliot Fisk. | Guitar Player, June 1980 |
| Eliot Fisk. | Guitar & Lute, July 1981 |
| Interview. | Classical Guitar, May 1985 |
| Interview. | Classical Guitar, March 1991 |

# WILLIAM FODEN

**Born – St Louis, USA**

**23 March 1860**

**Died – St Louis , 9 April 1947**

*William Foden*

William Foden was of English ancestry. His father was the owner of a music store in St Louis. Foden's instrument was the violin, and he began his musical studies at the age of seven. By the time he was sixteen he had already become the leader of a local orchestra. At the same age, he became attached to the guitar, an instrument played by one of his school friends.

In 1887 he became a member of a professional trio comprising violin, flute and guitar. In the same year he organized the Beethoven Mandolin and Guitar Orchestra, later known as the Foden Mandolin and Guitar Orchestra.

Foden's first concert as a guitar soloist was on 29 January 1904, when he appeared at the Carnegie Hall, New York. By that time he was accepted as a virtuoso of the guitar, and his frequent public performances were highly acclaimed by critics and audiences alike.

In 1921 William Foden published in two volumes his Guitar School (William J. Smith & Company, New York). The work proved very practical in its development of technique through easy pieces to more difficult pieces. He also published a graded series of guitar lessons as a correspondence course, as well as two books of guitar chords and chord progressions. His most important work, begun in 1904 and completed in 1941, was his Grand Sonata for Guitar.

William Foden spent many years as a leading teacher and recitalist in New York. In his later years he returned to St Louis, continuing to devote his life to teaching and playing the guitar. An outstanding musician, William Foden was one of the foremost guitar personalities and players the United States has produced.

**SELECTED MUSIC**

Six Short Preludes. CO 159

# DANIEL FORTEA

**Born - DANIEL FORTEA GUIRMERA**

**Bennloch, Castellón de la Plana, Spain**

**28 April 1878**

**Died – Castellón, 5 March 1953**

*Daniel Fortea*

Daniel Fortea is regarded by many as one of the most important guitarists and teachers that Spain has produced. He began to study the guitar at an early age, using the methods of Aguado and Tárrega. At the age of twenty he began to take lessons with Francisco Tárrega in Castellón. He made such good progress that on several occasions Tárrega devoted part of his concert programmes to guitar duos with him.

In 1909, after Tárrega's death, Daniel Fortea moved to Madrid, where he became a popular and successful concert artist. It was in Madrid that he founded the Academia de Guitarra and also the Biblioteca Fortea, which eventually became a world-famous publisher of guitar music.

Fortea also edited and published a regular news sheet, Boletin Revista de la Biblioteca Fortea, which first appeared in 1935 and which, apart from its news items, contained a regular music supplement.

Daniel Fortea was a prolific composer for the guitar. He also made hundreds of transcriptions from classical and modern composers, as well as a Method for Guitar (based on the studies of Sor and Aguado), which was published in 1921. A second edition, in two volumes, was published in 1930.

Daniel Fortea continued to devote his life to the guitar right up to his death, following a heart attack at the age of 75, in 1953.

# FRANÇOIS DE FOSSA

**Born – Perpignan, France**

**31 August 1775**

**Died – Paris, 33 June 1849**

*François de Fossa*

COURTESY: EDITIONS ORPHEE

It was only after the publication of Matanya Ophee's book 'Luigi Boccherini's Guitar Quintets – New Evidence' (Editions Orphée, 1981) that François de Fossa's ability as a guitarist, composer and arranger became widely recognized.

François de Paule Jacques Raymond de Fossa joined an army regiment in 1793 at the age of seventeen. This unit, the Legion de Pyrenees, was one of many French emigré groups that joined the Spanish coalition, fighting the new revolutionary government in France. From this time, and for most of his life, de Fossa was to lead a long and distinguished career as a military officer in various regiments of the French army. Parallel to this career, it has now been revealed that de Fossa was active as a fine musician and guitarist.

De Fossa was a friend of Dionisio Aguado (1784-1849). He collaborated with Aguado on that famous guitarist's method, which was first published in 1825. He was also the copyist of Boccherini's well-known guitar quintets. Around 1826, Richault of Paris published his own three guitar quartets Opus 19. De Fossa also made many arrangements for classical guitar of popular opera overtures of the day by Piccinni, Boieldieu, Spontini and others. These arrangements and de Fossa's original works reveal the influence of some of the leading contemporary composers, including Beethoven, Haydn and Boccherini. The technical demands of the guitar parts in de Fossa's quintets, which give full status to the instrument in the ensemble, prove the high calibre of his ability on the instrument.

**SELECTED READING**

Luigi Boccherini's Guitar Quintets New Evidence — Matanya Ophee (Editions Orphée 1981)

François de Fossa's Three Quartets op.19 — Classical Guitar, April 1985

**SELECTED MUSIC**

Three Guitar Trios, op.18. — Chanterelle
Three Guitar Quartets, op.19 — Chanterelle

**SELECTED RECORDING**

François de Fossa — Three Guitar QuartetsOp.19
Simon Wynberg and the Gabrieli String Quartet. — Chandos ABRD 1109

# ALEXANDER FRAUCHI

**Born –**

**Rostov, Yaroslavski, USSR**

**4 January, 1954**

*Alexander Frauchi*

Alexander Kamilovich Frauchi first learnt to play the violin, receiving lessons from his father. At the age of ten he changed to the guitar, and in 1969 entered the guitar class at the Tchaikovsky Conservatory in Moscow. His teacher was Natalia Ivanova-Kramskaya. He graduated in 1973 with honours, and in 1974 went on to study with Professor Dezun at the Sverdlovsk Conservatory.

In 1979 Alexander Frauchi completed the course at the Mussorgsky Conservatory and went on to win the first prize in a national music competition held in Leningrad. Then, in 1986, he won first prize in the Havana International Guitar Competition, Cuba. Since then he has led a busy career as a concert artist and teacher, and is now recognized as one of the best classical guitarists to appear in the Soviet Union in recent years.

Alexander Frauchi is professor of guitar at the Gosudarstvenny Musicalno-Pedagichesky Institut imeni Gnesinykh in Moscow.

**SELECTED RECORDINGS**

Alexander Frauchi. — Melodiya C10-17193-4

**SELECTED READING**

Interview. — Guitar International, November 1986
Interview. — Classical Guitar, December 1986

# PAUL GALBRAITH

**Born –**

**PAUL MICHAEL GALBRAITH**

**Edinburgh, Scotland, 18 March 1964**

*Paul Galbraith*

Paul Galbraith studied the piano at first, but changed to the guitar when his parents bought him one for his ninth birthday. After playing folk and popular music for a year he was advised to begin classical guitar. His first classical teacher was Graham Wade, who at that time, like the Galbraith family, was living in London. After a few months the Galbraiths moved to Cornwall, where the young guitarist continued his studies with Ian Jackson. In 1975 Paul returned to Edinburgh with his family, where he attended St Mary's Specialist Music School. There he studied piano with Francesca Uhlenbruek and guitar with Barry Shaw.

Encouraged by the distinguished Venezuelan guitarist Alirio Díaz, Galbraith studied with Gordon Crosskey in Manchester. From 1975 to 1978 he studied at Chetham's School of Music in Manchester, and from 1978 to 1981 he completed his studies at the Royal Northern College of Music. During this period he studied guitar with Gordon Crosskey and took part in many school concerts and recitals for guitar societies.

In 1980 he gained third prize in the string section of BBC TV's prestigious Young Musician of the Year Competition, going on in 1982 to win first prize in the same competition. This success, and his second prize in the 1981 Segovia International Competition held at Leeds Castle, Kent, led to many television, radio and concert appearances throughout Great Britain and Europe. Later study was done with the pianist and composer George Georgiadis.

Paul Galbraith is a guitarist of great talent, and is well on the way to establishing himself as one of Britain's foremost classical guitarists.

**SELECTED RECORDING**

| | |
|---|---|
| Music of Ponce. | Watercourse Records |

**SELECTED READING**

| | |
|---|---|
| Interview. | Guitar, September 1982 |
| Article. | Classical Guitar, October 1984 |

# GERALD GARCIA

**Born –**

**Hong Kong**

**11 August 1949**

*Gerald Garcia*

Gerald Garcia studied chemistry at New College, Oxford, graduating in 1971. At the same time he showed great talent, mainly self-taught, as a classical guitarist. Encouraged by John Williams, Garcia developed his natural talents on the guitar and made his Wigmore Hall debut in 1979.

Since that time Gerald Garcia has made several tours of Europe and the Far East. He has played with many leading ensembles and musicians including the London Sinfonietta, Paco Peña and the cellist Rohan de Saram. With his own group 'Attacca' he has written and performed many of his own arrangements. As a teacher and lecturer he has been involved in workshops with the English National Opera and Kent Opera.

Gerald Garcia has broadcast in numerous countries on both radio and television and is much in demand as a concert artist offering a wide repertoire, both as a soloist and an ensemble artist.

**SELECTED RECORDINGS**

Garcia/Conway – Flute & Guitar Duo Psyche Records PSY 1
Chinese Popular Music for Violin & Guitar. HK Records
Concierto de Aranjuez/Granados/Albéniz. Naxos CD 8.550220
Brazilian Portrait. Naxos CD 8-550226
Latin American Guitar Festival. Naxos CD 8-550273

**SELECTED READING**

Interview. Guitar, September 1980
Gerald Garcia & New Music. Classical Guitar, July 1986
Interview. Classical Guitar, December 1987

# HECTOR GARCIA

**Born –**

**Havana, Cuba**

**19 November 1930**

Hector García's first guitar teachers were Eduardo Saborit and Fela Gonzáles Ruberia. He completed his education, receiving Master of Guitar and Master of Music degrees from Peyrellade Conservatory. On graduation in 1954, he joined the faculty at Peyrellade as an instructor of classical guitar, and remained there until 1960. During this period he also performed as a concert guitarist and as a soloist with various orchestras. He then decided to further his education by studying with Emilio Pujol in Barcelona, Spain.

In 1960 Hector García left Cuba, but was taken prisoner after the 'Bay of Pigs' invasion of that country. Although he had no musical instrument in prison, he did continue to compose a lot of music for the guitar. He was released on 24 December 1962 and went to the United States of America. He moved to Albuquerque, New Mexico, in 1963 and resumed his career as a concert guitarist. He gave concerts on the West Coast and also performed as soloist with the Los Angeles Symphonette. He also performed in New

*Hector García*

York's famed Town Hall, the Smithsonian Institute in Washington D.C. and other principal cities in the east. An extensive concert tour of major European cities included Madrid, Barcelona, Bilbao, Paris, London, Stockholm, The Hague, Amsterdam, Brussels and the Canary Islands.

He was honoured by the outstanding contemporary composer Mario Castelnuovo-Tedesco, who wrote a guitar composition on the name of Hector García. In 1967 García was appointed to the faculty of the University of New Mexico when the chair in classical guitar was established. He has generated a high degree of interest there in the classical guitar, drawing students from throughout the United States. The programme includes intensive study and research in the history of the guitar and its literature.

In 1969 García was appointed assistant to Emilio Pujol in the masterclasses held for guitarisrts in Cervera (Lerida), Spain.

**SELECTED READING**

Hector García. Guitar Player, June 1975

# OSCAR GHIGLIA

**Born –**

**Livorno, Italy**

**13 August 1938**

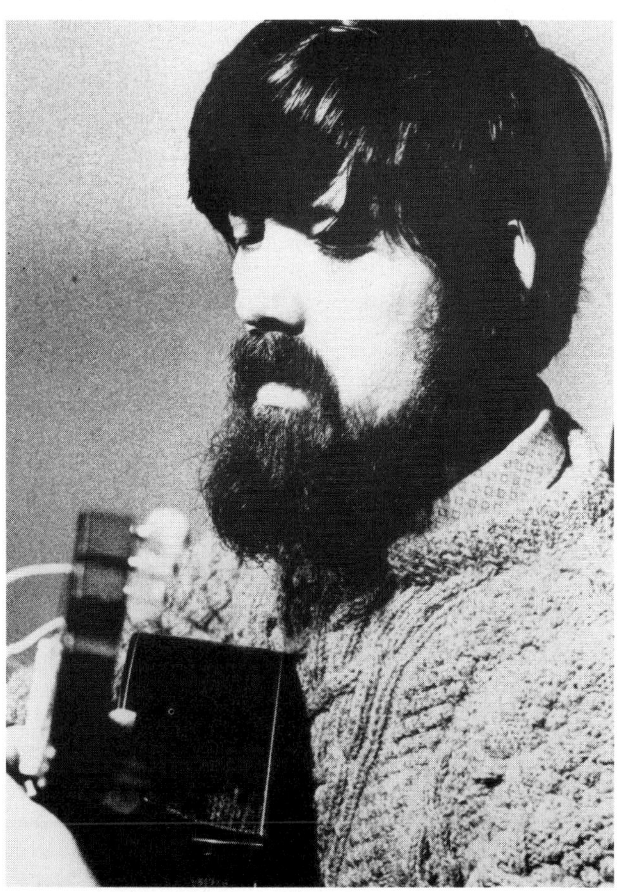

*Oscar Ghiglia*

Oscar Ghiglia grew up in an artistic atmosphere: his mother was a pianist, his father a painter. Initially it was thought he would become a painter. His father wanted to paint a family portrait one day, and to entice his son to remain still during the long sittings put a guitar into his hands, each session teaching him a bit more of the rudiments of playing. By the time the painting was done, Oscar Ghiglia had decided to become a professional guitarist and not a painter.

Ghiglia enrolled in Rome's Santa Cecilia Conservatory. His teacher was Benedetto di Ponio. After graduating with honours in 1961, he was admitted to Andrés Segovia's masterclasses in Siena, and made his professional debut at the Festival of Two Worlds in Spoleto the following year. In 1963 he was the judges' unanimous choice for the first prize at the International Guitar Competition in Paris, and he then won first prize at the Guitar Competition in Santiago de Compostela, Spain. Then came an invitation from Segovia to be his assistant for two years at the University of California, at Berkeley. With this rare honour, Oscar Ghiglia's career took on great momentum, and many international recitals and concerts soon followed. In addition to appearing extensively in all parts of North and South America and Europe, Oscar Ghiglia is a frequent performer in the Far East, Israel, Australia, New Zealand and the South Pacific.

Oscar Ghiglia is very much in demand as a teacher all over the world. In North America he has given masterclasses in, among others, Chicago, Detroit, Los Angeles, Salt Lake City and Toronto. He has also taught at the University of Missouri, Southern Methodist University, Florida State University, the San Francisco and Cincinnati Conservatories, and the Juilliard School and Mannes College. Since 1969 he has been Artist-in-Residence at the Aspen Festival, and from 1976 he taught annually in Siena.

**SELECTED RECORDINGS**

| | |
|---|---|
| Schubert & Carulli for Guitar. | World Record Club ST 1040 |
| Paganini for Guitar and Violin | EMI/HMV CSD 3511 |
| Guitar Music of Four Centuries | Angel S 36282 |
| The Guitar in Spain. | Angel S 36508 |
| Spanish Guitar. | Angel S 36849 |
| Ghiglia Plays Baroque Masters | Angel S 39715 |

**SELECTED READING**

| | |
|---|---|
| Oscar Ghiglia | Guitar Player, March 1972 |
| Oscar Ghiglia. | Guitar, August 1974 |

*Mauro Giuliani*

# MAURO GIULIANI

**Born – Bisceglie, near Bari, Italy**

**27 July 1781**

**Died – Naples, Italy, 8 May 1829**

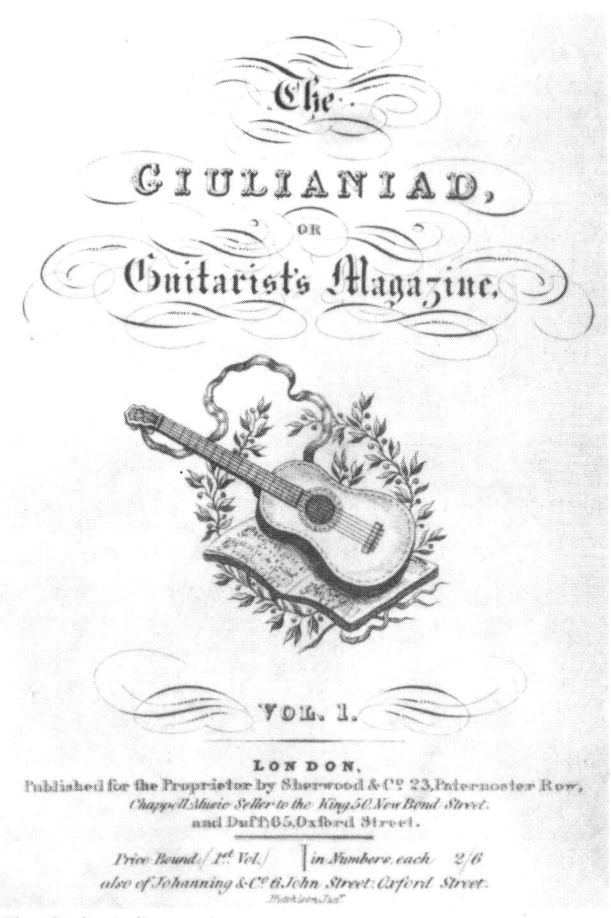


*The 'Giulianiad' magazine*

Mauro Giuliani was one of the most famous nineteenth century guitarists and probably one of the most brilliant guitar virtuosos ever.

As a young boy, Giuliani could play the violin, flute and guitar well, but by his teens the young musician had decided to devote his life to the guitar. A self-taught player, Giuliani not only was a great guitarist, but also became one of the instrument's supreme composers.

By the time he was twenty years old, Giuliani was already regarded as a virtuoso in his native Italy. A European concert tour in 1800 established his reputation throughout the continent. For the next seven years he continued to give recitals in the major cities of Europe.

In 1806 Giuliani settled in Vienna, one of the great musical centres of Europe. There he led a highly successful career as a teacher and recitalist. His musicianship and artistry are said to have inspired Beethoven to say that 'The guitar is a miniature orchestra', a comment used by Berlioz years later. He was appointed Chamber Musician and Teacher to the Arch-Duchess Marie Louise. Many members of the Austrian royal family and nobility studied the guitar with him. He developed close friendships with Moscheles, Hummel and Diabelli, who was himself a fine guitarist.

Giuliani was a prolific composer for the guitar. Over three hundred of his compositions were published, ranging from very simple exercises and studies to works demanding virtuoso ability. Among these are several concertos with orchestral accompaniment, duets for violin, and duets for flute and guitar. The first guitar magazine ever published, the 'Giulianiad', was named in his honour. It was first published in London in 1833.

Mauro Giuliani died in Naples at the age of forty-eight. One hundred and sixty years later his reputation is undiminished, and his outstanding contribution is celebrated daily in performances of his remarkable music throughout the world.

**SELECTED MUSIC**

Complete Works. — Tecla Editions
Various Works. — Suvini, etc.

**SELECTED RECORDINGS**

Handel Variations/
Grand Sonata (Pepe Romero). — Philips 9500 513
Guitar Concertos op.36 & op.70 (with Pepe Romero). — Philips 9500 320
Guitar Concertos op.30 & op.70 (with Angel Romero). — EMI CDC 7 479862
Guitar Concertos (with Julian Bream) — RCA SB 6826
Le Rossiniane : (Angel Romero) — Angel SZ 37326
Le Rossiniane (Julian Bream). — RCA ARLI 0711
Guitar Duets composed and arranged by Mauro Giuliani: Kämmerling & Christensen. — Paula 34
Gran Duetto Concertante op.52: North (guitar), Beznosiuk (flute). — Amon Ra CD-SAR 33
Deux Rondeaux op.68: Prunnbauer (guitar), Heller (hammerklavier). — Christophorus SCGLX 74044

**SELECTED READING**

The Birth of the Classic Guitar – Thomas F. Heck. — Dissertation, Yale University (1970).
Guitar Concertos of Giuliani. — Guitar, November 1976
Mauro Giuliani. — Guitar Review No.18, 1955
Mauro Giuliani. — Guitar Review No.37, 1972.
The Guitar Concertos of Mauro Giuliani: Magula. — Soundboard, May 1976
The Genius of Mauro Giuliani. — Classical Guitar, August 1986

# VICENTE GOMEZ

**Born –**

**Madrid, Spain**

**8 July 1911**

*Vicente Gomez*

Vicente Gomez began to play the guitar when he was seven years old. His father owned a tavern, and by the time he was eight years old the young Gomez was already entertaining customers with flamenco music on his guitar. His obvious talents were quickly recognised, and he was encouraged by his schoolteacher to take private lessons in solfeggio.

Gomez turned to the classical guitar after he became a pupil of Don Quintin Esquembre, a former pupil of Tárrega. He made rapid progress, and furthered his classical training when he entered the Madrid Conservatory.

Vicente Gomez made his first public appearance at the age of thirteen in the Teatro Español. A highly successful concert tour of Spain soon followed, and in 1932-33 he toured France and North Africa. An extensive tour of Russia and Poland was made in 1936, and later in the same year he gave recitals in Cuba, Mexico and the United States of America.

For the next twenty years Vicente Gomez enjoyed enormous success both in Spain and in the United States. He gave numerous public recitals and radio broadcasts, and his guitar playing and original music were featured in several Spanish and Hollywood films. In 1948 he opened a night-club, 'La Zambra', in New York, and late in 1953 he established a school in Los Angeles, with the title 'The Academy of Spanish Arts'.

Since 1959 Vicente Gomez has dedicated most of his time to teaching and the writing of music.

**SELECTED MUSIC**

| | |
|---|---|
| Vicente Gomez Guitar Album. | Belwin |

**SELECTED RECORDINGS**

| | |
|---|---|
| Guitar Recital. | Decca DL 8018 |
| Guitar Extraordinary. | Decca DL 4312 |
| Blood Wedding Suite. | Decca DL 78918 |
| Artistry of Vicente Gomez. | Decca DL 78965 |

**SELECTED READING**

| | |
|---|---|
| Vicente Gomez. | Guitar Player, December 1977 |
| Vicente Gomez. | Guitar & Lute, July 1979 |

# JOSÉ LUIS GONZALEZ

**Born –**

**JOSÉ LUIS GONZALEZ JULIA**

**Alcoy, Spain, 2 July 1932**

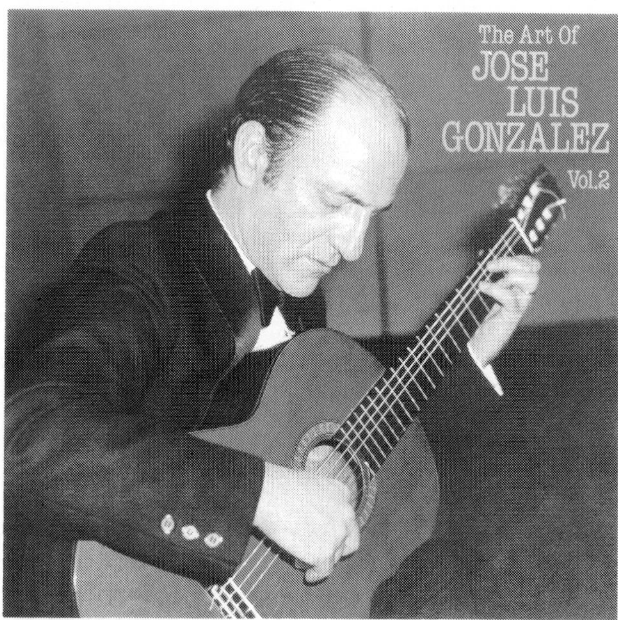


*José Luis González*

José Luis González gave his first public guitar recital at the age of sixteen in Madrid's Realto Theatre. In 1957 he graduated from the Valencia Conservatory. His talents were recognised very early in his career, and the young guitarist became a scholarship pupil of Regino Sainz de la Maza in Madrid. Later he studied several times with Andrés Segovia at Santiago de Compostela.

In 1961 he won the Margarita Pastor prize in a competition organised by the Orense Conservatory which was being held in conjunction with the Santiago de Compostela Festival. José Luis González has given many highly successful concerts in Europe and North Africa, emerging as one of the most important classical guitarists since the end of World War II.

In 1962 González decided to move to Australia. There he settled in Sydney and soon established himself as a busy recitalist and teacher. He continues to give many guitar concerts throughout the world, achieving particular success in Japan. He has now once again settled in Alcoy, Spain.

**SELECTED RECORDINGS**

| | |
|---|---|
| El Arte de la Guitarra Española. | CBS S 73656 |
| Portrait of the Guitar. | CBS 61654 |
| Art of José Luis González: Vol.1. | CBS/Sony 28AC 1184 |
| Art of José Luis González: Vol.2. | CBS/Sony 28AC 1239 |

# PAUL GREGORY

**Born –**

**Beirut, Lebanon**

**26 January 1956**

*Paul Gregory*

The British guitarist Paul Gregory's first teacher was Robert Sutton in Brighton. Subsequently he studied with Carlos Bonell, Baltazar Benitez and Oliver Hunt.

Gregory gave his first public concert in 1972. Many concerts throughout Great Britain followed. In 1973 he was nominated one of 'Tomorrow's Musicians' by the Croydon Music Council, which led to a major concert at the Fairfield Halls. In 1978 he won the prestigious Andrés Segovia Competition in Mallorca, Spain. Since that time he has been much in demand as a concert artist throughout Europe. As well as being a fine solo artist, Paul Gregory has shown a keen interest in integrating his instrument into general music making. This has been aided by studies on the cello and the composition of numerous chamber works. He has performed with the Lontano ensemble, the De Fossa Trio, the violinist Andrew Sherwood and the harpsichordist Sharon Gould among many others. He broadcasts frequently for the BBC.

**SELECTED READING**

| | |
|---|---|
| Interview. | Classical Guitar, September 1984 |

**SELECTED RECORDINGS**

| | |
|---|---|
| Encore. | Airship AP 128 |
| Bach/Scarlatti/Alberti Recital. | Opus 1 821 Cassette |
| 20 Studies: Fernando So. | Opus 1 841 Cassette |
| Romantic Guitar Music. | Meridian E 77092 |
| Guitar Music of Four Centuries. | Meridian CD E 84146 |

**SELECTED VIDEO**

| | |
|---|---|
| Guitar Music of Villa-Lobos. | Stentor Music Co. |

# OLE HALÉN

**Born –**

**Hameenlinna, Finland**

**3 April 1944**

*Ole Halén*

Ole Anders Halén started to play the guitar at the age of thirteen. He studied electric guitar with the well-known Finnish studio guitarist Ingmar Englund. At the age of fifteen he joined a touring pop/rock music band which made several hit records.

At the age of seventeen, Halén became fascinated with the guitar style of Chet Atkins, and began to study the classical guitar a year later to improve his fingerstyle technique. He studied with Ivan Putilin who, impressed by the young guitarist's ability, encouraged him to study classical music at the Sibelius Academy in Helsinki. In 1979 he received a degree in music as a guitar teacher at the Academy, and is now on the teaching staff there.

Ole Halén retains an intense love of all styles of music, and his endeavours have helped to make Finland one of the most active guitar centres in the world. He owns the Helsinki-based Chorus publishing company, which features several important names in its catalogue including Stepán Rak and Jorge Morel. His Chorus recording company has made several important recordings by various artists including Robert Brightmore and Seppo Siirala. Halén has also been involved in guitar string production, and has personally built several classical guitars. He is a director of the Scandinavian International Guitar Festival and is the organizer of the annual Midnight Sun Guitar Festival held in Ikaalinen.

# NICOLA HALL

**Born –**

**Ipswich, England**

**3 March 1969**

*Nicola Hall*

Nicola Hall began to play the guitar at the age of eight. At ten, sponsored by the City of Derby, she studied with Robin Pearson at the Spanish Guitar Centre in Nottingham. She continued to show exceptional talent on the guitar, and in 1982 she was awarded a place at Chetham's School of Music in Manchester. There she studied with Gordon Crosskey, Professor of Guitar at the Royal Northern College of Music. In her final year at Chetham's she was awarded the Midwood Prize, the highest honour the school awards to string players. In 1987 she continued her studies at the Royal Northern College of Music with John Williams and the violist Roger Bigley. In 1989 she was awarded the Professional Performer's Diploma (PPRNCM), two years early and with distinction.

Nicola Hall made her London recital debut at the age of fifteen, at which age she also performed her first public concerto (Rodrigo's Aranjuez ) with a professional orchestra. Since then she has given many concerts as a solo player and in ensemble throughout the United Kingdom. She has also played in Hungary, Poland, Holland, Yugoslavia, Denmark, Finland and Canada. In 1986 she won first prize in the first Polish International Guitar Competition, and in 1987 she won second prize in the Toronto International Guitar Competition. In May 1989 she was the winner of the Eagle Star Award for strings in the Royal Over-Seas League Music Competition in London. She went on to win the gold medal and Champagne Pommery award in the grand finale of the same competition. In February 1990 she won the Malcolm Sargent Music Award. A recording contract with Decca International was signed during the same year, and her first recording will be released in 1991. Her virtuoso technique and mature musicianship continue to dazzle audiences in her many performances in the concert hall and on radio and television.

**SELECTED READING**

| | |
|---|---|
| Interview. | Classical Guitar, January 1987 |

# FREDERICK HAND

**Born –**

**Brooklyn, New York, USA**

**15 September 1947**

Frederic Hand attended the High School of Music and Art in New York, and is a graduate of the Mannes College of Music, where he is now a member of the faculty. He has taught several of the new generation of American guitarists including Stephen Funk Pearson and Benjamin Verdery. Hand began to play the guitar at the age of nine, inspired by some recordings of Andrés Segovia. He made good progress during the next few years and in 1972 he received a Fulbright Scholarship to study with Julian Bream in England.

As a guitar soloist he has performed in North and South America and in Europe. He has been an affiliate artist with the state art councils of Arizona, Alabama, California, Colorada, New York and Washington. He has been a guest artist with the Marlboro and Newport Music Festivals.

In addition to his concert performances, Frederick Hand has composed and arranged numerous scores for the cinema and television. His arrangement and performance of Vivaldi's Mandolin Concerto in C for the film Kramer v Kramer earned him special recognition for his treatment of Renaissance and Baroque music.

**SELECTED MUSIC**

| | |
|---|---|
| Trilogy. | Theodore Presser PRE 41441152 |
| Late One Night. | Theodore Presser PRE 11440393 |
| Five Studies. | G.Schirmer S 47945 |

*Frederick Hand*

**SELECTED RECORDINGS**

| | |
|---|---|
| Trilogy: The Guitar Music of Frederick Hand. | Music Masters MM 20065 |
| Baroque and On The Street. | Columbia FM-36687 |
| Jazzantiqua. | RCA AMLI 7126 |

**SELECTED READING**

| | |
|---|---|
| Interview. | Guitar Player, November 1986 |

# JOSEP HENRIQUEZ

**Born –**

**Barcelona, Spain**

**22 December 1951**

*Josep Henríquez*

Josep Henríquez was a pupil of Graciano Tarragó and Eduardo Sainz de la Maza. In 1971 he began his professional career as a founder member of the Tarragó Guitar Quartet. He left the ensemble in 1977, his place being taken by Jaume Torrent.

In 1976 Josep Henríquez obtained his Ph.D degree in music at the Conservatorio Municipal de Música de Barcelona. In 1982 he was appointed professor at the San Francisco Music and Arts Institute. He is currently head of the Guitar Department at the Music Conservatory of Granollers, Barcelona.

Josep Henríquez has a busy performing career. In recent years he has played throughout Europe, the USSR, the USA, Canada, Central and South America, Africa and Israel.

**SELECTED RECORDING**

Recital. BCD FM-68745

**SELECTED READING**

Interview. Classical Guitar, November 1984
Interview. Guitar International, August 1987
Profile. Classical Guitar, November 1990



# JOSEF HOLECEK

**Born –**

**Prague, Czechoslovakia**

**28 October 1939**

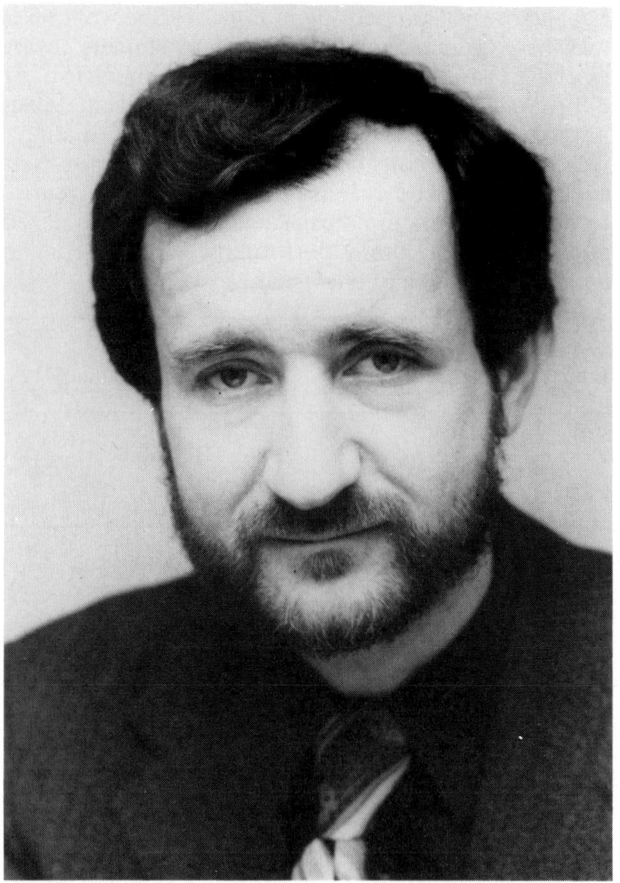

*Josef Holecek*

Josef Holecek showed obvious talent on the guitar at an early age. After examinations he entered the guitar class of Prague Conservatory, finishing his studies there under Professor Sádlik and receiving his diploma in 1966.

In the same year he was one of the five finalists in the ORTF (French radio and television) International Guitar Competition in Paris. He was awarded a scholarship to study under Professor Karl Scheit at the Academy of Music in Vienna, where he completed his studies, receiving an honours diploma in 1967 after only one year.

From 1961 to 1967 Josef Holecek was engaged as a guitarist in the National Theatre of Prague. As well as teaching the guitar at the State School of Drama in Prague from 1961 to 1966, he also led a guitar class at the Conservatory of Pilsen during his last year in Prague.

After finishing his studies with Karl Scheit in Vienna, Holecek went to Sweden and was engaged as a teacher of the guitar at the Framnas Folkhogskola. He also directed several international summer guitar courses in Sweden and Finland. Since 1970 he has been a guitar teacher at Gothenburg Conservatory. He has given concerts throughout Czechoslovakia, and also in the major cities of Austria, Sweden and Finland.

Among those who have written works for Josef Holecek is the prominent Finnish composer Einojuhani Rautavaara, whose Serenades of the Unicorn was premiered by Holecek in Gothenburg.

**SELECTED MUSIC**

| | |
|---|---|
| Six Aquarelles. | Schirmer S 3497 |
| Swedish Romance. | Schirmer |
| Nevergreens. | Schirmer S 3496 |
| Guitar Jokes. | Parodies and Transcriptions. CG 5946 |
| Guitar Moods. | CG 5915 |
| Ministudies. | CG 5914 |

**SELECTED RECORDINGS**

| | |
|---|---|
| With Marta Schele. | BIS LP-31 |
| Romantic Guitar Music from Sweden. | BIS LP-203 |

# JOHN HOLMQUIST

**Born –**

**Wyoming, USA**

**7 February 1955**

*John Holmquist*

John Holmquist began his guitar studies at the age of seventeen with Jeffrey Van. He later attended the University of Minnesota, where he received a Bachelor of Fine Arts degree in guitar performance. He also studied with Alirio Díaz, first in Banff, Canada, and later in Castres, France. In 1978 he was awarded the first prize in the Toronto International Guitar Competition. From 1978 to 1980 he lived in London, where in addition to teaching and performing he studied with the guitarist-composer Gilbert Biberian.

In 1985 John Holmquist was the recipient of a National Endowment for the Arts Solo Recitalist Fellowship. In addition to performing, John Holmquist is in great demand as a teacher and lecturer. He is currently Head of the Guitar Department at the Cleveland Institute of Music. He has also served on the faculties of the Wisconsin Conservatory of Music and Northwestern University.

**SELECTED RECORDINGS**

| | |
|---|---|
| Las Folias de España. | Cavata CV 5001 |
| Music of Edvard Grieg, for Two Guitars (with Daniel Estrem). | Cavata CV 5002 |
| Gershwin by Guitar. | Pro-Arte/Pro-Jazz CDJ 226 |
| In The Still of the Night. | Pro-Arte/Pro-Jazz CDJ 606 |
| Love You Madly: Duke Ellingt | Pro-Arte/Pro-Jazz CDJ 628 |

**SELECTED READING**

| | |
|---|---|
| Interview. | Classical Guitar, July/August 1983 |
| Interview | Classical Guitar, May 1990 |

# HARVEY HOPE

**Born –**

**2 Stratford-upon-Avon, England**

**27 May 1943**

*Harvey Hope*

Harvey Hope began to play the guitar at the age of fourteen. He became interested in the music of the Baroque period early in his professional career and, during the 1960s, embarked upon an intensive study of the performing styles and repertoire of the five-course guitar. His research into what was then a neglected field led him abroad to the conservatories of Paris, Rome and Barcelona to study surviving source material at first hand. During the course of his studies he formed what is now regarded as one of the finest private collections in the world of rare 17th and 18th century guitars. His unique playing collection includes magnificent instruments by some of the greatest 17th century luthiers: Tielke, Fleischer and the Voboams.

Harvey Hope has lectured and given recitals in most of the universities in Great Britain and also in many similar establishments abroad. He has performed at leading European early music festivals, and has established an international reputation through his concerts, recordings and broadcasts of early guitar music played on original 17th century instruments. In addition to solo recitals, Hope regularly performs with the London Concert Orchestra, the Bournemouth Symphony Orchestra and BBC orchestras. He has provided music for the Royal Ballet and the Royal Shakespeare Company. He has contributed articles to a number of music journals and is currently the history editor of Classical Guitar magazine.

**SELECTED RECORDINGS**

| | |
|---|---|
| Baroque Guitar. | Pye/Response RE 800 |
| Italian Baroque Guitar. | Pye/Response RE 804 |
| Gitarrenmusik des Barock. | Bellaphon 68 07 001 |
| Harvey Hope: French Baroque Guitar. | Lyric LYR 303 |

**SELECTED READING**

| | |
|---|---|
| Harvey Hope. | Article. Observer, January 1979 |
| Harvey Hope. | Article. Music Week, April 1979 |
| Harvey Hope. | Article. Soundboard, January 1982 |
| Interview. | Classical Guitar, October 1989 |

## MIKIO HOSHIDO

**Born –**

**Tokyo, Japan**

**19 September 1947**

*Mikio Hoshido*

Mikio Hoshido is one of Japan's leading classical guitarists. He first appeared as a soloist at a concert in Tokyo at the age of nineteen in 1966. Two years later in 1968 he gave his first solo guitar concert, also in Tokyo. Since that time he has given concerts throughout Japan and has appeared in radio and television. From 1968 to 1970 he studied guitar with José Tomás, Andrés Segovia and Alirio Díaz. In 1972, with the Japan Philharmonic Symphony Orchestra, he performed the Japanese première of the work by Albert Pizzini, Concierto para Tres Hermanas. In Tokyo in 1976 he gave a joint recital of contemporary works with the German guitarist Siegfried Behrend.

From 1977 to 1978 Mikio Hoshido studied in Spain with Narciso Yepes at the invitation of the Spanish Government. In 1978 he gave a recital at the Château de Sorbonne, Paris, and following this played in the major cities of Spain and Belgium.

**SELECTED MUSIC**

| | |
|---|---|
| Method of Guitar. | Zen-On 240190 |
| 'Las Cantigas de Santa Maria' para Guitarra. | Zen-On ZG 33 |

**SELECTED RECORDINGS**

| | |
|---|---|
| Hoshido Recital. | Audio Lab ALC 1044 |
| Favourite Showpiecesof Guitar. | CBS/Sony 25AG 628 |
| M. Carcassi: 25 Studies. | CBS/Sony 20AG 680 |
| Method of the Guitar I. | CBS/Sony 20AG 354 |
| Method of the Guitar. | CBS/Sony 20AG 541 |

## DON A. F. HUERTA

**Born – Orihuela, Valencia, Spain**

**6 June 1804**

**Died – Paris, France, 1875**

*Don Huerta*

Don A. F. Huerta was one of the great guitar virtuosos of the nineteenth century. As a child he showed a strong inclination for music, and from the age of fourteen studied music at the San Pablo College in Salamanca. His special subjects were singing and guitar playing, and he achieved distinction in both. His most important guitar teacher was the renowned Manuel García.

During the unsettled period following the Peninsular War in Spain, Huerta enlisted in the army in the cause of General Riego, but had to flee to France when Riego was defeated. In Paris he devoted himself entirely to music, in particular the guitar and singing.

Very impulsive by nature, Huerta suddenly decided to cross the Atlantic to go the United States of America. There he was to make his living singing and playing the guitar. After a visit to Martinique, he lost his voice and was forced to devote himself exclusively to the guitar. He began an intense study of the instrument and was soon giving solo recitals throughout the United States. He became generally regarded as one of the greatest guitarists of the period on the North American continent.

Huerta returned to Europe in 1826 and settled in London, where he became associated with many distinguished musicians including La Pasta, Moscheles, Donizetti and La Blanche. He married one of the daughters of the guitar maker Louis Panormo, and enjoyed enormous success as a guitarist in London.

In 1830 Huerta returned to France and once again decided to live in Paris. As in England, he enjoyed great popularity and success in France and Europe as a whole. Over the next few years he toured throughout Europe and the Middle East, dazzling audiences with his guitar virtuosity. He was made a Knight of the Order of Gregory the Great, an honour of which he was particularly proud. While in Spain, he declined an offer from Queen Isabella II to become her permanent court guitarist. He preferred to continue living in Paris, and it was there that he died in 1875 at the age of seventy-one.

*Dr Walter James Leckie – patron, friend and confidant of the great Spanish guitarist, Francisco Tàrrega*

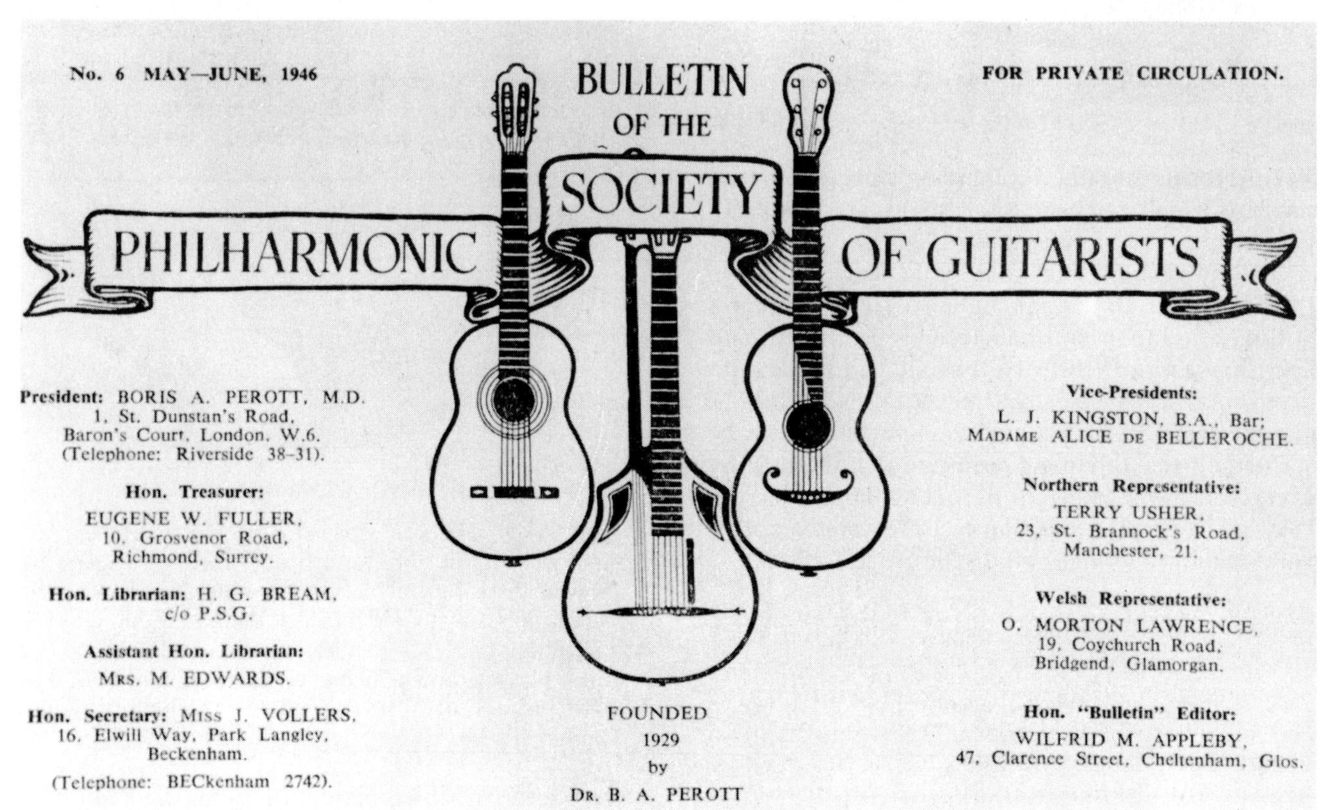

No. 6 MAY—JUNE, 1946

FOR PRIVATE CIRCULATION.

BULLETIN OF THE PHILHARMONIC SOCIETY OF GUITARISTS

**President:** BORIS A. PEROTT, M.D.
1, St. Dunstan's Road,
Baron's Court, London, W.6.
(Telephone: Riverside 38-31).

**Hon. Treasurer:**
EUGENE W. FULLER,
10, Grosvenor Road,
Richmond, Surrey.

**Hon. Librarian:** H. G. BREAM,
c/o P.S.G.

**Assistant Hon. Librarian:**
MRS. M. EDWARDS.

**Hon. Secretary:** MISS J. VOLLERS,
16, Elwill Way, Park Langley,
Beckenham.
(Telephone: BECkenham 2742).

FOUNDED
1929
by
DR. B. A. PEROTT

**Vice-Presidents:**
L. J. KINGSTON, B.A., Bar;
MADAME ALICE DE BELLEROCHE.

**Northern Representative:**
TERRY USHER,
23, St. Brannock's Road,
Manchester, 21.

**Welsh Representative:**
O. MORTON LAWRENCE,
19, Coychurch Road,
Bridgend, Glamorgan.

**Hon. "Bulletin" Editor:**
WILFRID M. APPLEBY,
47, Clarence Street, Cheltenham, Glos.

*1946 Bulletin of the Philharmonic Society of Guitarists*

# SHARON ISBIN

**Born –**

**Minneapolis, Minnesota, USA**

**7 August 1956**

*Sharon Isbin*

Sharon Isbin began to play the guitar at the age of nine. Her first serious study of the instrument was with Aldo Minella in Italy. Her father, a professor at the University of Minnesota, had taken the family with him to Italy for a year's sabbatical.

On her return to Minneapolis, Sharon Isbin continued her studies with Jeffrey Van, and later with Sopohocles Papas. She made rapid progress, and attended masterclasses given by Oscar Ghiglia and Alirio Diaz.

In 1979 Isbin received her master's degree in music from Yale University, where she had conducted weekly masterclasses for three years. She also studied with the renowned Bach interpreter and scholar, Rosalyn Tureck, in Oxford, England.

Since 1974, when she gave her first European tour at the age of seventeen, Sharon Isbin has been acclaimed by guitar enthusiasts and critics alike all over the world. In 1975 she was awarded the first prize in the international competition 'Guitar '75' held in Toronto, Canada. The following year she won the top prize in the guitar division of the Munich International Competition. Her performances for this event were televised and broadcast throughout the world. As a winner of the Queen Sofia 1979 International Competition in Madrid, she performed Rodrigo's Concierto de Aranjuez in a nationwide broadcast with the Spanish National Radio Orchestra.

In May 1977 Sharon Isbin made a highly acclaimed debut at the Wigmore Hall, London, followed by the first of several BBC broadcasts. Her New York debut, at Alice Tully Hall, Lincoln Centre, in March 1979 was again well received. The previous year she performed as a guest soloist with the Minnesota Orchestra, premiering Concerto for Guitar , a work written for her by the Israeli composer Ami Maayani. In June 1978 she made her first solo tour of Japan, and later that summer gave masterclasses and performances for the Rubin Academy Summer Festival in Jerusalem. She has also appeared as a guest artist at the Grand Teton Music Festival in Wyoming, the Festival les Arcs in Bourg Saint Maurice, and the Strasbourg International Music Festival.

Sharon Isbin has proved herself to be one of today's foremost guitarists in the United States of America. She now lives in New York City, and as well as leading a busy life as recitalist is a member of the guitar department at the Manhattan School of Music. She has recently been appointed the first professor of guitar at the Juilliard School of Music.

**SELECTED RECORDINGS**

| | |
|---|---|
| Bach, Britten, Brouwer. | Sound Environment TR 1013 |
| Concierto de Aranjuez. | Denon/PCM OX 7210 ND |
| Guitar Recital. | Denon/PCM OX 7224 ND |
| Spanish Works for Guitar. | Denon/PCM OF 7012 |
| Road to the Sun : Latin Romances. | Virgin Classics CD |

**SELECTED READING**

| | |
|---|---|
| Sharon Isbin. | Guitar, September 1977 |
| Sharon Isbin & Rosalyn Tureck. | Guitar, September 1980 |
| Sharon Isbin. | Guitar & Lute, April 1981 |
| Sharon Isbin. | Guitarra, September 1980 |
| Sharon Isbin. | Guitar Player, May 1980 |
| Interview. | Classical Guitar, December 1985 |
| Interview. | Classical Guitar, October 1990 |

## ALEXANDER IVANOV-KRAMSKOY

**Born – Moscow, Russia, 1912**

**Died – Minsk, Russia**

**11 April 1973**

*Alexander Ivanov-Kramskoy*

Alexander Ivanov-Kramskoy was one of the best-known contemporary Russian guitarists. He devoted himself to the classical guitar rather than to the seven-string instrument which from the time of Andrei Sychra (1773-1850) dominated the Russian guitar world until fairly recently.

Ivanov-Kramskoy published a method for the six-string guitar which, although specially adapted for self-study, is still widely used in schools of the Soviet Union. He gave many concerts and radio performances of his own compositions and those of other Russian composers, as well as music from the standard concert repertoire.,

Ivanov-Kramskoy was a very capable musician, and wrote a large number of original pieces for the guitar. He transcribed for the guitar all kinds of interesting music by Soviet and other composers, and was also a talented and respected chamber music player. He made a recording of his own variations on Russian themes for guitar and orchestra, now out of print, on the Monitor label. This record confirms the fine technical ability of Alexander Ivanov-Kramskoy.

**SELECTED RECORDINGS**

Concert for Guitar and Strings. Monitor MG 2024
A. Ivanov-Kramskoy. Melodiya CM 03111-12
A. Ivanov-Kramskoy. Melodiya CM 02579-80
Paganini: Violin & Guitar Duets (with Leonid Kogan). Melodiya M10 44933 005

## RICARDO IZNAOLA

**Born – RICARDO FERNANDEZ IZNAOLA**

**Havana, Cuba**

**21 February 1949**

COURTESY: RICARDO IZNAOLA

*Ricardo Iznaola*

Ricardo Iznaola was born in Cuba, but his parents moved shortly after the revolution, first settling in Colombia, where he began to play the guitar. The family later moved to Caracas, Venezuela, where the young guitarist continued to teach himself for four years, using the available written methods and listening to records. He then entered the Escuela Superior de Música in Caracas and studied under Professor Manuel Perez Díaz. Iznaola soon made remarkable progress, and in 1968 won third prize in the Manuel Leonicio Porras Competition in Caracas. In the same year he went to Madrid, Spain, to study with Regino Sainz de la Maza, eventually becoming his assistant in 1973 and working closely with him until his death in 1981.

In 1968 he won the first prize at the Francisco Tárrega Competition in Benicasim, Spain. In 1969 and 1971 he also won prizes in competitions held in Munich, Granada, Madrid and Caracas.

Ricardo Iznazola has been a naturalized Venezuelan since 1970. He returned to the United States in 1980, and is now the chairman of the Guitar Department at the University of Denver's Lamont School of Music.

He also directs the University's annual International Guitar Week Festival.

Ricardo Iznaola has composed a variety of works for the guitar, his Monologue II winning a prize at the Stroud Festival International Composers' Competition in 1983. His Monologue I for double bass was described by the famous double bass player Gary Karr as 'a wonderful work...I shall continue to play it for my own enjoyment, just as I do with the Bach Suites.'

**SELECTED RECORDINGS**

| | |
|---|---|
| Original Guitar Music. | Belter 70912 |
| Venezuelan Music for Guitar, Vol.1. | Promus LPP 2048 |
| Venezuelan Music for Guitar Vol.2. | Promus LPPS 20154 |
| South American Music for Guitar. | Columbia CS 8566 |
| The Guitar in Latin America. | Promus LPPS 20238 |
| Iznaola – Valses Venezolanos. | Alcasa No.8 |
| Vibraciones con Iznaola. | Toison de Oro |
| Iznaola interprets Ponce. | Promus LPPS 20294 |
| Originales para Guitarra: Lauro/Sonata. | America LPA 20 |
| Dream of Icarus. | IGW 22874 |

**SELECTED READING**

| | |
|---|---|
| Ricardo Fernández Iznaola. | Guitar, December 1975 |
| Ricardo Fernández Iznaola. | Guitar, April 1980 |
| Ricardo Fernández Iznaola. | Guitar & Lute, March 1977 |

# PER-OLOF JOHNSON

**Born –**

**Västra Vingåker, Sweden**

**8 October 1928**

Per-Olof Johnson began playing the guitar at the age of fourteen but only became seriously interested in the instrument after completing his military service. After studying with David Berg and Sven Hammarberg-Kritschevsky in Stockholm, he went to Vienna in 1955 to study with Karl Scheit for two years. He continued his studies for several more years, completing them in 1960-61 at the Schola Cantorun Basiliensis in Basle, Switzerland. In 1962 he came second in the Concours International de la Guitare in Paris.

Per-Olof Johnson returned to Sweden and held a variety of positions in Malmö and Arvika as a guitar teacher. In 1966 he received an offer to work in Copenhagen, and two years later he was given the lectureship in classical guitar at the Royal Danish Conservatory. As Johnson still retained a part-time position at the Malmö State College of Music, there began a sixteen-year period of commuting between Sweden and Denmark.

*Per-Olof Johnson*

In 1980 Per-Olof Johnson was knighted as 'Ridder af Dannebrogen' by Queen Margarethe of Denmark. In July 1982 the Swedish authorities created a personal professorship for him at the University of Lund/Malmö State College of Music, the first of its kind in Sweden, and a position he has held since.

For many years Per-Olof Johnson has performed widely throughout Europe and Scandinavia. At the same time he has established himself as Sweden's foremost classical guitar teacher and it is for this he is most widely known Göran Söllscher is one of his many pupils. In 1989 he was invited to Yale University School of Music as a research affiliate in notation, performance technique and transcriptions for lute and vihuela.

**SELECTED RECORDINGS**

| | |
|---|---|
| Per-Olof Johnson. | EMI SCLP 1037 |
| Per-Olof Johnson. | EMI LP 34395 |
| Swedish Guitar Music. | Caprice CAP 1236 |

# JEAN-PIERRE JUMEZ

**Born –**

**Hesdin, Pas de Calais, France**

**9 February 1943**

*Jean-Pierre Jumez*

Jean-Pierre Jumez came from a family of pianists and organists. He first studied the guitar with Jean Lafon in Paris, from 1959 to 1961. From 1962 to 1963 he studied under José Sierra at the Music Conservatory of Saint Germain en Laye, near Paris. The following year he studied the art of flamenco with Pedro Soler, and in 1966 he went to the USA to study jazz with Charlie Byrd in Washington.

Returning to Europe, Jumez completed his music studies at the Santa Cecilia Academy in Rome, with the conductor Gianluigi Gelmetti and with Professor Nataletti, a specialist in the study of popular music around the world.

In 1972 Jean-Pierre Jumez made his United States debut at the Carnegie Recital Hall, New York. He has since become one of the most travelled of contemporary classical guitarists, appearing in over one hundred countries, including concert tours of the Soviet Union. In 1977 he became the first classical guitarist to ,perform in Peking, China.

Many works have been dedicated to Jumez, among them the Petite Suite Française by John Duarte, and Pictures at an Exhibition by the Soviet composer Piotr Panin. Jumez has given the first performances of a large number of compositions, particularly in the French repertoire. They include Concerto for Guitar and Symphony Orchestra (Jacques Casterede, 1978), Swing No.2 (Jacques Bondon), Deux Etudes de Concert (André Jolivet), Soliloque en Souvenir de Manuel de Falla (Henri Sauguet), and Hommage à Alonso Mudarra (Georges Auric).

Jean-Pierre Jumez is the founder of the Martinique International Guitar Festival, and a permanent member of the Yehudi Menuhin Foundation jury (France). He is also President of the International Guitar Information and Documentation Centre ('Guitarothèque') in Saint Germain en Laye. He has conducted various masterclasses around the world.

Aside from the classical field, Jumez has constructed a unique repertoire of works inspired by folk music discovered through his many travels. These include pieces from Africa, Asia, Russia and South America, as well as Eskimo and Arab music.

**SELECTED RECORDINGS**

| | |
|---|---|
| Les Couleurs de la Guitar No.1. | Festival FLD |
| Les Couleurs de la Guitar No.2. | Festival FLD 700 |
| Les Couleurs de la Guitar No.4. | Festival FLD 709 |
| Nimble Fingers of Jean-Pierre Jumez. | Westminster WGS 8240 |

**SELECTED READING**

| | |
|---|---|
| Jean-Pierre Jumez. | Guitar, May 1977 |
| Jean-Pierre Jumez. | Guitar Player, November 1974 |
| Jean-Pierre Jumez. | Guitar & Lute, March 1982 |
| Interview. | Classical Guitar, Nov/Dec 1982 |

## DEAN KAMEI

**Born –**

**Honolulu, USA**

**20 November 1950**

*Dean Kamei*

Dean Kamei began to play the guitar at the age of thirteen. For a period of about seven years his interest lay in the field of popular music and rock and roll. After completing his studies in engineering, Kamei at the age of twenty-one began his involvement with other styles of music and the guitar. It was then that his love for the classical guitar began, and in 1974 he opened his first guitar shop and teaching studio in San Francisco.

Under Kamei's enthusiastic and expert management, his establishment became the most important of its type in California. The introduction of an extensive mail-order catalogue, concentrating on classical guitar products, spread his business throughout the USA, and indeed internationally. In 1985 he began his Guitar Solo Publications (GSP) business with the publication of two works by Antonio Lauro. In a relatively short period of time the GSP catalogue has blossomed, and with the benefit of Kamei's exceptional energies is now one of the most important publishing houses for classical guitar music. Kamei has on his current roster of composers and arrangers for GSP many prominent names including Carlos Barbosa-Lima, Eliot Fisk, David Tanenbaum, William Kanengiser, Luis Bonfá and Stephen Funk Pearson.

1989 saw Kamei extending his interests into manufacturing with the introduction of his GSP classical guitar string line.

## MARIA KÄMMERLING

**Born –**

**Leverkusen, West Germany**

**20 February 1946**

*Maria Kämmerling*

Maria Kämmerling studied with Karl Scheit at the Hochschule für Musik und Darstellende Kunst in Vienna, where she received her degree with honours in 1971.

Since her debut as a concert guitarist, she has performed widely as a soloist and chamber musician. In addition to numerous concerts in Denmark and other European countries, she has performed at international music festivals such as Guitar Québec, the Copenhagen Summer Festival and the Volos Guitar Festival. She has also appeared at many contemporary music festivals including ISCM World Music Days and The Nordic Music Days.

In Scandinavia Maria Kämmerling has established herself as an important interpreter of contemporary music, and a number of distinguished Danish composers have written guitar works especially for her. She has given the first Danish performances of guitar works by Apostel, Henze, Halffter, Maderna, Takemitsu and others.

Over the past few years, she has been active in working with historical original instruments as well as with the modern guitar. She has given concerts on the baroque guitar regularly since 1977 with the Danish recorder player Leif Ramlov Svendsen, and in 1981 she began performing with the Danish guitarist, the late Leif Christensen, who was also her husband, as a duo specializing in the performance of classical and romantic guitar duets on original 19th century instruments.

Maria Kämmerling has lived in Denmark since 1971, where she holds the post of assistant professor of guitar at the Royal Danish Academy of Music in Aarhus.

**SELECTED RECORDINGS**

Maria Kämmerling: Recital. Paula 3
Recorder/Baroque Guitar Duos. Kämmerling/Svendsen. Paula 7
Maria Kämmerling plays Gunnar Berg Guitar Works. Paula 9
Fernando Sor Guitar Duos: Kämmerling/Christensen. Paula 14
Maria Kämmerling plays Vagn Holmboe. Paula 30
Giuliani Guitar Duos: Kämmerling/Christensen. Paula 34
Giuliani Virtuoso Overtures: Kämmerling/Christensen. Paula 44
Baroque Works for Guitar/Recorder:Kämmerling/Svendsen. Horizon 8601

# HUBERT KÄPPEL

**Born –**

**Bensberg, West Germany**

**3 July 1951**

*Hubert Käppel*

Hubert Käppel first studied classical guitar at the Musikhochschule, Cologne. He went on to complete his studies under Konrad Ragossnig at the Musikakademie in Basel. He also attended master-classes given by Narciso Yepes. In 1978 Hubert Käppel won first prize at the Concorso Internazionale di Interpretazione in Gargnano, Italy. This success established him as one of Europe's finest young guitarists and led to a busy concert and teaching career. His version for the solo guitar of Bach's 6th keyboard Partita BWSV830 set new standards in the transcription of Bach's music.

**SELECTED RECORDINGS**

Bach (BWV1006a), Granados, Rodrigo, Brouwer. Exaudio 2982/S
Bach (BWV830), Kellner. GSP 1003 CD

**SELECTED READING**

Interview. Classical Guitar, April 1985
Interview. Guitar International, October 1988

# ELI KASSNER

**Born –**

**Vienna, Austria**

**27 May 1924**

*Eli Kassner*

As a boy of fifteen Eli Kassner escaped the Nazi Holocaust in Europe, leaving Austria to work on a kibbutz in Palestine. In 1951 he emigrated to Canada to join his elder brother. Within two years he had established himself as a classical guitar teacher in Toronto.

In 1958 Andrés Segovia heard Kassner play and invited him to study with him in Spain at Santiago de Compostela. On his return to Canada he was invited to join the faculties of both the University of Toronto and the Toronto Conservatory of Music as their first teacher of classical guitar.

In 1967 he founded his own Guitar Academy in Toronto, and it has become the most important institution of its type in Canada. His many pupils have included Liona Boyd and Norbert Kraft.

Eli Kassner is also a founder of the Guitar Society of Toronto, which sponsored in 1975 its first international guitar festival. This event is now held every three years and has become one of the largest and most important guitar festivals in the world. In 1978 he formed the University of Toronto Guitar Ensemble and has been its artistic director since.

Kassner has also been instrumental in persuading prominent Canadian composers, including Milton Barnes, Lothar Klein, Harry Somers, Kenin Talivaldis, John Weinzeig and others, to compose for the guitar.

**SELECTED READING**

Eli Kassner: A Biography. Guitar Canada, Spring 1989

# MARCELO KAYATH

**Born –**

**Belem-State, Brazil**

**15 January 1964**

*Marcelo Kayath*

Marcelo Kayath first studied with Leo Soares, Jodacil Damacino and Turibio Santos in Brazil.

In 1980 he won the Andrés Segovia Prize at the International Villa-Lobos Competition, and in 1982 he won the coveted Young Concert Artists of Brazil Award. He then went on to win, in 1984, two major international competitions – the Paris Concours International de Guitare and the Fourth Toronto International Guitar Competition.

Although still only twenty-five years old, Marcelo Kayath has already established himself as one of the most talented guitarists of the eighties. He also holds a degree in electrical engineering from the University of Rio de Janeiro. He has given many concerts to wide critical acclaim throughout Europe and the USA, and has made several recordings on the Hyperion and IMP labels.

**SELECTED RECORDINGS**

| | |
|---|---|
| The Twentieth Century Guitar. | Hyperion A 66203 |
| Latin Guitar. | MCA Classics MCAD 25963 |
| Guitar Classics from Latin-America. | IMP Classics CIMP 853 |
| Guitar Classics from Spain | IMP Classics PCD 876 |
| Marcelo Kayath. | 3M/RCA (Brazil) 7M5/0003 |

**SELECTED READING**

| | |
|---|---|
| Interview. | Guitar International, February 1985 |
| Interview. | Classical Guitar, June 1986 |

Classical Guitar

JUNE 1986 £1.00

Marcelo Kayath

Classical Guitar

WIN A £2000 CAMACHO GUITAR IN OUR ANNUAL PRIZE DRAW

8 PAGE MUSIC SUPPLEMENT

# CHRIS KILVINGTON

**Born –**

**18 June 1944**

**York, England**

*Chris Kilvington*

Chris Kilvington first played the guitar at the age of thirteen. After receiving his degree from Hull University, he spent several years in the Bahamas, where he won first prize in the National Music Festival in 1972. Upon returning to England he established himself as a soloist with a series of recitals in 1977, eventually moving to Cambridge in 1979.

During the last ten years Chris Kilvington has become recognised as one of Britain's foremost teachers of the instrument. He taught from 1977-1990 at the Cannington International Guitar Summer School, where he was Deputy Director; from 1980-1990 he was Director of the Cambridge Summer School for Guitar. He resigned both posts in order to become a Co-Director of the Cambridge International Guitar Festival at Girton College, The University of Cambridge. Since 1985 he has been Director of the Scottish International Guitar Festival. He is Lecturer in Guitar on the BA Degree course of Anglia College Cambridge. He is the Secretary of EGTA (UK), the British representative body of the European Guitar Teachers' Association.

Chris Kilvington has given concerts in Austria, Germany, Spain, Italy and Venezuela, also teaching courses in the latter two (for the British Council and the Caracas Conservatory). He has taught ensemble classes for the Guitar Foundation of America's International Festival in Los Angeles. He travels widely in the UK, giving masterclasses and directing a variety of guitar ensembles.

Chris Kilvington has a number of published compositions to his credit, some of which have been used by the examining bodies of both the Associated Board and the Guildhall School of Music. He is also the editor of a composer series with Ricordi under the title 'Chris Kilvington's Choice'. He is well known internationally as Reviews Editor of Classical Guitar magazine, a post he has held since 1983, and in addition to his editorial duties he has contributed many articles concerned with the development of the guitar.

**SELECTED MUSIC**

| | |
|---|---|
| Progressive Guitar Technique. | Hampton Music Publishers |
| Rain Suite | Hampton Music Publishers |
| Dowland's Dozen | Ricordi |
| Dowland's Half Dozen | Ricordi |
| Dream of Black Isle | Ricordi |
| Chanson du Soir. | Editions Musicales Transatlantique |

**SELECTED RECORDING**

| | |
|---|---|
| Images. | Gemini |

**SELECTED READING**

| | |
|---|---|
| Nervousness. | Classical Guitar, October 1984 |
| The Performance of Ensemble Music. | Classical Guitar, February 1988 |
| Start at the Top, parts 1/2/3. | Classical Guitar, March, June, July 1989 |
| Step by Step Analysis | Classical Guitar, August 1989 |
| Scales for Guitarists – Series. | Classical Guitar, 1990/1991 |

# HORST KLEE

**Born –**

**Bad Kreuznach, West Germany**

**1 April 1952**

*Horst Klee*

Horst Klee first started to play the guitar at the age of twelve. His first interest was in popular music, and he gave many concerts in semi-professional groups. From 1973 to 1977 he studied classical guitar with Gunter Alenburg at the Conservatory of Wiesbaden. He also studied with Robert Brojer, a professor at the Vienna Conservatory. From 1977 to 1981 he studied with Michael Teuchert in Frankfurt.

Since 1977 Horst Klee has taught in the Wiesbaden Conservatory and given many recitals throughout Germany.

**SELECTED RECORDINGS**

| | |
|---|---|
| Meisterwerke der Gitarre. | Sonata 96080 |
| Die Spanisch Gitarre. | Sonata 96082 |
| Gitarrenmusik des Barock. | Sonata 86000 |
| Gitarrenmusik von Manuel Ponce. | Sonata 96085 |
| Gitarrenmusik des 18 und 19 Jahrhunderts. | Sonata 96088 |

# FRANCIS KLEYNJANS

**Born –**

**Paris, France**

**15 April 1951**

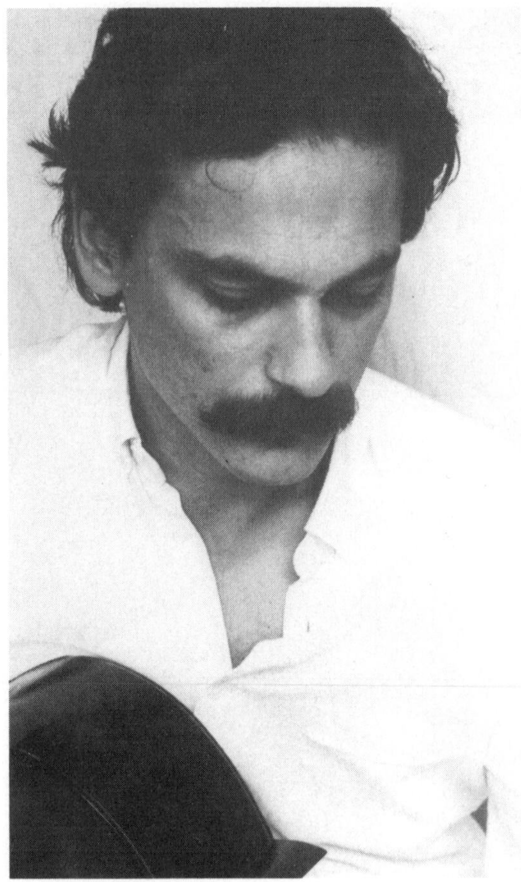

*Francis Kleynjans*

Francis Kleynjans began his serious guitar studies at the Conservatoire National Supérieur de Musique in Paris with Alexandre Lagoya. He went on to study with Alirio Díaz. His ability as a concert performer soon showed, and won him a first prize from the Yehudi Menuhin Foundation. Since that time he has given concerts throughout Europe and has made several broadcasts on French radio stations.

Kleynjans is also an important composer, having written over 300 pieces for the guitar including pedagogical and concert works, pieces for two, three and four guitars, and film scores. He was awarded the prize for composition at the 22nd International Guitar Competition organized by Radio France with his work, A l'Aube du Dernier Jour, which has been recorded by Roberto Aussel.

In April 1984 Francis Kleynjans wrote his first concerto for guitar and string orchestra, Op.62. He performed the work with the Philharmonic Chamber Orchestra of Nice at the 2nd Nice International Guitar Festival.

**SELECTED MUSIC**

| | |
|---|---|
| A L'Aube du Dernier Jour. | LEM 25017 |
| Arabesque en Forme de Caprice, Op.99. | LEM 25062 |
| Cinq Nocturnes. | LED 25866 |
| Cinq Nouvelles Estudines. | LED 25945 |
| Impromptu et Berceuse Op.65. | LEMOINE |
| Passacaille en A, Op.87. | LEM 24944 |
| Suite Brésilienne, Op.51. | LEM 25001 |
| 24 Preludes Vol.1. | LEM 24748 |
| 24 Preludes Vol.II. | LEM 247482 |
| Concerto No.1 (guitar part). | LED 27166 |

**SELECTED RECORDINGS**

| | |
|---|---|
| 14 Etudes de Concert pour Guitare. | EL Classique SEL 300 247 |
| Music of Satie and Kleynjans. | Context GX 311105 |
| Ouevres de Kleynjans. | Daminus DR 885CD |

**SELECTED READING**

| | |
|---|---|
| Francis Kleynjans. | Classical Guitar, May 1980 |

# NIKITA KOSHKIN

**Born –**

**Moscow, USSR**

**28 February 1956**

Nikita Koshkin enjoyed music from a very early age. At the age of four, two of his favourite composers were Shostakovich and Stravinsky, yet he did not start to study music and the guitar until he was fourteen. He received his first guitar as a present from his grandfather, together with a record by Andrés Segovia. Koshkin was so impressed by the recording that he made a decision to make music his career. His first guitar teachers were Vladimir Kapayev (at primary school) and George Emanov (at secondary school). He later studied at the Gnessin Conservatory in Moscow with Alexander Frauchi. He also studied composition with Victor Egorov.

Although his chosen instrument is the guitar, Koshkin regards himself now as mainly a composer. He believes that guitarists should interest themselves in music of all kinds, and this is reflected in his own highly original music for the guitar and other instruments. His musical style contains elements of the post-Stravinsky Russian composers, notably Shostakovich and Prokofiev.

Nikita Koshkin lives in Moscow, where he divides his time between composing and teaching.

**SELECTED MUSIC**

| | |
|---|---|
| The Prince's Toys. | Gendai Guitar 24 |
| Suite 'Les Elfes'. | LEM 25069, Orphée |
| Maskarades Vols. I & II. | LEM 24886/ LEM 24887 |
| Russian Collection Vol.5. | Orphée |

COURTESY: OLE HALEN

*Nikita Koshkin*

**SELECTED READING**

| | |
|---|---|
| The Guitar in Russia. | Guitar International, October 1985 |
| Interview. | Guitar International, September 1986 |

**SELECTED RECORDING**

| | |
|---|---|
| Vladimir Mikulka plays Koshkin & Rak. | BIS LP-240 |

# ELEFTHERIA KOTZIA

**Born –**

**Alexandroupolis, Greece**

**24 January 1957**

*Eleftheria Kotzia*

Eleftheria Kotzia studied at the National Conservatory in Athens with Dimitri Fampas and A. Paleoglogos. She later studied at the Conservatoire National Supérieure in Paris with Alexandre Lagoya, having earned a scholarship from the French Government. Kotzia then gained a scholarship to take part in a masterclass given by Julian Bream in Lichtenstein in 1977. In the same year she was awarded the first prize of the Athens Conservatory and also the first prize of the Sixth International Guitar Competition in Milan. In 1982 she won first prize in guitar at the Ville de Juvisy competition in France.

In 1984, under the auspices of the British Council and the Hellenic Foundation, Eleftheria Kotzia came to London to study at the Guildhall School of Music. Since that time she has maintained a busy career as a solo recitalist throughout Europe and Scandinavia. She made her first visit to the United States in 1990. Her debut recording contains the first recorded version of Sir Michael Tippett's The Blue Guitar.

**SELECTED RECORDING**

| | |
|---|---|
| The Blue Guitar. | Pearl/Pavilion SHE CD 9609 |

**SELECTED READING**

| | |
|---|---|
| Interview. | Guitar International June 1986 |
| Interview. | Classical Guitar, September 1989 |

# NORBERT KRAFT

**Born –**

**Linz, Austria**

**21 August 1950**

*Norbert Kraft*

Norbert Kraft emigrated to Canada with his family in 1954. He first studied the guitar seriously at the Royal Conservatory of Music in Toronto with Carl van Feggelen. He later studied with John Mills and Aaron Shearer.

In 1979 Kraft was the Grand Prize Winner of the CBC (Canadian Broadcasting Corporation) Young Artist Competition. In 1985 he won the first prize in the Andrés Segovia Competition held in Mallorca, Spain. Since that time he has become an international concert artist. He has appeared with every major orchestra in Canada and with the Boston Pops and the Baltimore Symphony in the USA. He is a regular performer on both Canadian radio and television. He has been featured in his own series on CBC television featuring the guitar and the guitar in chamber music, called 'The Art of Guitar'. He also often appears with his ensemble 'Kraft & Company' in concerts to the smaller communities throughout Canada. Kraft was a representative for Canada in 'The Year of Canadian Music' held in Washington DC in 1987.

Norbert Kraft has commissioned and premiered several new works for guitar, including a new guitar concerto by R. Murray Schafer. He is currently Professor of Guitar and Chamber Music at the faculty of Music, University of Toronto. He is also on the faculty at the Royal Conservatory of Music of Toronto. He is responsible for introducing their graded guitar repertoire series. Kraft was also Artistic Director at the first Toronto GuitarFest held in the summer of 1990.

**SELECTED RECORDINGS**

Duets for Cello and Guitar (with Ofra Harnoy). Moss MMG CMG 1144
Music for Guitar & Harpsichord (with Bonnie Silver) Fanfare DFL-6003
Villa-Lobos & Rodrigo Concertos. CBC SM5000
Tippett, Schafer & Britten. Chandos 8784

COURTESY: CBS RECORDS. PHOTO: HAUGHTON

*Alexandre Lagoya*

# ALEXANDRE LAGOYA

**Born –**

**Alexandria, Egypt**

**21 June 1929**

*Alexandre Lagoya with Ida Presti*

Alexandre Lagoya is without doubt one of the foremost guitarists of the twentieth century. Born in Alexandria, Egypt, the son of an Italian mother and a Greek father, Lagoya began to play the guitar at the age of eight.

He gave his first concert at the age of thirteen and, despite some objections from his parents, decided to make the guitar his career – although at one time he found professional boxing almost equally attractive. He gave many recitals in the villages of Egypt and toured other parts of the Middle East and Europe. At the age of eighteen he moved to Paris, France, and furthered his musical education at the Ecole Normale de Musique. By the time he was nineteen he had given more than five hundred concerts, and his career as a professional guitarist was assured. It was in Paris that he was able to perfect his technique, at the same time studying harmony and counterpoint with Saudry and meeting such famed musicians as Milhaud, Poulenc, Dutilleux, Messiaen, Rodrigo and Villa-Lobos.

In 1950 Lagoya went to Siena to study with Andrés Segovia. In the same year he met Ida Presti, a guitarist he much admired. They met in the home of André Verdier and a mutual love for the instrument developed into a love for each other. They married in 1952 and not only joined lives but musical forces as well to become the legendary concert duo Presti-Lagoya. Though they had made formidable reputations as solo performers, their work together brought them even more fame. They founded a guitar class at the Schola Cantorum in Paris and also made regular world tours. In fifteen years they played 2,000 concerts and also worked out many brilliant new techniques for the guitar.

In 1967 the Presti-Lagoya duo was at the height of its fame when Ida Presti, whilst preparing for a concert in New York City, suddenly fell ill and died. Lagoya, grief-stricken, continued teaching but did not perform in concert. Emotionally he had been devastated, and it took him a year and a half to re-study his repertoire. After a break of five years he began a new career as a solo guitar recitalist.

Alexandre Lagoya is now one of the world's busiest guitarists, playing at least one hundred concerts a year. He is also Professor at the Paris National Conservatoire, a position he has held since 1969, when he created a guitar class for the institution. In the summer, he teaches at the International Academy of Music in Nice, a position he has held since 1960, as well as in other parts of the world.

**SELECTED RECORDINGS**

| | |
|---|---|
| L'Extraordinaire Alexandre Lagoya. | Philips 6521 013 |
| La Guitare est mon Maître. | Philips 6504 041 |
| Lagoya. | Philips 6504 120 |
| Lagoya Plays Sor and Villa-Lobos. | Philips 6504 131 |
| Concerto for Classical Guitar and Jazz Piano (Bolling). | RCA CY 3007 |
| Rampal and Lagoya in Concert (2 LPs). | RA ARL 2-2631 |
| The Spanish Guitar | CBS M35857 |
| *With Ida Presti* | |
| Music for the Classical Guitar. | Nonesuch H 71161 |
| Musique Baroque pour deux Guitares | Philips 6504 003 |
| Concertos pour deux Guitares. | Philips 6504 018 |
| Musique Espagnole pour deux Guitares. | 6504 020 |
| Presti-Lagoya: Oeuvres pour deux Guitares. | Philips 6504049 |
| Masters of the Guitar: Volume One. | RCA RTB 6589 |

**SELECTED READING**

| | |
|---|---|
| Alexandre Lagoya. | Guitarra, May 1980 |
| Alexandre Lagoya. | Guitar Player, February 1982 |
| Interview. | Classical Guitar, December 1989, January 1990 |

**SELECTED MUSIC**

| | |
|---|---|
| Caprice. | Ric. R1608 |
| Rêverie. | Ric. R1607 |

# ROBERTO LARA

**Born – Tres Arroyos, Argentina**

**23 May 1927**

**Died – Buenos Aires, Argentina, 1988**

*Roberto Lara*

Roberto Lara completed his musical studies at the Music Conservatory in Buenos Aires, subsequently making several concert tours of South America and Europe. A noted teacher, he also recorded Qualiton record company. Several of his recordings were released by Lyrichord Disc Incorporated in the United States of America. Lara also made many transcriptions for the guitar, including a large amount of traditional Argentine melodies.

**SELECTED RECORDINGS**

| | |
|---|---|
| The Guitar of the Pampas. | Lyrichord LLST7253 |
| The Classic Guitar. | Lyrichord LLST7299 |

*Typical French nineteenth century guitar*

# ANTONIO LAURO

**Born – Ciudad Bolivar, Venezuela**

**3 August 1917**

**Died – Caracas, Venezuela, 18 April 1986**

COURTESY: RADIO FRANCE

*Antonio Lauro*

The popularity of Antonio Lauro's music has grown enormously in recent years. He has made a great contribution to the library of contemporary classical guitar music, not only through his own compositions but also through his many arrangements for the guitar of the music of fellow Venezuelan composers such as Sojo, Borges, Cisneros, Ramón y Rivera, and Landaeta.

Lauro had an academic musical background. He studied at the Academy of Music in Caracas under Vicente Emilio Sojo and Juan Bautista Plasis. His original instrument was the piano, but on hearing the Paraguayan guitar virtuoso Agustín Barrios Mangoré in concert, he decided to devote his musical study to the guitar.

Lauro wrote and arranged many works, the bulk of which are as yet unpublished. Most of them are for the guitar, but he also composed works for a cappella choral group, orchestra, orchestra and choir, piano, piano and voice, organ and voice, string quartet, wind quartet and other instrumental combinations. More often than not, the inspiration for his compositions was derived from the folkore, instruments and regional dance rhythms of Venezuela.

It was the Venezuelan virtuso guitarist Alirio Díaz who really first drew the guitar world's attention to the genius of his fellow countryman. Lauro and Díaz enrolled as students of Raúl Borges around the same time, and became close friends. Díaz revised and fingered many of Lauro's original compositions and arrangements for the guitar, and has often included a selection of them in in his concert tours around the world. As a result, the music of Antonio Lauro has featured prominently in the concert repertoires of many other leading guitarists. Lauro is now regarded as one of the great 20th century composers for the guitar.

**SELECTED MUSIC**

Angostura: Valse Venezolano, ed. Díaz. B 901
Carora: Valse Venezolano, ed. Díaz. B 903
El Marabino: Valse Venezolano, ed. Díaz. B 904
Four Venezuelan Waltzes, ed. Díaz. B 794
María Luisa: Valse Venezolano, ed. Díaz. B 905
Sonata. ZA 5539
Suite Venezolano, ed Díaz. B 793
Two Venezuelan Pieces: Valse Criollo & Pavana, ed. Papas. CO 166A
Variations on a Venezuelan Children's Song, ed. Díaz. B 940
Aire de Joropo: Canonico arr. Lauro. B 902

**SELECTED RECORDINGS**

David Russell plays Antonio Lauro. Guitar Masters GMR 1001
Guitar Music of Spain and Latin America: Alirio Díaz. EMI/HMV HQS 1175
Concerto for Guitar: Miloslav Matousek. Panton 8111 0318

**SELECTED READING**

Antonio Lauro. Guitar & Lute, January 1980
Antonio Lauro. Guitar, October 1980
Antonio Lauro: complete list of works. Guitar & Lute, January 1980
Antonio Lauro: special tribute issue. Guitar International, August 1986
Article. Classical Guitar, November 1986

# LUIGI LEGNANI

**Born – Ferrara, Italy**

**7 November 1790**

**Died – Ravenna, Italy, 5 August 1877**

*Luigi Legnani – original music cover*

Luigi Rinaldo Legnani began his musical education at the age of eight when his parents moved to Ravenna. As a singer and guitarist he soon showed immense talent, and by the time he was seventeen he was taking a prominent part in the opera at the Ravenna Theatre.

Legnani's first public recital as a guitar virtuoso was in Milan in 1819. From that time he was regarded as one of the foremost guitarists in Europe. He toured Europe extensively from 1822, appearing in Austria, Italy, Switzerland and Russia, where he played before the Grand Duke Nicolas. In 1836 a close friendship developed between Legnani and the violinist and guitarist Nicoló Paganini.

Legnani became very interested in the construction of the guitar, and when he visited the leading guitar makers in Vienna – Staufer and Ries – he left with them designs of several new models, including a terz guitar (a guitar tuned a minor third higher than the standard instrument). Both these makers produced guitars bearing Legnani's name. In 1850 Legnani decided to give up his career as a concert recitalist, and returned to Ravenna to devote his life to the construction of guitars.

Legnani was not only a talented luthier and a virtuoso guitarist, but also a prolific composer for the guitar. He wrote over two hundred and fifty compositions for the instrument, including a Method for the Guitar, op.250, which was published by Ricordi of Milan. The bulk of his compositions was published in Vienna by the publishing house of Leidesdorf.

Luigi Legnani, an honorary member of the Philharmonic Societies of Rome, Florence, Ferrara and Munich, and one of the greatest classical guitarists of the nineteenth century, died in Ravenna in 1877 at the age of eighty-seven.

**SELECTED MUSIC**

| | |
|---|---|
| Caprices in all Major and Minor Keys op.20, Nos.1-18 & 19-36 | Kalmus |
| Caprices in all Keys op.20, Books 1 & 2. | GA 35/GA 36 |
| 36 Caprices, op.20, ed. Wynberg. | ECH 440 |
| Introduction, Theme, Variations & Finale, op.64. | SZ 7765 |
| Introduction, Theme & Variations, op.224. | GA 74 |
| Introduction & Theme, op.237. | Kalmus |
| Six Little Caprices, op.250, ed. Pomilio. | BA 11240 |
| Six Caprices, op.250. | Bèrben 2240 |
| Ten Selected Caprices, ed. Storti. | Bèrben 1383 |
| Twelve Selected Caprices, ed. Savio. | BA 11363 |
| Variations on theduet 'Nel cor píu' from La Molinara, op.16, ed. Chiesa. | SZ 8359 |

# DAVID LEISNER

**Born –**

**Los Angeles, California, USA**

**22 December 1953**

*David Leisner*

Since his success as a prizewinner in the 1975 International Guitar Competition in Toronto, Canada, David Leisner has come to be regarded as one of the best classical guitarists in the United States of America, an opinion that is confirmed by his recent concert performances and his record release on the Titanic label. He also won the Silver Medal at the 1981 International Guitar Competition held in Geneva, Switzerland.

Although born in California, Leisner is a graduate of Wesleyan University in Connecticut, and is now a resident of New York. Over the years he has studied the guitar and music with several important teachers, both in the USA and in Europe. He has studied the guitar with John Duarte, Angelo Gilardino, Theodore Norman and David Starobin; interpretation with Karen Tuttle and John Kirkpatrick; and composition with Richard K. Winslow.

Leisner is also a talented singer and composer, and in the latter capacity had two works commissioned by a London choral group and a New York theatre company. He has appeared several times on national radio in the USA, and also in concert with the famous harmonica player Larry Adler.

David Leisner holds an appointment in the faculty of the New England Conservatory of Music in Boston, and is also on the roster of Affiliate Artists Incorporated.

**SELECTED MUSIC**

| | |
|---|---|
| Suite Op.1. | Bèrben |
| 'Billy Boy' Variations. | Merion Music |
| Passacaglia and Toccata. | Merion Music |
| The Cat that Walked by Himself. | Merion Music |
| Three Moons (cello & guitar). | Merion Music |
| Outdoor Shadows (voice & guitar). | Merion Music |

**SELECTED RECORDING**

| | |
|---|---|
| The Viennese Guitar. | Titanic TI-46 |

# PHILIPPE LEMAIGRE

**Born –**

**Vise, Belgium**

**16 February 1950**

*Philippe Lemaigre*

Philippe Lemaigre first studied the piano, but at the age of thirteen he changed to the guitar. His first guitar teacher was Gonzalez Mohino in Liège, although earlier he had studied harmony, counterpoint and musical analysis with Félix Mahieu. He entered the Liège Conservatory when he was seventeen and graduated in 1971. He won first prize for guitar and chamber music on his graduation. Later he studied with Leo Brouwer and Alberto Ponce.

Philippe Lemaigre also plays the lute, and has given concerts throughout Europe on both this instrument and the guitar. In recent years he has established himself as one of Belgium's leading guitarists, often appearing with his fellow Belgian Guy Lukowski, and also as a composer of note. Some of his recordings have featured the works of contemporary Belgian composers including P.Boesmans, H.Pousseur, J. Absil and J. L. Robert.

**SELECTED MUSIC**

Douze Etudes
Equisses (Mourat)

Miniatures (Mourat)
Six Preludes en Hommage à Debussy.

**SELECTED RECORDINGS**

| | |
|---|---|
| The Guitar works of Leo Brouwer. | Ricercare RIC 028 |
| Carulli Guitar Duos (with Guy Lukowski) | EMI C 069-19069 |
| Sor Guitar Duos (with Guy Lukowski). | Pavane ADW 7016 |
| Virtuoso: Giuliani, Tárrega, Sor, Coste, Albert. | EMI 1 A 065 1654671 |
| Compositions by Lemaigre. | Pavane ADW 7148 |
| Recital de Guitare: Sor & Villa-Lobos. | Alpha DB 208 |
| La Guitare à Versailles. | Alpha DB 234 |
| La Guitare Romantique. | Music Magna Mag 20004 |
| Fernando Sor. | Music Magna Mag 50018 |
| Philippe Boesmans: Intrusion. | Music Magna Mag 50024 |
| Lemaigre: Improvisations. | Music Magna Mag 20008 |

# WOLFGANG LENDLE

**Born –**

**Ludwigsburg, Germany**

**5 January 1948**

*Wolfgang Lendle*

Wolfgang Lendle began his guitar studies in Trier with H.J.Volkholz, continuing with Jiri Jirmal at the Musikhochschule in Saarbrücken. There was further study with Andrés Segovia, Alirio Diaz, José Tomás, Alvaro Company and Regino Sainz de la Maza. He built up a considerable part of his repertoire with the German pianist Martin Galling.

Lendle won the 15th competition of the German Music Council as well as the international Competition 'Maria Canals' in Barcelona in 1969 and the 'Francisco Tárrega' in Benicasim in 1974. He has given concerts in nearly all European countries, the USSR, North and South America, and has appeared in international festivals such as Esztergom, Volos, Krakow, Istanbul, Jerusalem, Paris and Havana. Since 1985 he has been teaching at the Music Academy of Kassel. In addition to his career as a solo concert guitarist, he performs in a duo with his wife, the mezzo-soprano Bertha Casares. He is also a talented composer, whose works are published by Editions Orphée.

**SELECTED MUSIC**

| | |
|---|---|
| Variations Capricieuses d'aprés Paganini. | Orphée |

**SELECTED RECORDINGS**

| | |
|---|---|
| Saudade (with Françoise Reuter, voice) | Luxembourg Sound SA 76 23691 |
| Scarlatti/Rodrigo Sonatas. | Leico Records 8155 |
| Songs by Ginastera, Guastavino, Villa-Lobos, Almeida, Lendle/Bertha Casares, mezzo-soprano, with Wolfgang Lendle. | TGF Records 20-8504 |
| Recuerdos de la Alhambra – Highlights. Spanish Guitar Music. | Teldec 243 717-2 CD |
| Villa-Lobos:Complete Solo Works for Guitar. | Teldec 8.44143 ZK, 244 2197-2 CD |

**SELECTED READING**

| | |
|---|---|
| Interview. | Classical Guitar, August 1985 |
| Wolfgang Lendle. | Classical Guitar, August 1989 |

# WULFIN LIESKE

**Born –**

**Linz an der Donau, West Germany**

**6 March 1956**

**SELECTED RECORDINGS**

| | |
|---|---|
| Bach/Schubert for Guitar | Intercord CD INT 830-804 |
| La Catedral: Barrios. | Intercord CD INT 830-846 |
| Preludio Latino | Saphir INT 830.877 |

**SELECTED READING**

| | |
|---|---|
| Interview. | Classical Guitar, July 1990 |

*Wulfin Lieske*

Wulfin Lieske began to study the guitar at the age of twelve. In 1973 he studied the classical guitar with Karl-Heinz Bottner and Hubert Käppel at the Musiktheorie am Konservatorium der Stadt Köln. At the same time he studied jazz with Manfred Schoof at the Musikhochschule Köln. His first recording, Bitternis, was with a jazz quartet and was released in 1979.

Since that time Wulfin Lieske has concentrated on the classical guitar, winning several important international competitions including Alicante, Spain, in 1981, Gargagno, Italy, in 1982, and the Andrés Segovia Competition in Almuñecar, Spain, in 1985. Following these successes, Lieske has performed throughout Europe, establishing himself as one of Europe's finest young classical guitarists.

Wulfin Lieske lives in Cologne and has been teaching at the Hamburg State School of Music.

# DAGOBERTO LINHARES

**Born –**

**São Paulo, Brazil**

**9 September 1953**

*Dagoberto Linhares*

Dagoberto Linhares started his guitar studies with Manuel São Marcos at the age of nine, continuing with his daughter Maria Livia São Marcos at Geneva Conservatoire. At fourteen he won first prize at the City of São Paulo City Competition as well as the Young Instrumentalists' award. In 1971 he played the solo guitar part in the South American première of Castelnuovo-Tedesco's Romancero Gitano (based on García Lorca) for chorus and guitar.

Linhares moved to Europe in 1972 and was appointed professor at the Fribourg Conservatoire, Switzerland. Currently he holds diploma and virtuosity classes at Lausanne Conservatory.

He attended masterclasses given by Turibio Santos and Julian Bream, and continued his success in international competitions when he won first prize in the Geneva Conservatory 'Virtuosité' examination in 1973. He was also granted the Swiss Musician Association Award. The following year he was laureate at the Maria Canals Competition in Barcelona and, in 1975, at the International Competition of Musical Performance in Geneva.

Since his debut at the Wigmore Hall, London, in 1974, Dagoberto Linhares has given numerous concerts throughout Europe, the United States (where he performed at the Lincoln Centre, New York) and Latin America, and has made several broadcasts for continental radio stations. He also appears frequently at music festivals, including the Esztergom International Guitar Festival, the Bratislava Festival (where he played Rodrigo's Concierto de Aranjuez ), the Tibor Varga Festival (Villa-Lobos Concerto), the Festival Estival in Paris, and Lisbon's First International Festival. He has performed with orchestras such as the Suisse Romande, Birmingham, Sofia, Detmold and Gulbenkian Foundation, and is also the founder of his own chamber group, the Linhares Guitar Quartet.

Dagoberto Linhares currently lives in Geneva, Switzerland.

**SELECTED RECORDINGS**

Villa-Lobos: Cinq Preludes, Suite Populaire Brésilienne. Alvarez 817
Dagoberto Linhares: Musique espagnole pour guitare. Gallo 30507
Ouevres pour choeur et guitare. Tedesco, Nobre, Prado. Arion 36641
Trios: Paganini. SMS 2843
Yanomamy: Nobre. EMI 063422921
Musique pour quatre guitares:
Piazzolla, Joplin, Granados, Falla, Dowland. Gallo CD 517
Villa-Lobos. 12 Etudes/5 Preludes. Gallo CD 572

# MIGUEL LLOBET

**Born – Barcelona, Spain**

**17 October 1878**

**Died – Barcelona , 22 February 1938**

*Miguel Llobet*

Miguel Llobet's father was a noted wood carver of religious images. Many distinguished artists and musicians used his studio as a meeting place, and as a result Llobet was brought up in an artistic atmosphere. His father had hoped that he would follow in his footsteps and also become an artist. In fact Llobet was a skilful artist, as can be seen by the excellent sketches he made throughout his life.

Llobet's uncle gave him his first guitar when he was eleven years old. He began to study the instrument with Macan Alegre at the Municipal School of Barcelona. Alegre immediately recognised his special musical talent and introduced him to the leading guitarist in Spain at that time, Francisco Tárrega. Llobet soon made great progress under Tárrega's tutelage, and in 1900 he made his recital debut in Málaga. The concert was a resounding success, and as a result he was invited to play for the Spanish royal family in Madrid. True international fame came to Llobet after his first concert in Paris at the Salon Washington-Palace on 26 January 1905. A series of highly acclaimed concerts followed.

Llobet's reputation was established in Paris with the help of his friend, the pianist Ricardo Viñes, whose influence often resulted in the presence of musicians such as Debussy, Ravel, Fauré, Dukas and Stravinsky at Llobet's concerts.

Continuing his highly successful career as a recitalist, Llobet toured throughout Europe, South America and the United States of America. There is no doubt that he was one of the most influential guitarists of the era. He was probably the first guitarist to make a recording with a microphone. These first records were made by Parlophon Electra in Barcelona in 1926. He also made several duo recordings with the Argentinian guitarist Maria Luisa Anido.

Miguel was not only a great guitar virtuoso, but also a fine transcriber and arranger for the instrument. It was as a result of his repeated requests that Manuel de Falla wrote his only guitar work, Homenaje pour le Tombeau de Claude Debussy in 1920.

Llobet died in Barcelona at the age of 59 during the Spanish Civil War. Despite rumours that he was the victim of a bombing raid, there is positive proof that he died of natural causes after a bout of pleurisy.

**SELECTED MUSIC**

| | |
|---|---|
| Le Mestre: Catalan Folk Song. | BA 12124 |
| Estilo Popular Argentino No.1. | UME 21317 |
| Estilo Popular Argentino No.2. | UME 21318 |
| Five Catalan Folk Melodies, ed. Papas. | CO 232 |
| La Filla del Marxant. | BA 12123 |
| Leonesa. | UME 21939 |
| Respuesta. | UME 20370 |
| Romanza (in C minor). | UME 21695 |
| Scherzo: Waltz. | UME 20371 |
| Ten Popular Catalan Songs. | UME 20372 |

**SELECTED RECORDINGS**

The Recordings of Miguel Llobet (2 LPs). — El Maestro EM 8003

Miguel Llobet: The Guitar Recordings c.1925 (cassette). — Chanterelle CHR 001

**SELECTED READING**

Miguel Llobet,Chitarrista dell Impressionismo – Bruno Tonazzi. — Bèrben, Milan, 1966

# MICHAEL LORIMER

**Born –**

**Chicago, USA**

**13 January 1946**

COURTESY: SHAW CONCERTS INC.

*Michael Lorimer*

Born in Chicago, Michael Lorimer was raised in Los Angeles, California. He became interested in the classical guitar at the age of ten when he heard one of his father's records of Andrés Segovia. Lorimer's first teacher was the Los Angeles guitarist Guy Horn, and he studied with him until he was fourteen years old.

Dorothy de Goede, a former pupil of Segovia, introduced Lorimer to Segovia in 1962. The master guitarist was impressed by the young player and suggested a visit to Siena, Italy, in order to study with him. This Lorimer did after graduating from high school at the age of seventeen. He continued his studies with Segovia at Santiago de Compostela, Spain.

After returning to the United States, Michael Lorimer began a busy career, giving a minimum of thirty recitals a year and teaching on a regular basis at Berkeley, California, and at the San Francisco Conservatory of Music.

In 1980 he was the visiting professor of guitar at the University of Carolina, at Wilmington, USA. For several years he wrote a column on the classical guitar for the magazine Guitar Player.

Michael Lorimer has also made a study of the baroque guitar, and has included it in many of his concert recitals.

One of the leading recitalists and teachers in the United States today, Michael Lorimer has also achieved prominence as a transcriber of several excellent books of guitar music, for Charles Hansen Music, USA, and for the Mel Bay Publishing Company.

**SELECTED READING**

| | |
|---|---|
| Michael Lorimer. | Guitar Player, October 1973 |
| Michael Lorimer. | Guitar Player, December 1975 |
| Michael Lorimer. | Frets, September 1980 |
| Michael Lorimer. | Guitar & Lute, July 1980 |

# GUY LUKOWSKI

**Born –**

**Brussels, Belgium**

**7 March 1942**

*Guy Lukowski*

The son of a Polish father and a French mother, Guy Lukowski began his studies on the guitar at the age of thirteen. After leaving university he attended the Conservatory of Liège, where he was a pupil of Gonzalez Mohino.

In 1972 Lukowski was chosen by Alexandre Lagoya to join the Ensemble Français de Musique de Chambre Pupitre XIV, performing throughout France. Since then he has led a busy concert career in Europe, North and South America and the Middle East. He has made over twenty recordings.

Guy Lukowski teaches classical guitar at the Academie de Musique César Franck in Belgium. He is the founder and artistic manager of the Festival International de la Guitare in Liège, and is regarded by many as Belgium's most important guitarist and guitar personality.

**SELECTED RECORDINGS**

| | |
|---|---|
| Ma première guitare. | Decca 146Y |
| Guitar Romance. | WEA 58071 |
| Guitare. | RKM 805 |
| Spanish Guitar. | IBC 97212 |
| Romance. | Barclay 93021 |
| Guitar Music of Barrios. | EMI Angel S-37844 |
| Vivaldi, Boccherini, Rossini Paganini, Mozart. | EMI 1A 067-2702521 |
| Carulli Guitar Duets (with Philippe Lemaigre) | EMI PM C 069-19069 |
| Fernando Sor Duets (with Philippe Lemaigre). | Pavane ADW 7016 |
| Sor-Carulli. | EMI 37845 |
| Piazzolla: Histoire du Tango (with M. Grauwels, flute). | Carrere CA 681 66.325 |
| Alternances for guitar & flute. | EMI 99544 |
| Guy Lukowski. | Vogue DIA 336 |
| Patchwork. | EMI 2401261 |

# VINCENZO MACALUSO

**Born –**

**Milwaukee, Wisconsin, USA**

**9 January 1941**

COURTESY: VINCENZO MACALUSO

*Vincenzo Macaluso*

Vincenzo Macaluso began his studies on the guitar at the age of ten with his father. His first interest was jazz, and he eventually studied with the jazz guitarist Barney Kessel. Macaluso made great progress and soon established himself as a prominent jazz/studio guitarist in the Los Angeles area.

It was during his late teens that Macaluso began a serious study of classical music. Within a few years he developed a fine technique on the classical instrument and became generally accepted as one of the leading classical guitarists on the West Coast of America.

Macaluso was one of the few American guitarists to change over to the ten-string guitar originally designed by Narciso Yepes. He played this instrument exclusively for several years, recording four albums for the Klavier label. More recently, he returned to playing the six-string guitar exclusively, feeling that the sonority of this instrument could not be duplicated on the ten-string guitar.

Vincenzo Macaluso is currently Artist-in-Residence and Professor of Guitar at Whittier College, California.

**SELECTED RECORDINGS**

| | |
|---|---|
| 10-String Guitar Interprets the Classics. | Klavier KS 508 |
| 10-String Guitar Interprets theFrench Classics. | Klavier KS 523 |
| 10-String Guitar Interpretsthe Spanish Classics. | Klavier KS 552 |

COURTESY: MARIO MACCAFERRI

*Mario Maccaferri in 1926*

# MARIO MACCAFERRI

**Born –**

**Cento, Bologna, Italy**

**20 May 1900**

COURTESY: MAURICE J. SUMMERFIELD

*Mario Maccaferri in 1989*

Mario Maccaferri gained his diploma and left school at the age of nine. He began to work as a dish washer and then later as an apprentice carpenter. After a while he heard of a vacancy in the workshops of the famous Italian luthier Luigi Mozzani, which he was to fill in 1911.

It was during his apprenticeship with Mozzani that Maccaferri took an interest in the playing of the classical guitar. By the age of sixteen he had gained a high reputation as a concert guitarist. He studied music seriously at the Academy in Siena from 1916, and during the period 1920-1923 he gave many guitar recitals. Throughout this period he maintained his interest, as a techncial adviser in the Mozzani workshops, in the technical side of guitar making and engineering as a whole. In 1926 he received the highest possible diploma for music and guitar playing from the Academy in Siena, and in the same year became that institution's first professor of guitar.

In 1923 Maccaferri left Mozzani and embarked on a European concert tour that included Italy, Switzerland, France and Germany. In the eyes of some press reviewers he was an artist of the highest calibre, equal in both artistry and interpretation to the then young Andrés Segovia. During this period he advertized as a maker of all fretted instruments, violins, violas and cellos, and in 1926-1927 he won top prizes in the violin and cello making contests held in Rome, Fiume and Montecatini. In 1926 Maccaferri visited London, appearing in concert at the Wigmore Hall. He decided to stay for a while to try and earn a living as a guitar teacher, and it was in London that he developed the prototypes of the distinctive and famous Maccaferri guitars that were to be built later in Paris and used by Django Reinhardt and other top European jazz guitarists. Those revolutionary guitars had closed, lubricated and geared tuning machines, predating those on today's instruments.

In 1933 Maccaferri continued his career as a concert artist, playing in Berlin, Hamburg, Cologne, Brussels and Antwerp. This suddenly came to a halt when he broke his hand in a swimming pool accident. Having studied the manufacture of saxophone reeds in Paris, he founded the French American Reed Mfg Company, moving it from Cento to the United States in 1938. Within a short period of time his company became the leading supplier in the United States of clarinet and saxophone reeds.,

Maccaferri then went into plastics, and his company, Mastro Industries, developed a line of best-selling plastic guitars and ukuleles. His engineering genius undoubtedly helped millions of children throughout the world to buy a playable guitar at an affordable price.

In 1981 Mario Maccaferri finally closed Mastro Industries. In his eighties, he designed some new guitars for the Saga company in Japan. In 1990, within a few weeks of his ninetieth birthday, he heard one of his plastic violins played in a recital at Carnegie Hall, New York.

Maccaferri had a strong friendship with artists such as Andrés Segovia and, among his earlier pupils, Ida Presti and Len Williams, the father of John Williams. As he enters his tenth decade, Mario Maccaferri remains a guitarist, luthier and innovator of unusual ability.

**SELECTED READING**


Mario Maccaferri. Guitar Player, April 1974
Mario Maccaferri. Guitar, May 1975
Mario Maccaferri. Guitar Player, November 1976
Mario Maccaferri. Guitar, January 1976
Mario Maccaferri. Guitar, August 1977
Interview. Classical Guitar, September 1984
The Rebirth of Django's Guitar. M.J. Summerfield. CSL Booklet, 1974

# IVOR MAIRANTS

**Born –**

**Rypin, Poland**

**18 July 1908**

COURTESY IVOR MAIRANTS

*Ivor Mairants*

Ivor Mairants is well known throughout the world to guitarists of all styles. In recent years he has devoted more of his time to the classical guitar, and has composed several original works for the instrument, made many transcriptions of classical melodies, and written a best-selling flamenco guitar method.

He became a professional guitarist at the age of twenty. Over the past sixty years he has come to be regarded throughout the world as one of the leading authorities on the guitar in all its forms. Although not strictly a classical guitarist, his contribution to the promotion of the classical guitar in Britain over the years has been enormous.

He was a featured member of many of Britain's leading dance bands in the nineteen-thirties and forties, including those of Ambrose, Roy Fox, Lew Stone, Geraldo and Ted Heath. In later years he was often heard with the popular Mantovani orchestra, and more recently with Manuel and his Music of the Mountains.

Of particular importance to guitarists is the fact that Ivor Mairants has devoted so much of his time to writing music and methods for the guitar. He established a school of music in London (1950-60), and among his many pupils were several players who today are some of Britain's top guitarists. He has devoted a lot of his energies to developing his music store in the West End of London, offering one of the world's finest selection of classical guitars.

Ivor Mairants still spends every spare moment writing for the guitar – jazz, classical and flamenco. Many of his methods and solos, old and new, are used by thousands of guitarists throughout the world. He is a regular contributor to Classical Guitar magazine.

**SELECTED MUSIC**

| | |
|---|---|
| 6 Solos for Classic Guitar. | EMI |
| 6 Bagatelles. | EMI |
| A Bundle of Blues. | Chappells/Hansen |
| 6 Progressive Pieces for Solo Guitar. | EMI |
| 6 Easy Pieces. | EMI |
| 6 Lute Pieces. | EMI |
| 6 Part Suites. | Breitkopf & Härtel |
| Sonata (to a Sonic Age). | Brons/Hansen |
| Sonata No.2. | AP |
| Meditation. | Chappells/Hansen |
| The Spirit of New Orleans. | Chappells/Hansen |
| Travel Suite. | EMI |
| 3 Rhythmic Dances. | EMI |
| Four Biblical Sketches | FENTONE |
| Triptych. | FENTONE |

**SELECTED READING**

My Fifty Fretting Years:An Autobiography: Ivor Mairants. Ashley Mark, 1980

Interview. Classical Guitar, February 1986

# CARMEN MARINA

**Born – MARIA DEL CARMEN MANTEGA PASCUAL**

**Santander, Spain**

**17 July 1936**

PHOTO: J. ABELES

*Carmen Marina*

Carmen Marina showed a natural ability for music at an early age. When she was sixteen she won a scholarship to the Royal Conservatory of Music in Madrid, from where she graduated in the classical guitar and composition. She also won an honorary award for her opera 'The Old Man and the Sea' based on the Ernest Hemingway novel of the same name.

At the age of eighteen she made a highly successful concert tour of North Africa and France. For several years she attended Segovia's annual masterclasses in Siena, Italy, and Santiago de Compostela in Spain. As well as a hectic concert schedule, she made several European television and radio broadcasts.

In the United States of America, where she has lived since 1971, she made a very successful concert debut at the Carnegie Hall, New York. She currently divides her time teaching at the Institute of Guitar Music, New York (established with her husband in 1976), and a busy schedule of concerts, recording and broadcasting on both radio and television.

In 1979 a grant from the US-Spanish Joint Committee for Educational and Cultural Affairs allowed her to write a series of song cycles based on the poetry of Miguel de Unamuno, Gerardo Diego, Rafael Alberti, Garcia Lorca and others, which later were performed in the United States and Spain. In 1981 she premiered, on the Spanish-American television in New York, Channel 47, a cycle of songs based on Rafael Alberti's 'Poems of Parana'.

Carmen Marina is not only a fine guitarist and composer but also a talented singer, as can be heard on her recordings on the IGM label.

**SELECTED RECORDS**

| | |
|---|---|
| Recordando a España. | SMC 1121 |
| Nineteenth Century Guitarists. | SMC 1122 |
| Albéniz for Guitar. | SMC 1123 |
| Bach for Guitar. | SMC 1124 |
| Spanish Gold: Guitar and Voice. | IGM 333-01 |

# DEBORAH MARIOTTI

**Born –**

**Zürich, Switzerland**

**26 September 1959**

*Deborah Mariotti*

Deborah Mariotti began to play the guitar at the age of four under the instruction of her father Luigi Mariotti, a guitarist and luthier. Through him the young guitarist benefited from personal contact with many prominent guitarists, including Manuel López Ramos, Ernesto Bitetti and Alfonso Moreno, who were regular visitors to the Mariotti home.

In 1978 Deborah Mariotti won first prize in the Concours des Jeunesses Musicales Suisses and was awarded the Villa-Lobos interpretation medal in Milan, Italy. In 1979 she continued her studies at the Academy Estudio de Arte Guitarristico in Mexico City with Manuel López Ramos, and in the same year was awarded the soloist diploma. In 1982 she was a prizewinner at Guitar '81 in Toronto, Canada, and she also made a highly acclaimed debut recital at the Wigmore Hall, London.

Since 1980 Deborah Mariotti has maintained a very active concert schedule, performing throughout Europe, Scandinavia, North America, Mexico and the Far East. She has also appeared on radio and television and recorded with major orchestras including the London Symphony Orchestra.

**SELECTED RECORDINGS**

| | |
|---|---|
| Deborah Mariotti, Gitarre. | Ex Libris PAN 130 053 |
| Rodrigo: Concierto Madrigal. | EMI Digital ASD 1651411 |
| Deborah Mariotti spielt. | Jecklin 240 |
| Musik aus Spanien und Sudamerika. | Jecklin JS 263-2 CD |

**SELECTED READING**

| | |
|---|---|
| Interview. | Classical Guitar, September 1986 |
| Interview. | Guitar International, March 1987 |
| Interview. | Guitar International, May 1989 |

# BARRY MASON

**Born –**

**Cottingham, Yorkshire, England**

**6 September 1947**

Barry Mason was educated at Hull College of Technology. He studied classical guitar at the Royal Academy of Music in London, where he studied with Anthony Rooley and David Munrow, specializing in early guitar and the lute. He made his concert debut at the Purcell Room in 1973.

Mason left the Academy in 1974 and went on to study with Diana Poulton at the Royal College of Music for a year. By this time he was recognized as a leading performer on the lute, vihuela and other early fretted instruments. He became director of the early music group Camerata of London in 1974, and in 1977 he was director of the First Early Music Centre Festival in London.

Barry Mason is today a leading international concert recitalist of early music and a prolific recording artist.

*Barry Mason*

**SELECTED RECORDINGS**

| | |
|---|---|
| Popular Music of Elizabeth I. | Saga 5447 |
| 16th Century Music. | Saga 5454 |
| The Queen's Men. | CRD 1055 |
| Music in Pictures. | NGS 100 |
| Portraits in Music. | NGS 101 |
| The Music of Thomas Campion. | Meridian E 77009 |
| Music of Kings & Courtiers. | Saga 5467 |
| English Social Music (with James Tyler). | Saga 5479 |
| English Ayres & Duets. | Hyperion A 66003 |
| Italian Bel Canto Arias (with James Tyler). | Hyperion A 66153 |
| Masters of the Baroque Guitar. | Amon Ra CDSAR45 |

**SELECTED READING**

| | |
|---|---|
| Interview. | Guitar International, December 1985 |
| Interview. | Classical Guitar, 1990 |

# AKINOBU MATSUDA

**Born – AKINOBU JIRO MATSUDA**

**Himeji, Japan**

**28 June 1933**

*Akinobu Matsuda*

Akinobu Matsuda graduated at Kobe University in 1957, where he read Economics. He had begun to play the guitar at the age of fourteen and had immediately shown great promise.

His first public recital, in Kobe, Japan, 1958, was a great success. In 1959 his playing was commended by Andrés Segovia, who was principal artist at the Osaka International Festival in Japan that year. In 1969 Matsuda travelled to Europe, where for two years he studied with Segovia and Alirio Díaz. During this time he also studied with John Williams at the Royal College of Music in London.

In 1962 Akinobu Matsuda made the first of three concert tours in the United States, going on to make his debut in Singapore and Hong Kong in 1964. His debut at Carnegie Hall, New York, took place in 1969. In the same year he also appeared for the first time at the Wigmore Hall, London. In 1973 he undertook a successful concert tour of Great Britain, and made radio broadcasts in Dublin and Paris. He also gave a recital in Bergen, Norway. The following year he performed at the Hong Kong Arts Festival as a soloist.

Akinobu Matsuda has been awarded many prizes, including the Papas-Puyana Prize at the International Guitar Competition under the auspices of Andrés Segovia and sponsored by the Conservatory of Music at Orense, Spain. In 1963 he received the Japan Critics Club Prize of the Year, and in 1979 he became an honorary member of the Board of Directors of the International Castelnuovo-Tedesco Society. In the same year he was given the award of the Cultural Services from Himeji City. He performs widely in addition to recording and teaching.

**SELECTED RECORDINGS**

| | |
|---|---|
| The Classic Sound of the Guitar. | Argo ZDA 205 |
| Sound of the Guitar. | ARM 30011 |

**SELECTED READING**

| | |
|---|---|
| Jiro Matsuda. | Guitar, March 1973 |

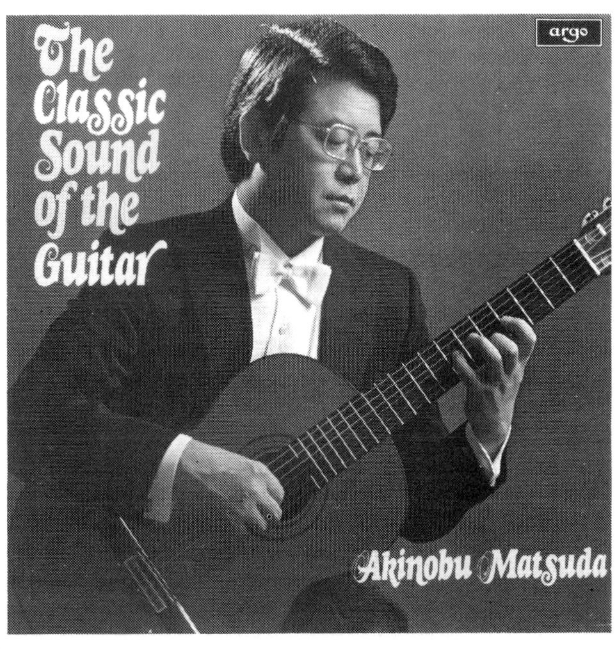

# JOHANN KASPAR MERTZ

**Born – Poszony, Hungary**

**17 August 1806**

**Died – Vienna, Austria , 14 October 1856**

*Johann Kaspar Mertz*

Johann Kaspar Mertz began his study of music, on both the guitar and the flute, at an early age. A child prodigy, he was able at the age of twelve to support his parents from the income he earned as a teacher.

In 1840 he left Poszony (later known as Pressburg, and now the Czechoslovakian city of Bratislava) for Vienna, less than forty miles distant. There, on 29 November 1840, he made his concert debut in front of the Empress Carolina Augusta at the Court Theatre. The recital was a great success, and Mertz embarked on a concert tour of several European countries.

Whilst living in Vienna, Mertz met and marrfied Josephine Plantin. She was a pianist, and they often appeared together in concert. They enjoyed great success and popularity, and as a result were much in demand as teachers, especially to the society élite of Vienna.

Johann Kaspar Mertz was not only a virtuoso guitarist, but also a prolific composer. He composed, arranged and transcribed over one hundred works for the guitar. His composition Concertino won the first prize at the Brussels Competition in 1856, but his untimely death at fifty from a heart complaint of long standing meant that the award had to be made posthumously.

**SELECTED MUSIC**

| | |
|---|---|
| Capriccio, op.13 no.3. | Bèrben 2138 |
| Kindermärchen (Children's Fairytale), ed. Leisner. | Presser 11440262 |
| Polacca, ed. Leisner. | Presser 11440259 |
| Romanze. | Presser 11440261 |
| Tarantelle. | Presser 11440260 |
| Three Nocturnes, op.4 . | N 3326 |
| Selected Works: 4 volumes. | ECH 417/420 |

**SELECTED READING**

| | |
|---|---|
| Mertz's Last Compositions. | Soundboard, Spring 1982 |

**SELECTED RECORDING**

| | |
|---|---|
| Guitar Music of Mertz: Szendrey-Karper. | Hungaroton SLPD 12894 |

# VLADIMIR MIKULKA

**Born –**

**Prague, Czechoslovakia**

**11 December 1950**

*Vladimir Mikulka*

Vladimir Mikulka started playing the classical guitar at the age of thirteen. Within two years he was a student of the foremost Czech guitarist Jiri Jirmal at the State Conservatory in Prague. At the age of nineteen, he proved to the world his outstanding ability on his chosen instrument by winning the international guitar competition in Paris, organized by the French radio and television organization ORTF.

Mikulka's success in this competition led to many concert bookings throughout the world. He played to enthusiastic audiences in most countries in Europe, Scandinavia, the Soviet Union, Cuba and Australia.

One of the finest guitarists to have emerged in recent years, Mikulka is not only a great player but also a talented teacher, and as a result he has been called upon to conduct many international masterclasses for guitarists.

Since 1980, Vladimir Mikulka has established himself among the élite of today's classical guitarists. He has participated in many international music festivals, including those held in Helsinki, Paris, Rome and Amsterdam. His several recordings are outstanding. He currently lives in Paris, where he is Professor in the conservatoires of the XIIIth and XXth arrondissements. He is also an editor for the publishers Henri Lemoine of Paris for their guitar series 'Vladimir Mikulka Presents...'

**SELECTED RECORDINGS**

| | |
|---|---|
| Vladimir Mikulka Plays Bach. | Supraphon 1-11-15 |
| Guitar Recital. | Denon (Japan) OX-7164 ND |
| Rodrigo/Tedesco Concertos. | Panton 11-0608 G |
| Haydn Quartet/Giuliani Op.3. | Supraphon 1100-2700 |
| The Music of Stepán Rak. | GHA 126-003 |
| Koshkin, Rak, East European Music. | BIS LP 240 |
| Ibero-American Guitar . | BIS CD 340 |

**SELECTED READING**

| | |
|---|---|
| Interview. | Classical Guitar Jan/Feb 1983 |
| Interview. | Classical Guitar, October 1984 |
| Interview. | Classical Guitar, July 1989 |

# JOHN MILLS

**Born –**

**Kingston-upon-Thames, England**

**13 September 1947**

*John Mills*

John Mills was initially a self-taught player from the age of nine. After making exceptional progress as a pupil at the Spanish Guitar Centre in London, he studied from 1966 to 1969 at the Royal College of Music, London, with John Williams. In 1968 he went to Spain to take part in masterclasses given by Andrés Segovia at Santiago de Compostela.

John Mills has been giving recitals regularly throughout the British Isles for many years. He has performed a number of times at the Wigmore Hall, the Purcell Room and the Queen Elizabeth Hall in London. In 1972 he made his international debut with a concert tour of Eastern Canada, and has since returned many times to perform throughout Canada and the United States. In the summer of 1975 he was chosen to play one of the major evening recitals at the Guitar '75 Festival in Toronto. He has also made concert tours of Australia, Sweden and Japan. In one period of ten years, John Mills gave over two thousand recitals.

John Mills is recognized world-wide not only as one of Britain's finest guitarists but also for his excellent teaching. His guitar method, The John Mills Guitar Tutor, was published by Musical New Services of Britain. He has also given many masterclasses, both at home and abroad, and has several records to his credit. He appeared several times on the BBC Radio programme The Classical Guitar, and has also been featured on television and local radio stations in Great Britain. In recent years he has spent some time in New Zealand, but has now settled once again in England.

**SELECTED RECORDINGS**

| | |
|---|---|
| Five Centuries of Classical Guitar. | Discourses ABK 10 |
| Student Repertoire: Volume One. | Guitar G 101 |
| Student Repertoire: Volume Two. | Guitar G 102 |
| 20th Century Guitar Music. | Guitar G 105 |

**SELECTED READING**

| | |
|---|---|
| John Mills. | Guitar, December 1973 |
| John Mills. | Guitar, June 1978 |

# SIMON MOLITOR

**Born Neckarsulm, Wurtemburg, Austria**

**3 November 1766**

**Died Vienna, Austria, 21 February 1848**

*Simon Molitor*

Simon Molitor originally studied the guitar with his father, Johann Michael Molitor. He continued his studies with the Abbe Vogler and was soon regarded as one of the best guitarists in Vienna at the end of the eighteenth century. After a short period as an orchestral conductor (1796-97) in Venice Molitor returned to Vienna in 1798 to take up a position in the War Office. He was to become a superintendent of the Italian and Dalmatian borders. During his period as a clerk and official Molitor composed many works for the guitar and also collaborated on a guitar method in his spare time, but his work as a guitarist was obviously limited. Molitor retired from the War Office in 1831 and was then able to devote the rest of his years entirely to music.

**SELECTED READING**

Simon Molitor,Viennese Guitarist& Composer – Josef Zuth
Anton Goll, Vienna 1919

MARIA LUISA ANIDO marca con su actividad interpretativa un capítulo fundamental de la historia guitarrística universal. En pág. 13 "Guía de intérpretes" sintetiza su vida dedicada a la guitarra.

EN ESTA EDICION:

- EL NACIMIENTO DE UNA ESCUELA — Emilio Colombo
- LA GUITARRA DEL FUTURO — Eduardo Muscari

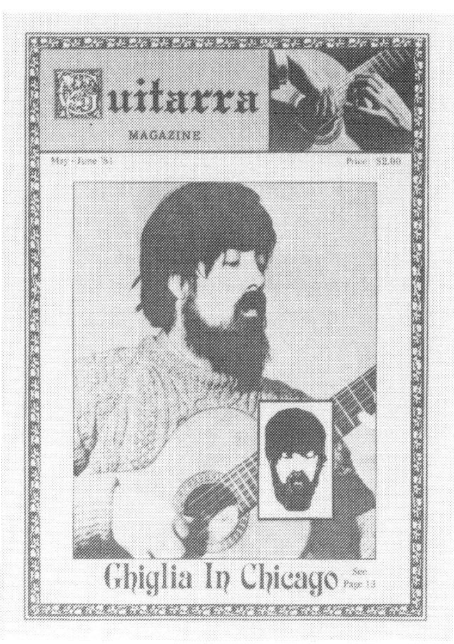


*A selection of guitar magazines*

*Jorge Morel*

# JORGE MOREL

**Born – JORGE SCIBONA**

**Buenos Aires**

**9 May 1931**

*Jorge Morel*

Jorge Morel showed a musical aptitude at a very early age. His father, an actor and an accomplished guitarist, began teaching his talented son the rudiments of the instrument when he was only eleven years of age. It soon became apparent that the youngster was destined for a career in music. He entered the University of Musical Studies in Buenos Aires, where he learned all the basic music subjects and majored in guitar under the guidance and inspiration of the renowned South American guitarist and composer Pablo Escobar. It was Escobar who gave Morel his professional debut at the age of sixteen, in a radio programme featuring both teacher and pupil. The young guitarist was immediately recognized as a major talent, and began his concert career at that time, while still a student at university.

Not until he received his degree at the age of eighteen did Jorge Morel begin to experiment and develop the unique style and brilliant technique that today are so much a part of his artistic identity. As is the case with all great virtuosos, his own arrangements and compositions are the most tangible examples of his aims, standards and ideals as a creative and performing musician. Jorge Morel's prime calling is based in contemporary modes of expression. His compositions abound in bracingly modern rhythms and harmonies, leading naturally towards the melodies and idioms of South America. A fine interpreter of the standard classical repertoire, Morel has also dazzled audiences throughout the world with his exciting transcriptions for guitar of the music of Gershwin, Bernstein, Lennon & McCartney and other modern composers.

Jorge Morel first went to the United States in 1961, making a highly successful debut at Carnegie Hall. Since that time he has toured throughout North America and in Hawaii and Puerto Rico, but remained virtually unknown to European audiences until his London debut at the Wigmore Hall in October 1979. That was a great success, and Jorge Morel has since made frequent visits to Great Britain and Europe, in addition to the very many concerts he gives in North America. He holds the post of Professor of Guitar at the Lehman College in New York.

**SELECTED MUSIC**

| | |
|---|---|
| Virtuoso South American Guitar Vol.1. | Ashley Mark |
| Virtuoso South American Guitar Vol.2. | Ashley Mark |
| West Side Story/Porgy and Bess. | Ashley Mark |
| Virtuoso South American Guitar Vol.4. | Ashley Mark |
| Sonatina. | Chorus |
| Allegro in Re. | Chorus |
| Four Pieces. | Chorus |
| Latin Impressions. | Chorus |
| Variations on a Gershwin Theme. | Chorus |
| Danzas para Emiko. | Chorus |
| Prelude. | Chorus |
| Little Rhapsody. | Chorus |
| Preludio y Gigua. | Chanterelle |
| Guitareando. | Chorus |

**SELECTED RECORDINGS**

| | |
|---|---|
| The Warm Guitar. | Decca DL 4167 |
| Artistry of Jorge Morel. | RCA LSP 3953 |
| Guitar Moods. | SMC 1110-2 |
| Magnificent Guitar. | Decca DL 4966 |
| The Fabulous Jorge Morel. | Village Gate VGLP 2001 |
| Virtuoso South American Guitar. | Guitar Masters GMR 1002 |
| Jorge Morel Plays Broadway. | Guitar Masters GMR 1004 |
| Latin Impressions | Guitar Masters GMR 1005 |
| Morel y su Guitarra | Panart LP-3068 |
| Meet Morel | Sesac S-601/602 |
| Encore | Sesac S-603/604 |

**SELECTED READING**

| | |
|---|---|
| Jorge Morel. | Guitar Player, March 1970 |
| Jorge Morel. | Frets, September 1979 |
| Jorge Morel. | Guitar, December 1979 |
| Interview. | Classical Guitar, Nov/Dec 1982 |
| Jorge Morel. | Classical Guitar, March/April 1983 |
| Jorge Morel. | Guitar Player, June 1987 |
| Jorge Morel. | Classical Guitar, November & December 1985 |

# ALFONSO MORENO

**Born –**

**Mexico,**

**1950**

*Alfonso Moreno*

Alfonso Moreno began his musical training at the age of eight, studying violin and composition. In 1964 he took up the guitar and studied with Manuel López Ramos in Mexico City. In 1968 he won first prize at the Radio France International Classical Guitar Competition in Paris. Since that time he has led a busy concert career playing throughout Mexico, the USA, Europe and the Soviet Union. He has also recorded for the EMI company.

Alfonso Moreno is regarded as one of Mexico's leading classical guitarists.

**SELECTED RECORDINGS**

Fantasia para un Gentilhombre: Rodrigo. EMI ESD 7145
Alfonso Moreno. GAMMA CG-351
Ponce: Concierto del Sur. EMI ESD 1651051
Rodrigo: Concierto de Aranjuez. EMI ASD 4159
Rodrigo: Concierto Madrigal (with Deborah Mariotti). EMI ASD 1651411

# LUIGI MOZZANI

**Born –**

**Faenza, Italy, 9 March 1869**

**Died – Rovereto, Italy, 12 August 1943**

COURTESY: MARIO MACCAFERRI

*Luigi Mozzani*

Luigi Mozzani showed a great interest in music at an early age, and dedicated every free moment he had to the study of the guitar. He later studied the oboe and composition at the Conservatory of Music in Bologna under Professor Castelli, earning his diploma at the age of eighteen. For two years he was first oboist at the San Carlo Theatre, Naples, after which he travelled throughout Europe and Asia. At the age of twenty he went to North America with a symphony orchestra, but the tour proved a financial disaster and Mozzani decided to make the guitar his career rather than the oboe.

His first public recitals on the guitar met with great success, and he was regarded as a virtuoso. He returned to Europe and lived in Paris, where at the age of twenty-five he became one of the most sought-after teachers of the guitar by Parisian high society. He continued to give many highly acclaimed recitals in France, Austria and Germany. A distinctive feature of his guitar technique was the use of a metal thumb pick on the right hand, a technique also used by Mario Maccaferri throughout his concert career in the 1920s.

During these years as a recitalist, Mozzani became frustrated with some of the limitations of the guitar as it was then constructed, and decided to return to Italy to study guitar construction in depth. He eventually founded important schools for luthiers in Cento, Bologna and Rovereto. One of his most famous pupils was Mario Maccaferri. Mozzani continued to study the construction of the guitar right up to his death, and his workshops produced a large number of instruments. Among his many patents was the well-known guitar-lyre, an instrument with an adjustable neck.

Although latterly much of his time was devoted to instrument construction, Mozzani was also a talented composer and transcriber of guitar music. Quite a lot of his works were published, but many of his compositions remain unedited and unpublished.

**SELECTED MUSIC**
Esercizi Di Tecnica Superiore. Berben

# MARTIN MYSLIVECEK

**Born –**

**Prague, Czechoslovakia**

**12 June 1950**

*Martin Myslivecek*

Martin Myslivecek studied classical guitar at the Brno Conservatory under Prof. A. Sadlik from 1966 to 1972 and with Prof. Roland Zimmer at the Franz Liszt University of Music at Weimar from 1972 to 1978.

He began his concert career while still a student at the Brno Conservatory. While he was at the Liszt University, he entered and won prizes at several important guitar competitions including Markneukirchen (1975), Paris (1976) and Caracas (1977). These successes led to many concert engagements throughout Europe, the USSR, Cuba and Venezuela.

Martin Myslivecek, who is also a fine lute player, is regarded as one of Czechoslovakia's finest classical guitarists. He currently holds a teaching appointment in Graz, Austria.

**SELECTED RECORDINGS**
Martin Myslivecek Plays. Panton 8111 0174
Martin Myslivecek plays Bach Sanz, Weiss. Supraphon 1111 3425

**SELECTED READING**
Interview. Guitar International, December 1983
Interview. Classical Guitar, March/April 1984

## SANTIAGO NAVASCUES

**Born –**

**Madrid, Spain**

**23 July 1933**

COURTESY: EURODISC RECORDS

Santiago Navascues is a graduate of the Real Conservatorio in Madrid, and also of the Music Academy in Munich, Germany.

Navascues is highly regarded as one of Europe's finest teachers. Although he gives frequent recitals and has made several recordings for the German company Arcola Eurodisc, it is as a teacher that he spends most of his year. He is currently professor of the guitar at the Richard Strauss Conservatory in Munich, where he has been teaching since 1972. He conducts the International Guitar Seminar annually in Reisbach, and is the editor of guitar works for the publishing house Biblioteca de la Guitarra.

**SELECTED RECORDINGS**

| | |
|---|---|
| Music for the Spanish Guitar. | Vanguard 10137 |
| Santiago Navascues. | Eurodisc 86852 |
| Santiago Navascues. | Eurodisc 86853 |
| Santiago Navascues. | Eurodisc 88597 |
| Santiago Navascues. | Eurodisc 89247 |
| Santiago Navascues. | Eurodisc 28902 |

Santiago Navascues

## MICHAEL NEWMAN

**Born –**

**New York, USA**

**21 December 1957**

*Michael Newman*

Since his Carnegie Hall debut in March 1974, Michael Newman has established himself as one of the United States' most accomplished classical guitarists.

He was brought up in a musical environment. His father, who worked for the Guild Guitar Company in New York, was a lover of music and had a large record collection in which were many classical guitar recordings. They were to influence the young musician.

At the age of seven, however, Newman began to study the piano. Losing interest in this instrument, he took up the guitar and studied with a local teacher, Thomas Anthony, for three years. He made such good progress that, in 1971, he began studying with Albert Valdes Blain at Mannes College of Music, New York. On the advice of Blain, he enrolled full time at Mannes College, where he eventually earned his Bachelor of Music degree. He also studied with Oscar Ghiglia at the Aspen Music Festival and the Accademia Musicale Chigiana in Siena, Italy.

Michael Newman has been a guest soloist with the Hartford and Rochester Chamber Orchestras, the Omaha Symphony, the Cleveland and Fort Wayne

Philharmonics, and the renowned Atlanta Symphony. He has given solo guitar recitals throughout the United States, and was a recipient of the Concert Masters' 'Young Artist Award' in 1973. He was a prizewinner at the International Guitar Competition at the Guitar '78 Festival held in Toronto, Canada.

Michael Newman is also highly regarded as a teacher, and is currently on the faculty of both Mannes College of Music and Rutgers University as instructor in guitar. In addition he has conducted many workshops and masterclasses.

**SELECTED RECORDINGS**

| | |
|---|---|
| Michael Newman. | Sheffield Lab SL 10 |
| Italian Pleasures. | Sheffield Lab SL 16 |

**SELECTED READING**

| | |
|---|---|
| Michael Newman. | Guitar & Lute, October 1981 |

# DOUGLAS NIEDT

**Born –**

**St Louis, Missouri, USA**

**8 October 1952**

*Douglas Niedt*

It was hearing Andrés Segovia on a record that first inspired Douglas Niedt. His father, also a guitarist, gave him his first lessons at the age of seven. By the time he was fourteen he had received first-prize awards in competitions sponsored by the American Guild of Music in Pittsburgh, Louisville and Kentucky. The young player continued his studies at the Juilliard School, Segovia masterclasses in Spain and privately with Narciso Yepes, Christopher Parkening, Jorge Morel and Oscar Ghiglia.

At the age of twenty-one, Niedt made his debut recital at the Carnegie Recital Hall in New York, since when he has given many concerts throughout the USA. In 1987 he was awarded a Solo Recitalist Fellowship by the National Endowment for the Arts.

Douglas Niedt has made several recordings, and is currently Chairman of the Guitar Department of the Conservatory of Music, University of Missouri at Kansas City.

**SELECTED RECORDINGS**

| | |
|---|---|
| Classic Guitar Artistry. | Antigua S-1000 |
| Virtuoso Visions. | Antigua S-2000 |
| After Hours. | Antigua S-3000 |

**SELECTED MUSIC**

| | |
|---|---|
| Classic Guitar Artistry. | Sherry-Brener |
| Virtuoso Visions. | Sherry-Brener |

**SELECTED READING**

Bi-monthly technique articles in Guitarra Magazine.

# NIGEL NORTH

**Born –**

**London, England**

**5 June 1954**

*Nigel North*

Nigel North began to study the violin from the age of seven, and won scholarships to study at the junior department of the Guildhall School of Music from 1964 to1970. In 1964 he began to teach himself the classical guitar. In 1969 he began to teach himself to play the lute.

From 1971 to 1974 North studied classical guitar with John Williams and Carlos Bonell at the Royal College of Music in London. He also studied viols with Francis Baines. In 1974 he gained an ARCM Diploma with distinction, for lute performance. He returned in 1974 to the Guildhall, where he joined the new postgraduate course in Early Music. In 1975 he became a member of staff as lute teacher, and since 1976 he has been Professor of Lute there.

His knowledge and experience in the art of continuo playing led him to write the first modern practical continuo method for the lute and theorbo, published by Faber in 1987.

Nigel North has given many workshops and master-classes for lutenists and guitarists throughout Europe and North America. He is recognized as one of the world's foremost lutenists, yet he also remains a great exponent of the early classical guitar. A soloist on both lute and guitar, he gives many concerts all over the world. His recordings range in style from the mid-sixteenth century to the mid-nineteenth. As an ensemble player he has made many more recordings and concert appearances with leading Early Music groups of the day, including the English Concert, the London Baroque, Romanesca, and the Taverner Players. He has also made several broadcasts on both radio and television for the BBC.

**SELECTED MUSIC**

Continuo Playing on the Lute, Archlute and Theorbo. Faber 1987

**SELECTED RECORDINGS**

De Visée. Decca 'Florilegium' L'Oiseau-Lyre DSLO 542
Dowland Lute Works. Decca 'Florilegium' L'Oiseau-Lyre D187 D5
Pieces de Luth. UEA 81704
Guitar Collection. Amon Ra RA SAR 18
Bach Lute Music. Amon Ra RA SAR 23
Concord of Sweet Sounds (with Lisa Beznosiuk). Amon Ra CD SAR 33

**SELECTED READING**

Interview. Classical Guitar, September 1987

# STEIN-ERIK OLSEN

**Born –**

**Bergen, Norway**

**8 September 1953**

*Stein-Erik Olsen*

Stein-Erik Olsen was educated at the Bergen Conservatory of Music and the Norwegian State Academy of Music. He then studied with Alexandre Lagoya for two years at the Paris Conservatoire National Supérieur de Musique. He has also studied with Per-Olof Olson and Manuel Barrueco.

Stein-Erik Olsen has played at international festivals throughout Norway, and has made several television and radio broadcasts there. He has also given concerts throughout the rest of Scandinavia and Europe. In 1986 he made his concert debut at the Wigmore Hall in London.

Several eminent contemporary composers, including Ketil Hvoslev and John W. Duarte, have written works especially for him.

**SELECTED RECORDINGS**

| | |
|---|---|
| Guitar. | Simax PS 1008 |
| Stein-Erik Olsen Guitar plays – Kucera, Duarte, Castérède, Brouwer. | Samt 184 |
| Panorama. | FXLP 60 |
| Double Delight: Flute/Guitar Duo. | BD 7004 |
| Blue Sonata. | Simax PSC1029 |
| Mosaic. | For-X FXCD 81 |

**SELECTED READING**

| | |
|---|---|
| Interview. | Guitar International, January 1986 |
| Interview. | Classical Guitar, July 1987 |

# JORGE ORAISON

**Born –**

**Montevideo, Uruguay**

**26 June 1946**

*Jorge Oraison*

Jorge Oraison's first guitar teacher was Lola Gonella de Ayestaran, in Montevideo. He also studied music theory at the Conservatorio Municipal, then musicology at the University of Montevideo.

In 1969 Oraison was granted a scholarship from the Instituto de Cultura Hispanica to study in Spain with José Tomás at Santiago de Compostela. In 1971 he won the silver medal at the XIII Radio-France Concours International de Guitarre in Paris. Shortly after that, he moved to the Netherlands, where he has lived since.

Jorge Oraison performs widely throughout Europe, and is professor of guitar at the Rotterdam and Twents Conservatories of Music in the Netherlands.

**SELECTED RECORDINGS**

| | |
|---|---|
| South American Guitar Music. | EMI 037-26 019 |
| Castelnuevo-Tedesco Guitar Works. | Etcetera ETC 1001 |
| Astor Piazzolla Guitar Works. | Etcetera ETC 1023 |
| Leo Brouwer Guitar Works. | Etcetera ETC 1034 |

# JESÚS ORTEGA

**Born –**

**Havana, Cuba**

**1935**

*Jesús Ortega*

Jesús Ortega's introduction to the guitar and music came through listening, as a child, to his grandfather's record collection of flamenco music. It was not until he was seventeen that, with the encouragement of his friend Leo Brouwer, he began to study the guitar. He studied with Isaac Nicola at the Conservatorio Musical de Havana. Here he developed a love for chamber music, and decided also to study the cello.

After finishing his studies, Ortega performed professionally as a soloist, in a duo with Leo Brouwer and also as an ensemble player. He has given concerts throughout Latin America and Europe. His repertoire has always emphasized Cuban, Latin American and contemporary works. He has toured the USA as an accompanist for a Cuban dance company.

Ortega was director of the Conservatorio Amadeu Roldán (1966-68), National Co-ordinator of Music in the Consejo Nacional de Cultura (1961-65), and is currently professor of guitar at the Instituto Superior de Arte in Havana. He also heads a state publishing concern for guitar music, and plays a prominent part in the organization of the biennial Havana International Guitar Competition.

An enthusiastic musicologist, Jesús Ortega divides his time between playing, teaching, composing and writing about the guitar. He has had many works for guitar dedicated to him by leading contemporary Cuban composers.

**SELECTED RECORDING**

Solistas Cubanos – Jesús Ortega. Egrem LD-3553

**SELECTED READING**

Interview. Guitar Review, Summer 1988

Gaspar Sanz y su Instrucción de Música Sobre la Guitarra Española. 1972

Brouwer y la Guitarra. 1985

# JULIO MARTINEZ OYANGUREN

**Born – Uruguay, 3 July 1905**

**Died – Montevideo, Uruguay**

**15 September 1973**

*Julio Martínez Oyanguren*

Julio Martínez Oyanguren established himself as a concert performer when he was a teenager, giving his first concert in Montevideo. He had studied music and the guitar with Alfredo Hargain. After some years in the Uruguayan and Italian navies, Oyanguren settled in the USA in the 1930s and established himself as a leading performer on the classical guitar.

Although much of his repertoire was devoted to South American music, he did include classical works in his concert programmes. In the 1930s and 1940s he made many recordings for the American Decca company, establishing himself as one of the foremost players of the period. A high spot of his career was his appearance with the New York Philharmonic Orchestra. He was also a regular broadcaster on the NBC radio network in the USA.

Oyanguren resettled in Uruguay in the 1960s and was not involved in music since that time.

**SELECTED RECORDING**

| | |
|---|---|
| Latin American Folk Music. | Decca DL 8018 |
| Un Retrata de Espana. | Decca LTC 9558 |

## To Jane, With a Guitar

By

PERCY BYSSHE SHELLEY

The artist who this idol wrought,
To echo all harmonious thought,
Felled a tree, while on the steep
The woods were in their winter sleep
Rocked in that repose divine,
On the wind-swept Appennine;
And dreaming some of Autumn past
And some of Spring approaching fast,
And some of April buds and showers
And some of songs in July bowers
And all of love; and so this tree,—
O that such our death may be!
Died in sleep, and felt no pain,
To live in happier form again;
From which, 'neath Heavens fairest star,
The artist wrought this loved Guitar
And taught it justly to reply,
To all who question skilfully
In language gentle as its own
Whispering in enamoured tone
Sweet oracles of woods and dells
And summer winds in sylvan cells;
For it had learnt all harmonies
Of the plains and of the skies,
Of the forests and the mountains
And the many-voicèd fountains
The clearest echoes of the hills
The softest notes of falling rills
The melodies of birds and bees
The murmuring of summer seas
And pattering rain, and breathing dew
And airs of evening; and it knew
That seldom heard mysterious sound
Which, driven in its diurnal round
As it floats through boundless day
Our world enkindles on its way
All this it knows, but will not tell
To those who cannot question well
The spirit that inhabits it—
It talks according to the wit
Of its companions; and no more
Is heard than has been felt before
By those who tempt it to betray
These secrets of an elder day
But sweetly as it answers will
Flatter hands of perfect skill,
It keeps its highest, holiest tone
For our beloved friend alone —.

# NICOLO PAGANINI

**Born – Genoa, Italy**

**27 October 1782**

**Died – Nice, France, 27 May 1840**

*Nicoló Paganini*

Until comparatively recently only a few music lovers realized that the nineteenth century virtuoso violinist Nicoló Paganini was also a virtuoso guitarist. Ferdinand Carulli, a contemporary of Paganini, wrote in his guitar tutor 'The fact may not be generally known that Paganini was a fine performer on the guitar, and that he composed most of his airs on this instrument, arranging and amplifying them on the violin according to his fancy.'

Nicoló Paganini's first instrument was the mandolin. His father had a great love of music, and from the day his son was able to hold the mandolin he ensured that every spare moment was spent in practising. Paganini's musical talent was soon very obvious, and he began to study the violin with the noted teachers Casta and Servetto.

It was in 1795, at the age of thirteen, that Paganini began to study the violin with Alessandro Rolli. Rolli was not only a violin virtuoso but also a talented guitarist. It seems likely that Paganini also studied the guitar with him. Nevertheless, for the next few years Paganini devoted his talents entirely to the violin, his virtuoso performances exciting audiences throughout Italy.

In 1801 Paganini became attached to an aristocratic lady whose favourite instrument was the guitar. During the three years he lived in this lady's château, he devoted himself to the guitar. His first composition for the instrument was written in 1801. In 1805 he returned to touring the continent, his concerts once again devoted to his violin playing. Among his close friends was the guitar virtuoso Luigi Legnani.

In Turin, on 9 June 1837, Paganini gave what was to be his last public concert. His health began to deteriorate in 1838-39, and in 1840 he moved to Nice in the South of France in order to miss the winter and try to recuperate. Unfortunately, his health deteriorated very rapidly, and he died in Nice on 27 May 1840 at the age of fifty-seven.

Nicoló Paganini, the legendary violinist, was not only a virtuoso guitarist but also a prolific composer for the instrument. He composed at least one hundred and forty solos for the guitar, many duets for violin and guitar, and several trios and quartets which included a guitar part. His most outstanding composition for the guitar is probably the Grand Sonata in A .

**SELECTED MUSIC**

| | |
|---|---|
| Caprice No.24, arr. John Williams. | B & H |
| Five Compositions for Solo Guitar, ed. Pila. | RIC 132432 |
| Five Pieces for Guitar, ed. Behrend. | EMT 1420 |
| Grand Sonata, arr. Meyerriecks. | CO 214 |
| La Campanella, ed. Casuscelli. | BA 8442 |
| Minuet & Sonatina op.25, tr. Prat. | BA 9548 |
| Perpetual Motion, for 1 or 2 guitars, tr. Fleury. | BA 11585 |
| Pièce Intime. | ZM 1863 |
| Romanze, ed. Scheit. | UE 13068 |
| Six Original Compositions, ed. Scheit. | UE 14465 |
| Sonatina, ed. Scheit. | UE 14455 |
| Twenty-six Original Compositions for Guitar. | Z 11250 |
| Complete Guitar Works of Paganini. | Chanterelle |

**SELECTED RECORDINGS**

| | |
|---|---|
| John Williams plays Paganini. | CBS 73745 |
| Grand Sonata in A: Oscar Ghiglia. | EMI |
| Quartets with guitar, Op.4 Nos. 1, 2, 3: Prunnbauer & strings. | EMI 067 169600 1 |
| Quartet Op.4 Nos.3, 7, 14 : Quartteto Paganini. | Dynamic CDS 46 |
| Sonatas Op.2, Op.3 etc. for violin & guitar: Mezzena/Sebastiani. | Dynamic CDS 62 |
| Sonata in E minor, Op.3 No.6: Norge | CD CBS 45581 |

**SELECTED READING**

| | |
|---|---|
| Nicoló Paganini. | Guitarra, March 1979 |
| New Light on Paganini. | Guitar Review, Nos. 2,3,5 |
| Paganini. Sheppard/Axe/Rod. | Paganini Publications, 1979 |
| Paganini: Ruggero Chiesa. | Classical Guitar, July, August, September, 1988. |

# SOPHOCLES PAPAS

**Born – Sopiki, Epirus, Greece, 18 December 1893**

**Died – Washington D.C., USA**

**26 February 1986**

*Sophocles Papas*

Sophocles Thomas Papas was born in a small town in Greece, and received his first musical instruction from his father, an amateur violinist. Later, whilst living in Cairo, Egypt, he took lessons on the mandolin, but soon changed to the guitar.

Papas went to the United States in 1914 to study agriculture in Massachusetts. In World War I, he joined the American Army, in which he served as a gunsmith. He took his guitar with him, having taught himself to play with the aid of Carcassi's Classical Guitar Method, and his playing was much admired by other soldiers. It was during his army service that he formed the idea of becoming a guitar teacher.

Papas in fact played and taught almost every kind of plucked instrument, but it was as a guitar teacher that he established himself in Washington D.C. after the War. In 1922 he founded his Columbia School of Music. Papas's talents as a solo guitarist and teacher were quickly recognized. His school of music, offering instruction in nearly all instruments but specializing in the guitar, was a great success. The school became the only such establishment in the United States where a student could work for a bachelor's degree in music with the guitar as the principal instrument.

Sophocles Papas became a close friend of Andrés Segovia, and many of his teaching methods were based on the technique and musical approach of Segovia. His pupils have included Burl Ives, Peter Ustinov, the poet Carl Sandburg, the Hollywood actors Gregory Peck and Bette Davis, and the famous jazz guitarist Charlie Byrd.

Papas wrote a guitar method for the classical guitar which has proved over the years to be a worldwide best seller. He was a founder of the prestigious Washington Guitar Society, and also involved himself as a prominent publisher of guitar music.

**SELECTED MUSIC**

| | |
|---|---|
| Five Solos for Guitar. | CO 102 |

**SELECTED READING**

| | |
|---|---|
| Sophocles Papas. | Guitar Player, February 1975 |

# CHRISTOPHER PARKENING

**Born –**

**Brentwood, California, USA**

**14 December 1947**

*Christopher Parkening*

Christopher Parkening began to play the guitar at the age of eleven after hearing his cousin Jack Marshall, who was a leading Californian studio guitarist.

Parkening's first teachers were Celedonio and Pepe Romero. They soon noticed the young guitarist's exceptional talent, and within one year Parkening gave his first public recital. At the age of fourteen he entered the annual state-wide auditions of the Young Musicians Foundation. Among the judges were Jascha Heifetz, Gregor Piatigorsky and Mario Castelnuovo-Tedesco. The Foundation at that time offered no category in which guitarists could compete; but so impressed were the judges with Parkening's virtuosity that he was scheduled as a special 'out-of-competition' performer.

After this competition Parkening developed a friendship with Castelnuovo-Tedesco, and a little later made his formal concert debut playing his Concerto in D for Guitar and Orchestra under the auspices of the Young Musicians Foundation of Los Angeles on 10 March 1963. This highly acclaimed performance led to further engagements with the Los Angeles Philharmonic Orchestra, the Pasadena Symphony Orchestra and numerous other orchestras in Southern California.

With letters of recommendation from Castelnuovo-Tedesco and the cellist Joseph Schuster, Parkening was accepted as a scholarship student by Andrés Segovia in a masterclass at the University of California at Berkeley. Segovia chose him from three hundred students present to perform daily before the class, later selecting him as a soloist when the masterclass was televised nationally.

In January 1966 Parkening gave the first performance of the Second Concerto in C for Guitar and Orchestra by Castelnovo-Tedesco. In the same year he took up academic and musical studies at the University of Southern California; and he again attended on full scholarship a Segovia masterclass held at the North Carolina School of Arts. In July 1968 he was named one of the outstanding young artists of the year by High Fidelity magazine. The following September he made his first concert tour of the United States and Canada. In the same year he began to make the first of several recordings for Angel Records, several of which have been best sellers. His recording of the music of Bach reputedly sold over one hundred thousand copies.

In the autumn of 1968 Parkening was invited by Segovia to serve with him on the panel of judges for the International Guitar Competition in Santiago de Compostela, Spain. Parkening then became one of the United States' busiest recitalists, making his New York debut at the Alice Tulley Hall in November 1972. In August and September of that year he completed his first tour of Japan. While there, he was chosen to be the principal soloist at the country's first Rodrigo Festival.

Christopher Parkening is the author of The Guitar Method and a number of books of classical transcriptions for the guitar. For several years he was head of the guitar department of the University of Southern California School of Music. He now lives in Montana, where he holds a series of annual masterclasses for the guitar at Montana State University.

**SELECTED RECORDINGS**

In the Classic Style. Angel S.36019
In the Spanish Style. Angel S.36020
Romanza. Angel S.36021
Parkening Plays Bach. Angel S.36041
Parkening and the Guitar. Angel S.36053
Christopher Parkening Album. Angel S.36069
Christopher Parkening and Kathleen Battle (Soprano). EMI EL 27 0307 1
Virtuoso Guitar Duos with David Brandon. EMI CDC 7494062

**SELECTED READING**


Christopher Parkening. Guitar Player, June 1970
Christopher Parkening. Guitar Player, June 1972
Christopher Parkening. Frets, June 1980
Interview. Classical Guitar, February 1987

# MARIO PARODI

**Born – Istanbul, Turkey**

**5 March 1917**

**Died – 27 October 1970 Buenos Aires, Argentina**

COURTESY: JAQUES CHAÎNE

*Mario Parodi*

Mario Parodi was born in Istanbul of Italian parents. From an early age he was drawn to music, his first instrument being the piano. On hearing a concert given by an Argentinian orchestra that included a number of guitarists, Parodi decided that the guitar was to be his instrument. As there were virtually no guitar teachers in Turkey at that time, Parodi was self-taught.

As a concert artist, Parodi toured throughout Turkey, Greece, Italy, Switzerland, Germany and Argentina, performing in a style that was very individual and probably unique. He recorded in both Italy and Argentina and published numerous transcriptions and compositions of his own. He dedicated most of his concert programmes to his own transcriptions of the romantic composers, including Liszt, Schumann, Chopin, Debussy, Beethoven and Brahms. One of his records sold 30,000 copies in Britain alone.

**SELECTED MUSIC**

| | |
|---|---|
| Seis Instantaneas. | BA 12564 |
| Poema. | BA 12565 |
| Prelude No.1. | BA 10270 |
| Three Preludes, Nos. 3, 4, 8. | BA 11823 |

**SELECTED RECORDINGS**

| | |
|---|---|
| The Classical Guitar. | Music for Pleasure MFP 2094 |
| Transcriptions for Classical Guitar. | MFP 2140 |
| Guitarra Romantica. | Angel/EMI LPA-11205 |
| Magia en la Guitarra. | Angel/EMI LPA-11207 |
| Instantaneas. | Angel/EMI LPA-11208 |
| Facetas – Mario Parodi. | Angel/EMI SLPA-11211 |
| Concierto sobre Seis Cuerdas. | TK LD 80.003 |

# STEPHEN FUNK PEARSON

**Born –**

**Poughkeepsie, New York, USA**

**22 January 1950**

*Stephen Funk Pearson*

Both Stephen Funk Pearson's parents are musicians. His father, an organist and harpsichordist, was a professor at Vassar College. His mother is a pianist, organist and choir director. His first instrument was the piano, which he studied with his mother and later with a member of the Vassar faculty. Despite good progress, he lost interest in the piano and turned to a steel-strung guitar belonging to his brother. For some time the young musician developed his guitar technique on this instrument in the styles of folk and bluegrass. He also experimented with other instruments, including the cello, saxophone, string bass, banjo and mandolin.

Stephen Funk Pearson soon realized that he wanted to devote his life to the guitar and music, and decided to study classical guitar technique with Alexander Bellow. Having qualified in philosophy and studied ecology at Vassar, he returned there to study music and composition. He also studied guitar with Luis Garcia-Renart at Vassar, and then went to study in New York with Frederic Hand and later with Alice Artzt. In 1980 he won first prize in the Bunyan Webb National Guitar Competition in Memphis, Tennessee, and was placed second in the International Guitar Competition in Puerto Rico. In 1981-82 he was awarded the Maguire Fellowship for study in Europe, where he worked with John Mills and David Russell in England, José Tomás in Spain, and Oscar Ghiglia at the Accademia Musicale Chigiana in Siena, Italy. On his return to the USA he won the national Mohonk Music Fund competition for instrumentalists.

With this unique musical background, Pearson has developed into a highly individual composer/guitarist. He has composed for several instruments including the bassoon, flute, oboe, harpsichord and organ, but now performs his own music exclusively on the classical guitar. Some of his compositions have been premiered by Paul Gregory, the Buffalo Guitar Quartet, the Newman/Oltman Duo and Neil Anderson amongst others.

Stephen Funk Pearson is at present Visiting Artist in the programme of the North Carolina Arts Council, serving Alamance County as a performer and composer.

**SELECTED MUSIC**

| | |
|---|---|
| Four Skaals. | Theodore Presser |
| Thusslegarth. | Theodore Presser |
| Tsamaloon. | Theodore Presser |
| Brunella the Dancing Bear. | Theodore Presser |
| Six Mixtures. | Guitar Solo |
| Mummychogs (Le Monde). | Doberman-Yppan |
| Not Just Classical Guitar (6 teaching cassettes). | Homespun Tapes |

**SELECTED RECORDINGS**

| | |
|---|---|
| Hudson River Debut. | Kyra KR 1001 |

**SELECTED READING**

| | |
|---|---|
| Interview. | Classical Guitar, November 1984 |
| Composer/Performer Capsule Series. | Classical Guitar, December 1988 to April 1989 |
| Interview. | Classical Guitar, February 1991 |

# BORIS A. PEROTT

**Born –**

**St Petersburg, Russia, 1882**

**Died – London, England, 12 March 1958**

COURTESY: M. PEROTT

*Boris A. Perott*

For many years Boris Perott was one of the most important guitar personalities in Great Britain. Born in Russia, he became a naturalized British subject. By profession a doctor of medicine, he had studied the piano at an early age, later turning his attention to the balalaika and the mandolin.

Perott's introduction to the guitar took place at the age of eight. His first lessons (on the seven-string guitar) were with the famous guitar virtuoso J.Decker-Schenk. It was not long before he took up the six-string guitar under the guidance of V.P.Lebedev, making his first public appearance as a soloist in St Petersburg in 1903, a performance that was warmly acclaimed by the press.

The following year he toured Siberia, Germany and France with Lebedev and V.Ivanov. Perott made an appearance before the Imperial Court, for which he was presented with a gold watch by the Emperor of Russia, Nicholas II.

Boris Perott continued his career in medicine, but gave many public and private performances on the guitar for a period of twelve years. After the death of Lebedev, his widow chose Perott to be her teacher and to guide her with her studies of the guitar, together with several of her husband's pupils.

Following the revolution in Russia, Boris Perott came to Britain and set up in practice as a doctor in London, where for many years he was a noted teacher of the classical guitar. His most outstanding pupil was Julian Bream. It was Perott who introduced Bream to Segovia, who quickly recognized the young guitarist's enormous talent. Help in promoting the early career of the young prodigy came from the Philharmonic Society of Guitarists, which Perott had founded in London in 1929.

In 1930 Boris Perott began to contribute a regular series to B.M.G. magazine in London, proving himself to be an expert historian of the guitar.

Although Boris Perott's professional career was in medicine – he became an eminent heart specialist – his first love throughout his life was always the guitar.

# RICHARD PICK

**Born –**

**St Paul, Minnesota, USA**

**20 October 1915**

COURTESY: MANTANYA OPHEE

*Richard Pick*

Richard Pick's first encounter with music was through his father, who taught him the piano and the violin at the age of five. On the death of his parents, Pick became the foster son of Max Pick, who was the concert master of Minneapolis, Minnesota, and a professor of musicology, violin and piano.

Living in such a musical environment, it was natural that Pick developed a great love for music. The piano was his first instrument, although he did play the guitar to accompany his singing. Pick then met Frank Lannom, a well-known Chicago guitar teacher. For the next six or seven years he took guitar lessons from Lannom, then went to Urbana to enter the University of Illinois. Needing money to finance his studies, Pick worked in local dance bands, playing the plectrum guitar. A few opportunities arose for him to play the classical guitar on radio, and Pick suddenly realized that the classical guitar was the instrument through which he was able to express his musical talent. He entered DePaul University of Chicago, and earned his B.Sc. degree. Soon afterwards, on 2 March 1941, he gave his first public guitar recital, sponsored by the University of Chicago Music Department.

Today, Richard Pick is known throughout the United States as a fine classical guitarist and a composer of many pieces for the guitar. Over the years he has lectured on music and the guitar at many American universities, including the Chicago School of Music. He retired from teaching in 1986.

**SELECTED MUSIC**

| | |
|---|---|
| Favourite Classic Guitar Solos. | MB 93613 |
| Richard Pick School of Guitar. | Editions Orphee RTFT-7 |

**SELECTED RECORDINGS**

| | |
|---|---|
| Above & Beyond. | International IRC 3324 |
| Guitar. | Music Library MLR 7066 |

# ALVARO PIERRI

**Born –**

**Montevideo, Uruguay**

**1953**

*Alvaro Pierri*

Alvaro Pierri was born into a musical family. José Pierri Sapere, his grandfather, was a composer; Ada Estades, his mother, a pianist; and Olga Pierri, his aunt, a well-known Uruguayan guitarist.

Pierri began his studies at the age of eleven. His talent soon showed, and he began to win prizes in competitions for young guitarists in Uruguay. He went on to win first prizes at the Concurso Internacional de Guitarra in Buenos Aires, Argentina, and the International Guitar Competition in Porto Alegre, Brazil. Moving to Europe, Alvaro Pierri won the 18th Radio France International Concours in Paris, which established him as a guitar soloist of world class. He made his USA debut at the Kaufmann Concert Hall, New York, in 1978.

Since 1981 Alvaro Pierri has taught at the University of Santa Maria in Brazil. He is also professor of guitar at the University of Québec in Montréal, Canada.

**SELECTED RECORDINGS**

| | |
|---|---|
| Alvaro Pierri. | Blue Angel BA29002 |

**SELECTED READING**

| | |
|---|---|
| Article. | Guitar International, March 1985 |
| Interview. | Classical Guitar, May/June 1983 |

# BARBARA POLASEK

**Born –**

**Reichenberg, Germany**

**8 March 1939**

COURTESY: RCA RECORDS

*Barbara Polasek*

Barbara Polasek was born into a family of Bohemian musicians in Reichenberg, Germany (now Liberec, Czechoslovakia). Her exceptional musical talents were obvious at an early age and, encouraged by her family, she made great progress on the guitar.

At the age of twelve Barbara Polasek gave her first public recital. She continued her music studies at the Weimar Academy and the Prague Music Conservatory. She then went to Spain and studied with Andrés Segovia. In 1959 she won the First International Prize of Vienna, and in 1964 she won the First Prize for Interpretation at the Concours de Guitare in Paris, organized by the ORTF (French Radio and Television Service).

Since that time Barbara Polasek has continued an active career as a guitar recitalist and teacher. Her highly successful British debut took place at the Wigmore Hall, London, on 26 October 1966. She also appeared at the Festival Malais in Paris, and the Flanders Festival in Louvain in 1969. She is married to the prominent cellist Jan Polasek.

**SELECTED MUSIC**

| | |
|---|---|
| Gitarre im Gruppenunterricht. | 9 SY 2221 |

**SELECTED RECORDINGS**

| | |
|---|---|
| Anthology of the Guitar: Volume One. | RCA VICS 1038 |
| Barbara Polasek Plays Bach. | Erato STU 70573 |

## ALBERTO PONCE

**Born –**

**Madrid, Spain**

**13 March 1935**

COURTESY ARION RECORDS

*Alberto Ponce*

Alberto Ponce's first guitar tutor was his father. He later went to the Barcelona Municipal Conservatory for seven years, where he completed his course with honours.

The young guitarist was introduced to Emilio Pujol, who invited him to study with him at the Lisbon Conservatory of Music. Ponce became very taken with Pujol's approach to music and the guitar, studying with him in Lisbon for three years and later in Siena.

While he was in Siena, Alberto Ponce specialized in the music of Spain's golden age, in particular the vihuela and its music. He studied the vihuela in addition to the guitar, and in 1961 was awarded the first prize for the vihuela by the Accademia Musicale Chigiana in Siena.

In 1962 Ponce won the First Prize for Interpretation at the Concours de Guitare in Paris, organized by ORTF (French Radio and Television). In the same year he began teaching at the Ecole Normale de Musique, Paris, under the directorship of Alfred Cortot.

Alberto Ponce has remained in this important teaching position, at the same maintaining a busy concert schedule throughout Europe and Canada. He has also made several recordings for the French company Arion.

**SELECTED RECORDINGS**

| | |
|---|---|
| Ohana: Oeuvres de Guitare. | Arion ARN 38240 |
| La Guitare au 20ème Siècle. | Arion ARN 30S150 |
| Sourire de la Guitare. | Arion ARN 36341 |
| Masterpieces of 20th Century Guitar Music. | Musical Heritage Society MHS 3603 |

## DOMINGO PRAT

**Born – MARSAL DOMINGO PRAT**

**Barcelona, Spain, 17 March 1886**

**Died – Buenos Aires Argentina , December 1944**

*Domingo Prat*

Domingo Prat originally studied the guitar at the Municipal Music School of Barcelona. Later he was a pupil of the outstanding guitarist Miguel Llobet.

Prat established himself in Buenos Aires, where he became highly regarded as an authority and teacher of the classical guitar. He was the first exponent of the Tárrega method in South America, and was a prolific writer of guitar methods, studies and transcriptions. His most lasting achievement is the 'Dictionary of Guitarists', published in Spanish in 1934 by Romero and Fernandez of Buenos Aires.

**SELECTED MUSIC**

| | |
|---|---|
| Bajo el Sauce: Milonga Criolla. | BA 11675 |
| Danza Española No.1. | BA 9579 |
| El Escondido: Danza Argentina. | BA 8989 |
| El Palito: Danza Argentina. | BA 8991 |
| Gran Jota, Con Variaciones. | BA 11549 |
| Gueya (1 or 3 guitars). | BA 9501 |
| La Firmeza: Danza Argentina. | BA 8990 |
| Pasionaras: Vidalitas. | BA 11676 |
| Recuerdos de Saldungaray: Triste Argentino. | BA 9561 |
| Recuerdos de Santiago del Estero: Triste. | BA 9562 |

**SELECTED READING**

Diccionario de Guitarras, Guitarristas y Guitarreros: Prat. Romero & Fernandez, Buenos Aires 1934 (reprinted Editions Orphée, 1986).

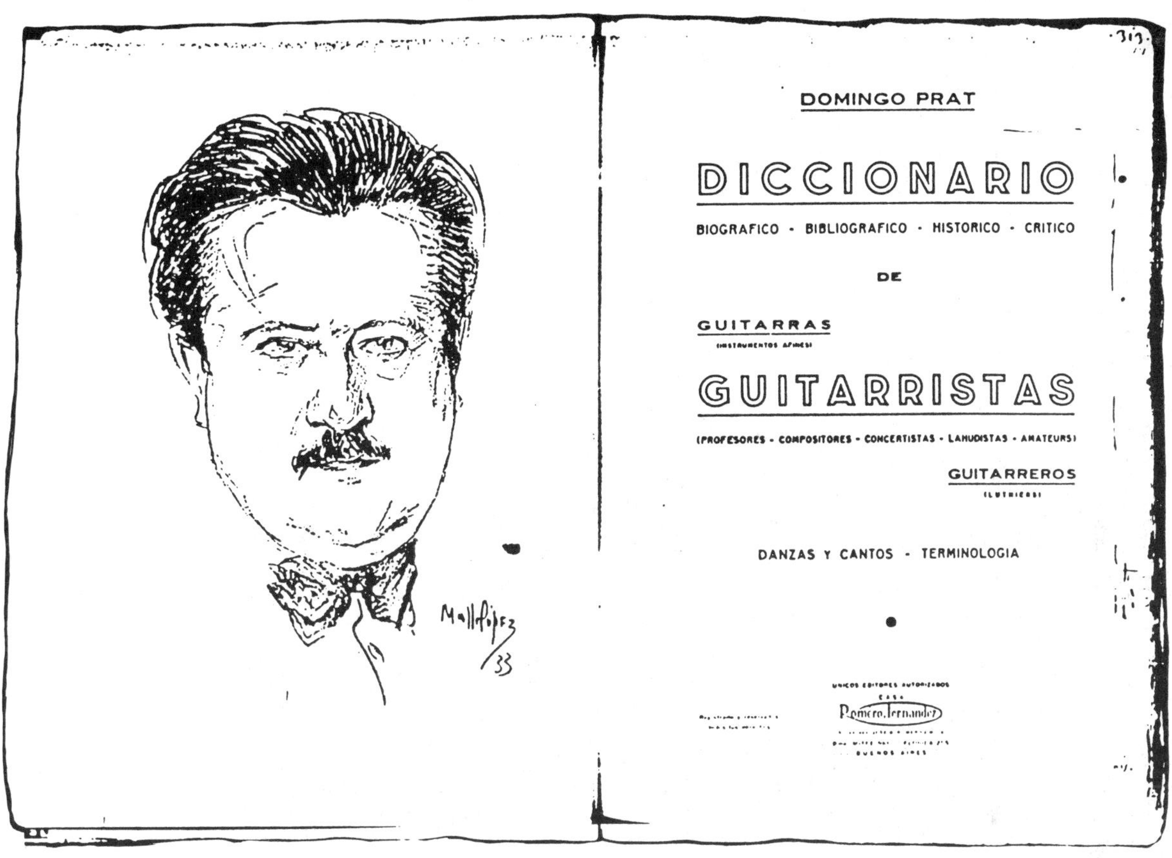

DOMINGO PRAT

DICCIONARIO

BIOGRAFICO · BIBLIOGRAFICO · HISTORICO · CRITICO

DE

GUITARRAS

GUITARRISTAS

(PROFESORES · COMPOSITORES · CONCERTISTAS · LAHUDISTAS · AMATEURS)

GUITARREROS

DANZAS Y CANTOS · TERMINOLOGIA

Romero Fernandez

*Portrait of Hector Berlioz with his guitar on a French ten franc banknote*

## MADAME SIDNEY PRATTEN

**Born – CATHERINE JOSEPHA PELZER**

**Mulheim, Germany, 1821**

**Died – London, England, 10 October 1895**

*Madame Sidney Pratten*

Madame Sidney Pratten was one of the most important classical guitarists of the nineteenth century. Her first guitar teacher was her father, Ferdinand Pelzer. By the time she was seven years old, she was already regarded as a highly accomplished guitarist.

In 1829 the Pelzer family moved to London. Here Catherine Pelzer dazzled British audiences with her appearances with the opera singer Madame Gringi, and also with another young guitar prodigy, Giulio Regondi.

After establishing herself as a teacher in Exeter. she was persuaded to return to London by one of her pupils, Lady John Somerset, in order to teach the guitar to members of the nobility. This she agreed to do, and it was in London that she met the distinguished flautist Robert Sidney Pratten. They married in 1854.

In 1868 Robert Pratten died, and his distressed widow gave up her public performances for three years. In 1871 she returned to the concert stage to perform Giuliani's third Concerto, a work she had played (using her terz guitar) in her tour of Europe in 1837. Giuliani's niece played the piano part for this concert.

Madame Sidney Pratten gave her last public performance at the age of 72 in 1893. There is no doubt that she was one of the outstanding figures of the nineteenth century guitar. She also wrote several popular guitar methods, and the prominent guitar makers, Panormo and Lacôte, labelled hundreds of guitars with her name in order to promote sales of their instruments.

# IDA PRESTI

**Born – YVETTE IDA MONTAGNON**

**Suresnes, France, 31 May 1924**

**Died – Rochester, NY State, USA, 24 April 1967**

*Ida Presti*

Ida Presti's father, Claude Montagnon, was a French piano teacher. Her mother, Olga Lo-Presti, was of Italian birth. Ida Presti received her first music lessons on the piano at the age of five from her father. At the age of six she changed to the guitar and soon showed that this was the instrument on which her extensive musical talents would be exposed. For two years from 1932 she studied the guitar with Mario Maccaferri, who was living in Paris at the time. Her father continued to teach her harmony and musical theory.

Ida Presti gave her first public recital in 1932, at the age of eight. She made her concert debut in Paris two years later. On 13 February 1938 she was invited to play at the Société des Concerts du Conservatoire de Paris, the first time a guitarist had performed there since Napoléon Coste claimed to have played his Op.15 (dedicated to Berlioz). In 1940, on the occasion of the centenary of Paganini's death, Ida Presti played his guitar in a commemorative concert. Her performances were outstanding, and over the next twenty years she was to make extensive concert tours both in France and abroad. She also appeared in a French film entitled La Petite Chose.

In 1952 she met the classical guitarist Alexandre Lagoya at the home of a mutual friend, André Verdier. A year later, on 23 May 1953, they were married; and two years later the Lagoya-Presti guitar duo made its appearance. Widely regarded as the finest classical guitar duo ever, Presti and Lagoya were to perform two thousand concerts all over the world. Together they founded a prestigious guitar class at the Schola Cantorum in Paris, and made several magnificent recordings for the Philips Record Company, which bear testimony to their greatness.

Tragically, while preparing for a concert in New York in 1967, Ida Presti, one of the finest classical guitarists of the twentieth century, suddenly fell ill and died shortly afterwards from an internal haemorrhage resulting from an aneurysm.

**SELECTED RECORDINGS**

*With Alexandre Lagoya:*

| | |
|---|---|
| Music for the Classical Guitar. | Nonesuch H 71161 |
| Musique Baroque pour deux Guitares. | Philips 6504 003 |
| Concertos pour deux Guitares. | Philips 6505 018 |
| Musique Espagnole pour deux Guitares. | Philips 6504 020 |
| Oeuvres pour deux Guitares. | Philips 6504 049 |
| Masters of the Guitar: Volume One. | RCA RB 6589 |

**SELECTED READING**

| | |
|---|---|
| Ida Presti. | Guitar Review No.31, Memorial Issue, 1969 |
| Ida Presti. | Les Cahiers de la Guitare Winter, 1984 |

*Presti-Lagoya Duo*

# SONJA PRUNNBAUER

**Born –**

**Hamburg, West Germany**

**28 August 1948**

*Sonja Prunnbauer*

Sonja Prunnbauer started playing the guitar at the age of thirteen and had her first professional lessons from Eike Funck in Hamburg. After receiving her high school diploma, she studied with Karl Scheit in Vienna for four years.

In 1972 she earned her soloist's diploma with distinction and returned to Hamburg, where she was offered a teaching position at the Hochschule für Musik und Kunst. In the same year she won first prize in the West German National Competition for Young Artists. Since then she has performed extensively throughout Europe, Africa, North America and Asia.

Sonja Prunnbauer has made many recordings, both solo and ensemble. She has appeared on all major German radio and television stations, and in 1982 she made the first videotape lessons for classical guitar beginners. In addition to her many concert performances, she teaches at guitar seminars in Germany and abroad.

**SELECTED RECORDINGS**

Klassisch-RomantischeGitarrenmusik. Harmonia Mundi HM 805 D/067
Modern Solo Guitar Works. Aurophon AU-11057
Gitarrenmusik. Da Camera Magna SM 93609
Musik für Gitarre und Hammerklavier. Christophorus DMM 74044
Paganini: Tre Gran Quartetti Op.4. Harmonia Mundi 067EL169600 1
Musik des Besonderen Klanges Vol.1. Schwann Musica VMS 1050-1
Musik des Besonderen Klanges Vol.2. Schwann Musica VMS 1051-2
Virtuose Gitarrenkonzerte. Schwann Musica VMS 2062 E
Giuliani Violin/Guitar Duos. Marco Polo 6.220151
Paganini Violin/Guitar Duos. Telefunken 6.35574
Eine Kleine Nachtmusik. Telefunken 6.42171 AW

**SELECTED READING**

Interview. Classical Guitar, March 1989

# EMILIO PUJOL

**Born – EMILIO VILLARUBI PUJOL**

**Granadella, Spain, 7 April 1886**

**Died – Barcelona, Spain, 15 November 1980**

*Emilio Pujol*

Emilio Pujol's introduction to music was through singing and the bandurría, on which he became a soloist with a mandolin and guitar orchestra. The orchestra appeared with enormous success at the Paris Exhibition of 1900. It was in 1900 that Pujol changed to the guitar and became a pupil of Francisco Tárrega in Barcelona. In 1907 Pujol, who had already made a name for himself throughout Spain as a guitar virtuoso, left for a concert tour of Argentina, Uruguay and the United States.

Pujol married the talented flamenco guitarist Mathilde Cuervas. They appeared in concert together in many countries, including a successful tour of Great Britain in 1923. In 1924 Pujol discovered in a Paris museum an ancient vihuela. The instrument interested him very much, and over the years he became one of the leading personalities behind its revival.

In 1947 Pujol was appointed professor of guitar at the National Conservatory of Music in Lisbon, Portugal. He retained this position until his death in 1980.

Emilio Pujol was not only a fine guitarist and teacher, but also one of the foremost musicologists of the twentieth century. He wrote several important books about the guitar, including 'Rational Method for the Guitar', 'The Dilemma of Timbre on the Guitar' and a biography of his teacher Francisco Tárrega.

**SELECTED MUSIC**

| | |
|---|---|
| Atardecer: Crepuscule. | ESC |
| Bagatella. | BA 11006 |
| Becquerian (Endecha-Complainte). | ESC |
| Canción de Cuna: Berceuse. | ESC |
| Canto de Otoño. | ESC |
| Caprice Varié sur un thème d'Aguado. | ESC |
| Cubana. | Celesta |
| Deuxième Triquilandia: 5 selections. | ESC |
| El Abejorro. | BA 11109 |
| Els Tres Tambors (The Three Drums). | BA 11111 |
| Endecha a la amada ausente. | ESC |
| Fantasía Breve. | BA 11110 |
| Festival: Danza Catalana. | BA 12046 |
| Four Short Pieces. | Kalmus |
| Homenaje a Tárrega. | GA 150 |
| Manola del Avapies. | BA 11448 |
| Pequeña Romanza. | ESC |
| Preludio Romantico. | BA 11007 |
| Rapsodia Valenciana. | ESC |
| Salve. | BA 1112 |
| Seguidilla. | BA 1113 |
| Sevilla: Evocación. | ESC |
| Tonadilla. | ESC |
| Troisième Triquilandia: 3 selections. | ESC |
| Two Preludes. | ESC |
| Variations sur un thème Obsedant. | ESC |
| Veneciana. | ESC |
| Villanesca: Country Dances. | BA 12342 |
| Guitar School | Editions Orphee RTFT-1 |

**SELECTED READING**

| | |
|---|---|
| Emilio Pujol. | Guitar Review No.5, 1948 |
| Tárrega: Ensayo Biográfico: Emilio Pujol. | Ramos & Alfonso, 1960 |
| El Dilema del Sonido en la Guitarra: Emilio Pujol. | Ricordi, 1960 |
| Emilio Pujol: Juan Riera. | Instituto de Estudios Llerdenses, Lerida, 1974 |
| Emilio Pujol: Juan Riera. | Lerida, 1974 |
| The Pujol XI Curso Internacional: Ickes. | Soundboard No.3, 1976 |
| Emilio Pujol. | Guitar, July 1977 |
| Emilio Pujol. | Guitar Player, April 1977 |
| Guitar Travels: J. D. Roberts. | Valencia, 1977 |
| Emilio Pujol. Complete list of works. | Guitar & Lute, May 1978 |
| Interview. | Guitar & Lute No.9, 1979 |
| Emilio Pujol In Memoriam: Purcell. | Soundboard, May 1981 |
| Emilio Pujol: Purcell (short biography) | TheOrphée Catalogue, 1986 |

# IVAN PUTILIN

**Born –**

**St Petersburg, Russia**

**18 September 1909**

*Ivan Putilin*

Ivan Feodorovitch Putilin's family settled in Finland in 1918. Putilin studied the double bass at the Sibelius Academy in Helsinki under Lauri Nissinen (1934-1938), under Ludvig Juht in the United States and privately under Alfred Burg-Schwendtner at the Mozarteum in Salzburg. He played double bass in the Helsinki City Orchestra and in the Radio Finland Symphony Orchestra (1947-1972). As a guitarist, he is practically self-taught. He also plays most other fretted instruments, including the balalaika and the mandolin. Playing all these instruments, he made many broadcasts on Radio Finland from 1927 until his retirement. The broadcasts included chamber music with guitar.

Putilin's contribution to the development of the classical guitar in Finland is quite extraordinary. He began teaching the guitar professionally in 1930, and was the first guitar teacher to be appointed at the Sibelius Academy (1967-1978). Most of the current teaching staff in the guitar department are his former pupils. He was the main driving force in the formation (on 5 November 1950) of the Helsinki Guitar Society, which has been instrumental in extending knowledge and appreciation of the guitar in Finland as a whole right up to the present day.

Ivan Putilin published a guitar tutor in 1960, and has also published several arrangements of Finnish music for guitar. Although now retired from professional performing, he continues to teach privately from his studio in central Helsinki.

# RAFAEL RABELLO

**Born –**

**Petropolis, Rio de Janeiro, Brazil**

**31 October 1962**

*Rafael Rabello*

Rafael Baptista Rabello began to study the guitar at the age of twelve with the well-known guitarist/teacher Jaime Florence. A talented classical guitarist, he also developed a great interest in the popular music of Brazil. In 1981 he received the 'Best Guitarist' award from the music reviewers of the magazine Playboy. In the same year he was awarded the title 'Best Instrumentalist' by the Associado Brasileira de Produtores de Discos.

Rabello enjoyed an association with the prominent Brazilian composer Rádames Gnattali during the last few years of Gnattali's life. He has made several recordings and is regarded as one of Brazil's most important young guitarists.

**SELECTED RECORDINGS**

Rafael: Sete Cordas. — Fontana 6488 174

Tributo a Garoto (with Rádames Gnattali, piano). — Funarte PA 82001

Rafael Rabello interpreta Rádames Gnattali. — Visom LPVO-006

# KONRAD RAGOSSNIG

**Born –**

**Klagenfurt, Austria**

**6 May 1932**

*Konrad Ragnossnig*

Konrad Ragossnig received his first guitar lessons at the age of nine. In order to widen his musical studies, he also took lessons on the piano and cello at the Klagenfurt Conservatory of Music. He went on to complete his musical studies as a pupil of Karl Scheit, professor of guitar at the Academy of Music and Performing Arts in Vienna.

In 1960 Konrad Ragossnig was appointed a professor of guitar at the same Academy, a position he held until 1964. In 1960 he studied with Andrés Segovia in Spain. He won first prize at the Cheltenham Festival in England in the same year. A year later, in 1961, he won first prize for interpretation at the Concours International for Guitar in Paris. Following this, he made extensive concert tours of Europe as well as many appearances on radio and television.,

About this time, Ragossnig began to take an intense interest in the lute. He mastered the Renaissance instrument, and now often includes it with the guitar in his concert recitals. Numerous composers have written works especially for him, including H.E.Apostel, J.Bondon, Mario Castelnuovo-Tedesco, H.Haug, J.Rodrigo and A.Schibler.

An outstanding classical guitarist, Konrad Ragossnig has lived in Switzerland since 1964, where he is professor of guitar at the Basel Music Academy. He also continues an active career as a recitalist and recording artist on both the guitar and the lute.

**SELECTED RECORDINGS**

| | |
|---|---|
| Master of the Guitar: Volume Three. | RCA RTB 6599 |
| Dances and Songs for Two Guitars (with Walter Feybli). | Turnabout TV 34605RS |
| Anthology of the Guitar: Volume Two (with Werner Tripp, flute). | RCA VICS 1504 |
| Bondon: 'Concerto de Mars'. | RCA VICS 1367 |
| The Spanish Guitar. | Turnabout TV 34494S |
| Guitar Recital. | Supraphon 1-11-1040 |
| Concertos pour Guitare 18me Siècle. | VOX Musicalis 35050 |
| Spanische Guitarre Musik. | Claves P 806 |
| Duo with Hans-Martin Linde (flute). | EMI 065-45-386 |
| Serenade Espagnole (guitar & cello duo). | Harmonia Mundi HM 686D |

**SELECTED READING**

| | |
|---|---|
| Handbuch der Gitarreund Laute: Konrad Ragossnig. | B. Schott, 1978 |
| Interview. | Classical Guitar, September 1990 |

EMI
HANS-MARTIN LINDE
und KONRAD RAGOSSNIG spielen
Mozart, Schubert, Praeger und Fürstenau

# STEPAN RAK

**Born –**

**Ukraine, USSR**

**8 August 1945**

*Stepán Rak*

Stepán Rak was born in a village in the Ukraine during the closing stages of World War Two, but the precise date is obscure. Advancing Soviet troops took him to Czechoslovakia, where he was adopted by the Rak family. He studied at the Fine Arts School in Prague, after which he went on to study guitar at the Prague Conservatory from 1965 to 1970. He also studied composition at the Prague Academy of Arts in 1975.

It was during his student period that Stepán Rak began to establish himself as a talented performer and an individual composer. In 1973 his symphonic composition Hiroshima won second place in the Czechoslovakian National Competition for Young Composers. In the following year his song Until, based on the lyrics of the poet V.Nezval, was placed among the winning compositions. In 1975 he was invited to teach in Finland at the Jyväskylä Conservatory. He maintained this position until 1980.

Rak's many innovative compositions for the guitar have been admired by guitarists everywhere. He has appeared at many international guitar events and made several recordings in Czechoslovakia with the Prague Marimba Trio and as a soloist on the UK record labels Chandos and Nimbus.

**SELECTED MUSIC**

| | |
|---|---|
| Temptation of the Renaissance. | Chorus |
| Farewell to Finland. | Chorus |
| Romance. | Chorus |
| Decem. | Chorus |
| Remembering Prague. | Chorus |
| Cry of the Guitar. | Chorus |
| Five Preludes. | Chorus |

**SELECTED RECORDINGS**

| | |
|---|---|
| Remembering Prague. | Chandos CHAN 8622 CD |
| The Guitar of Stepán Rak. | Nimbus NI 5177 CD |
| Prague Marimba Trio. | Supraphon 104118-1 |
| Stepán Rak played by Vladimir Mikulka. | GHA 126.003 |
| Dedications. | Nimbus NI 5239 CD |

**SELECTED READING**

| | |
|---|---|
| Interview. | Guitar International, January 1985 |
| Article. | Classical Guitar, October 1986 |
| Stepán Rak. | Classical Guitar, February 1988 |

# MANUEL LOPEZ RAMOS

**Born –**

**Buenos Aires, Argentina**

**1929**

*Manuel López Ramos*

Manuel López Ramos studied the guitar from an early age. His teacher was Miguel Michelone. At the age of nineteen Ramos was already regarded as one of Argentina's finest guitarists.

In 1948 he won the Argentine Chamber Music Associates first prize. In 1952 he embarked upon a highly successful international concert tour, appearing as a solo artist and with several leading symphony orchestras. He appeared in Mexico City in the same year, and soon afterwards accepted the position of professor of guitar at the Music School of the University of Mexico. In 1963 he toured the USSR, playing fourteen recitals.

Manuel López Ramos continues to lead a busy life as a recitalist and teacher. He has appeared at several international guitar festivals, and has also directed special courses for guitarists at the University of Arizona, the National School of Music of the UNAM, and the Conservatoire of Guatemala.

**SELECTED RECORDS**

| | |
|---|---|
| Masters of the Guitar: Volume Two. | RCA RB 6599 |
| Anthology of the Guitar. Volume Three. | RCA VICS 1541 |
| Castelnuovo-Tedesco. Quintet for Guitar and String Quartet. | RCA VICS 1367 |
| La Guitarra Clásica. | Boston B-216 |

**SELECTED READING**

| | |
|---|---|
| Manuel López Ramos. | Guitarra, September 1979 |
| Manuel López Ramos. | Classical Guitar, April 1987 |

# GIULIO REGONDI

**Born – Lyons, France, 1822**

**Died – London, England**

**6 May 1872**

*Giulio Regondi*

One of the greatest guitar virtuosos of the nineteenth century, Giulio Regondi was originally taught the guitar by his father. By the time he was seven he had already made his first public recital in Paris. He amazed his audience with his immense talents, and was dubbed 'The Infant Paganini' by the critics. His father took advantage of his son's unique gifts by presenting him in concert in most of the principal cities of Europe.

In 1831 Giulio Regondi, who was also a virtuoso performer on the concertina, gave concerts in several British provincial cities. At the end of his concert tour his family settled in London, where Regondi lived until his death in 1872.

Giulio Regondi continued an active career as a virtuoso of both the guitar and the concertina. He was also a prolific composer. Much of his music has been out of print for most of the twentieth century, but there has been a revival of interest, and several of his republished works have found their way into public performances.

**SELECTED MUSIC**
Rêverie (Notturno) per Chitarra, op.19, ed. Chiesa. — Zerboni
The Guitar Works of Giulio Regondi. — ECH 415
Complete Guitar Works of Giulio Regondi. — Chanterelle
Ten Etudes. — Edition Orphee PWYS-17

**SELECTED RECORDINGS**
The Guitar Works of Regondi: Leif Christensen. — Paula 10

**SELECTED READING**
Giulio Regondi. — Guitar & Lute, January 1982

*Giulio Regondi as a child prodigy*

# ISTVAN RÖMER

**Born –**

**Zagreb, Yugoslavia**

**27 August 1962**

*István Römer*

István Römer studied guitar with Darko Petrinjak at the Zagreb Music Academy. He graduated in 1983, going on to study at the Hochschule für Musik und darstellende Kunst in Graz, Austria, with Marga Bäuml-Klasinc, graduating in 1984. He also took part in masterclasses with John Williams and Julian Byzantine.

István Römer won first prize at the Mettmann International Guitar Competition, West Germany, in 1983. He went on to win three major prizes at international guitar competitions in the following year: third prize in Gargnano, Italy, second prize at the Maria Callas Competition in Athens, Greece, and first prize at the Andrés Segovia Competition in Palma, Spain. He also won the Milka Trnina Annual Award given by the Association of Croatian Composers in 1984.

Since 1980, he has taught guitar at the Zagreb Music Educational Centre, and since 1984 he has been assistant professor at the Zagreb Music Academy. A member of the Zagreb Guitar Trio, István Römer is a fine solo artist in his own right, and has given concerts throughout Europe and the USSR.

**SELECTED RECORDING**
Music by Bach, Papandopulo, Granados, Bogdanovic. — Yugoton LSY 66275

# ANGEL ROMERO

**Born –**

**Málaga, Spain**

**17 August 1946**

*Angel Romero*

Angel Romero, the youngest son of the guitarist Celedonio Romero, made his debut as a guitar soloist with the family quartet at the age of six. A year later, he gave his first solo recital in Valencia, Spain.

In 1958 the Romero family emigrated to the United States and settled in the Los Angeles area. Celedonio founded a guitar school there, at the same time maintaining a concert career for himself and his three talented sons.

In 1964 Angel Romero became the first guitarist to appear at the famous Hollywood Bowl, where he performed Rodrigo's Concierto de Aranjuez with the Los Angeles Philharmonic Orchestra.

In 1970, together with his brother Pepe, Angel performed the world première of Rodrigo's Concierto Madrigal for two guitars and orchestra.

Angel Romero has developed into one of the world's most outstanding classical guitarists. He maintains a busy concert schedule throughout the United States and abroad. He currently has an exclusive recording contract with Angel Records in America as well as appearing on Philips and Mercury recordings by the Romero Guitar Quartet.

**SELECTED RECORDINGS**

| | |
|---|---|
| Virtuoso Works for Guitar. | Angel S 37312 |
| Rodrigo Concerto and Fantasia. | Angel S 37440 |
| Classical Virtuoso. | Angel S 36094 |
| Music of Celedonio Romero. | Angel S 37311 |
| Angel Romero: Rodrigo and Torroba. | Angel S 37312 |
| The Divine Giuliani. | Angel SZ 37326 |
| Rodrigo: Concerto for Four Guitars: The Romeros. | Philips 3677 |
| Guitar Concertos for Two Guitars (with Pepe Romero). | Philips 6500-918 |
| Classical Music for Four Guitars: The Romeros. | Philips 9500-296 |
| A Touch of Class. | Telarc CD-80134 |
| Granados 12 Danzas (with Celedonio Romero). | Telarc CD-80216 |

**SELECTED READING**

| | |
|---|---|
| Interview. | Classical Guitar, March/April 1983 |

# CELEDONIO ROMERO

**Born –**

**Málaga, Spain**

**2 March 1918**

COURTESY: COLUMBIA ARTISTS

*Celedonio Romero*

Celedonio Romero was the youngest son of the Spanish architectural engineer who designed the harbour of Gibraltar. Introduced to the guitar when he was five years old, Romero's talent convinced his family that he should follow a career in music. As a result he was enrolled at and later graduated from the Conservatory of Madrid. He was a student of Daniel Fortea, who had been a pupil of Tárrega.

Celedonio Romero's first public recital was in Madrid when he was twenty years old. His performance was well received by the audience and critics alike. Soon after his Madrid debut, he married a young actress from Málaga's Teatro Cervantes. During the Spanish Civil War he played the guitar many times for his fellow loyalists. When Málaga surrendered to General Franco's forces, Romero was imprisoned but later released. He then earned his living by entertaining the troops.

Celedonio Romero's reputation as a fine classical guitarist continued to grow, but because he refused to commit himself to the opposition, the Franco regime denied him the right to give concerts outside Spain. In 1957, after considerable pressure and governmental red tape, Romero and his family were granted a passport to visit Portugal. The following year, with the help of sympathetic American friends, they were able to emigrate to the United States. Celedonio Romero now lives in the Los Angeles area of California.

A fine classical guitarist in his own right, Celedonio Romero has made a unique contribution to the classical guitar in that, under his tuition, all his three sons have developed into highly talented guitarists. In particular, Angel and Pepe have become two of the great guitar virtuosos of the twentieth century. For many years, Celedonio Romero has appeared with great success in concert all over the world with his three sons as a guitar quartet, 'Los Romeros'.

**SELECTED RECORDINGS**

| | |
|---|---|
| European Court Music. | Philips (Universo) 6582-001 |
| Compositions for Two Guitars. | Philips 9500-352 |
| Classical Music for Two Guitars. | Philips 9500-296 |
| Rodrigo Concertos Andaluz/Aranjuez. | Mercury 75021 |
| An Evening with the Romeros. | Mercury 75022 |
| Royal Family of the Guitar. | Mercury 75027 |
| Vivaldi Concertos. | Mercury 75054 |
| Evening of Guitar Music. | Delos D/CD 1004 |
| Bach/Sanz Guitar Music. | Delos D/CD 1005 |
| Granados 12 Danzas (with Angel Romero). | Telarc CD-80216 |

**SELECTED READING**

| | |
|---|---|
| The Romeros. | Guitar Player, April 1972 |
| The Romeros. | Guitar & Lute, September 1978 |
| Los Romeros. | Classical Guitar, September/October 1982 |

**SELECTED MUSIC**

| | |
|---|---|
| Classic Guitar Method. | Orozco, New York 1990 |

# PEPE ROMERO

**Born –**

**Málaga, Spain**

**8 March 1944**

COURTESY: COLUMBIA ARTISTS; PHOTO: KEN VEEDER

*Pepe Romero*

Pepe Romero began his studies on the guitar at the age of three with his father, Celedonio Romero. He gave his first public performance with his father at the Teatro Lope de Vega in Seville, Spain, when he was only ten years old.

The Romero family moved to California in 1958. A year later, when he was fifteen, Pepe – by this time regarded as a highly talented flamenco guitarist – made his first recording, for the Contemporary record label.

Pepe Romero's only guitar teacher was his father, but he studied music both in Spain and in New York with the Basque pianist-composer Francisco de Medina. For well over twenty years he has appeared as a member of the family quartet, 'Los Romeros'. He has also appeared in duos with Celin or Angel, his older and younger brothers respectively. More recently, he has appeared more often as a soloist or in a duo with Angel. Together they gave the first performance of Rodrigo's Concierto Madrigal for two guitars and orchestra, in 1970.

Seven of Boccherini's Quintets have been recorded by Pepe Romero for Philips. Together with his concert performances, they have established him as one of the great virtuosos of the day.

When he is not giving concerts, Pepe Romero teaches at the University of Southern California. He has written a guitar method entitled Guitar Style and Technique, which is published by Bradleys of New York.

**SELECTED RECORDINGS**

| | |
|---|---|
| Compositions for Two Guitars. | Philips 9500-352 |
| Guitar Concertos for Two Guitars (with Angel Romero). | Philips 6500-918 |
| Rodrigo (Fantasia) and Giuliani. | Philips 9500-042 |
| Carulli Concertos / Moreno Concertos. | Philips 426 263-2 |
| Famous Guitar Music. | Philips 9500-295 |
| Classical Music for Four Guitars. | Philips 9500-296 |
| Boccherini Guitar Quintets Nos.4 & 5. | Philips 9500-621 |
| Boccherini Guitar Quintets Nos.1, 2 & 7. | Philips 9500-985 |
| Boccherini Guitar Quintets Nos.3 & 9. | Philips 9500-789 |
| Sor's Guitar Sonatas, Op.22 & Op.25. | Philips 9500-586 |
| Rodrigo for Solo Guitar. | Philips 9500-915 |
| Carulli/Moreno Concertos. | Philips 426 263-2 |

**SELECTED READING**

| | |
|---|---|
| Pepe Romero. | Guitar, April 1979 |
| Pepe Romero. | Guitar Player, 1981 |
| Interview. | Classical Guitar, Nov/Dec 1983 |
| Pepe Romero. | Classical Guitar, March 1987 |

*David Russell*

# DAVID RUSSELL

**Born –**

**Glasgow, Scotland**

**1 June 1953**

PHOTO: COLIN COOPER

*David Russell*

Regarded as one of the greatest guitar virtuosos to have emerged in recent years, David Russell was born in Scotland, and spent most of his childhood on the Spanish island of Menorca, where his parents had decided to live.

He was attracted to the guitar at an early age by the records of Andrés Segovia. His father, a professional artist, was also a keen guitarist and was his son's first teacher. At sixteen David Russell, already recognized as a highly talented guitarist, moved to London to study at the Royal Academy of Music, where he twice won the Julian Bream Guitar Prize. Over the years he studied with several teachers, but his two main influences were Hector Quine in London, and José Tomás in Spain.

Russell's career developed rapidly after he won several of the major guitar competitions in Spain, amongst them the 'Ramírez' Competition, the 'Franciso Tárrega' Competition and the Concurso 'Andrés Segovia'.

Since the late 1980s David Russell has lived in Vigo, Spain. He spends much of his working year touring North America, most countries of Western Europe, and the United Kingdom, giving recitals and master-classes. He has appeared many times on BBC television and radio. He has also taken part in many major international music festivals, including the Edinburgh Festival, the Esztergom International Guitar Festival, the Concours of Radio France, the Toronto Guitar Festival, the Scandinavian Guitar Festival, and the International Guitar Festival of Havana.

**SELECTED RECORDINGS**

Musique pour Basse et Guitare. Festival FC 501
Something Unique. Overture OR 1001
David Russell plays Antonio Lauro. Guitar Masters GMR 1001
Bach, Handel & Scarlatti. Guitar Masters GMR 1007
David Russell (with Raphaëlla Smits & Jos van Immerseel): Castelnuovo-Tedesco solos and duets. Academix AX 850218
Sor & Kaufman: duets with Raphaëlla Smits. Pocketino PL 0008
David Russell plays Mertz, Regondi, Coste. GHA 5256003
Rodrigo/Concierto de Aranjuez; Giuliani/Concerto in A Op.30. Polskie Nagrania SX 2611.

**SELECTED READING**

David Russell. Guitar, November 1978
David Russell. Guitar Player, October 1981
Interview. Classical Guitar, November/December 1982
Interview. Classical Guitar, July, 1985
Interview. Classical Guitar, June 1989

*Historic photograph of (left to right): Andrés Segovia, Daniel Fortea, Miguel Llobet and Emilio Pujol, c.1918*

*Historic photograph of two of the greatest twentieth century composers for the guitar and their wives. Left to right, Clara Castelnuevo-Tedesco, Heitor Villa-Lobos, Mario Castelnuevo-Tedesco and Arminda Villa-Lobos*

# MICHEL SADANOWSKY

**Born –**

**Maulde, Lille, France**

**11 January 1950**

*Michel Sadanowsky*

Of Russian and French parentage, Michel Sadanowsky began to play the violin at the age of seven. He continued studying for ten years, and played in a symphony orchestra. During this time he discovered the guitar, and at the age of eighteen decided to devote himself entirely to this instrument.

Sadanowsky settled in Paris in 1969, where he studied with Turibio Santos and later with Oscar Cáceres. Subsequently he was greatly influenced by Abel Carlevaro's approach to playing the guitar. In 1976 he obtained the Maîtrise of the Music University of Paris.

In 1979 he won the first prize at the Concours International de Guitare de Paris, organized by Radio France. Since that time he has given concerts and taught throughout Europe, Africa, Asia, Australia, South and North America. In 1984 he formed the Paris Guitar Trio, consisting of Yves Godeau, Jean-Françcois Ruzel and himself.

Sadanowsky has taught the guitar at the International Music University of Paris, and gives a regular masterclass at the Royal Conservatory of Ghent, Belgium. He is the editor of a collection of guitar transcriptions, including the complete works for cello and lute by J.S.Bach, published by Billaudot.

**SELECTED RECORDINGS**

| | |
|---|---|
| The Guitar of Michel Sadanowsky. | Verseau M 10.034 |
| Michel Sadanowsky Plays. | Podium 8004.17 |
| The Art of Michel Sadanowsky. | Istria DI 3533 |

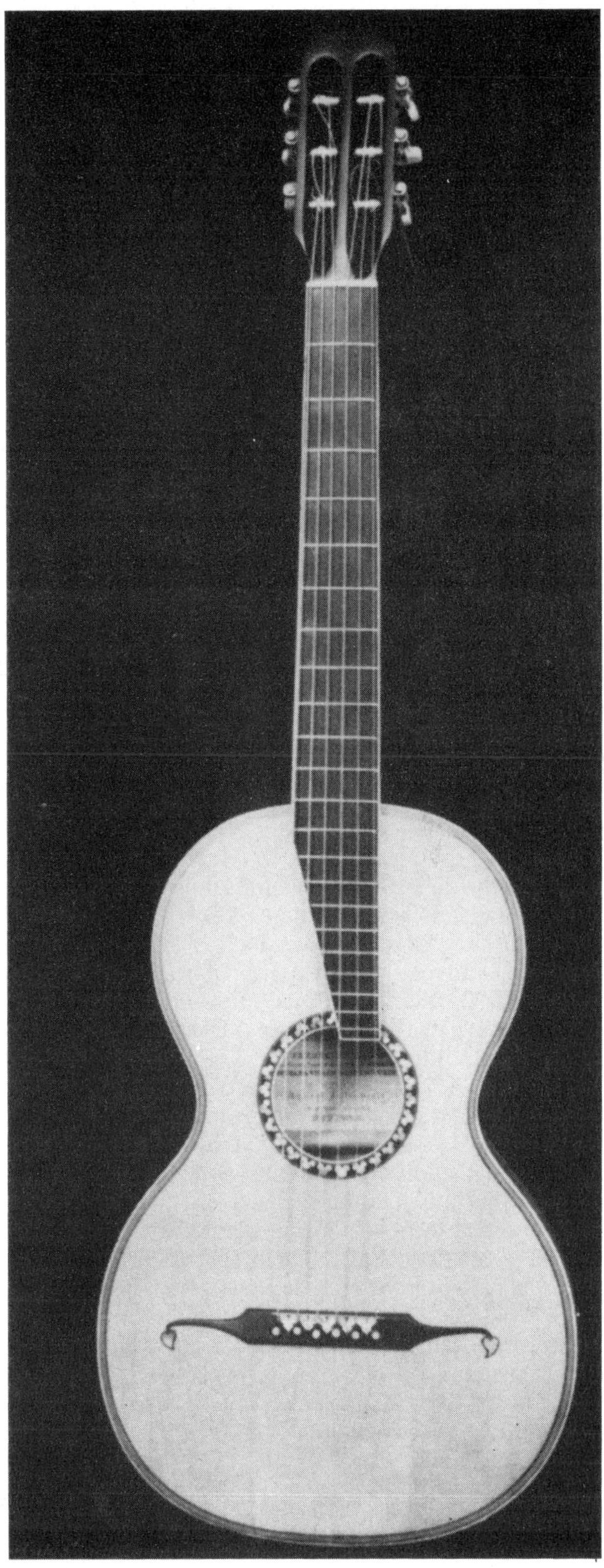

*Superb classical guitar made c.1834 by Christian Frederick Martin (1796-1873)*

# REGINO SAINZ DE LA MAZA

**Born – Burgos, Spain,**

**7 September 1896**

**Died – Madrid, Spain , 26 November 1981**

*Regino Sainz de la Maza*

Regino Sainz de la Maza began his musical studies on the piano in his native town of Burgos. He then attended the Academia de Bellas Artes de San Sebastián, studying harmony with Beltrán Pagola and piano with Germán Cendoya. His studies took him later to both Barcelona and Madrid, where he continued to study the piano.

Madrid turned out to be an important turning point in Sainz de la Maza's career, for it was there that he began formal studies of the guitar with Daniel Fortea. It was at that time that he realized that the guitar was the instrument through which he could best display his musical talent. At the age of eighteen, he gave his first public recital at the Círculo de Belles Artes in Madrid. His performance was well received by audience and critics alike. On the recommendation of important musicians, including Tomás Breton and Emilio Serrano, he earned a grant to further his musical studies from the municipality of Burgos.

Regino Sainz de la Maza moved to Barcelona to study composition with Enrique Morera and Jaime Pahissa. He then completed a highly successful concert tour of Spain, and this led to further tours of South America and Europe.

When he returned to Spain, he worked with Manuel de Falla in the National Music Society, and was appointed to the newly established professorship of guitar at the Conservatory of Madrid in 1935. In 1937 he went to the United States to perform, returning after the Spanish Civil War to become a music critic for the Spanish daily journal ABC. He also became very involved in transcribing early Spanish works, and in doing so found himself in close contact with many of Spain's foremost musicians. In 1938 he met Joaquín Rodrigo and the Marquís de Bolarque. The latter was a famous music patron and an enthusiast for the guitar. The result of their meeting was Rodrigo's Concierto de Aranjuez, which he completed in the autumn of 1939. Sainz de la Maza was given the double honour of having the work dedicated to him and of giving the first performance in Barcelona on 9 November 1940. The work has since won world-wide acclaim, and is probably the most popular concerto ever written. Regino Sainz de la Maza was to perform it a further sixty times in Europe and the Americas.

Regino Sainz de la Maza was a very active teacher, not only in the Madrid Conservatory but also in private study and in masterclasses. He was an avid researcher on many aspects of the guitar and early Spanish music, and made numerous transcriptions as well as producing several original compositions. In 1955 he wrote a brief history of the guitar, La Guitarra y Su Historia. His erudition won him election to the Spanish Academy in 1958, making him the first guitarist to be elected since its foundation in 1752.

**SELECTED MUSIC**

| | |
|---|---|
| Alegrías. | UME 16943 |
| Canciones Castellanas. | UME 22146 |
| Cantilena. | UME 15645 |
| Cuatro Fantasías del Siglo XVI. | UME 18827 |
| El Vito: New Version. | UME 19768 |
| Frontera de Dios. | UME 20207 |
| Petenera | UME 20347 |
| Rondeña. | UME 19900 |
| Seguidilla; Sevillanas. | UME 16944 |
| Soléa. | UME 22145 |
| Zapateado. | UME 19901 |

**SELECTED RECORDINGS**

| | |
|---|---|
| Rodrigo – Concierto de Aranjuez and Fantasia. | RCA VICS 1322 |
| Regino Sainz de la Maza. | Barclay 920-230 |
| Recital. | RCA (Spain) 3L-16.118 |
| La Guitarra de Regino Sainz de la Maza. | RCA (Spain) LM-16.337 |
| Encuentro con la Guitarra de Regino. | RCA (Spain) VictoLM-16.330 |

**SELECTED READING**

| | |
|---|---|
| Regino Sainz de la Maza. | Guitar & Lute, April 1980 |

# GEORGE SAKELLARIOU

**Born –**

**Athens, Greece**

**2 May 1944**

*George Sakellariou*

George Sakellariou was the youngest of eight children. He was introduced to the guitar at an early age by one of his brothers.

Sakellariou studied at the Hellenikon Odeion (conservatory) in Athens with Professor Charalambos Ekmetsoglou. At the age of fifteen he gave his first recital, at the Parnassus Hall in Athens, and at eighteen he graduated, receiving first prize for an outstanding musical performance.

He emigrated to the United States in 1963, originally to study medicine at the University of California. He soon decided that music should be his career, and established himself as one of the finest guitarists and teachers on the West Coast of America. In 1964 he studied privately with Andrés Segovia, and attended some of his international masterclasses. Sakellariou has performed throughout the United States, Canada and South America. He has appeared in concert in many universities, and at the Carmel Bach Festival and Universidad de los Andes, Bogota, Colombia. He has been a soloist with several symphony orchestras and chamber groups in the United States. Over the years he has made numerous appearances on the CBC Television network in Canada and the NET network in the USA.

George Sakellariou now lives in San Rafael, California, giving many concerts and also teaching at the San Francisco Conservatory of Music.

**SELECTED RECORDING**
Music from South America. — Amat AGS 181

**SELECTED READING**
George Sakellariou. — Guitar & Lute, May 1978

# MARCO DE SANTI

**Born –**

**Brescia, Italy**

**3 November 1957**

*Marco de Santi*

Marco de Santi began studying the guitar at an early age with Fausto Bettelli. From 1972 to 1978 he studied with Angelo Gilardino at the Liceo Musicale G.B.Viotti in Vercelli and then graduated with distinction at the Conservatoire C.Pollini in Padua.

Santi won four national competitions and in 1974 was awarded the Mario Castelnuovo-Tedesco prize for the best Italian guitar student. In 1981 he won second prize at the International Competition for Musical Performers in Geneva, and in 1982 won the 'Andrés Segovia' Competition in Palma de Mallorca.

Marco de Santi made his debut as a concert soloist in 1974, and since then has performed extensively both as a soloist and with orchestras or chamber groups throughout Europe. In 1987, together with the chamber group Carme and Astor Piazzolla, he gave the first Italian performance of Piazzolla's Double Concerto for guitar, bandonéon and strings. He has also made many radio and television broadcasts.

**SELECTED RECORDING**

| | |
|---|---|
| Giuliani, Regondi, Legnani. | Lira 0028 |
| Piazzolla, Santórsola, Ginastera. | Lira 0022 |

# TURIBIO SANTOS

**Born – TURIBIO SOARES SANTOS**

**São Luis, Maranhao, North Brazil**

**7 March 1940**

*Turibio Santos*

Turibio Santos was attracted to the classical guitar at the age of ten. His first teachers were Antonio Rebello and, later, Oscar Cáceres. His first recital took place in 1962, in Rio de Janeiro, and was followed by a series of concerts all over Brazil. In the following year the Villa-Lobos Museum invited him to play the Brazilian composer's complete Twelve Studies for Guitar (1929) and to take part in the first public hearing of the Mystic Sextet (1917).

In 1964 Santos formed a duo with Oscar Cáceres and made several tours of South America. In 1965 he decided to establish himself in Europe, and attended masterclasses given by Andrés Segovia in Italy and Julian Bream in England. In the same year he won the first prize in the ORTF's International Guitar Competition in Paris. His subsequent appearances on both ORTF and BBC programmes, as well as his recording on disc of Villa-Lobos's Twelve Studies, made him well known to European audiences. From 1965 to 1969 he was professor of guitar at the Conservatoire Municipal in Paris.

Turibio Santos has performed with many orchestras as a soloist. They include the Monte Carlo Orchestra, the Philharmonic Orchestra of the ORTF, the English Chamber Orchestra, and the Royal Philharmonic Orchestra. Santos has also taken part in numerous festivals in Europe, including the fifth Croisière Méditerranée de Musique. In 1974 he joined Yehudi Menuhin and Mstislav Rostropovich in the opening concert for the Creation of International Funds for Musical Collaboration organised by UNESCO.

Santos established himself in North America with appearances in New York, Boston, Houston, Dallas, Minneapolis, Cincinnati and Washington DC. He was also featured at the Guitar '78 and Guitar '81 Festivals in Toronto, Canada. He was appointed General Director of the Sala Cecilia Meireles in Brazil.

**SELECTED RECORDINGS**

| | |
|---|---|
| Concierto de Aranjuez: Rodrigo. | Musidisc 30 RC 894 |
| Villa-Lobos: Twelve Studies for Guitar. | Erato STV 70496 |
| Villa-Lobos: Prelude, Concerto, Sextour Mystique. | Erato STV 70566 |
| Classiques d'Amerique Latine. | Erato STV 70658 |
| Musique Française pour Guitare. | Erato STV 70767 |
| Musique pour deux Guitares: Volume One (with Oscar Cáceres). | Erato STV 70794 |
| Danses Espagnoles: Volume One. | Erato STV 70844 |
| J. S. Bach. | Erato STV 70885 |
| Musique Brésilienne. | Erato STV 70913 |
| Danses Espagnoles: Volume Two. | Erato STV 71076 |
| Musique pour deux Guitares: Volume Two (with Oscar Cáceres). Erato STV 71092 | |
| Fernando Sor. | Erato STV 71268 |
| Chôros do Brasil. | Erato ERA 9155 |
| Valsas et Chôros. | Erato ERA 9231 |
| Duo for Flute and Guitar(with Christian Lardé, flute). | Erato ERA 71127 |

**SELECTED READING**

| | |
|---|---|
| Interview. | Classical Guitar, December 1984 |

# MARIA LIVIA SÃO MARCOS

**Born –**

**São Paulo, Brazil**

**8 April 1942**

*Maria Livia São Marcos*

Maria Livia São Marcos began to study the guitar at the age of five. Her first teacher was her father, Professor Manuel São Marcos. It was soon obvious that she had enormous musical talent, and at the age of thirteen she gave her first public recital.

At the age of seventeen she was awarded a diploma with honours at the Conservatorio Dramático e Musical in São Paulo. Her first recording followed soon afterwards.

Maria Livia São Marcos went to Portugal, where she gave the first public performance of the guitar concerto Domingos Brandao.. Following this highly acclaimed concert, she went to Paris, where she gave several successful solo guitar recitals. In 1964 she went to Santiago de Compostela, Spain, to study with Andrés Segovia, and then to Lisbon for further study with Emilio Pujol.

After a highly successful career as a classical guitarist in Brazil, Maria Livia São Marcos accepted in 1970 a teaching post as professor of guitar at the Conservatory of Music in Geneva, a position she has held since. A highly respected teacher, she continues to give recitals in the principal cities of Europe and North and South America.

**SELECTED RECORDINGS**

| | |
|---|---|
| Classical Guitar and Strings. | Everest 34209 |
| A Internacional. | Fermata 303-1009 |
| Saudades do Brasil. | Fermata 303-1013 |
| Villa-Lobos: 12 Etudes. | Fermata 305-1039 |
| Maria Livia São Marcos plays Baroque Music. | Classic Pick Music 70-124 |

**SELECTED READING**

| | |
|---|---|
| Maria Livia São Marcos. | Guitar Player, January 1976 |

*Manuel Sao Marcos*

# JUKKA SAVIJOKI

**Born –**

**Helsinki, Finland**

**8 June 1952**

*Jukka Savijoki*

Jukka Savijoki began to play the guitar at the age of thirteen but only took up the classical guitar seriously at the age of eighteen. He studied the guitar in Finland with Ivor Putilin at the Sibelius Academy in Helsinki. He then studied in London with John W. Duarte (1975-76) and then with Oscar Ghiglia in Italy, in 1976 at a Siena masterclass.

Jukka Savijoki has given concerts throughout Scandinavia, Europe and also in Japan. Several important composers, including Paavo Heininen, Erik Bergman, Magnus Linberg, Jouni Kaipainen, Kalevi Aho, Usko Merilainen and Atli Heimir Sveinson, have composed for him or for the ensembles in which he plays.

Jukka Savijoki is currently a senior lecturer at the Sibelius Academy in Helsinki.

**SELECTED RECORDINGS**

| | |
|---|---|
| Baroque Suites for Guitar. | BIS LP 176 |
| Contemporary Finnish Guitar. | BIS LP 207 |
| Guitar Music by Manuel Ponce. | BIS LP 255 |
| Giuliani: Complete works for flute & guitar (with Mikael Helasvuo): 3 vols. | BIS CD-413 |

**SELECTED READING**

| | |
|---|---|
| Interview. | Guitar, September 1983 |
| Interview. | Classical Guitar, April 1986 |
| Interview. | Guitar International, November 1986 |

# ISAIAS SAVIO

**Born – Montevidedo, Uruguay**

**1 October 1902**

**Died – São Paulo, Brazil, 12 January 1977**

*Isaias Sávio*

Isaias Sávio began his musical education at the age of nine. After studying the piano for four years, he began to study the guitar. He made rapid progress on the instrument, and it was soon obvious that he had very special talents.

He became a highly successful concert artist, playing throughout South America. In 1931 he went to Brazil and decided to make his home there. He continued an active career as a guitarist, promoting the classical guitar throughout Brazil's cities, towns and villages.

Isaias Sávio was also a fine composer. Over one hundred of his original works for the guitar have been published. Many of his compositions are based on Brazilian folk melodies that he had heard and learnt while visiting Brazilian country villages.

Towards the latter part of his life, Sávio devoted most of his time to teaching. He was professor of guitar at the Conservatorio Dramático e Musical de São Paulo, the first person to hold this post. He was also the director of the Escola Violinistica Jose do Patrocinio.

**SELECTED MUSIC**

| | |
|---|---|
| A Casinha Pequenina & | |
| Minha Terra Tem Palmeiras. | BR 150 |
| Cajita de Música. | BA 11505 |
| Cênas Brasileiras, 1st series (seven pieces). | BR 1593 |
| 2nd series (two pieces). | MCM 0271 |
| Celeste y Blanco: Estilo. | BR 2301 |
| Duas Guitarras: Canção Cignana. | BR 1811 |
| Nesta Rua: Theme & Variations. | BR 2252 |
| Ojos Negros (Dark Eyes – Russian song) | |
| & A Casinha Pequenina. | BA 11217 |
| Para Nilo Brincar: 9 popular children's songs. | BR 1079 |
| Pensamientos, op.3 (short works). | R & F |
| Pequeña Romanza. | RF 7448 |
| Preludes Nos.3, 4, 5, 6. | BR 3193 |
| Four Preludes Pitorescos. | BR 1808 |
| Sarabande & Gigue. | BR 2170 |
| Three Original Pieces, 1927. | BR 3076 |
| Two Pieces, Vidalita Popular, Dança de Boneca. | BR 2337 |
| Variações de Gato. | BR 2302 |
| Variations on an Infant's Theme. | R & F |

**SELECTED RECORDING**

Yone Perreira Interpreta Isaias Sávio. Brasidisc LP 14037

*Karl Scheit*

# KARL SCHEIT

**Born –**

**Schönbrunn, Austria**

**21 April 1909**

Karl Scheit's musical studies began on the violin at an early age. Although his father was a military band conductor, he did not want his son to become a professional musician.

Scheit joined a youth group when he was fifteen years old, and it was then that he began to study the guitar in order to accompany himself when he sang. Soon afterwards the young musician became aware of the guitar's full potential, and began to study the instrument in earnest.

Karl Scheit left his home for Vienna and began to study music theory and harmony on the guitar at the Academy of Music there. After hearing both Miguel Llobet and Andrés Segovia in concert, Scheit decided to make the classical guitar his career. He continued his music studies with the eminent Austrian composer N.David.

At the age of twenty-four Scheit was appointed professor of the guitar at the Vienna State Academy, a position he still holds today. He is regarded as one of the foremost guitar teachers in Europe, and has published many transcriptions for guitar in addition to a Method for Guitar in two volumes.

**SELECTED RECORDING**

Music for Guitar. Turnabout TV 341238

# JOHN SCHNEIDER

**Born –**

**Pasadena, California, USA**

**8 November 1950**

*John Schneider*

John Schneider began to play the guitar at the age of nine after having experimented with the ukulele and the banjo. During his teenage years he performed in various amateur folk, rock and jazz groups before turning to the classical guitar. He first studied the instrument with Vincenzo Macaluso. Schneider went on to study composition at the University of California. From California he went to the University of Wales in Cardiff, where he earned a Masters Degree in Electronic Music and a Ph.D. in Physics and Music in 1977. He also studied the guitar at the Royal College of Music, London.

Upon his return to the USA John Schneider began producing and hosting his weekly two-hour radio programme SOUNDBOARD, the longest running guitar series in the USA. Schneider served as President of the Guitar Foundation of America from 1979 to 1983.

Since the early 1980s Schneider has performed almost exclusively on the 'well-tempered guitar', an instrument which uses a system of interchangeable fingerboards that attach to the neck of the guitar by magnetic means. Each fingerboard uses a different pattern of fretting which produces acoustically pure intervals (unlike the standard equally tempered system) that are tuned according to either the key or the tuning system desired. With this unique capability Schneider interprets music from past eras in their original temperaments, as well as the modern quartertone music of Alois Haba and Juan Carrillo, and the repertoire specifically written for the instrument by Lou Harrison and LaMonte Young.

John Schneider has written widely on the history and repertoire of the guitar for Guitar Review, Soundboard and Guitar & Lute. He is a specialist in contemporary music, and his book, The Contemporary Guitar, has become a standard text in this field of music.

**SELECTED RECORDING**

| | |
|---|---|
| Sonic Voyage. | El Maestro Records EM 8004 |
| Music for Guitar and Percussion. | Etcetera CD KTC 1071 |

**SELECTED READING**

| | |
|---|---|
| The Contemporary Guitar. | University of California, 1985 |
| Article: The Well Tempered Guitar. | Guitar, November 1983 |
| Interview. | Classical Guitar, July/August 1984 |

# FRANZ SCHUBERT

**Born – FRANZ PETER SCHUBERT**

**Lichtental, near Vienna, Austria, 31 January 1797**

**Died – Vienna 19 November 1828**

*Franz Schubert*

Perhaps the greatest composer ever to have played the guitar, Franz Schubert produced an enormous amount of music, but unfortunately nothing of any consequence for the guitar.

He was given a sound music education by his father, a schoolteacher, who recognised his son's musical talents at a very early age. From him, Franz learned to play the violin; from his brother Ignaz, the piano. He learned to sing at the Chapel of the Court. He befriended the poet Theodor Korner, who was an enthusiastic guitarist. Much impressed with the instrument, Schubert decided that he would master it, and in a short time had become an accomplished guitarist.

The classical guitar became Franz Schubert's main instrument during the early part of his career. Before he could afford to buy a piano, he conceived all his vocal compositions on the guitar, and most of his songs at that time were written with a guitar accompaniment.

Franz Schubert lived in virtual poverty, achieving little success or recognition during his short life. His activities as a song writer lasted for almost seventeen years, yet it was not until 1819 that one of his songs was publicly performed, and it was not until 1821 that the first one was published.

There has recently been a revival of interest amongst guitarists in the guitar accompaniments of Schubert, the master of the Lied. Some of his other compositions include a guitar part. The Kantata zur Namensfeier des Vaters, for two tenors and bass, has an arpeggio accompaniment for guitar. In 1819 his 15 Original Dances for flute, violin and guitar were published by Diabelli, and he adapted a trio by Matiegka for flute, viola and guitar, adding a cello and turning it into a quartet.

Franz Schubert suffered ill health for many years. He died on 19 November 1828 at the age of thirty-one. One of his guitars, bearing his name, is on display in the Vienna Museum,.

**SELECTED MUSIC**

| | |
|---|---|
| Terzetto for male voices & guitar: ed.Scheit. | Doblinger |
| Die Nacht (voice & guitar). | Universal UE 18 957 |

COURTESY: ICM ARTISTS

*Andrés Segovia*

# ANDRÉS SEGOVIA

**Born – ANDRÉS TORRES SEGOVIA**

**Linares, Granada, Spain, 21 February 1893**

**Died – Madrid, Spain, 2 June 1987**

*Andrés Segovia, c.1927*

Andrés Segovia was one of the greatest musicians of the twentieth century, and certainly the most important guitarist the world has ever known. His exceptional genius and determination overcame very heavy prejudices against the guitar, and the instrument is now widely accepted as the equal of any other. There is not one classical guitarist alive today who has not been influenced by Andrés Segovia in one way or another.

At the age of five, Andrés Segovia was taken to live with his uncle in Granada. The uncle tried to encourage his nephew to learn the violin, but with little success. Andrés Segovia became fascinated with the sound of a guitar played by a flamenco guitarist who happened to be in his uncle's house. At the age of ten, Segovia received his first guitar, and from that moment, despite his uncle's opposition, he devoted every spare moment to it. After his uncle's death, Segovia, then twelve years old, went to live with his mother and brother in Córdoba. A little later, the young guitarist decided to rent his own room, so that he could fully develop his study of the guitar and music. He made friends with several musicians, including a pianist, Luis Serrano, who introduced him to a young pianist, Rafael de Montis. Montis was much impressed by Segovia's transcriptions of classical music for the guitar.

At the age of sixteen Andrés Segovia left school, determined to make the guitar his life. In 1909 he gave his first public recital, at the Granada Art Centre. The young guitarist then went to Seville to the home of Rafael de Montis. There he met and impressed many influential people who would patronise his future concerts. Segovia stayed in Seville for over a year, and played sixteen recitals while he was there. He then went to play in other major cities in Spain, but found enormous opposition to the classical guitar from musicians and critics alike.

In 1912 Segovia went to Madrid to make his debut in Spain's capital. There he met the luthier Manuel Ramírez, who was so impressed with the guitarist's ability that he gave him one of his finest guitars as a gift. Segovia's Madrid concert, despite an excellent performance, was not well received.

He went to Valencia, where he made contact with Tárrega's most prominent pupil, Miguel Llobet. They became good friends, and Llobet invited Segovia to his home in Barcelona. Segovia played three concerts in Barcelona, and they were generally well received.

On his return to Madrid Segovia was introduced to the concert promoter Ernesto de Quesada. Quesada was greatly impressed by Segovia's musicianship and technical ability, and offered to be his concert agent. The first booking arranged by Quesada was a tour of South America. It was highly successful. In 1920 Segovia was invited to play for Queen Victoria of Spain at the Palace of Madrid, a positive sign of the young guitarist's growing reputation and great musical talent.

From 1920 to 1935 Andrés Segovia gave concerts throughout the major cities of Europe. He appeared in London and Paris in 1924, and in Moscow in 1926. In 1928 he crossed the Atlantic again to make his United States debut in New York's Town Hall. Everywhere he went, he astounded his audiences with his performances. It was during this period that Segovia began his campaign to encourage leading composers to write for the guitar. The first to reply was Federico Moreno Torroba. Many more prominent composers, including Manuel Ponce, Heitor Villa-Lobos, Joaquín Turina, Mario Castelnuovo-Tedesco and Joaquín Rodrigo, were to compose original music for solo guitar and guitar and orchestra.

At the beginning of the Spanish Civil War in 1936, Segovia left Spain. His home in Barcelona was looted. He did not return until after the end of World War II. During these years he made his home in New York and Montevideo, Uruguay.

After the end of World War II, Segovia was instrumental in bringing about a revolution for classical guitarists. For many years he had suffered from the unreliability of gut strings. With the help of his friend Albert Augustine, Segovia persuaded the chemical company Du Pont to investigate the possibility of producing a nylon guitar string. Augustine took charge of the project, and in 1947 the first nylon guitar strings were made. Another big step forward, instigated by Andrés Segovia, had been made for the classical guitar.

During the 1950s and 1960s, Segovia continued a highly successful career as a concert and recording artist. Averaging one hundred concerts a year during this period of his career, he also recorded thirty albums for the Decca label. It was during this time that he began his annual masterclasses in Siena, Italy, and Santiago de Compostela, Spain. Many of the guitarists who attended them are among the leading players today.

Up to the time of his death, Segovia still held occasional masterclasses, in countries as far apart as the USA and Japan. The teaching movement instigated by him has ensured more guitar virtuosos than ever before. Segovia also encouraged colleges and conservatories of music in the major cities of the world to include the guitar in their curriculum, and today there are few colleges that do not have a professor of guitar.

Early in his career, Andrés Segovia set himself several goals, all of them designed to raise the level of the classical guitar. The seeds which had been sown by Francisco Tárrega and Miguel Llobet were cultivated and brought to full bloom by the superhuman efforts of Andrés Segovia. There is little doubt that he achieved all his goals, and more. The classical guitar now enjoys worldwide acceptance and popularity in all musical circles.

**SELECTED MUSIC**

Five Short Works for the Guitar-Impromptu, Tonadilla, 3 Preludes. Kalmus
From 'Follies of My Youth': Five Anecdotes Belwin Mills
Lessons Nos.11 and 12 Belwin Mills
Macarena Belwin Mills
Neblina (a Olga) Belwin Mills
Prelude on Chords. Celesta

**SELECTED RECORDINGS**

The Art of Segovia 1927-1939 (2 LPs). EMI RLS 745
Andrés Segovia 1949. EMI HLM 134
Concerto. MCA S-26044
International Classics. MCA MACS 2359
Andrés Segovia Plays. MCA MACS 1354
Recuerdos de la Alhambra: Tárrega and Sor. MCA S26091
Interprete les Italiens. MCA MACS 6123
Segovia and the Guitar. MCF 3073
Golden Jubilee Set (3 LPs). Decca DXT 148
Maestro. Brunswick SXA 4535
Boccherini/Cassado and Bach Suite. MCA MACS 125
Five Pieces from 'Platero and I'. MCA MACS 1967
Granada. MCA MACS 1968
Sonata Romantica. MCA S-26087
Tansman & Mompou. Brunswick AXA 4532
On Stage. Brunswick SXA 4550
Mexicana. MCA MACS 100
España. MCA S-26-037
Castles of Spain. MCA MACS 3045
The Unique Art of Andrés Segovia. Decca DL 71067
The Guitar and I: Volume One. MCA MACS 3965
The Guitar and I: Volume Two. MCA MACS 6281
Nocturno. Intercord INT 160 815
The Intimate Guitar: Volume One. RCA ARL 1-0864
The Intimate Guitar: Volume Two. RCA ARL 1-1323
Reveries. RCA RL 12602

**SELECTED READING**

Andrés Segovia. Guitar, December 1972
Andrés Segovia. Guitar, December 1974
Andrés Segovia. Guitar, October 1976
Andrés Segovia. Guitar, June 1977
Andrés Segovia. Guitar, December 1977
Andrés Segovia. Guitar Player, June 1971,
Andrés Segovia. Guitar Player, October 1971
Andrés Segovia. Guitar Player, February 1972
Andrés Segovia. Guitar Player, April 1974
Andrés Segovia. Guitar Player, June 1978
Andrés Segovia. Frets, December 1981
Andrés Segovia. Guitarra, January 1979
Andrés Segovia. Guitarra, September 1980
The Sound of Segovia. Guitar Review No.42, 1977
A Conversation with Segovia. Guitar Review No.43, 1978
Andrés Segovia: Bernard Gavoty. Kister, 1955
Andrés Segovia: ed. Clinton. Musical New Services, 1978
Segovia: An Autobiography 1893-1920. Macmillan, 1976
Andrés Segovia: Contributions to the World of Guitar: Ronald C. Purcell. Belwin Mills, 1975
The Segovia Technique: Vladimir Bobri. Macmillan, 1972
The Guitar and Myself: Series of articles, Guitar Review Nos.4, 6, 7, 8, 10, 13.
Andrés Segovia: M. Vaisbord. Musika, Moscow, 1981
Interview. Classical Guitar, Jan/Feb 1983
Reminiscences: Alice Artzt. Classical Guitar, Jan/Feb 1983
Special Issue. Guitar International, April 1986
Segovia's Strings of Destiny: Julian Bream. The Guardian, reprinted in Classical Guitar, August 1987
The Father of Them All: Vollers. Classical Guitar, August 1987
Segovia and Falla: Graham Wade. Classical Guitar, April 1988
Andrés Segovia and Guitar Artin the 20th Century: M. Vaisbord.Soviet Composer, Moscow 1989
The Segovia-Ponce Letters. Editions Orphée, 1989
Tras la Huella de Andrés Segovia – Pérez-Bustamente de Monasterio. University of Cádiz, Spain 1990

PHOTO: RADIO FRANCE

*Andrés Segovia and family, 1983. (Left to right): Son Carlos Andrés, wife Emilia, Segovia, granddaughter, Mr and Mrs Andrés Segovia Junior*

PHOTO: COLIN COOPER

*Andrés Segovia receives the gold medal of the Royal Philharmonic Society after his concert at the Wigmore Hall, London on 26 April 1986*

There exists a legend regarding the origin of the guitar that is more beautifully suggestive than historic fact: Apollo was running in pursuit of a beautiful nymph, gallantly repeating to her all the while: "Don't tire yourself, don't tire yourself, I promise not to catch up with you." When, finally, he did succeed in taking her into his arms, she called out to her semidivine father, who instantly changed her into a laurel tree. Apollo made the first guitar from the wood of this tree and gave it as form the graceful, curved contours that forever reveal its feminine origin. That is why the guitar is of a reserved and changeable nature, even hysterical at times; but that is also why it is sweet and smooth, harmonious and delicate. When it is played with love and skill, there issues from its melancholy sounds a rapture that holds us fast to it forever.

From my youthful years I dreamed of raising the guitar from the sad artistic level in which it lay. At first my ideas were vague and imprecise, but as I grew in years and my love for it became intense and vehement, my will to do so became more assertive, and my intentions clearer.

Since then, I have dedicated my life to four essential tasks. The first: To separate the guitar from mindless folklore-type entertainment. It was born for something more and something better. Can you imagine Pegasus drawing a cart laden with vegetable greens?

My second item of labor: To endow it with a repertoire of high quality, made up of works possessing intrinsic musical value, from the pens of composers accustomed to writing for orchestra, piano, violin, etc. The masters, in accordance with usage, had written for it with passion, but with incompetence, allowing it to sink even lower than when Flamenco *tocaores*—some of whom were wonderful within their field—strummed it. Three names stand out in the modern history of the guitar: they are Sor, Giuliani and Tárrega, although the little works of this last are not of transcendental import. The first symphonic composer to heed my request, offering to collaborate with me, was Federico Moreno Torroba; then, Falla and Turina; later, Manuel Ponce, Villa-Lobos, Castelnuovo-Tedesco, Tansman, Roussel, Cyril Scott, Rodrigo, Jolivet, Duarte, and others. Assisted by professional musicologists, I also dedicated myself to capturing delightful works written for the vihuela and the lute, and among the latter is a magnificent collection composed by Johann Sebastian Bach. Today, new works for the guitar number more than three hundred.

My third purpose: To make the beauty of the guitar known to the philharmonic public of the entire world. I began by giving concerts in Spain, disproving the truth of the saying "No one is a prophet in his own country." Theaters and music halls were filled and the public's interest and respect for the "classical" guitar grew. In 1919 I made my first tour of Latin America, and five years later the doors of the Paris Conservatory's hall opened to me. The French critics praised the guitar as an expressive medium for serious music, and mentioned the works of Bach in their words of praise. Concert societies and impresarios began to call me from London, Berlin, Vienna, Zurich, Amsterdam, Rome, Stockholm, etc. My first appearance in the United States took place in 1928, and during the summer and early autumn of that same year I undertook a tour of the Far East for the first time. Today, at seventy-seven, I continue my artistic activities throughout the civilized world. Like the poet, I can say: "I have felt the roundness of the world beneath my feet."

I am still working on my fourth and perhaps last task: That of influencing the authorities at conservatories, academies and universities to include the guitar in their instruction programs on the same basis as the violin, cello, piano, etc. I have placed pupils of mine as teachers in four conservatories in Switzerland, as well as five in Italy, two in Spain, one in England, two in Australia, two in Argentina, three in the United States, and others in Germany, Holland, France and the Scandinavian countries.

The future of the guitar is, therefore, assured. I have broken the vicious circle in which adverse fate had held it enclosed. Guitarists of worth did not appear because great composers did not write for the guitar, and the latter did not write for the guitar because it lacked virtuosos of talent. My disciples—many of whom are already famous teachers and artists—will continue my work, fervently adding their own artistic contributions to the history of this most beautiful instrument.

COURTESY: MCA RECORDS

*Sleevenotes by Segovia from his record 'The Guitar and I', MCA 3965*

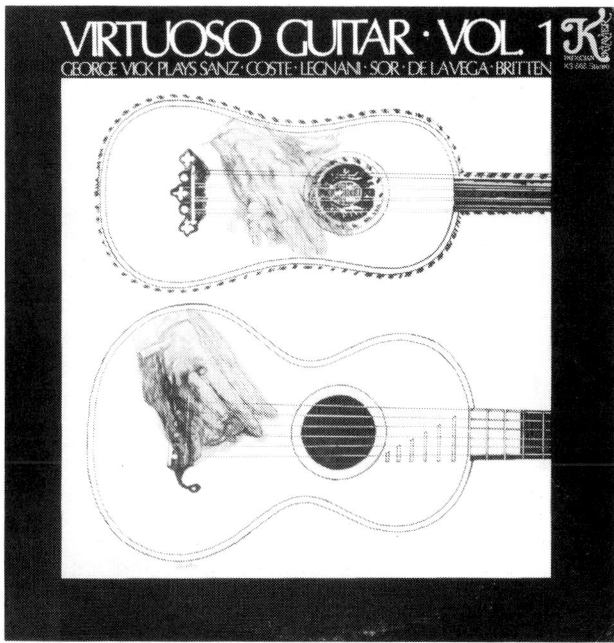

*A selection of classical and modern guitar art on record sleeves.*

# PETER SENSIER

**Born – Ealing, London, England**

**20 January 1918**

**Died – Gateshead, England, 24 September 1977**

*Peter Sensier*

Peter Sensier was one of the most important guitar personalities in Britain for many years. Although his playing was generally restricted to a popular South American vocal duo 'Dorita y Pepe' for most of his career, Sensier was an authority on the classical guitar repertoire. He made many transcriptions of early lute music and classical melodies for the guitar, and he was also the original presenter of the BBC Radio 3 programme 'The Classical Guitar'. He was also a fine constructor of guitars and vihuelas. His journalism embraced regular contributions to B.M.G. magazine for many years, and a wide range of articles for various other periodicals and reference books.

Peter Sensier's first music studies were on the piano at the age of eight. After leaving school he took up the plectrum guitar, and by the age of nineteen was playing professionally in dance bands. During World War II he served with the Royal Signals. He continued to play the guitar in an army dance band, and also studied the oboe and clarinet.

In 1945 Peter Sensier returned to a career as a professional guitarist, playing in several London night-clubs. In 1948 he began to take an interest in the classical guitar, and studied it with Geoffrey Sisley, Desmond Dupré and Angel Iglesias. In 1952 his wide knowledge resulted in an invitation to give a series of lecture-recitals in Middlesex County Schools.

In Dorothy Holcombe, whom he met in 1956, Sensier found a mutual interest in South American music and the guitar, and over the next five years the couple collected and built up an extensive repertoire of South American vocal and instrumental music. As 'Dorita y Pepe', they made their recital debut at the Wigmore Hall in 1961. It was a great success. In the same year they visited Mexico, where they were awarded a diploma, a silver plaque and a gold statuette, the much coveted 'El Pipila', for their work in spreading and popularizing Latin American folk music. About this time they became much in demand for radio and televison programmes, in mainland Europe as well as Britain (where they had a 39-week series on Southern TV).

In 1964 Dorita y Pepe went to Argentina and Paraguay. They were invited back to Argentina in 1965 for the Fifth National Festival of Argentine Folklore in Cosquín, where they appeared beside the great folk artists of Argentina on equal terms and with great success. During that visit they also appeared in the National Festival of Poetry and Folk Music at Carlos Paz, and in the first Festival of Latin American Folk Music at Salta, where they were a part of the delegation of professional Argentine folk artists.

Despite the burden of failing health, Peter Sensier continued to write about the guitar in various journals, construct many fine fretted instruments, and also broadcast for the BBC on guitar matters, until his death in 1977 at the age of fifty-nine.

**SELECTED RECORDINGS**

| | |
|---|---|
| Latin American Folk: Dorita y Pepe. | Pye NSPL 18215 |
| Si! Dorita y Pepe. | Argo ZFB 24 |
| Dorita y Pepe in Buenos Aires. | Parlophone PCS 7007 |
| Dorita y Pepe. | Hallmark HM 546 |
| Dorita y Pepe. | Society SOC 954 |

**SELECTED READING**

| | |
|---|---|
| Peter Sensier. | Guitar, August 1972 |

# ERNEST SHAND

**Born – ERNEST WATSON**

**Hull, England, 31 January 1868**

**Died – Birmingham, England, 30 November 1924**

*Ernest Shand*

Ernest Shand was best known to the British public as an actor and comedian, but he was also one of the best guitarists in Britain at the end of the nineteenth century.

Shand studied the violin for five years, then began to teach himself the guitar. He later studied with Madame Sidney Pratten, and with her guidance made great progress on the instrument. Before he was thirty years old, he had written one hundred and fifty compositions for the guitar, many of which were published by Barnes & Mullins, Schott & Co., Weekes and Co., and Essex & Cammeyer.

In 1896 Shand opened a guitar teaching studio in Bryanston Street, London, but he could not get enough pupils and it was not a success. Although he continued to play the guitar, he never used it in his theatre appearances. He would occasionally play the guitar at concerts, some of which took place at the London Conservatoire of Music.

Ernest Shand was one of Britain's most prolific composers for the guitar. At the time of his death he had composed nearly two hundred and fifty works for the guitar, the most important of which was his Premier Concerto pour Guitar, op.48. He performed this work for the first time at the Glasgow Arts Club in February 1896. He was also the author of a guitar method, published by Barnes & Mullins of London.

**SELECTED READING**

| | |
|---|---|
| Ernest Shand. | Classical Guitar, May 1985 |

# MARIA ISABEL SIEWERS

**Born –**

**Buenos Aires, Argentina**

**22 October 1950**

*Maria Isabel Siewers*

Maria Isabel Siewers studied music and the guitar at the Manuel de Falla Conservatory in Buenos Aires. Her teacher was Maria Luisa Anido. She graduated with honours in 1974. She earned grants from the Spanish and Italian governments, enabling her to study with Andrés Segovia and José Tomás in Santiago de Compostela, and with Oscar Ghiglia, Ruggiero Chiesa and Alan Meurnier at the Accademia Musicale Chigiana in Siena, from which she received a diploma with honours.

In 1974 Maria Isabel Siewers won several prizes in Argentinian music competitions, and also won second prize in the 16th International Classical Guitar Competition held in Paris by Radio France under the direction of Robert Vidal. In the same year she gave concerts throughout Europe, the USA and Latin America, and since that time has maintained a busy international concert schedule.

Maria Isabel Siewers has also played in many radio broadcasts, and has presented a series of radio programmes on the classical guitar in Argentina. A fine teacher, she has taught at the Manuel de Falla Conservatory in Buenos Aires and at the Morón Conservatory. She is currently professor of guitar at the Musikhochschule Mozarteum in Vienna, Austria.

**SELECTED RECORDING**

| | |
|---|---|
| Music of Argentina. | Guitar Masters GMR 1003 |

**SELECTED READING**

| | |
|---|---|
| Interview. | Classical Guitar, Jan/Feb 1984 |
| Interview. | Classical Guitar, April 1986 |

# SEPPO SIIRALA

**Born –**

**Helsinki, Finland**

**29 February 1952**

*Seppo Siirala*

Seppo Siirala's first musical instrument was the violin, which he began to play at the age of six. He began to play the classical guitar after a short time, playing both the electric and the folk instrument. In 1972 he won first prize at the Lanchester International Guitar Competition, England. He made his debut in London in 1975, and since that time has performed throughout Scandinavia, Europe, Australia and the USA. He has made several recordings which reflect his interest in ensemble music and his wide variety of musical styles.

Since 1977 Seppo Siirala has been teaching classical guitar at the Sibelius Academy in Helsinki, and since 1981 he has been chairman of the Helsinki Guitar Society. He is the author and co-author of a number of pedagogical and performance publications, and is regarded as one of Finland's finest players and foremost teachers. He appears frequently as both teacher and performer at international guitar events, including the Scandinavian Guitar Festival, the Danish festivals in Aalborg and Aarhus, Gdansk in Poland, the Esztergom Guitar Festival in Hungary and the GFA Festival in Lubbock, Texas, USA.

**SELECTED RECORDINGS**

| | |
|---|---|
| Seppo Siirala and Ilari Lehtinen. | Love 140 |
| Rantalaitumella: Siirala & others. | Ponsi 12 |
| Zingara: Siirala & others. | Beta 4016 |
| Lorca, Granados etc. Siirala and Airas. | Beta 4018 |
| Guitar Souvenir: Finnish Music. | Chorus CH 8702 |

# RONOEL SIMÕES

**Born –**

**São Paulo, Brazil**

**24 March 1919**

*Ronoel Simões*

Ronoel Simões began to play the guitar in 1939. In 1941 he began to study the classical guitar seriously with Attilio Bernardina. He studied with this well-known guitarist for six years, after which he went on to perform, mainly in guitar duos and trios. He also began to teach, and in 1953 opened his guitar school, the Academia Brasileira de Violão.

Simões' passion for the guitar led him to become a collector of records, music books and guitar memorabilia. He is reputed to have one of the largest collections of such material in the world. For many years he had a weekly programme of guitar music, 'Solos de Violão', on Radio Gazeta in São Paulo. He also wrote a regular guitar column in the São Paulo newspaper, 'A Gazeta'. Over the years Simões' home became the centre of guitar activity in Brazil.

Ronoel Simões closed his Academy in 1984 and retired from teaching altogether, but continues to devote his energies to the guitar. No one has contributed more to the advancement of the guitar in Brazil in the last fifty years.

**SELECTED READING**

Ronoel Simões: A Profile. Guitar Review, Summer 1988

*A Grobert guitar originally owned by Paganini and then later by Berlioz. Now in the Paris Conservatoire museum*

*A Staufer guitar owned by Franz Schubert. Now in the Vienna museum*

# NEIL SMITH

**Born –**

**Horwich, Lancashire**

**6 January 1945**

*Neil Smith*

Neil Smith began to play the plectrum guitar at the age of sixteen. He was self-taught on this instrument, and soon became a well-known dance band and session guitarist in the Lancashire area.

At the age of twenty-two, Neil Smith heard some records by Andrés Segovia, and decided that he wanted to make his career on the classical guitar. He took lessons with the guitarist Michael Strutt in Manchester, and lessons in theory and harmony with the pianist Robert Marsh. He went on to study in London with the composer/guitarist John W. Duarte, and later with professors at the Royal College of Music and the Guildhall School of Music. He gained a fellowship of the London College of Music at the end of his course.

In 1975 he was the only English guitarist invited to study in Canada with the Venezuelan guitarist Alirio Díaz in a masterclass recorded by CBC.

Since 1975 Neil Smith has established himself as one of Britain's finest classical guitarists. He has made several broadcasts on BBC radio and television, and continues an active career as a recitalist and teacher throughout Great Britain and Europe.

**SELECTED RECORDINGS**

| | |
|---|---|
| Classical Guitar. | Pennine Sound PS 186 |
| Neil Smith plays John W. Duarte. | Guitar Masters GMR 1006 |
| Virtuoso – Neil Smith | LCR 1 (Cassette) |

**SELECTED READING**

| | |
|---|---|
| Interview. | Classical Guitar, January 1985 |
| Various contributions. | Classical Guitar, from 1982 |

# REGINALD SMITH BRINDLE

**Born –**

**Preston, England**

**5 January 1917**

PHOTO: COLIN COOPER

*Reginald Smith Brindle*

Reginald Smith Brindle studied at the Bangor College of the University of Wales under D.E.Parry Williams and was awarded the Gynnedon Scholarship.

His first interest in the guitar began before World War II, when he played in jazz bands. His main instruments were the saxophone, the clarinet, the guitar, the organ and the double bass. He realised the full potential of the guitar when he heard some records by the Gypsy jazz guitarist Django Reinhardt. In 1939 he joined the army, and during his military service (until 1946) took the guitar with him everywhere to continue his music studies. He became aware of the classical guitar in early 1946 when he went to Florence and met Professor Giuseppe Gullino, who introduced him to the classical literature of the guitar. Smith Brindle was particularly impressed by the many records of Segovia he heard at this time.

A university fellowship had enabled Reginald Smith Brindle to continue his studies under Ildebrando Pizzetti at the Santa Cecilia Academy in Rome. Here he received a diploma for advanced composition, and also the Luigi Sturo Prize. He studied twelve-tone technique with Luigi Dallapiccola for a period of two years.

Reginald Smith Brindle lived for much his life in Italy, writing music for documentary films, conducting British music and writing as a music critic. He has composed over sixty original works for guitar, which have made him one of the most important composers for the classical guitar in the twentieth century.

**SELECTED MUSIC**

| | |
|---|---|
| Danza Pagana | Schott |
| Do Not Go Gentle. | SZ 8021 |
| El Polifemo de Oro. | Bruzz |
| Etruscan Preludes. | Schott |
| Four Poems of García Lorca. | Schott |
| Fuego Fatuo. | Schott |
| Guitarcosmos: Progressive Pieces for Guitar. | Schott |
| Memento in Two Movements. | Bèrben 1986 |
| Nocturne. | Schott |
| November Memories. | SZ 8020 |
| Sonata: El Verbo. | G21 |
| Sonatina Fiorentina. | Schott |
| Ten Simple Preludes, ed. Duarte. | UIE 29162 |
| Variants on Two Themes of J. S. Bach. | Peters 7131 |
| Vita senese. | Schott |
| *For two guitars:* | |
| Las Doces Cuerdas. | Schott |
| The Pillars of Karnak. | Schott |
| *For four guitars:* | |
| Concerto de Angelis. | Schott |

**SELECTED RECORDINGS**

| | |
|---|---|
| El Polifemo de Oro: Julian Bream. | RCA Victor RB 6723 |
| Trio Chitarristico Italiano. | RCA RL 31277 |
| Sonata 'El Verbo': Forbes Henderson. | Musical New Services G121 |

**SELECTED READING**

| | |
|---|---|
| Reginald Smith Brindle: Article. | Guitar, June 1973 |
| Reginald Smith Brindle: Article. | Guitar & Lute, October 1980 |
| Interview. | Classical Guitar. January & February 1988 |
| Autobiography. | Classical Guitar January and February 1989 |

# RAPHAËLLA SMITS

**Born –**

**Mortsel, Antwerp, Belgium**

**1 February 1957**

*Raphaëlla Smits*

Raphaëlla Smits was brought up in an artistic environment. She studied at both the Antwerp and Brussels Royal Conservatories of Music in Belgium. In 1978 she received the first prize in the Antwerp Conservatory annual awards, and in 1981 she received the Diploma Superior from the Brussels Conservatory. She studied with José Tomás at the Andrés Segovia classes in Spain, and in 1986 won first prize in the 10th Certamen Internacional de Guitarra Francisco Tárrega Competition.

Raphaëlla Smits began her professional performing career in 1975, since when she has given many concerts throughout Europe and the USA. She has established a fine reputation as a teacher, giving masterclasses at many important centres as well as her own summer course in Belgium. She is currently teaching guitar and chamber music at the Louvain Lemmens Institute in Belgium.

**SELECTED RECORDINGS**

| | |
|---|---|
| Fernando Sor: Guitar Duets with David Russell. | Poketino PL0008 |
| Napoléon Coste: Guitar Music. | DOR 1 |
| Romantic Guitar: Mertz & Giuliani. | CD Accent ACC2 8863D |
| 20th Century Guitar Music | CD Accent ACC2 8966D |

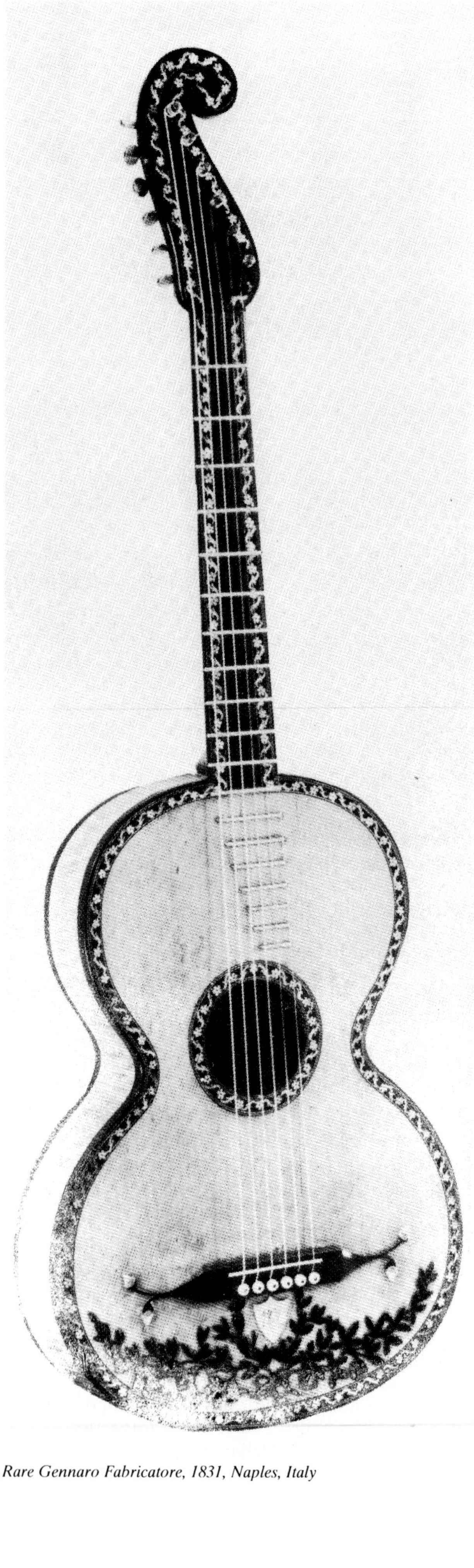

*Rare Gennaro Fabricatore, 1831, Naples, Italy*

AUTHORS PERSONAL COLLECTION

# GÖRAN SÖLLSCHER

**Born –**

**Vaxjo, Sweden**

**31 December 1955**

PHOTO: COLIN COOPER

*Göran Söllscher*

Göran Söllscher grew up in Kalmar on the east coast of Sweden. He started to play the guitar at the age of seven, and studied at the Kalmar Municipal School of Music from 1965 to 1970. His studies continued under Professor Per-Olof Johnson, privately at first, and later at the Malmö Conservatory (from 1975 to 1977) and the Copenhagen Conservatory (from 1976 to 1979).

Göran Söllscher's recital debut took place in Kalmar in 1973, and he made his first appearance on Swedish television in 1975. In 1978 he won first prize at the Concours Internationale de Guitarre in Paris. This led to an important recording contract with Deutsche Grammophon. Since that time, he has established himself as one of the guitar's finest exponents. He has a wide repertoire, playing on both the regular six-string guitar and an eleven-string alto guitar. He has given numerous concerts throughout Scandinavia, Europe, North America, Eastern Europe and China.

**SELECTED RECORDINGS**

Bach & Sor. Deutsche Grammophon DG 2531-195
Bach Lute Suites. Deutsche Grammophon DG 410 643-1
Bach Works for Lute Vol.1. Deutsche Grammophon DG 413 719-1 CD
Bach Works for Lute Vol.2. Deutsche Grammophon DG 413 719-2 CD
Cavatina. Deutsche Grammophon DG 413 720-1
Rodrigo: Concierto de Aranjuez; Fantasía para un Gentilhombre. Villa-Lobos: Concerto. Polygram 429-232 2

**SELECTED READING**

Interview. Guitar International, April 1985

*Fernando Sor*

# FERNANDO SOR

**Born – JOSEPH FERNANDO MACARI SORS**

**Barcelona, Spain 14 February 1778**

**Died – Paris, France, 8 July 1839**

PHOTO: COOPER COOPER

*Fernando Sor's grave in Paris*

Fernando Sor, one of the guitar's greatest composers and performers, received his first musical education in singing, harmony and counterpoint at a monastery, the Escolania at Montserrat. His tutor was Father Anselmo Viola. As a child, Sor had played his father's guitar, and in the monastery he studied the organ and the violin as well as singing.

After completing his studies at the age of sixteen, Sor left the monastery and returned to Barcelona. There he joined the military academy in which he was to spend the next four years. During this time he never lost his interest in music, and at the age of nineteen he presented his first opera in a Barcelona theatre. By that time he was already accepted as one of Spain's most brilliant young musicians. After hearing some guitar music by Moretti, he decided to make the guitar his main instrument.

On a visit to Madrid, Sor was commissioned by the Duke of Medina and the Duchess of Alba to write music. When the French invaded Spain, Sor wrote patriotic songs. He became a captain in the Cordoban Volunteers, but later, when virtually the whole of Spain was occupied and many thoughtful Spaniards had come to admire the ideals of the French Revolution, he made contact with French musicians in Madrid. It made his position impossible after the defeat of the French armies by Wellington, and when the French left Spain in 1813, Sor left too and made his home in Paris. Here, encouraged by Cherubini, Méhul and Berton, he resumed his musical career.

From 1815 to 1823 Fernando Sor lived in London, where his great talent on the guitar was recognized, and where he was highly successful as a guitarist, teacher and composer. His singing was also appreciated by London audiences, and while there he published more compositions for the voice than for any other instrument. His ballet Cendrillon was performed for the first time at the Kings Theatre in 1822. It was a great success, and in the following year it was performed in Paris, and later in Moscow.

From 1823 to 1826 Sor lived in Russia. Here, as in London, he enjoyed enormous popularity. In 1827-28 he was once again living in Paris, and there he decided to devote his life totally to the guitar. Other great nineteenth century guitarists were living in Paris at the same time, and Sor appeared often in concerts with Aguado and Coste.

Fernando Sor was to spend the remaining years of his life in Paris. It was during this period that he wrote his famous guitar method. It was originally published in France in 1830, and the first English translation was made by the organist and professional translator Arnold Merrick. This English edition was published in 1832 by Robert Cooke Co., London. It is one of the most remarkable guitar methods ever published, and is a lasting memorial to the genius of its author.

Fernando Sor composed over four hundred pieces for the guitar including studies, fantasies, themes with variations, and sonatas.

**SELECTED MUSIC**

| | |
|---|---|
| Complete Works for Guitar, facsimile editions, ed. Jeffery. | Tecla Editions |

**SELECTED RECORDINGS**

| | |
|---|---|
| Diego Blanco plays Sor. | BIS LP 133 |
| Alice Artzt plays Sor. | Meridian E 77006 |
| Turibio Santos plays Sor. | Erato STU 71268 |
| Segovia plays Sor and Tárrega. | MCA S 26091 |
| La Guitarre en Duo: Lemaigre/Lukowski. | Pavanne ADW 7016 |
| Rey de la Torre plays Sor. | SMC 517 |
| Fernando Sor: Complete Works for Guitar. Kazuhito Yamashita. | RCA V VDC-14 VDC-29 |

**SELECTED READING**

| | |
|---|---|
| Fernando Sor: Composer and Guitarist. Brian Jeffery. | Tecla, 1977 |
| Fernando Sor: Article. | Guitar Review No.26, 1962 |
| Fernando Sor: Article. | Guitar Review No.39, 1974 |

The Significance of Fernando Sor: Stuart Button.
Article in 'The Guitar in England 1800-1924', Garland, 1989

# DAVID STAROBIN

**Born –**

**New York City, USA**

**27 September 1949**

*David Starobin*

David N. Starobin began his guitar studies at the age of seven with Manuel Gayol in New York. From 1963 to 1967 he studied with Alberto Valdes Blain, going on to study with Aaron Shearer at the Peabody Institute in Baltimore, 1967-73.

It was during his student years at the Peabody Institute that Starobin first became involved with ensemble music. He was invited to make a recording with the Chamber Players of the Kennedy Centre in Washington D.C. Aaron Shearer, who had recommended Starobin to play the guitar with this group, soon put the young guitarist in charge of Peabody's Guitar Ensemble, 1971-73. Starobin's passion for and dedication to the advancement of the guitar in ensemble music has continued since that time.

David Starobin moved back to New York in 1974, where he joined the faculty at Brooklyn College in 1976 as Adjunct Assistant Professor, a position he holds today. He also holds associate positions at several other USA colleges, and has given masterclasses and seminars throughout the USA and Europe. He has also led an important career as a solo performer, both in the USA and in Europe. He has given première performances of over one hundred new works written and dedicated to him, including works by Elliott Carter, David Del Tredici and Charles Wuorinen.

David Starobin has also made an important contribution to Bridge Records, both as performer and as producer, and also as a music editor for numerous guitar publications for companies such as Boosey & Hawkes and G. Schirmer.

**SELECTED RECORDINGS**

| | |
|---|---|
| New Music with Guitar Volume 1. | Bridge BDG 2001 |
| New Music with Guitar Volume 2. | Bridge BDG 2004 |
| New Music with Guitar Volume 3. | Bridge BDG 2006 |
| A Song from The East. | Bridge BCD 9004 |
| New Music with Guitar Volume 4. | Bridge BCD 9022 |

**SELECTED READING**

| | |
|---|---|
| Interview. | Guitar International, March 1985 |
| David Starobin. | Classical Guitar, November 1985 |
| David Starobin. | Guitar Player, May 1986 |
| David Starobin. | Guitar Review, Autumn 1986 |
| David Starobin. | Guitar Review, Winter 1986 |
| Interview. | Guitar International, June 1987 |
| David Starobin. | Guitar Player, August 1987 |
| David Starobin. | Gramophone, August 1987 |
| Interview. | Classical Guitar, November 1989 |

# ERIK STENSTADVOLD

**Born –**

**Oslo, Norway**

**10 March 1948**

*Erik Stenstadvold*

Erik Stenstadvold began playing the guitar at the age of eleven. He studied first with a local teacher and then with Per-Olof Johnson. From 1970 to 1973 he studied at the Royal College of Music in London, where his teachers were John Williams (guitar) and Diana Poulton (lute). From 1975 to 1976 he continued his lute studies at the Schola Cantorun Baseliensis in Basle, Switzerland, with Eugen Dombois, and also medieval music under Thomas Binkley.

In 1973 Erik Stenstadvold was appointed professor of guitar at the Norwegian State Academy of Music in Oslo. He has been active as a concert performer, both as a soloist and in chamber groups, on both guitar and lute. He has performed with several of the major Norwegian orchestras and appears frequently on Norwegian radio and television. His scholarship is also impressive, and has resulted in many well-researched articles.

**SELECTED RECORDINGS**

Visions: Duo with Lars Klevstrand. Fugitive ALP 11001
Norwegian Guitar Music. Veps CD 1012

**SELECTED READING**

Coste's Contribution to Sor's 20 Studies. Soundboard Vol. XI, No. 2, 1984
Giuliani's Sixth Finger. Guitar International, August 1985
The Bother over Broken Chords. Classical Guitar, May 1987
The Guitar Methods of Dionisio Aguado. Classical Guitar, March & April 1990

# ICHIRO SUZUKI

**Born –**

**Kobe, Japan**

**9 May 1948**

*Ichiro Suzuki*

Ichiro Suzuki began to play the guitar at an early age. He gave his first public recital in Kobe, Japan, in March 1965 at the age of sixteen. He showed great talent, and won second prize in both the 11th and 12th Tokyo International Guitar Competitions, held in 1968 and 1969.

Since 1970 Ichiro Suzuki has lived in Europe, where he studied guitar with Andrés Segovia, José Tomás, Oscar Ghiglia and Leo Brouwer. At present he is music director of the Palamós International Music Festival. He lives in Paris, and gives fifty to sixty concerts annually in many countries, including Czechoslovakia, Hungary, Poland, Yugoslavia, the USSR, Japan, Australia, Africa, North and South America, Asia and the Caribbean countries. As a soloist he has performed with the Paris Concerts Colonne Orchestra, the Lyon Symphony Orchestra, the Orchestra Solistas de Cataluña, and the Tokyo Philharmonic Orchestra, amongst others. He has also accompanied the soprano Victoria de los Angeles in many of her concerts of Spanish songs.

**SELECTED RECORDINGS**

Suzuki plays Britten's Nocturnal. CMT 1045
Concertos by Hirayoshi & Tedesco. Camerata CMT 4015
From Yesterday to Penny Lane Codep-Auvidis A4846

**SELECTED READING**

Interview. Classical Guitar, May 1988

# LASZLO SZENDREY-KARPER

**Born –**

**Budapest, Hungary 28 January 1932**

**Died – 12 February 1991, Budapest**

COURTESY: COLIN COOPER

*László Szendrey-Karper*

László Szendrey-Karper began to play the guitar at the age of seven. He studied the guitar with E. Kaparti and Barna Kovats, and music with Janos Hammerslag, Aladar Racz, Ede Zathureczy and Rezso Sugár. His first public appearance as a soloist took place in 1948 in a Hungarian radio broadcast.

Szendrey-Karper was awarded first prize at the Warsaw World Youth Festival in 1955. He was also well placed in the Radio France Competition in Paris in both 1961 and 1962. In Hungary in 1962 he was awarded the Second Degree of the Liszt Prize, and in 1973 the First Degree of the same prize.

From 1957 Szendrey-Karper performed widely and made several recordings. He began teaching the guitar in 1962 at the Liszt Academy of Music in Budapest. In 1972 he wrote a method for teaching classical guitar, now the basis of the curriculum for the guitar department at the Academy of Music. László Szendrey-Karper was also an important figure in the organisation of the Esztergom International Guitar Festival, which he directed from its inception in 1972 to 1990.

**SELECTED RECORDINGS**

| | |
|---|---|
| Guitar Recital. | Qualiton LPX 1161 |
| Guitar Recital. | Hungaroton LPX 1162 |
| Vivaldi Guitar Concertos | Hungaroton SLPX 11970 |
| Geminiani: Six Sonatas. | Hungaroton SLPX 12013 |
| Guitar Music of Mertz. | Hungaroton SLPD 12894 |

**SELECTED READING**

| | |
|---|---|
| Interview. | Classical Guitar, July 1986 |

# DAVID TANENBAUM

**Born –**

**New York City**

**10 September 1956**

PHOTO: COLIN COOPER

*David Tanenbaum*

David Tanenbaum is the son of two classical musicians. He studied both the piano and the cello when very young but gave them up in favour of the electric guitar at the age of ten. A year later, after hearing Segovia play, he began classical guitar studies with Rolando Valdes-Blain in New York. He made his solo debut at the age of sixteen, and began touring the USA as a guest soloist with the Joffrey Ballet. He then studied with Aaron Shearer at the Peabody Conservatory.

After completing his studies, Tanenbaum won the first prize at the 1977 Carmel Classical Guitar Competition, and second prize at the 1978 Toronto International Competition. Since then he has appeared on concert platforms throughout the USA, Canada and Europe. He has been heard with the London Sinfonietta, the Kronos Quartet and the Steve Reich Ensemble, and has been a soloist at many festivals, including those in Bath, Lucerne, Frankfurt and the 2nd American Classical Guitar Congress, of which he was the President. He has had important new works written for him, including a guitar concerto by Hans Werner Henze entitled An Eine Aeolsharfe. David Tanenbaum has also recorded the complete Royal Winter Music by Henze on the Audiofon label. His transcriptions of Scarlatti sonatas and a Mozart Divertimento have been published by Guitar Solo Publications.

David Tanenbaum is a recipient of grants from the Martha Baird Rockefeller Fund and the NEA, and has given masterclasses at many leading universities. He is currently the chairman of the guitar department at San Francisco Conservatory of Music, and artist-in-residence of Manhattan School of Music.

**SELECTED MUSIC**

The Essential Studies: Carcassi, Sor, Brouwer. Guitar Solo

**SELECTED RECORDINGS**

Royal Winter Music: Henze. Audiofon CD 72029
Lute Masterworks . Innova Digital Archive IDA 1001-1
Estudios: The Essential Recording. Guitar Solo GSP 1000C (cassettes), GSP 1000CD (CD)
Acoustic Counterpoint. New Albion Records NA 032 CD

**SELECTED READING**

Interview. Guitar International, July 1987
Interview. Classical Guitar, October & November 1987
Article. Guitar Player, September 1986
Article. Guitar Player, September 1987

# RENATA TARRAGO

**Born –**

**Barcelona, Spain**

**1927**

*Renata Tarragó*

Renata Tarragó was first taught the guitar by her father, Graciano Tarragó, a well-known professor of guitar in Barcelona. She gave her first public recital at the age of fourteen. At sixteen she won a silver medal in the Premio del Conservatorio del Liceo. She was soon regarded as one of Spain's most leading guitar recitalists. In 1944 she finished her studies at the Conservatory of Music in Barcelona, and was appointed Assistant Professor of Guitar to her father at the same conservatory.

In 1948 Renata Tarragó appeared in London to take part in the BBC's presentation of Manuel de Falla's La Vida Breve. She also appeared in London in a recital of popular Spanish songs in collaboration with her father and the soprano Victoria de los Angeles. In 1951 she won the Premio Extraordinario award for unusual achievement created by the Conservatorio del Liceo of Barcelona. Following this, she embarked on a highly successful concert tour of Europe. In 1960 she made her first tour of the United States, her performances there receiving high critical acclaim. She officially represented Spain in the International Guitar Congress in Tokyo in 1962, receiving the award of a gold medal for her performances. In 1963 she returned to Japan for a highly successful concert tour. During the next three years she continued to give guitar recitals in most countries of the world.

In 1968 Renata Tarragó was featured with the London Philharmonic Orchestra on the soundtrack of the British film thriller Deadfall. In recent years she has spent most of her time teaching in the Barcelona area.

**SELECTED RECORDINGS**

La Guitarra de Renata Tarragó. Phillips (Spain) 843 138PY
Romance for Guitar and Orchestra (J. Barry). Stateside SL 10263
Torroba: Concerto de Castille. Erato EFM 8080 GU
Rodrigo Concerto: MorenoTorroba Suite. Columbia ML 5345
Music of Francisco Tárrega. Columbia ML 5454
Renata Tarragó. Columbia ML 5722

*Heitor Berlioz featured on French postage stamps, 1983*

*Francisco Tarrega – honoured as one of Spain's foremost personalities on Spanish postage stamps 1977*

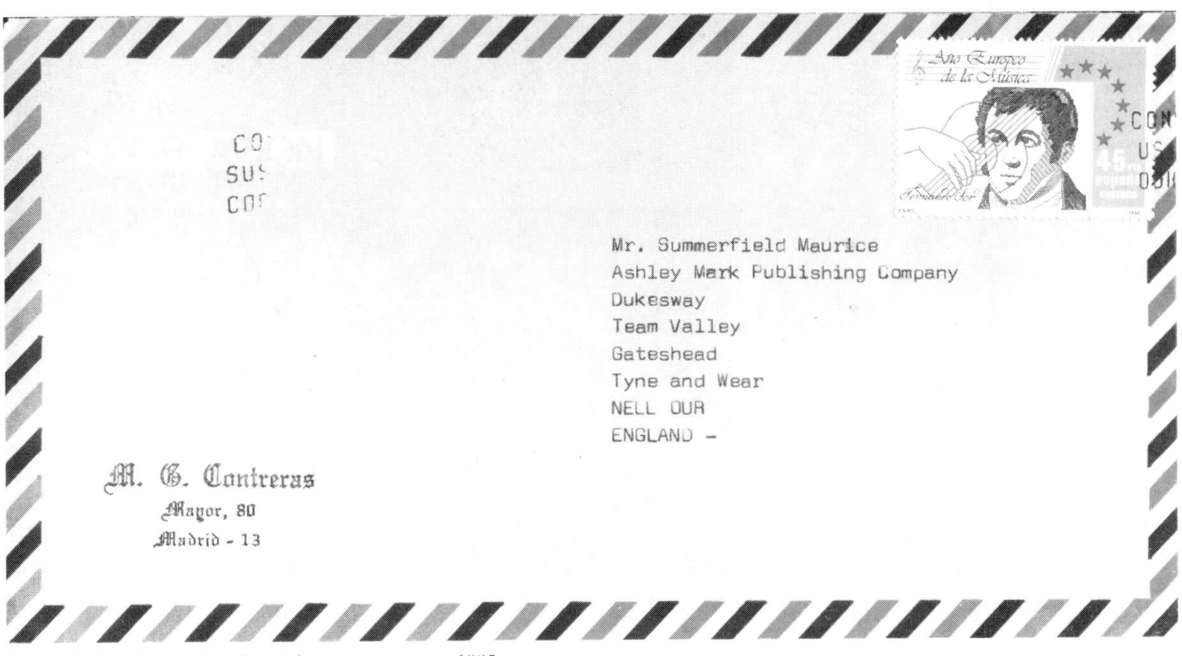


*Fernando Sor featured on Spanish postage stamps, 1985*

*Francisco Tarrega*

# FRANCISCO TARREGA

**Born – FRANCISCO DE ASSIS TARREGA EIXEA**
**Villareal de los Infantes, Castellón, Spain 21 November 1852**
**Died – Barcelona, Spain, 5 December 1909**

*Francisco Tarrega*

Francisco Tárrega's first teacher was a local player, Manuel González. The young guitarist's talent was first recognized when he played in public, in Villareal, a guitar concerto by Julián Arcas. In October 1874 Tárrega entered the Madrid Conservatory of Music as a student of harmony and composition. In 1875 he was awarded the first prize in these subjects. It has been recorded that at one of his early recitals he played half of the programme on the piano and the other half on the guitar, asking the audience to choose which they preferred. They chose the guitar, so Tárrega decided to dedicate his life to that instrument.

Francisco Tárrega then began a highly successful career as a recitalist and teacher. He toured throughout Europe, and audiences in most of the continent's major cities were able to hear his virtuoso guitar playing. He became Professor of Guitar at the Conservatories of Madrid and Barcelona. Among his many pupils were Emilio Pujol, Miguel Llobet, Daniel Fortea and Alberto Obregón.

Tárrega's vast knowledge of music enabled him to do two major things for the guitar. He improved sitting posture and the position of legs, arms and hands; he advocated the use of a footstool, and generally prepared the body to meet the demands imposed by not only the larger Torres guitar that he used but also the greatly expanded repertoire, to the creation of which he had devoted a large part of his energies. Particular attention was paid to improving the action of the fingers of each hand; and there seems little doubt that he drew on his expert knowledge of piano playing techniques, adapting their principles to the guitar.

Francisco Tárrega's other great contribution to the classical guitar was the improvement of the repertoire. Almost all other professional guitarists at that time played nothing but their own compositions. Napoléon Coste, one of Sor's pupils, made a few arrangements for the guitar of music written for other instruments, whereas guitarists of an earlier age, notably Giuliani and Carulli, had made many transcriptions. Tárrega continued and extended that tradition, transcribing works by Schumann, Chopin, Beethoven, Bach and other composers, including contemporary ones. He was especially successful with piano solos by Granados and Albéniz. It is said that Albéniz, on hearing Tárrega play one of his piano pieces on the guitar, declared that he preferred the guitar version to the original.

Francisco Tárrega has often been called the founder of the modern guitar school, a title well earned, although he did advocate the right-hand 'no nail' technique, a technique which today is not employed by most of the world's foremost guitarists. A man of great modesty and humbleness, Francisco Tárrega maintained his intense devotion to the guitar and music throughout his life. He died of apoplexy in 1909 at the age of 55.

Without doubt Francisco Tárrega was one of the greatest classical guitarists of all time. It was due to his commitment and energy through the latter half of the nineteenth century that the way was opened for the great guitarists of the twentieth century, in particular Andrés Segovia, to demonstrate to the world the enormous musical potential of the classical guitar.

**SELECTED MUSIC**

| | |
|---|---|
| Capricho Arabe. | Bèrben |
| The Carnival of Venice. | EMB |
| Complete Preludes. | Universal 13408 |
| Danza Mora. | Ricordi (BA) 9900 |
| Gavotta, Pavana, Mazurka | Bèrben |
| Gran Jota Aragonese. | Ricordi (BA) 7924 |
| Gran Vals. | Ricordi (BA) 7321 |
| La Alborada (Music Box). | Ricordi (BA) 7923 |
| Maria. | Ricordi (BA) 9068 |
| Marieta. | Ricordi (BA) 12075 |
| Danza Mora & Capricho Arabe | Guitar Archives – Schott 451 |
| Danza Odalisca. | Ricordi (BA) 12074 |
| Eighteen Original Studies. | Ricordi (BA) 11365 |
| Pavane, ed. Savio. | Ricordi (BA) 3215 |
| Recuerdos de la Alhambra. | Ricordi 2001 |
| Rosita: Polka. | Ricordi (BA) 12076 |
| Sueño! | Ricordi (BA) 11393 |
| Thirty Original Preludes. | Ricordi (BA) 12720 |

**SELECTED RECORDINGS**

| | |
|---|---|
| Alice Artzt plays Tárrega. | Meridian E77026 |
| Segovia plays Tárrega. | MCA S 26091 |
| Rey de la Torre plays Tárrega. | SMC 516 |
| Leif Christensen plays Tárrega. | Paula |

**SELECTED READING**

Tárrega: Ensayo Biographico.
Emilio Pujol: Ramos and Alfonso, 1960

Is There a School of Tárrega?
Guitar Review No.1, 1946

Complete list of works. Guitar and Lute No.5, 1977

*A sketch of Francisco Tarrega drawn by Miguel Llobet*

*Tarrega playing to an audience of his disciples*

# JOSÉ TOMAS

**Born –**

**Alicante, Spain**

**26 August, 1934**

*José Tomás*

Encouraged by his father, José Tomás was originally self-taught on the guitar. His first serious musical education was with the Spanish pianist Oscar Esplá.

It was soon realized that Tomás was a talented player, and he went to Madrid to study with Regino Sainz de la Maza. In Madrid he met Alirio Díaz who, after hearing the young guitarist play, advised him to go and study at the Guitar School in Siena, Italy. José Tomás went to Siena in 1955, and it was there that he first met Andrés Segovia.

From 1956 to 1957 José Tomás was in the Spanish army. In 1958 he went for two years to Santiago de Compostela, where he worked with Emilio Pujol. He had kept contact with Andrés Segovia since their first meeting in Siena, and Segovia, having recognized Tomás's exceptional teaching ability, asked him to be his assistant at his masterclasses. Since that time Tomás has devoted most of his career to teaching, although he is a fine recitalist and has appeared in concerts throughout Europe, the Middle East, Japan and the United States of America.

Around 1974 José Tomás changed to an 8-string guitar built by José Ramírez. The 7th string is tuned D below E, and the 8th string is tuned F above low E.

José Tomás lives in his native town of Alicante, where he teaches at the Oscar Esplá Conservatory and directs the guitar programme there. For many years he spent his summers at Santiago de Compostela directing Segovia's masterclasses.

**SELECTED READING**

| | |
|---|---|
| José Tomás. | Guitar Player, March 1981 |
| Interview. | Nova Giulianiad, 9/10 1986 |
| Interview. | Classical Guitar, March 1987 |
| Interview. | Classical Guitar, 1990 |

**SELECTED RECORDING**

José Tomás – Guitar Recital. Crown (Japan) SW-2001

*A classical guitar with a revolutionary design by guitarist Abel Carlevaro and constructed by Manuel Contreras since 1983*

# REY DE LA TORRE

**Born – JOSÉ REY DE LA TORRE**

**Gibara, Cuba**

**9 December 1917**

*Rey de la Torre*

Rey de la Torre began studying music and the guitar as a child in Havana, Cuba. His first teacher was Severino Lopez. After five years of study he astounded audiences with his ability after he had given several public recitals and some radio broadcasts.

Such was his success that the young guitarist travelled to Spain to continue his studies with Miguel Llobet in Barcelona. In 1933 he appeared in concert with great success at the Granados Academy.

In 1939 Rey de la Torre moved to New York, and established himself there as a leading recitalist and teacher of the guitar. His Town Hall concert in 1941 was widely acclaimed. Since that time he has made the USA his home, although he has appeared in concerts all over the world. He has appeared on numerous occasions on radio and television, and performed Rodrigo's Concierto de Aranjuez with the Cleveland Symphony Orchestra. He has had several pieces specially written for him by prominent contemporary composers including Julian Orbón, José Ardevol and Joaquín Nin-Culmell.

In recent times ill health has compelled Rey de la Torre to give up performing, but he continues to teach.

**SELECTED RECORDINGS**

| | |
|---|---|
| 20th Century Music for Guitar. | Elektra EKL 244 |
| Plays Classical Guitar. | Epic LC 3418 |
| Virtuoso Guitar. | Epic LC 3479 |
| Romantic Guitar. | Epic LC 3564 |
| Music for One and Two Guitars. | Epic LC 3674 |
| Spanish Music for the Classical Guitar. | Nonesuch 2590-001 |

**SELECTED READING**

Rey de la Torre. Guitar Player, October 1975

# MICHAEL TRÖSTER

**Born –**

**Schweinfurt, West Germany**

**26 October 1956**

*Michael Tröster*

Michael Tröster first studied the guitar with Gerhard Vogt in his home town of Schweinfurt, in 1966. He showed great promise and went on to study with Siegfried Behrend, Konrad Ragossnig, Karl Scheit and others. In 1972 he was a prizewinner in a national competition, Jugend Musiziert. In 1973 he won the first prize in his category in the Bavarian Guitar Competition.

Tröster continued his competition successes, winning a prize in 1977 in the 22nd national selection of young artists, Podium Junger Solisten. In 1980 he won first prize in the Deutschen Musikwettbewerb (German Music Competition), and in 1981 first prize at the Wettbewerb der Deutschen Musikhochschulen (German Music Colleges Competition). In 1983 he won a national award for the encouragement of young artists; and in the following year he won first prize at the 19th Milan International Guitar Competition and first prize in the Villa-Lobos Competition held in Milan.

Since that time Michael Tröster has performed throughout Europe, Australasia and Japan, and made many recordings for several companies. From 1980 to 1986 he was a teacher at the College and Conservatory of Würzburg. Since 1986 he has been director of a class at the Kassel Academy of Music.

**SELECTED RECORDINGS**

Etuden meisterhaft gespielt: Die Gitarre. Schwann VMS 712/13
Repertoire für junge Gitarristen. Calig CLG 30 902
Mertz, Carulli, Chopin, Mozart, Sor. EMI 567 747 5882
Berlin Guitar Ensemble & Michael Tröster. Electrola ASD 308 222
Walton, Sor, Legnani and Giuliani. Electrola ASD 308 223
Berlin Guitar Ensemble & Michael Tröster. Electrola ASD 741
Michael Tröster plays Villa-Lobos. Thorofon Capella CTH 2052
Music for Mandolin & Guitar (with Gertrud Weyhofen): Vivaldi etc. Thorofon
Michael Tröster plays Sonatas by Ponce, Berkeley, Rodrigo, Turina, Tedesco. Thorofon

**SELECTED READING**

Interview. Gitarre & Laute, Winter 1988

# JAMES TYLER

**Born – JAMES HENRY TYLER**

**Hartford, Connecticut, USA**

**3 August 1940**

*James Tyler*

James Tyler studied at the Hartt College of Music and the University of Connecticut. He took private tuition on the lute with Joseph Iadone. He made his concert debut at the Library of Congress, Washington D.C. in 1961, and played at the White House a year later. During this period he also performed as guest soloist with the New York Pro Musica, with whom he also recorded.

Tyler left the USA in 1967 for Germany to continue his research into the history of the lute and its music. In 1969 he came to London and soon established himself as one of the finest lutenists and early musicians around. He joined the Early Music Consort of London and Musica Reservata, and performed with them throughout the world.

For many years James Tyler has been a prominent member of The Julian Bream Consort. In 1976 he formed the London Early Music Group, an ensemble specializing in the performance of medieval and Renaissance music. Recognized internationally as an authority on early plucked instruments, Tyler has contributed articles to many learned journals, including Grove's Dictionary of Music & Musicians and Early Music magazine. His book The Early Guitar, published in 1980, is regarded as the definitive work on the instrument and its music.

**SELECTED RECORDINGS**

Music of the Renaissance Virtuosi. Saga 5438
The Early Guitar Saga 5455
English Social Music (with Barry Mason). Saga 5467
Italian Bel Canto Arias (with Barry Mason). Hyperion A 66153

**SELECTED READING**

The Early Guitar. Oxford University Press, 1980
A Brief Tutor for Baroque Guitar. Chorus, 1984

# TERRY USHER

**Born – TERENCE FLETCHER USHER**

**Manchester, England, 7 May 1909**

**Died – Manchester, 12 April 1969**

Terry Usher started to play the guitar in 1932. In 1936 he began to teach and write about the guitar for the musical press. In the same year he broadcast for the first time, and was then frequently heard on the radio playing guitar solos and with various instrumental ensembles. In 1937 he heard Andrés Segovia play at a concert in Liverpool, and was so impressed that he began a serious study of the classical guitar soon afterwards. Usher soon came to be regarded as one of Britain's authorities on the instrument and its music.

In 1945 Terry Usher began teaching the classical guitar, and embarked on a series of lecture-recitals to music societies under the auspices of the Hallé Concerts Society and the Arts Council of Great

COURTESY: JOHN W. DUARTE

*Terry Usher*

Britain. On 24 March 1954 he was appointed Tutor for the Guitar to the Royal Manchester College of Music.

Terry Usher wrote and arranged extensively for the guitar. His published compositions include Impromptu and Minuet, Canzoncina and Arabesque and Epitaph for Manuel Ponce. He was a member of the editorial board and editor of the academy section of Guitar Review, New York. He was also a regular contributor on the classical guitar to BMG magazine, and a founder member of the Manchester Guitar Circle.

Terry Usher continued his total involvement with the guitar until his death after a stroke in April 1969.

**SELECTED MUSIC**

Inmpromptu and Minuet. Schott
Canzoncina and Arabesque. Schott

**SELECTED READING**

The Spanish Guitar in the Nineteenth and Twentieth Centuries: Usher.
The Galpin Society Journal No.IX, June 1956

## ALBERT VALDES BLAIN

**Born –**

**Havana, Cuba**

**10 April 1921**

*Roland and Albert Valdes Blain*

In 1924 Albert Valdes Blain's parents moved to the United States of America and settled in New York. Blain's enthusiasm for the classical guitar was aroused by the early concerts of Andrés Segovia in that city.

Blain studied with the Uruguayan concert guitarist Julio Martínez Oyanguren for three years. He also studied piano and composition at the Greenwich House Music School and the Juilliard School of Music, New York.

For many years Albert Valdes Blain was regarded as one of the foremost classical guitar recitalists in the United States. He made his debut in 1941 at the Carnegie Chamber Music Hall, and appeared in concerts throughout the North American continent for many years. He has also broadcast on both radio and television on most of the important American networks.

It is as a teacher that Albert Valdes Blain has been one of the most important figures in the American guitar scene in recent years. He has taught the classical guitar at the Greenwich House Music School, The School for Musical Education, and at the Brooklands Conservatory for Music. He also has his own studio in New York, and many of today's best-known American guitarists have studied with him.

**SELECTED READING**

Albert Valdes Blain. — Guitar Player, November 1979

## ROLAND VALDES BLAIN

**Born –**

**Havana, Cuba**

**1922**

The younger brother of Albert Valdes Blain, Roland Valdes Blain originally studied with the Uruguayan guitarist Julio Martínez Oyanguren. He later went to Spain to give concerts and to work in advanced study with Regino Sainz de la Maza at the Royal Conservatory of Madrid, from which he graduated with the Grand Prize Award for concert guitar playing.

Since that time he has toured extensively throughout the main cities of the United States, Canada, South America and Spain. He has also appeared on the major radio and television networks in the United States, played and composed for various Broadway theatrical productions and appeared with several major symphony orchestras as guest soloist.

Roland Valdes Blain currently lives in New York, and maintains a busy career as a guitar recitalist and teacher.

**SELECTED RECORDING**

La Guitarra. — Roulette SR-25055

# BENJAMIN VERDERY

**Born – BENJAMIN FRANCIS VERDERY**

**Danbury, Connecticut, USA**

**1 October 1955**

*Benjamin Verdery*

Benjamin Verdery graduated in 1978 at The State University of New york at Purchase. He studied guitar with Frederic Hand and Phillip de Fremery.

Since his duo debut recital with his wife, the flautist Rie Schmidt, in New York in 1980, Benjamin Verdery has performed extensively throughout the USA, Canada and Europe. He has appeared at many major festivals, given masterclasses, and appeared on both radio and television. He has commissioned and performed several new works for guitar by Anthony Newman, Alvin Brehm, David Leisner, Frederic Hand, Roberto Sierra and Ernesto Cordero.

Verdery has appeared at the South Bank Festival in London with John Williams and Paco Peña. He has also performed or taught at other leading European festivals, including Paco Peña's International Guitar Festival in Córdoba, Spain.

A member of the roster of Affiliate Artists, Benjamin Verdery is also on the faculty at Yale University, the Artistic Director of the D'Addario Foundation for the Performing Arts and is a regular columnist for Guitar Player magazine.

**SELECTED RECORDINGS**

| | |
|---|---|
| Music by Anthony Newman. | Cambridge CRS B 2833 |
| Bach Transcriptions for Guitar. | Sine Qua Non 79040 (cassette only) |
| French Music for Flute & Guitar. | Newport Classics NC 0010 (cassette & CD) |
| Bach: Two Generations. | Musical Heritage Society 7397A (cassette, CD, LP) |
| American Guitar Music. | Newport NPD 85509 CD |
| Essentials of Classical Guitar – Instructional Video. | Workshop Arts, USA |

**SELECTED READING**

| | |
|---|---|
| Interview. | Guitar International, December 1984 |
| Article. | Classical Guitar, May/June 1984 |
| Interview. | Guitar Player, August 1984 |
| Interview. | Classical Guitar, March 1985 |
| Interview. | Guitar Player, June 1985 |

# ANDRE VERDIER

**Born – Paris, France**

**1 November 1886**

**Died – Paris, 13 December 1957**

*André Verdier*

André Verdier studied music from the age of six. He had a fine soprano voice as a child, and became a soloist in Paris churches. When his voice broke he studied the flute at the Paris Conservatoire. Later he studied the guitar under Rodriguez Aravena. Verdier met Miguel Llobet in Paris, and this great guitarist introduced him to the Tárrega method of playing.

At the age of eighteen André Verdier decided to enlist in the army to make his career as a military musician. He remained in this occupation until he was twenty-three, working at perfecting his flute playing and also studying harmony, but on returning to civilian life he could not make a living either as a flautist or a guitarist. He learnt to play the banjo, and within a relatively short time was known all over Paris for his virtuoso banjo playing in night clubs and cabarets.

Verdier's great contribution to the classical guitar in France was his foundation, in collaboration with Emilio Pujol, of 'Les Amis de la Guitare' in 1936. Verdier arranged regular meetings in his house in Ile St Louis, Notre Dame, Paris. One of the first important acts of the society was a pilgrimage to the tomb of Fernando Sor, which had been rediscovered by Verdier and the Danish guitarist W. Ostergoart in 1934. They arranged for a commemorative plaque to be placed on the tomb, and homage was thus paid to the great nineteenth century guitarist.

In 1939, during a recital of 'Les Amis de la Guitare', Verdier presented the child prodigy Ida Presti. The society made her an honorary member and greatly helped her in her career. It was in Verdier's house that Ida Presti met Alexandre Lagoya years later.

André Verdier was a teacher of music who specialised in teaching the guitar. He was also an enthusiastic collector of classical guitars and of guitar music and manuscripts. No single person did more to promote the classical guitar in France than André Verdier.


**SELECTED READING**

André Verdier. Guitar Review, No.22, 1958


# ROBERT J. VIDAL

**Born –**

**Paris, France**

**6 May 1925**

Robert Vidal is one of the most notable guitar personalities in the classical guitar world today. For almost forty years his promotions on behalf of the guitar have been prolific in number and generally excellent in quality. He has presented programmes on French radio and television devoted exclusively to the guitar. He has also produced an excellent series of classical guitar records for the RCA and Erato labels, featuring such famous guitarists as Turibio Santos, Oscar Cáceres, Leo Brouwer, Maria Luisa Anido, Betho Davezac and the Pomponio-Zarate Duo.

Vidal's Concours International de Guitare, held in Paris and sponsored by ORTF, has become of the most important annual international classical guitar

COURTESY: RADIO FRANCE

*Robert Vidal*

events. The first was held in 1958. The event has gone from strength to strength, and has been an important stepping-stone in the career of many of today's leading classical guitarists.

Robert Vidal travels widely, attending festivals, lecturing and adjudicating. In 1976 he organised the Festival Mondial de la Guitare in Martinique, in which guitarists from twenty-three countries participated.

Robert Vidal's exceptional efforts on behalf of the guitar have been applauded by Andrés Segovia, Emilio Pujol, John Williams and Leo Brouwer among many other prominent classical guitarists who have recognized his vital contribution to their instrument.


**SELECTED READING**

Notes sur la Guitare: Robert Vidal. EMT 1779

*Heitor Villa-Lobos*

# HEITOR VILLA-LOBOS

**Born – Rio de Janeiro, Brazil**

**5 March 1887**

**Died – Rio de Janeiro, 17 November 1959**

*Heitor Villa-Lobos*

Heitor Villa-Lobos began his musical studies at the age of six with his father, a writer and amateur musician. Encouraged by his father, he learnt to play cello, guitar, clarinet and piano. After his father's death, when he was eleven years old, Villa-Lobos became almost entirely self-taught in all aspects of music. At a very early age he began to improvize on popular Brazilian melodies, but his first original composition was a piece for the guitar, Panqueca. He began to play the guitar in one of the small music groups known as 'chôros', and at the age of seventeen played the cello in theatres, cinemas, cabarets and other small and large orchestras in Rio. About this time he enrolled in the National Institute of Music. He had intended to study composition but soon found that he did not like formal study, and left the institute. For five years he travelled in Brazil, studying the music of the people and absorbing the varied landscape and picturesque style of life, and recognizing it as something of his own which he would incorporate into his compositions.

In 1928 Villa-Lobos met the pianist Artur Rubinstein and the composer Darius Milhaud. This meeting, and his love of the music of Debussy, influenced Villa-Lobos in his decision to go to Paris in 1923. It was presumed that he was going there to study European music, but he made it known that he was going there to show European musicians what he had done. His music caused excitement in Paris, and attracted world-wide attention to him.

Villa-Lobos lived in Paris until 1929. It was during this period that he met Andrés Segovia. The result of their meeting was that Villa-Lobos would compose some of the most beautiful music in the modern guitar repertory.

Upon his return to Brazil, Villa-Lobos played an important part in the national campaign to provide general education. In 1932 he was appointed Supervisor and Director of Musical Education in Brazil, and became an educator and illustrator. He invented revolutionary ideas for musical instruction and was especially interested in the development of community singing. In recognition of his achievements and instruction in choral singing, the Federal Government of Brazil in 1943 made him Director of the newly founded Conservatorio Nacional de Canto Orfeônico.

Villa-Lobos received an impressive number of honours. In addition to a citation presented to him by the Mayor of New York for distinguished and exceptional service, he was awarded honorary degrees from several universities, was an Officer of the Legion of Honour in France, and an honorary member of the French Institute. He was an honorary member of the American Academy of Arts and Letters, and of the Accademia de Santa Cecilia in Rome. He was also President of the Brazilian Academy.

Villa-Lobos composed around 2,000 works. The best known of his guitar works are Suite Populaire Brésilienne (written in 1912, published in 1955); Twelve Studies (written in 1929, published in 1952); Five Preludes (written in 1940, published in 1954); and Concerto for Guitar and Small Orchestra (written in 1951).

**SELECTED MUSIC**

| | |
|---|---|
| Chôros No.1. | ESC 7418 |
| Five Preludes. | ESC 6731-35 |
| Suite Populaire Brésilienne. | ESC 6737, 6738, 6793, 6794, 6817 |
| Twelve Studies. | ESC 6679 |
| Mystic Sextet (1917). | ESC 6679 |
| Concerto for Guitar and Small Orchestra. | ESC 7993 |

**SELECTED RECORDINGS**

| | |
|---|---|
| Concerto for Guitar and Small Orchestra: Laurindo Almeida. | (Capitol) Master 8638 |
| Villa-Lobos Music for the Spanish Guitar: Laurindo Almeida. | (Capitol) Master 8497 |
| Manuel Barrueco: Etudes, Suite Populaire. | Turnabout TV 34676S |
| Barrueco plays The Music of Brazil. | Vox FSM 53-043 |
| Guitar Music of Villa-Lobos and Torroba: Julian Bream. | HMV CLP 1763 |
| Sexteto Místico, Bachianas Brasileiras No.5: Bergström. | Proprius PRCD 9021 |
| Julian Bream plays Villa-Lobos: Concerto, Preludes, Suite Populaire). | RCA SB 6852 |

Twelve Etudes & Suite Populaire:
Julian Bream. RCA RL 12499
Eduardo Fernández: 5 Preludes, 12 Studies. Decca 414 616-1
Eliot Fisk plays Villa-Lobos etc. EMI 14-6757-1
Guitar Music of Villa-Lobos: Eric Hill. Saga 5453
Lagoya plays Villa-Lobos & Sor. Philips 6504 131
Thomas Müller-Pering: 5 Preludes, 12 Etudes. Firebird K32Y 248
Konrad Ragossnig: Preludes. Supraphon 1-11-1040
Florilège de la Guitare 20: Brazilian Music:
Turibio Santos. Erato STU 70913
Twelve Studies: Turibio Santos. Erato STU 1007, Erato STU 70496
Concerto/Sextuor Mystique/
Preludes: Turibio Santos. Erato STU 70566
Maria Livia São Marcos: 12 Studies. Fermata 305-1039
Michael Tröster: 5 Preludes, 12 Studies, Suite Populaire, etc. Capella CTH 2052 CD
John Williams: Concerto CBS 76369
Narciso Yepes: 5 Preludes. DGG 2530 140

**SELECTED READING**


Villa-Lobos. Guitar Review, No.21, 1957
I Met Villa-Lobos: Segovia. Guitar Review No.22, 1959
Villa-Lobos. Guitar Review No.29, 1966
Villa-Lobos: Marcel Beaufils (French edition). Agir, 1967
Villa-Lobos. Guitar & Lute, October 1980
Voice-leading: Towards a better understanding: Schaffer. Soundboard, November 1980
Villa-Lobos. Guitar Player, July 1981
Heitor Villa-Lobos and the Guitar:
Turibio Santos (trans. Forde & Wade). Wise Owl Music, 1985
Grosse Fugue Villa-Lobos: Brian Hodel. Guitar Review, Fall 1987
Villa-Lobos and the Guitar: Brian Hodel. Guitar Review, Winter 1988
The Guitar Works of Heitor Villa-Lobos: Jukka Savijoki. Guitar International, May, June, July, August, September 1987, and March, April 1988.
Villa-Lobos: Lisa Peppercorn. Omnibus Press, 1989

*Segovia and Villa-Lobos and friends, Mrs Villa-Lobos is directly behind them*

# LUISE WALKER

**Born –**

**Vienna, Austria**

**9 September 1910**

*Luise Walker*

Luise Walker began to study the guitar at the age of eight. Her first teacher was the well-known Viennese guitarist Dr Josef Zuth. She subsequently studied at the State Musical Academy in Vienna under Professor Ortner. Luise Walker was also fortunate to be able to take lessons with Heinrich Albert and Miguel Llobet, both of whom were frequent guests at her parents' home in Vienna.

From 1940 Luise Walker devoted her life to guitar. Over the years she has made many concert tours of Europe, Russia and the United States. For many years she has been Professor of Guitar at the State Musical Academy of Vienna. She is also a highly respected composer, and many of her solos, studies and arrangements have been published, including Daily Studies for the Guitar and The Young Guitarist (published by V. Hladky, Vienna).

**SELECTED RECORDINGS**

| | |
|---|---|
| Guitar Recital | Supraphon 1-11-1230 |
| Paganini Quartet & Terzetto. | Turnabout TV 34322S |
| Guitar Music in Vienna. | Turnabout TV 34171S |

**SELECTED READING**

Ein Leben mit der Gitarre: Walker.
Zimmermann, Frankfurt a.M, 1989.

# TIMOTHY WALKER

**Born –**

**Durban, South Africa**

**13 May 1943**

*Timothy Walker*

Timothy Walker was born in South Africa of British parents. His father was a well-known journalist, writer, broadcaster and music critic.

Walker began playing the guitar at the age of twelve to accompany himself in the popular songs of the day. He eventually changed to the classical guitar, and when Narciso Yepes first toured South Africa he was invited by the Spanish guitarist to study with him in Madrid. This Walker did for two years before settling in London, where he gave his debut concert at the Wigmore Hall in 1970. He also studied with Ida Presti, Alexandre Lagoya and John Williams. The latter recommended him for work with the 'Fires of London', the modern classical group directed by Peter Maxwell Davies. Timothy Walker played regularly with this group until they disbanded in the middle 1980s.

Timothy Walker is currently the guitarist with the London Sinfonietta, and has played with the London Symphony Orchestra, the BBC Symphony Orchestra and the Royal Philharmonic Orchestra, amongst others. He has also appeared with small groups such as the Melos Ensemble and the Ensemble Musique Vivants. He has given concerts throughout Great Britain, Europe, South America and the United States.

Timothy Walker was the guitar soloist (playing electric guitar) in a 1977 Prom at the Royal Albert Hall, London. In 1978 he played duets with John Williams at the Queen Elizabeth Hall, London, in a Sor Bicentenary concert. His first solo tour of the United States took place in 1978, and was followed by a tour of South America with the soprano Mary Thomas. He has composed several original pieces for the guitar, including a concerto.

**SELECTED MUSIC**

| | |
|---|---|
| African Light Suite. | Belwin Mills SI 115 |
| Fantasia Celestina. | Belwin Mills SI 120 |
| Prelude. | Belwin Mills SI 122 |

**SELECTED RECORDINGS**

| | |
|---|---|
| Baroque Music. | Saga 5426 |
| Timothy Walker: Guitar. | Decca 6-42344 |
| Guitar Encores. | L'Oiseau-Lyre SOL 349 |
| Classical Folk Guitar. | Hyperion A66027 |
| Folk Songs and Music for Two Guitars. | Max Sound MSCB 27 |
| Viennese Songs & Sonata: Giuliani. | Max Sound MSCB 28 |

**SELECTED READING**

| | |
|---|---|
| Timothy Walker. | Guitar, January 1974 |
| Sir Peter Maxwell Davies with Timothy Walker. | Classical Guitar, December 1987 & January 1988 |
| Technical Articles. | Classical Guitar, 1986 & 1987 |

# NORIHIKO WATANABE

**Born –**

**Kobe, Japan**

**11 September 1948**

*Norihiko Watanabe*

Norihiko Watanabe is currently one of the leading classical players in Japan. He showed great progress on the guitar in his youth, and became a student of Jiro Matsuda. He was also enthusiastic about becoming a guitar maker, and studied the construction of the instrument with Masaru Kohno.

In 1966 Watanabe won first prize at the Guitar Concours of Japan. In 1969 he won first prize at the Concours International de Guitare in Paris. His success at these competitions has established him as one of the best classical guitarists to have emerged during the 1960s.

Norihiko Watanabe now spends most of his time in Japan, where he gives recitals, teaches and is also a recording artist for RCA.

**SELECTED RECORDINGS**

| | |
|---|---|
| Villa-Lobos, Tansman, Torroba. | RCA (Japan) RVC 2272 |
| In Concert. | Denon (Japan) OS 7033 ND |
| Guitar Recital. | RCA GG 1001 |

# BUNYAN WEBB

**Born – BUNYAN MONROE WEBB Jnr.**

**San Francisco, USA,1936**

**Died – San Francisco, 14 November 1978**

*Bunyan Webb*

Bunyan Webb received his Bachelor of Arts degree from South Western University in pre-medicine, then decided to pursue a career in music, in which he graduated at California State University at Fresno.

Webb then studied classical guitar at the Conservatory of Valencia, Spain, and later in masterclasses with Julian Bream, Andrés Segovia, Ida Presti and Alexandre Lagoya. Following this, he began a highly successful career as a guitar authority and teacher, giving concerts throughout the United States, Europe and Japan.

Webb made a valuable contribution to the promotion of the classical guitar in the United States of America as a member of the Affiliated Artists programme. He acquainted a large variety of audiences with the classical guitar, and performed and recorded with guitar in duos with viola, flute, voice and harpsichord. In addition to this active concert life, he held formal teaching positions at Blair Academy at Peabody in Nashville, the University of North Carolina at Raleigh, the Inter-American University in Puerto Rico, and held teachers' seminars for Guitar '78 in Toronto and for ASTA in New Orleans. He also held well-attended masterclasses and workshops for classical guitar throughout the United States.

Over the years Bunyan Webb collected an extensive library of manuscripts, books and records, now housed at the San Francisco Conservatory of Music. He died suddenly in 1978 while scuba diving in California.

# CARL MARIA VON WEBER

**Born – Eutin, Nr. Lübeck, Germany**

**18 December 1786**

**Died – London, England, 4 June 1826**

*Carl Maria von Weber*

Carl Maria von Weber was a founder of German national opera and is regarded as one of the most influential German composers of the early nineteenth century. The son of a travelling theatre director, he showed great musical talent from an early age. He wrote his first opera at the age of thirteen, and at seventeen was appointed as a conductor in Breslau. Later, after working for the Duke of Württemberg for a little while, the young composer had problems with his career and had to earn a living as a critic and writer, with some performing, in Darmstadt. In 1813 he was appointed conductor of the German theatre in Prague, and in 1816 he was appointed director of the court opera in Dresden. These appointments renewed Weber's success, and his operas continued to be acclaimed throughout Europe until his early death, of consumption, in London in 1826.

Weber, an excellent pianist (his large hands could stretch an interval of a twelfth), was also a very accomplished guitarist. He loved the instrument, and it was his constant companion. Many of his most beautiful songs were originally written with guitar accompaniment, and he wrote for the guitar throughout his short life. During his stay in Prague he wrote Five Songs with Guitar Accompaniment, Op.25, and in December 1816, whilst living in Berlin, he completed his Duo for Guitar and Pianoforte, Op.38. He also included a duet for two guitars in the incidental music he wrote in 1821 for Donna Diana, a musical version of a play by Moreto.

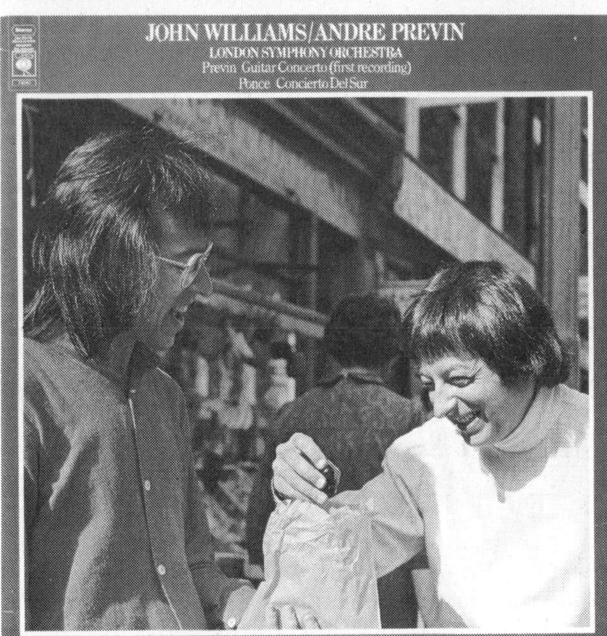

*Selection of John Williams recordings*

# JOHN WILLIAMS

**Born – JOHN CHRISTOPHER WILLLIAMS**

**Melbourne, Australia**

**24 April 1941**

*John Williams*

John Williams began playing the guitar at the age of seven, receiving his first lessons from his father, Len Williams, the well-known guitarist and teacher. He quickly showed himself to be a most gifted pupil, and when the family moved to London in 1952 he was taken to meet Segovia, who was deeply impressed by the eleven-year old boy's talent.

Williams began studying with Segovia, and on his recommendation undertook a full musical education. He entered the Accademia Musicale Chigiana in Siena, Italy, where Segovia himself taught at the Summer School each year. John Williams held a scholarship at the school for the following five years. During that time he gained one of its most coveted prizes, receiving the unprecedented honour of giving the first complete solo recital by a student of any instrument. He also gave a performance of the Castelnuovo-Tedesco Concerto in Siena.

In England, John Williams attended the Royal College of Music from 1956 to 1959, studying piano and musical theory. On 6 November 1958 he made his London debut at the Wigmore Hall. Other highly successful debuts followed, with appearances in Paris in 1959 and in Madrid in 1961. In 1962 he toured the USSR and visited Japan and the United States for the first time in 1963.

In recent years the career of John Williams has developed along many diverse lines, and his constant striving to cross musical barriers has led to some interesting ventures and collaborations. One of the most notable was his appearance at Ronnie Scott's jazz club in London. In 1970 he became one of the artistic directors, with John Dankworth, Cleo Laine and Richard Rodney Bennett, of the Wavendon Theatre. In April 1970 he appeared again at Ronnie Scott's, on the same bill as the rock group 'Soft Machine'. Also in 1970 he took part in a concert at the Royal Albert Hall, held in aid of the families of Greek political prisoners. Later that year he recorded with the Greek singer Maria Farandouri an album of music by Mikis Theodorakis. During 1970 he also played on the soundtrack of the film The Raging Moon. In the studios he met the composer and arranger Stanley Myers, and this led to the making of John Williams's first popular album Changes, arranged and produced by Myers. Williams had already recorded several classical albums for the CBS label.

Several important composers have dedicated works to John Williams. André Previn's Guitar Concerto was given its first performance in November 1971 under the direction of the composer, at a London Symphony Orchestra gala concert. Stephen Dodgson has written several works for Williams, including Partita No.1 in 1964, Fantasy-Divisions in 1969 and, more recently, Stemma in 1988.

John Williams has managed to bridge more musical barriers than any other living guitarist. For some years his classical/rock fusion group 'Sky' achieved enormous popular success. Likewise his concert appearances and recordings with the popular jazz singer Cleo Laine have attracted vast audiences who had never previously appreciated the classical guitar. His group 'John Williams and Friends', an occasional ensemble with a strong Latin American content, attracts large audiences wherever it plays. John Williams has also performed duo concerts with another celebrated guitarist, Julian Bream, the result of which was three very successful recordings. For three years Williams was the artistic director of London's South Bank Summer Festival.

John Williams currently spends part of each year in his native Australia, but continues to travel the world, make recordings and give a considerable number of concerts, a constant reminder that his ability and achievements with the classical guitar must be counted among the very highest the world has known.

**SELECTED RECORDINGS**

Guitar Recital: Volume One. Ace of Diamonds SDD R328
Guitar Recital: Volume Two. Ace of Diamonds SDD R329
Twenty Studies for Guitar: F. Sor. Pathé-Marion C-065 93404
Virtuoso Music for Guitar. CBS 72348
John Williams, Wilfred Brown: Songs and Poems with Guitar. CBS 61126

| | |
|---|---|
| Two Favourite Guitar Concertos. | CBS 72439 |
| More Virtuoso Music for Guitar. | CBS 72526 |
| John Williams Plays Guitar Concertos. | CBS 72661 |
| Haydn Guitar Quartet: with Paganini Trio. | CBS 72678 |
| Virtuoso Variations for Guitar. | CBS 72728 |
| John Williams plays Spanish Music. | CBS 72860 |
| Songs and Guitar Pieces by Theodorakis (with Maria Farandouri). | CBS 72947 |
| Music for Guitar and Harpsichord. | CBS 72948 |
| Gowers: Chamber Concerto; Scarlatti: Six Sonatas. | CBS 72979 |
| Gowers: Rhapsody; Villa-Lobos: Five Preludes. | CBS 73350 |
| Previn: Guitar Concerto; Ponce: Concierto del Sur. | CBS 73060 |
| Music from England, Japan and Latin America | CBS 73205 |
| Bach: Complete Lute Music. | CBS 79203 |
| Rodrigo Concerto, Villa-Lobos Concerto. | CBS 76369 |
| Duo: Paganini and Giuliani for Guitar and Violin (with Itzhak Perlman). | CBS 76525 |
| Castelnuovo-Tedesco/Dodgson/ Arnold Guitar Concertos. | CBS 76634 |
| John Williams plays Barrios. | CBS 76662 |
| Arnold and Brouwer Guitar Concertos. | CBS 76715 |
| John Williams plays Manuel Ponce. | CBS 76730 |
| Together: Duo with Julian Bream. | RCA SB 6862 |
| Together Again: Duo with Julian Bream. | RCA ARL1 0456 |
| Live: Duo with Julian Bream. | RCA RL 03090(2) |
| Boccherini Quintets. | CBS 6671 |
| Bach for Guitar and Organ (with Peter Hurford). | CBS 37250 |
| Portrait of John Williams. | CBS Masterworks 37791 |
| Rodrigo: Concertos for Guitar. | CBS Masterworks 37848 |
| Bach, Handel, Marcello Concertos. | IM 39560 |
| John Williams plays Paul Hart's Concerto for Guitar and Jazz Orchestra. | CBS MK 42332 |
| The Baroque Album. | CBS MK 44518 |
| Spirit of the Guitar. | CBS MK 44898 |

**SELECTED READING**

| | |
|---|---|
| John Williams. | Guitar, August 1973 |
| John Williams. | Guitar, September 1973 |
| John Williams. | Guitar, August 1977 |
| John Williams. | Guitar, August 1978 |
| John Williams and Sky. | Guitar, July 1979 |
| John Williams. | Guitar Player, February 1977 |
| John Williams. | Guitar Player, November 1980 |
| Interview. | Classical Guitar, February & March 1985 |
| Interview. | Classical Guitar, August & October 1987 |
| Interview. | Classical Guitar, December 1988 |
| Interview. | Classical Guitar, December 1989, January & February 1990 |

# LEN WILLIAMS

**Born –LEONARD ARTHUR WILLIAMS**

**London, England 11 August 1910**

**Died – Looe, England, 20 July 1987**

*Len Williams*

Len Williams began to play the piano at the age of six, and by the time he was fourteen was already playing professionally in a dance band. After three years he gave up his career as a professional musician and became an assistant in the fretted instrument firm of John Alvey Turner in London. It was there that he became interested in the guitar after hearing recordings made by the jazz guitarist Eddie Lang.

Williams studied both plectrum and classical guitar, taking lessons on the latter with Mario Maccaferri, who was living in London at the time. It was Maccaferri who made Williams aware of Andrés Segovia, and soon he preferred playing the classical guitar, although professionally he played and taught the plectrum guitar.

In 1939 Len Williams emigrated to Australia, where he established himself as a teacher at Suttons, in Melbourne. He was house guitarist for radio station 3DB, and soon became very well known as a plectrum guitar soloist and teacher. His decision in 1946 to give up the plectrum guitar and concentrate on the classical guitar did much to popularize the instrument in Australia.

Williams returned to England in 1952, and established his famous Spanish Guitar Centre in London. Since that time hundreds of pupils have passed through his school, many of whom have become fine players and teachers of the classical guitar. There is no doubt that Len Williams's most famous pupil was his son John, who became one of the most successful guitar virtuosos of all time. In addition to his teaching activities, Len Williams developed a new classical guitar trio, consisting of bass guitar played by Desmond Dupré, standard classical guitar played by Robert Wilson, and the Tarina soprano guitar played by himself.

For the latter part of his life Len Williams devoted most of his time to the study of monkeys (specifically Humboldt's Woolly Monkey), having sold his interest in the Spanish Guitar Centre. He made his home close to his monkey sanctuary at Looe, in Cornwall, where he died in July 1987.


**SELECTED READING**

Len Williams. Guitar, October 1978

Challenge to Survival: A Philosophy of Evolution: Len Williams. Allison and Busby, 1971

The Dancing Chimpanzee – Len Williams. Allison and Busby, 1980.

# LEO WITOSZYNSKYJ

**Born –**

**Vienna, Austria**

**23 June 1941**

*Leo Witoszynskyj*

Leo Witoszynskyj began to play the guitar at an early age. He completed his studies with Luise Walker at the Vienna Academy of Music, with honours. He later studied with Andrés Segovia and Narciso Yepes. At international competitions in Liège, Paris and Vercelli he was a finalist and prizewinner. In 1968 he won the 1st International Competition for Guitar in Alessandria, Italy.

Since that time Leo Witoszynskyj has maintained an active career as a recitalist in most countries of Europe, the Near East, Venezuela and the United States. He made his United States debut in 1974 in the Carnegie Recital Hall, New York. As a soloist, Witoszynskyj has played with many leading orchestras, including the BBC Concert Orchestra, the Birmingham Symphony Orchestra, and the Vienna Symphony Orchestra.

In 1974 Leo Witoszynskyj was appointed Professor at the Hochschule für Musik in Graz, Austria, and in 1980 elected as its Assistant Director. He combines his working year as a teacher at this important music establishment and as an international recitalist.

**SELECTED RECORDINGS**

| | |
|---|---|
| International Guitar. | Music for Pleasure CFP 122 |
| Music for Guitar and Piano. | Turnabout TV 34728 |
| Folk Songs & Music for Two Guitars. | Max Sound MSCB 27 |

**SELECTED READING**

| | |
|---|---|
| Leo Witoszynskyj. | Guitar, March 1975 |
| Interview. | Classical Guitar, September/October 1983 |

# SIMON WYNBERG

**Born –**

**Edinburgh, Scotland**

**4 October 1955**

*Simon Wynberg*

Simon Wynberg studied initially with Fritz Buss in South Africa, later attending masterclasses with Narciso Yepes in Paris. He returned to the United Kingdom in 1978, where he completed a master's degree in musicology at Goldsmiths' College, London. After this, he began his researches into the guitar's neglected repertoire. This ultimately led to the publication of over fifty volumes of unknown guitar music by Faber Music and Chanterelle Verlag.

Among the editions researched and edited by Wynberg are the complete works of Coste, Regondi and Ferranti, selected works of Aguado, Mertz and Ferrer, ensemble works by Carulli, de Fossa, Gaude and Molino, and the Faber Music 'First Repertoire' series.

As a performer, Simon Wynberg has established himself as a keen advocate of chamber music with the guitar, and has worked with some of Europe's and America's top ensembles, singers and instrumentalists, including the English Chamber Orchestra and the Gabrieli String Quartet. He has performed in many British and European Festivals, and made his American debut at the Newport Music Festival in 1984, where he is now a regular visitor. He is the author of a biography of the nineteenth century guitarist Zani de Ferranti.

**SELECTED RECORDINGS**

Guitar Music of Ferranti & Ferrer. Chandos ABRD 1222LP, CHAN 8512CD
François de Fossa Guitar Quartets. Chandos ABRD 1109LP
Duo concert with Oboe at Castle Howard. Chandos ABRD 1083LP
Coste Music for Guitar & Oboe. Chandos ABR 1031LP
Coste & Mertz Guitar Duets (with David Hewitt). Meridian KE 77095
My Minstrel Love (with Anne Mackay, soprano). Meridian E 45 77076LP
Pot Pourri (with William Bennett, flute). ASV CD DCA692

**SELECTED READING**

Interview. Classical Guitar, September 1985
Marco Aurelio Zani de Ferranti: A biography. Chanterelle, 1989
The Guitarist's ABC: Series. Classical Guitar, from April 1990

# KAZUHITO YAMASHITA

**Born –**

**Tokyo, Japan**

**25 March 1961**

*Kazuhito Yamashita*

Regarded as one of the most remarkable guitar virtuosos that Japan has produced, Kazuhito Yamashita was a child prodigy. His first public recital in Japan was at the MY Studio in Tokyo in 1974.

Yamashita came to public notice when he won the Kyushu 18th Guitar Competition in 1972. In 1976 he won the 19th Tokyo International Guitar Competition, which was sponsored by the Japanese Federation of the Guitar. Following his successes in Japan, he went to Europe in 1977. Here, at the age of sixteen, he won first prize in three important competitions: the 'Ramírez' Guitar Competition, Santiago de Compostela, Spain; the 10th Concorso Internazionale Chitarra Classica, Alessandria, Italy; and the 19th Concours International de Guitare organized by Radio-Television France in Paris.

Kazuhito Yamashita now leads a busy life as a recitalist in Japan, the Far East, Europe and the United States. He has an exclusive recording contract with RCA Victor of Japan, and, although still under thirty, has released many recordings.

**SELECTED RECORDINGS**

| | |
|---|---|
| Romance de Amor. | RACE RDC-8 |
| Guitar Recital. | Victor SJX-9538 |
| Concierto de Aranjuez. | RCA RUC-2280 |
| Guitar Recital II. | Victor SJX-9544 |
| Yamashita plays Bach. | RCA RCL-8014 |
| Pictures at an Exhibition. | RCA RCL 8042 |
| Duo with James Galway. | RCA RL 85679 |
| Castelnuovo-Tedesco Guitar Concertos. | RCA |

**SELECTED MUSIC**

Pictures at an Exhibition: Mussorksky arr. Yamashita. Gendai Guitar

**SELECTED READING**

| | |
|---|---|
| Interview. | Classical Guitar, September 1985 |
| Kazuhito Yamashita. | Classical Guitar, August 1989 |

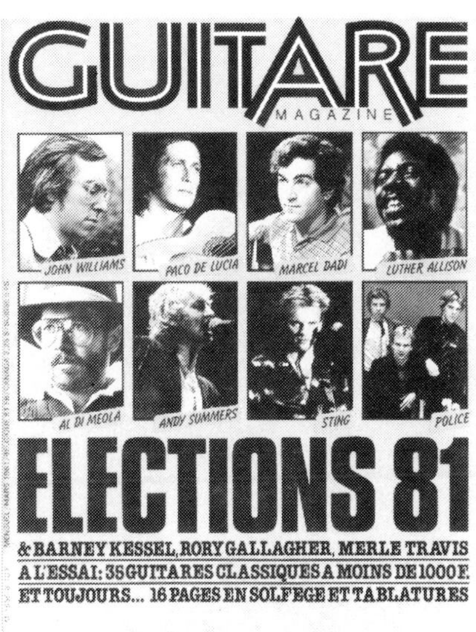

*A selection of guitar magazines*

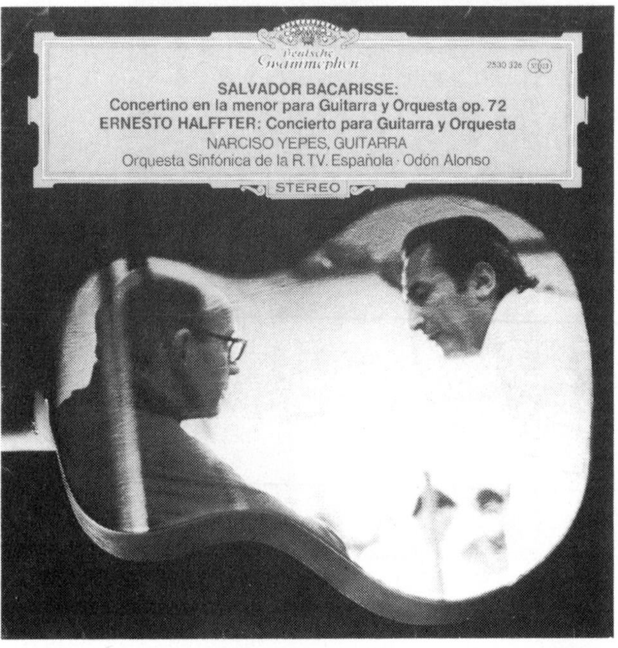


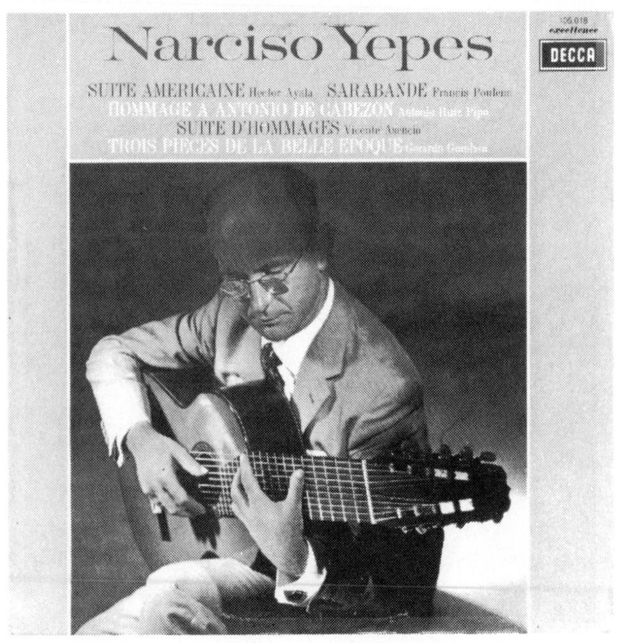


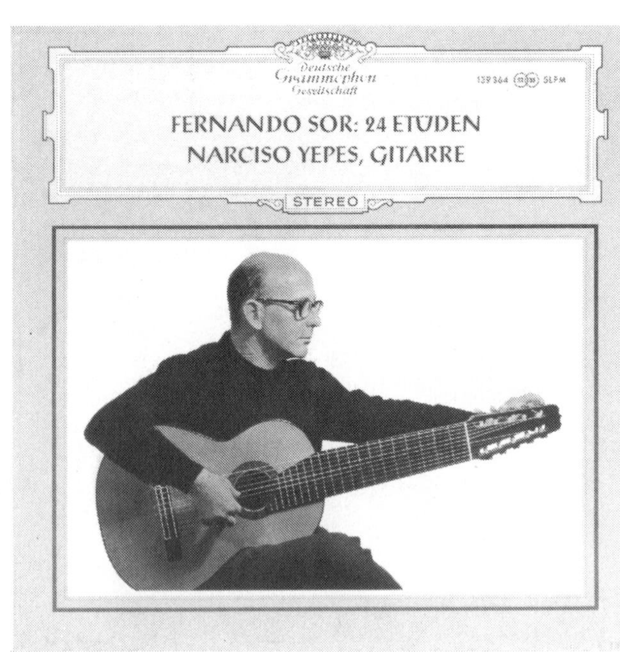

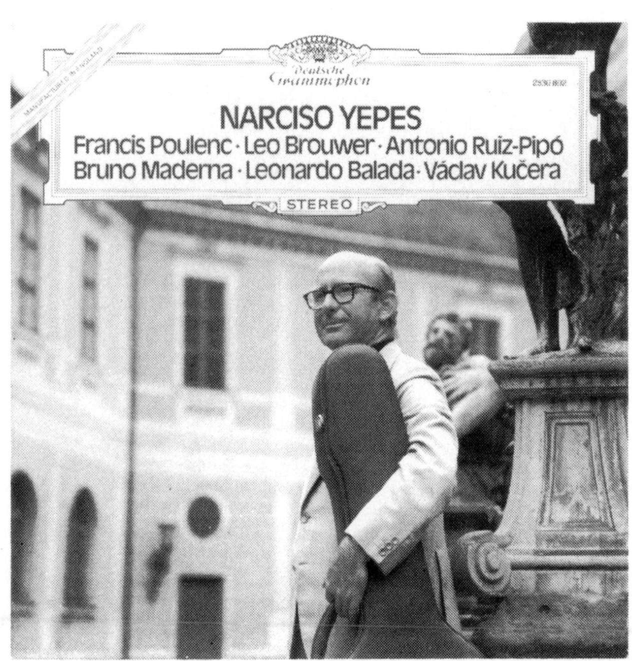


*A selection of Yepes recordings*

# NARCISO YEPES

**Born –**

**NARCISO GARCIA YEPES**

**Lorca, Spain, 14 November 1927**

COURTESY: DEUTSCHE GRAMMOPHON

*Narciso Yepes*

Narciso Yepes was given his first guitar at the age of four by his father, and took his first real lessons on the instrument at the age of six.

In 1940 he began his studies at the Conservatory of Music in Valencia, and in 1943 the pianist and composer Vicente Asencio became his teacher. Asencio's approach to music had a great influence in developing Yepes's guitar style.

In 1946 Ataulfo Argenta, the head of the Spanish National Orchestra, became aware of the nineteen-year old guitarist, and Yepes was invited to Madrid. The following year he made his debut as a soloist with the orchestra in a performance of Joaquín Rodrigo's Concierto de Aranjuez. By 1948 he was established as a guitarist of international standing, and made his first European tour. His highly acclaimed Paris debut took place in 1950, and in 1952 he achieved international fame as a composer and performer for the music to René Clement's film Jeux Interdits. During the next two years he continued to devote part of his career to composing more film music. The major part of his working year was devoted to expanding his concert career into nearly all countries of the world. In 1957 he made his first South American tour, in 1960 his Japanese debut, and in 1964 his first appearance in the United States of America.

Since 1963 Narciso Yepes has played a ten-string classical guitar of his own design. He commissioned José Ramírez to design a special instrument with four additional low-resonance strings tuned to c, b-flat, a-flat and g-flat. The purpose of this new instrument was to produce, through the extra bass strings, a more balanced or equalized group of sounds than with the traditional six-string guitar.

Since the middle 1960s Narciso Yepes has lived in Madrid, dividing his year between giving concerts and teaching. He is also a major recording artist for the Deutsche Grammophon company.

**SELECTED RECORDINGS**

| | |
|---|---|
| Rodrigo Guitar Concerto and Fantasia. | Decca SPA 233 |
| Musique Espagnole Pour Guitare. | Ace of Clubs ACL 907 |
| Narciso Yepes. | Decca 105-018 |
| Fernando Sor: 24 Studies. | Deutsche Grammophon 139 364 |
| Música Catalana. | Deutsche Grammophon 2530 273 |
| Bacarisse/Halffter Concertos. | Deutsche Grammophon 2530 326 |
| Ohana & Ruiz-Pipó: works with orchestra. | Deutsche Grammophon 2530 585 |
| Twentieth Century Guitar Music. | Deutsche Grammophon 2531 113 |
| Narciso Yepes. | Deutsche Grammophon 2531 113 |
| Telemann Guitar Duos. | Deutsche Grammophon 2531 350 |
| Domenico Scarlatti: Sonatas. | Deutsche Grammophon 413 783-2 CD |

**SELECTED READING**

| | |
|---|---|
| Narciso Yepes and the 10-string Guitar. | Guitar, August 1974 |
| Narciso Yepes. | Frets, February 1980 |
| Narciso Yepes. | Guitar Player, March 1978 |

# MILAN ZELENKA

**Born –**

**Prague, Czechoslovakia**

**4 June 1939**

*Milan Zelenka*

Milan Zelenka is regarded as one of Czechoslovakia's leading guitarists. As a student he won first prizes and medals in the Moscow (1957) and Vienna (1959) international guitar contests. Since 1957 he has been constantly performing in Czechoslovakia, Russia, Hungary, Germany and elsewhere in Europe.

Zelenka is a graduate of the Prague Conservatory of Music. He frequently performs modern Czechoslovakian music, much of which has been specially written for him. Much of his year is spent in teaching the guitar. He is a member of the Concert Artists Union, and has made recordings with the State Music Editor and Artia. Also active as an editor and lecturer on his chosen instrument, he is currently Professor of Guitar at the Prague Conservatory of Music.

Milan Zelenka was married to the composer Jana Obrovská (1930-1987).

**SELECTED MUSIC**

Interval Studies: M. Zelenka & J. Obrovská. B 1508

**SELECTED RECORDINGS**

| | |
|---|---|
| Guitar Concerto. | Rediffusion ROY 2004 |
| Moderni Ceske Skaldby. | Supraphon 1-11-0969 |
| Guitar Recital. | Supraphon SUB 10373 |
| Bellefleur. | Opus 3 8405 |
| Zelenka plays Bach. | Supraphon 1111-2263 |
| Obrovská: Concerto for two Guitars. | Panton 8110-0185 |
| Paganini: Works with Guitar. | Supraphon 1111-3647 |

# THE CLASSICAL GUITAR

# ITS DUOS, TRIOS, QUARTETS

# AND MORE

*Duo Presti-Lagoya, probably the greatest classical guitar duo of all time*

# THE CLASSICAL GUITAR
# ITS DUOS, TRIOS, QUARTETS AND MORE

The main section of this book has dealt with the foremost classical guitarists and guitar personalities since 1800. A prominent feature of the instrument's development since that time has been guitarists playing in duos, trios and quartets and other combinations of the instrument.

In the nineteenth century Dionisio Aguado appeared in concert several times in a duo with Fernando Sor. The twentieth century has seen a succession of great guitarists performing as duos. Francisco Tárrega with Daniel Fortea, Miguel Llobet and Maria Luisa Anido, Emilio Pujol and Mathilde Cuervas, Renata and Graciano Tarragó, and, regarded by many as the greatest guitar duo of all time, Ida Presti and Alexandre Lagoya. The Romero family quartet, often called the 'royal family of the guitar', achieved world-wide fame in the 1950s. Since then, this remarkable family of guitarists have established themselves as one of the most outstanding guitar quartets of all time.

In more recent times Turibio Santos has recorded and performed with Oscar Cáceres, and likewise Julian Bream with John Williams. All these great guitarists are included individually in the main section of the book.

This section of the book deals with the most important of those groups of guitar players not previously mentioned, who have established themselves as a vital part of the evolution of the classical guitar outside the sphere of the solo guitar.

PHOTO: COLIN COOPER

*Omega II Guitar Group*

# SERGIO AND EDUARDO ABREU

*Sergio and Eduardo Abreu*

The Brazilian brothers, Sergio (born 5 June 1948) and Eduardo (born September 1949), originally studied the guitar with their grandfather Antonio Rebello. They were then tutored by the Argentinian guitarist and lutenist Adolfina Raitzin Tavora, who had studied with Andrés Segovia.

Their duo playing began in 1963, when they enjoyed enormous success in tours sponsored by the Brazilian Government. Individually, both brothers won high honours in competions both in Brazil and in Europe.

This duo, regarded by many critics as the finest since Presti and Lagoya, split up after Eduardo decided to make his career in another profession (at the time of going to press, he was studying for a Ph.D. in computing). Sergio Abreu, whose biography is shown earlier in this book, was, for a time, a guitar soloist of international renown, but now devotes his career mainly to the construction of guitars.

**SELECTED RECORDINGS**

| | |
|---|---|
| The Guitars of Sergio and Eduardo Abreu. | CBS 61262 |
| The Guitars of Sergio and Eduardo Abreu. | Ace of Diamonds SDD 219 |
| Two Concertos for Two Guitars. | CBS 61469 |

# NICOLAS AND ILSE ALFONSO

*Nicolas and Ilse Alfonso*

Nicolas Alfonso (born 6 December 1918, Santander, Spain) studied music and the guitar in both Madrid and Barcelona. He became a successful recitalist in Spain and throughout Europe. In 1950 he settled in Brussels, establishing himself as a highly successful teacher, composer and editor of guitar works. Schott Frères of Brussels have published most of his original works and transcriptions, including a two-volume guitar method. In 1965 he was appointed professor of the newly founded Guitar Department of the Royal Academy of Music in Brussels.

For many years Nicolas Alfonso has performed and recorded in a successful guitar duo with his wife Ilse (born 15 February 1933).

**SELECTED RECORDINGS**

| | |
|---|---|
| Concerto pour Deux Guitares. | Erato EFM 8040 |
| Musique Espagnole pour Deux Guitares. | Zephyr Z05 |

# ASSAD DUO

*Sergio and Odair Assad*

Sergio Assad (26 December 1952) and Odair Assad (24 October 1956) were both born in São Paulo, Brazil. Their father's encouragement led them to take up the study of the guitar. After only two years they won São Paulo's most important guitar competition. One year later they moved to Rio de Janeiro to begin seven years of study with the renowned Argentine guitarist, Monina Tavora, a former student of Andrés Segovia.

In 1973 the Assad Brothers won the Brazilian Symphony Orchestra's first prize for young soloists. Following this success, they began a brilliant concert and recording career with their recital at the Municipal Theatre of Rio de Janeiro. Their superlative work has attracted many prominent composers, and among those who have dedicated works to them are Mignone, Nobre, Piazzolla, Gnattali and Lemaigre.

In recent times the brothers have lived in Europe, from where they lead their highly succesful international career. Sergio Assad is also a highly gifted composer and arranger.

**SELECTED RECORDINGS**

Sergio & Odair Assad. GHA Records GHA 5256001
Sergio & Odair Assad. Warner/Nonesuch 979 116-1
Alma Brasileira. Warner/Nonesuch 979 179-1

**SELECTED MUSIC**

Aquarelle (Sergio Assad)

**SELECTED READING**

Interview. Classical Guitar, January 1986

# DUO BATENDO

*Duo Batendo*

The Duo Batendo consists of the Dutch guitarists Ton Huijsman, born 1954 in Zaandam, and Sjaak van Vugt, born 1956 in Rotterdam.

Ton Huijsman began to play the guitar at fifteen. From 1971 to 1977 he studied with Dick Hoogeveen at the Twents and Rotterdam Conservatories. He also attended masterclasses given by Abel Carlevaro and Baltazar Benitez. Sjaak van Vugt began to play the guitar at eleven. From 1972 to 1980 he studied with Hans van Goch at the Rotterdam Conservatory.

It was during their studies at the Rotterdam Conservatory that Huijsman and van Vugt met and, in 1983, formed the Duo Batendo. Since that time they have given many concerts and made several radio broadcasts. Their special interest is the performance of neglected or little-known works.

**SELECTED RECORDING**

The Well-Tempered Guitars Op.199: Castelnuovo-Tedesco. Etcetera ETC 2009

# CASTELLANI-ANDRIACCIO DUO

*Castellani-Andriaccio Duo*

Since forming their duo at the Guitar '75 International Festival in Toronto, Joanne Castellani and Michael Andriaccio have established themselves as one of America's foremost classical guitar duos.

Both guitarists, now husband and wife, were born in Buffalo, New York (Castellani on 23 June 1952, Andriaccio on 25 September 1952), and led parallel careeers on the guitar. They began their studies with Oswald Rantucci. They both earned a B.A. degree in Fine Arts in Applied Music cum laude in 1974 at SUNY in Buffalo. They performed for masterclasses of Oscar Ghiglia, Angelo Gilardino, Gilbert Biberian and Sergio Abreu. On the recommendation of Andrés Segovia they were both awarded scholarships to study at Musica en Compostela.

Since 1975 Castellani and Andriaccio have concertized internationally as a classical guitar duo. In 1982 they were recipients of National Endowment for the Arts Recitalist Fellowships, and both are faculty members of the SUNY in Buffalo. Castellani is Chair of the String Faculty. Both guitarists have served as board members of the Guitar Foundation of America.

**SELECTED READING**

Interview. Classical Guitar, April 1988

**SELECTED RECORDINGS**

Joanne Castellani & Michael Andriaccio. Icarus 1002
Danzas and More for Two Guitars. Fleur de Son SD57916-2

# HENRY DORIGNY AND AKO ITO

*Henri Dorigny and Ako Ito*

Henry Dorigny was born in France in March 1939. He studied the guitar in Nice with the Presti-Lagoya Duo at the Academie Internationale d'Et. He attended various masterclasses and in 1963 was appointed Professor of Guitar at the Conservatoire Regional de Musique of Nice. He also began to perform widely as a guitar soloist. In 1966, while still attending the masterclasses of Presti-Lagoya, he met Ako Ito, whom he later married. They began performing as a guitar duo throughout France. They made many appearances on radio and television and have made several recordings.

Ako Ito was born in Japan, December 1942. She began to study the guitar as well as the piano and voice at an early age. Her talent soon became evident, and at the age of eighteen, she went to the United States to continue her music studies and to give numerous concerts as a guitar soloist. She studied in France and in Canada with the Presti-Lagoya Duo, and in the United States and Spain with Andrés Segovia. She married Henri Dorigny in 1967, and they now live in Nice. She was made Professor of Guitar at the Academie de Musique Rainier III in Monaco.

In 1970 the duo made their first international tour of Japan, including an appearance with the Tokyo Philharmonic Orchestra. Since then they have appeared regularly throughout Europe, the United Kingdom, the United States and Canada.

**SELECTED RECORDINGS**

Danses Espagnoles pour Deux Guitares. SFP 31-102
Compositions for Two Guitars. Delos FY 008

# EVANGELOS AND LIZA

*Evangelos and Liza*

The duo of Evangelos Assimakopoulos and his wife Liza Zoi was previously known as the Athenian Guitar Duo.

Both began their advanced studies on the guitar in 1954 at the National Conservatory of Athens under the direction of Dimitri Fampas. Each graduated and took First Prize with honours. Both guitarists gave their debut solo recitals in Athens in 1959. One year later they took the first two prizes in the international contest in Naples, and in 1962 both were appointed professors of the guitar in the National Conservatory in Athens.

The duo was formed in 1963, and Evangelos and Liza married in 1965. For three years they were awarded scholarships to study with the Presti-Lagoya duo in France, and in Spain with Andrés Segovia, who encouraged composers such as Castelnuovo-Tedesco to write works especially for them.

Since their arrival on the international music scene in 1967, Evangelos and Liza have played concerts in the major cities of Great Britain and Europe, in addition to Greece. They have also appeared regularly on television and radio. Since 1969 they have made several extensive tours of North America.

**SELECTED RECORDINGS**

| | |
|---|---|
| Musique Baroque pour Deux Guitares. | Edici Ed 21290 |

**SELECTED READING**

| | |
|---|---|
| Interview. | Guitar, August 1977 |
| Interview. | Guitar, August 1980 |
| Interview. | Guitarra, July 1980 |
| Interview. | Classical Guitar, November 1984 |

# FRANKFURT GUITAR DUO

COURTESY: JURGEN NIMBLER

*Frankfurt Guitar Duo*

The German guitar duo of Michael Teuchert and Olaf van Gonnissen was formed in 1971. Since their first public recital in 1972 they have established themselves as one of the finest guitar duos in the world today.

Michael Teuchert was born in 1948 in Frankfurt-am-Main. The son of a well-known guitar teacher, Heinz Teuchert, he began to play the guitar at the age of four and gave his first public solo recital at the age of eight in Frankfurt. He later continued his studies at the Akademie für Tokunst in Darmstadt.

Olaf van Gonnissen was born in 1954 in Tiengen, West Germany. He began to play the guitar at the age of eight and later also completed his musical studies at Dr Hochs Conservatory in Frankfurt. It was there that he met Michael Teuchert.

**SELECTED RECORDINGS**

| | |
|---|---|
| Renaissance Music. | Soloist Stereo 1176 |
| Virtuoso Guitar Music. | Soloist Stereo 1175 |
| Frankfurt Guitar Duo. | Soloist Stereo 1174 |

# GARAU-MILLET DUO

*Garau-Millet Duo*

Miguel Garau and Fernando Millet were both born in Buenos Aires, Argentina, in 1957 and 1956 respectively. They both hold diplomas from the Juan Jose Castro Conservatory in Buenos Aires, and both received the title of Senior Professor of Guitar with distinction.

Garau and Millet have performed regularly throughout South America and Europe. They made their first European tour in 1981, with a second in 1985. Since then they have lived in France, from where they follow an intensive schedule of concerts, also appearing on radio and television. They are now recognized as one of the finest classical guitar duos, having won first prize in a number of competitions including the Asociacón Estimulo Cultural 1978, Promociones Musicales 1979, and the Grand Prix and Médaille d'Or at the Festival de Jeunes Solistes, Bordeaux, in 1986.

**SELECTED RECORDING**

| | |
|---|---|
| Piazzolla, Villa-Lobos, Smith Brindle. | G-M 3336 |

**SELECTED READING**

| | |
|---|---|
| Garau & Millet. | Classical Guitar, February 1988 |

# GRONINGEN GUITAR DUO

*Groningen Duo*

Erik Westerhof and Remco de Haan studied at the Municipal Conservatory of Groningen (The Netherlands) with Willem van Lier. Both guitarists graduated in 1983 with a diploma for excellent performance. In the same year the duo gave the Dutch première of the Concerto for Two Guitars and Orchestra Op. 201 by Mario Castelnuovo-Tedesco.

In 1987 they reached the finals of the Concours for Chamber Music organized by Netherlands Impresariaat. In 1988 they won first prize at the 3rd International Guitar Duo Competition in Montélimar. In the same year they were invited by ORTF to give the first performance of the Concerto for two guitars and orchestra by Ton de Leeuw, with the orchestra of ORTF conducted by Leo Brouwer. They have recorded for the BBC, ORTF and NOIS.

As well as giving many concerts, the Groningen Duo have made several broadcasts on Dutch radio.

**SELECTED RECORDINGS**

| | |
|---|---|
| Bach, Brahms, Albéniz, Petit. | GG-Records GG 8501 |
| Duo Recital. | Ottavo OTR 118 818 |
| Danzas Espanolas. | Ottavo OTR 48710 |

# HILL-WILTSCHINSKY DUO

*Hill-Wiltschinsky Duo*

Robin Hill (born 1953, Huddersfield, Yorkshire) and Peter Wiltschinsky (born 1955, Doncaster, Yorkshire) formed their duo in 1979 after meeting and giving their first public recital at a music college in 1983.

Both guitarists studied with David Taplin at the Huddersfield School of Music. Robin Hill attended masterclasses given by Alirio Díaz.

In 1987 the duo made their debut at the Wigmore Hall, London, and since that time they have given many concerts throughout Europe, establishing themselves as one of the finest classical guitar duos.

**SELECTED RECORDINGS**

Virtuoso Music for Two Guitars. Hyperion A66113
Sound of Strings. Teldec 8.44140 ZK 243 716-2 CD
Les Deux Amis Music for 2 Guitar
Teldec 8.44141 ZK 244 181-2 CD

**SELECTED READING**

Hill-Wiltschinsky Duo. Classical Guitar, November 1988

# DUO MONTES KIRCHER

*Duo Montes Kircher*

The Duo Montes Kircher is made up of the husband-and-wife partnership of Alfonso Montes and his wife Irina Kircher.

Irina Kircher was born on 6 April 1966 in Stuttgart, West Germany. She began to play the guitar at the age of six, and later studied music and the guitar at the Hochschule für Musik und Darstellende Kunst in Stuttgart, where she studied with Mario Sicca. At the age of ten she won the German 'Young Musician of the Year' contest, a feat she repeated on the next occasion. In 1983 she moved to Caracas to study for a year with Antonio Lauro.

Alfonso Montes was born on 9 February 1955 in Ciudad Bolivar, Venezuela. His early involvement with folk music eventually developed into formal study with Leopoldo Igarza in Caracas. In 1976 he won a scholarship to study in London with John W. Duarte from 1976 to 1982, during which time he obtained the performance diploma of the Royal College of Music. Montes is also a composer, with many published works for theatre groups, ensembles and guitar.

Since 1983 Irina Kircher and Alfonso Montes have worked together as a duo, making their debut in 1984 at the Ateneo de Caracas. They now live in Germany, enjoying a busy career giving many concerts and appearing at international festivals.

**SELECTED RECORDING**

Guitar Duets. Vest-Norsk VNP 0086-11
Guitar Duets. Vest-Norsk VNP 0086-17
Dialogo. W.H.Ziefle 22 33 44

**SELECTED READING**

Interview. Classical Guitar, March 1990

# POMPONIO-ZARATE DUO

*Pomponio-Zárate Duo*

Jorge Martínez Zárate was born in Buenos Aires, Argentina, on 1 October 1923. He became interested in music at an early age, and later began to study at the National Conservatory of Music in Buenos Aires, where he studied guitar with Maria Luisa Anido. Soon after he left the Conservatory, he married the guitarist Graciela Pomponio, and they gave their first duo concert shortly afterwards.

As well as appearing throughout the world in duo performances with his wife, Jorge Martínez Zárate is a highly respected teacher of the guitar. He was appointed Professor of the Guitar at the Music School of Santa Fé, and later became Professor of the Guitar at the National Conservatory of Music in Buenos Aires. Zárate is also a composer, and has made over 600 transcriptions for one, two and four guitars.

Graciela Pomponio was born on the outskirts of Buenos Aires, Argentina, on 12 April 1926. Like most of the talented classical guitarists in Argentina at that time, she studied with Maria Luisa Anido. Pomponio performed her first public guitar recital at the age of eight.

She entered the National Conservatory of Music in Buenos Aires and studied the guitar, harmony and the theory of music. After completing her studies, she became the Professor of Guitar at the Music School of the National University of Littoral.

While studying at the National Conservatory of Music in Buenos Aires, Graciela Pomponio met Jorge Martínez Zárate. They married in 1948, and since that time have appeared together throughout the world, with great success, as the Pomponio-Zarate Duo.

**SELECTED RECORDINGS**

| | |
|---|---|
| Moreno Torroba. | Erato STV 70549 |
| Masters of the Guitar – Volume Two. | RCA RB 6599 |
| Masters of the Guitar – Volume Three. | RCA |

# AMSTERDAM GUITAR TRIO

*Amsterdam Guitar Trio*

The Amsterdam Guitar Trio was formed in 1978 at the Sweelinck Conservatorium in Amsterdam by Johan Dorrestein, Olga Franssen and Helenus de Rijke. Their London concert debut in 1981 and their outstanding recording of Vivaldi's Four Seasons in 1985 established them as one of the world's foremost guitar ensembles. They are now much in demand for concerts throughout the world, and have made four important recordings on the RCA label.

Johan Dorrestein (born Amsterdam, Holland, 1950) began to play the guitar at the age of twelve, yet only began to take it seriously when he was a drama student at the age of eighteen. Inspired by some of Narciso Yepes's recordings, he gave up drama and entered the Conservatory in Amsterdam.

Helenus de Rijke (born Holland 1954) was introduced to the guitar by his father, a jazz guitarist. After hearing, as a teenager, some of Segovia's recordings, he studied privately with Gerar Gest. At sixteen he decided to concentrate on his schooling, going on to study Latin and Greek at the University of Amsterdam. Whilst there his interest in the classical guitar was renewed, and under the guidance of Guido Topper he developed a serious interest in contemporary music and ensemble playing.

Olga Franssen (born Eindhoven, Holland, 1954) is from a musical family. She began to play the guitar at the age of nine. She also played piano, violin and oboe to a high standard. Her parents are musicians, and four of her brothers and sisters are professional musicians. She studied guitar with Hans Lutz Niessen and Guido Topper, and met the other members of the Amsterdam Trio while studying at the Conservatory in Amsterdam.

**SELECTED RECORDINGS**

| | |
|---|---|
| Vivaldi's Four Seasons. | RCA GL 70220 |
| J.S.Bach – Brandenburg Concertos 2, 3, 5, 6. | RCA RL 70903 |
| Ravel/Debussy/Poulenc. | RCA RD 87800 |
| Music of Chiel Meijering. | RCAS RDS 60165 |

**SELECTED READING**

| | |
|---|---|
| The Amsterdam Guitar Trio. | Classical Guitar, June 1985 |
| Interview. | Classical Guitar, April 1989 |

# THE FALLA TRIO

*Falla Trio*

The Falla Trio, formerly known as the De Falla Trio, consists of three excellent guitarists who have a common love of chamber music. In the tradition of string quartets and piano trios, Terry Graves, Ian Krouse and Kenton Youngstrom have established themselves internationally as a virtuoso guitar trio.

The three guitarists met initially at the University of Southern California in 1979 where they were all studying for their advanced music degrees. Since 1985 Dusan Bogdanovic, who studied at the Geneva Conservatory, Switzerland, has replaced Ian Krouse in the trio. All three guitarists mix a busy concert schedule, teaching and fulfilling an important recording contract for the Concord label.

**SELECTED RECORDINGS**

Virtuoso Music for Three Guitars. Concord Concierto CC 2007
The De Falla Trio. Concord Concierto CC 2011
West Side Story/Pulcinella/Jazz Sonata. Concord Concierto CC 2013

# ITALIAN GUITAR TRIO

*Italian Guitar Trio*

The Italian Guitar Trio (Trio Chitarristico Italiano) was formed in 1969 by three guitarists from Florence – Alfonso Borghese (born 1945), Roberto Frosali (born 1940) and Vicenzo Saldarelli (born 1946). All three studied in Florence with the guitarist Alvaro Company.

The three guitarists currently teach guitar in the music conservatories of Pesaro, Ferrara and Modena respectively.

**SELECTED RECORDINGS**

Trio Chitarristico Italiano. RCA RL 31277 (Italy)
Trio Chitarristico Italiano. RCA RL 31521 (Italy)

# THE NETHERLANDS GUITAR TRIO

*Netherlands Guitar Trio*

The Netherlands Guitar Trio was formed in 1981, and since then has become well known in the Netherlands for their varied programming and musicianship. The combination of three guitars, each with its own register (quarter, prime and quint-bass), gives the trio a unique sound. Dick Hoogeveen (requinto), Wim Spruyt (standard) and Henk Westhiner (7-string bass) are the members of the trio.

**SELECTED RECORDING**

| | |
|---|---|
| Grieg: Peer Gynt and Holberg Suites. | Etcetera ETC 1039 |
| Falla, Asencio, Halffter, Albéniz. | Globe GLO 5014 |

# THE THOMATOS GUITAR TRIO

*Spiro Thomatos*

The Thomatos Guitar Trio was formed in 1974 by Spiro Thomatos, professor of guitar at the Zürich Conservatory, Switzerland.

The trio consists of Marlies Waespe and Antonio Valero, who both teach at the Winterthur Conservatory of Music, and Spiro Thomatos.

**SELECTED RECORDINGS**

| | |
|---|---|
| Serenade Music For Three Guitars. | Spectrum SR 109 |

# ZAGREB GUITAR TRIO

*Zagreb Guitar Trio*

The Zagreb Guitar Trio consists of Darko Petrinjak, (b. 1 December 1954, Zagreb, Yugoslavia), Goran Listes (b. 1961) and Istvan Römer (b. 17 August 1962, Zagreb).

Petrinjak graduated from the Zagreb Music Academy in 1975, where he studied both guitar and double bass. He often includes this instrument in the Trio's repertoire. He went on to take post-graduate studies under Hector Quine at the Royal Academy of Music in London. He also studied lute under Robert Spencer. He was awarded the Julian Bream Prize and recital diplomas for both guitar and lute. After teaching for three years at the Birmingham School of Music, he returned to Yugoslavia in 1981 to become Professor of Guitar at the Zagreb Music Academy.

Listes and Römer were two of his best pupils at the Zagreb Academy, and they teamed up with Petrinjak in 1984 to form the now highly-regarded Zagreb Guitar Trio. All three guitarists are also established solo recitalists with many competition successes and recordings to their names.

**SELECTED RECORDING**
Zagreb Guitar Trio. Jugoton LP-6-S 2 021949

**SELECTED READING**
Interview. Classical Guitar, February 1990

# AIGHETTA QUARTET

*Aighetta Quartet*

The Aighetta Quartet was formed in 1979 in Monte Carlo by André-Michel Berthoux, Alexandre del Fa, Philippe Loli and François Szonyi. They were all students of Pier Domenico Amerio at the Academie de Musique Rainier III in Monaco.

The Aighetta Quartet give concerts throughout Europe, and have performed many times on television and radio. In 1989 they gave the first performance of Quartet No.2 and other music by Anthony Burgess, the distinguished novelist and man of letters.

**SELECTED RECORDING**
Oeuvres pour Quatuor de Guitares. REM 11032
Oeuvres pour Quatuor de Guitares: Burgess, Delanoff, Torroba. REM 311111 XCD

# ENGLISH GUITAR QUARTET

*English Guitar Quartet*

The original English Guitar Quartet was formed by Simon Munting (born 1947) early in 1978. Consisting of Peter Martin (born 1957), Alexander MacDonald (born 1950), Colin Thompson (born 1954) and Simon Munting, it built up a large and varied repertoire. Almost a quarter of a century later the English Guitar Quartet, now with new members, continues to achieve great success at home and abroad.

The current quartet consists of Roland Gallery (born Coventry 7 April 1957), treble guitar; Tom Dupré (born Matfield, Kent, 9 May 1959), guitar; Andrew Marlow (born Teddington, Middlesex, 7 October 1961), guitar; and Tim Pells (born 8 June 1954), bass guitar. Each member of the quartet studied with Hector Quine at the Royal Academy of Music in London. In 1986 the British Council invited the quartet to tour Canada, where they were broadcast by CBC radio. In 1988 they toured Australia in connection with the bi-centennial celebrations.

**SELECTED RECORDING**

| | |
|---|---|
| Romantic Guitar Quartets. | Saydisc 379 CD |
| Baroque Guitar Quartets. | Saydisc 386 CD |

# LOS ANGELES GUITAR QUARTET

*Los Angeles Guitar Quartet*

The Los Angeles Guitar Quartet was formed in 1979 by four young guitarists from the University of Southern California: Anisa Angarola, John Dearman, William Kanengiser and Scott Tennant. All four guitarists had been recognised as a talented soloists in their own right, and all four had been chosen to appear in Andrés Segovia's masterclass at USC in 1981.

They are now recognized as one of the finest classical guitar quartets, and have toured extensively in North and South America and in Europe.

**SELECTED RECORDING**

| | |
|---|---|
| Los Angeles Quartet. | GHA 126.001 CD |

**SELECTED READING**

| | |
|---|---|
| Interview. | Classical Guitar, June 1988 |

# THE OMEGA GUITAR QUARTET

*Omega Guitar Quartet*

The Omega Guitar Quartet was formed by Gilbert Biberian in 1969. At its inception it was the only classical guitar quartet in existence in England. Although nothing had been written specifically for guitar quartet at that time, the repertoire has now grown considerably. The group's repertoire included not only transcriptions of various renaissance and baroque works, but also a variety of new compositions written especially for the guitar quartet. The Omega's use of requintos – guitars tuned to a fourth higher – transformed the Omega Guitar Quartet's sound into something comparable to a string quartet. The Omega Guitar Quartet gave many concerts throughout Britain, and also appeared in Italy at the International Guitar Festival in Florence. In 1975 they made two tours of North America. The original group consisted of Colin Downs (born 1949), Gregory Pikler (born 1949), Bernard Watson (born 1949), and its founder Gilbert Biberian.

**SELECTED RECORDINGS**

| | |
|---|---|
| Omega Guitar Quartet. | President PTLS 1066 |
| Omega Guitar Quartet. | Guitar G131 |

**SELECTED READING**

| | |
|---|---|
| Omega Quartet. | Guitar, August, Vol.6 |

# THE ROMEROS

*The Romeros*

The Romeros are a family quartet consisting of Celedonio Romero and his three sons, Celin, Angel and Pepe. The main section of the book has already included biographies of Celedonio, Angel and Pepe, as they have all achieved individual success outside this famous guitar group. Celin, born in Málaga in 1936, has devoted his professional career to being an integral part of the quartet. When not working with the quartet, he is on the faculty of the University of California at San Diego.

Since the Romeros settled in the United States of America in 1958, they have been enthusiastically received throughout the North American continent for their solo, duo and quartet performances. In 1967, they commissioned Joaquín Rodrigo to compose his Concierto Andaluz for four guitars and orchestra. Since that time several other important composers, including Federico Moreno Torroba, have dedicated works to them. For over thirty years this outstanding group of guitarists has entertained audiences all over the world.

**SELECTED RECORDINGS**

| | |
|---|---|
| European Court Music. | Philips (Universo) 6582-001 |
| Compositions for Two Guitars. | Philips 9500-352 |
| Classical Music for Four Guitars. | Philips 9500-296 |
| Rodrigo: Conciertos Andaluz/Aranjuez. | Mercury 75021 |
| An Evening With the Romeros. | Mercury 75022 |
| Royal Family of the Guitar. | Mercury 75027 |
| Vivaldi Concertos. | Mercury 75054 |

**SELECTED READING**

| | |
|---|---|
| The Romeros. | Guitar Player, April 1972 |
| The Romeros. | Guitar & Lute, September 1978 |
| Los Romeros. | Classical Guitar, Sept/Oct 1982 |
| Article. | Classical Guitar, February 1985 |

# TARRAGO GUITAR QUARTET

*The Tarragó Guitar Quartet*

The Tarragó Guitar Quartet was founded in 1971 by four Barcelona guitarists, Laura Almerich, Manuel Calve, Jordi Codina and Josep Jan Henriquez. The quartet has appeared throughout Europe with great success and has inspired new music from several notable Spanish composers to write pieces especially for them, including Joaquín Homs, Antonio Ruiz-Pipó, Leonard Balada and Charles Guinovart.

**SELECTED RECORDING**

| | |
|---|---|
| Musica Espanola Contemporanea. | BASF 37-53901 |

# THE TOKYO NIIBORI GUITAR ENSEMBLE AND ORCHESTRA

The well-known Nihon Guitar Music Academy in Japan conducts a full-scale academic guitar education, adopting graduate school, college and high school systems in its methods of education focusing on the guitar.

The Academy's 200 students, mostly aged between fifteen and twenty-three, are encouraged in ensemble work. The director of the Niibori Guitar Orchestra introduced the use of alto, contrabass, guitarron and bass guitars in order to achieve an orchestral sound.

The Niibori Guitar Ensemble and Orchestra achieved popular success in Japan, playing over four hundred concerts a year. They made several recordings, including one of Vivaldi's Four Seasons arranged for the ensemble.

**SELECTED RECORDINGS**

| | |
|---|---|
| The Four Seasons/Vivaldi. | Fontec 5016 |
| Niibori 'Live' with Jorge Cardoso. | Apassionato 8009 |

COURTESY: ZENON COMPANY

*Niibori Guitar Ensemble*

*Niibori Guitar Orchestra*

COURTESY: ZENON COMPANY

# THE CLASSICAL GUITAR THE OTHER CLASSICAL GUITARISTS

The early nineteenth century has often been called the golden age of the guitar but few musicologists would disagree that the real golden age of the classical guitarist is now.

The major part of this book deals with the most important classical guitarists and guitar personalities since 1800. Needless to say, the classical guitar scene is now so vast that there are thousands of guitarists all over the world who, for one reason or another, have not yet received wide public recognition for their contribution to the instrument.

This section of the book pays tribute to these guitarists by including photographs of a few of those who seem likely to achieve wider recognition and fame in the near future.

*Tom Dupré and Richard Hand Duo*

PHOTO: NICK CORNISH

*Julian Gray and Ronald Pearl Duo*

*Novacek-Bissiri Duo*

*Neil Anderson and David McLelland Duo*

*Ignacio Rodes*

*Pablo de la Cruz*

PHOTO: LUIS LANOS

*Frederic Zigante*

PHOTO: COLIN COOPER

*Michael Strutt*

*Ruben Riera*

*Christopher Berg*

*Uros Dojcinovic*

*Susanne Mebes*

*Luis Zea*

PHOTO: MALCOLM CROWTHERS

PHOTO: THOMAS STRUTH
Frank Bungarten

Tadashi Sasaki

PHOTO: COLIN COOPER
Lex Eisenhardt

Vladislav Blaha

Nicholas Hopper

PHOTO: COLIN COOPER
Sven Lundestad

PHOTO: VIS-A-VIS PORTRAITS
Guillermo Fierens

PHOTO: LARS TORNDAHL
Per Skareng

PHOTO: DIDIER PRUVOT
Gerard Rebours

*Erling Møldrup*

*Stefano Grondõna*

*Leonardo de Angelis*

*Raymond Burley*

*Oscar Ohlsen*

*Christian Chanel*

*Andrew York*

*Yarom Hasson*

*Elena Papandreou*

# THE CLASSICAL GUITAR

# ITS COMPOSERS

*Segovia with guitarist composer Reginald Smith-Brindle*

PHOTO: COLIN COOPER

*Gareth Walters, BBC Producer and prominent musicologist, with Leo Brouwer and John Williams*

# THE CLASSICAL GUITAR
# ITS COMPOSERS

During the nineteenth century the repertory for classical guitarists consisted mainly of their own compositions and those of other guitarists. Sor, Giuliani and Paganini were the most outstanding of these, and to a lesser extent Aguado, Coste and Regondi, among others, also proved themselves to be talented composers. Towards the end of the nineteenth century Francisco Tárrega extended the range of music considerably with his numerous transcriptions of works by composers such as Mendellsohn, Schumann, Albéniz and Granados, a lead that was followed in the twentieth century by Miguel Llobet and Andrés Segovia. Subsequently more and more classical guitarists made their contribution in this field, so that today a great portion of the guitarist's repertoire consists of transcriptions of works written for other instruments. The works of J.S.Bach (1685-1750), D.Scarlatti (1685-1757), I.Albéniz (1860-1909) and E.Granados (1867-1916) are among those which have been most successfully transcribed for the guitar. A vast library of music originally written for the lute, vihuela and early guitar has also been transcribed successfully for the classical guitar. The most important of these composers are John Dowland (1562-1626), Alonso de Mudarra (1508-1580), Francesco Corbetta (1612-1681), Gaspar Sanz (1640-1710), Luis Milán (1500-1561), Enriquez de Valderr bano (1500-1547), Adrian de Roy (1520-1598), Diego Pisador (1509-1557), Franıois Campion (1686-1748), Sylvius Leopold Weiss (1686-1750), Robert de Visee (1660-1720) and Luis Narváez (1500-1551). Their works are often included in the concert programmes of guitarists today.

As we have seen, Andrés Segovia campaigned during the 1920s for new guitar music from prominent contemporary composers. Manuel de Falla had already written Homenaje pour le Tombeau de Claude Debussy for Miguel Llobet in 1920, and now Joaquín Turina and Federico Moreno Torroba answered Segovia's call. Turina's Fandanguillo and Moreno Torroba's Suite Castellana were both published in 1926, and were the first of many important works written by these Spanish composers especially for the guitar. Since that time more and more prominent contemporary composers have written for the guitar. These compositions, together with those written by the great twentieth century guitar-composers like Agustín Barrios, Antonio Lauro and Heitor Villa-Lobos, have now given the guitar a repertory equal to that of most other solo instruments.

This section of the book is devoted to biographies of the most important of these twentieth century composers, who have made such a vital contribution to the evolution of the classical guitar since 1800.

*Mario Castelnuovo-Tedesco with Vahdah Olcott Bickford at 40th Anniversary dinner of American Guitar Society*

# ANTON GARCIA ABRIL

**Born –**

**Teruel, Spain**

**19 May 1933**

*Anton Garcia Abril*

Anton Garcia Abril began his studies at the Conservatory of Music in Valencia. After earning the highest qualifications in piano and harmony, he went to the Madrid Conservatory of Music to complete his studies, after which he attended the Accademia Chigiana in Siena to study composition with Vito Frazzi, film music with Lavagino and conducting with Von Kempen. His composition Cantata a Siena for choir and orchestra won first prize at the Accademia.

Since that time, Abril has become one of Spain's foremost composers for theatre, film and television, with in addition many symphonic scores to his name. In 1971 his musical 'Un Million de Rosas' won the National Prize for Theatre. He has also won the National Prize for Film Scores several times.

Abril became interested in the guitar through Ernesto Bitetti. In 1979 Bitetti recorded Abril's Concierto Aguediano for guitar and orchestra, dedicated to Bitetti, for the Hispavox label. The recording was awarded the 1979 Premio Nacional para Empresas Fonográficas from the Spanish Ministry of Culture. The composer has gone on to write several more works for guitar, including Evocaciones, a solo work that won a prize in 1981 from the Spanish Ministry of Culture. Abril's second concerto for guitar and orchestra, Concierto Mudejar was completed in 1985 and premiered by Bitetti in 1986 with the Bilbao Symphony Orchestra.

Since 1974 Anton Garcia Abril has been Professor of Composition and Musical Forms at the Royal Conservatory in Madrid.

**SELECTED READING**

| | |
|---|---|
| Concierto Aguediano. | Real Madrid |
| Fantasia Mediterranea. | Real Madrid |
| Vademecum Vols I & II. | Real Madrid |
| Planton y Tocata. | Real Madrid |
| Concierto Mudejar. | Real Madrid |

**SELECTED RECORDING**

Concierto Aguediano – Homenaje a Sor. Hispavox S 60.294

**SELECTED READING**

Interview. Guitar International, October 1986

# MALCOLM ARNOLD

**Born – MALCOLM HENRY ARNOLD**

**Northampton, England**

**21 October 1921**

*Malcolm Arnold*

As a child Malcolm Arnold studied the violin and the trumpet. He won a scholarship to the Royal College of Music, and joined the London Philharmonic Orchestra as a trumpet player. He studied orchestration with Gordon Jacob, and in 1943 the great success of his overture Beckus the Dandipratt established him as a gifted composer. Later in 1948 he was awarded a Mendelssohn Scholarship, which enabled him to study in Italy for one year.

Since that time Malcolm Arnold has composed much orchestral music, including several symphonies, a great deal of highly successful incidental music for films (including 'The Bridge on the River Kwai') and fifteen solo concertos, including one for guitar (Op.67, written for and dedicated to Julian Bream) in 1959. Before that came his Serenade for Guitar and Strings in 1955.

**SELECTED MUSIC**

| | |
|---|---|
| Serenade Op.50. | Faber |
| Concerto Op.57. | Faber |
| Fantasy Op.107. | Faber |

**SELECTED RECORDINGS**

| | |
|---|---|
| Serenade – John Williams. | CBS 76634 |
| Guitar Concerto – Julian Bream. | RCA SB 6826 |
| Guitar Concerto – Eduardo Fernandez. | Decca 430-233-2 |

# RICHARD RODNEY BENNETT

**Born – Broadstairs, Kent, England**

**29 March 1936**

*Richard Rodney Bennett*

Richard Rodney Bennett won a scholarship to the Royal Academy of Music in 1953, where he studied with Lennox Berkeley and Howard Ferguson. In 1957 he went to Paris to study with Pierre Boulez for two years, having been awarded a scholarship by the French Government. In 1965 he was elected Composer of the Year by the Composers' Guild of Great Britain.

In 1968 Richard Rodney Bennett composed five short Impromptus for solo guitar, and in 1970 he completed his Concerto for Guitar, which was dedicated to Julian Bream.

**SELECTED RECORDINGS**

| | |
|---|---|
| Julian Bream '70. | RCA SB 6876 |
| Dedication – Julian Bream. | RCA RL 25419 |

**SELECTED MUSIC**

| | |
|---|---|
| Impromptus, ed. Scheit. | Universal |
| Sonata, ed. Bream. | Novello |

# LENNOX BERKELEY

**Born – Boars Hill, Oxfordshire, England**

**12 May 1903**

**Died – London, 26 December 1989**

*Lennox Berkeley*

Lennox Berkeley was partly of French descent. After receiving a general education at Oxford, he completed his music education in Paris as a pupil of Nadia Boulanger.

Berkeley, who was knighted in 1974, was without doubt one of Britain's most important composers of the twentieth century. He wrote piano music, chamber and choral music, orchestral music, and several operas. For over twenty years he was a professor of composition at the Royal Academy of Music in London.

With the encouragement of Julian Bream, Berkeley wrote several works for the guitar, of which Sonatina (1957) was the first. Then followed Songs of the Half Light (for Peter Pears and Julian Bream), Theme and Variations and, in 1974, the Guitar Concerto, dedicated to and first performed by Julian Bream.

**SELECTED MUSIC**

| | |
|---|---|
| Guitar Concerto Op.88. | JWC |
| Sonatina for Guitar Op.51. | JWC |
| Songs of the Half-Light Op.65. | JWC |
| Theme and Variations Op.77. | JWC |

**SELECTED RECORDING**

| | |
|---|---|
| Guitar Concerto – Bream/Monteverdi Orchestra. | RCA ARL 1 1181 |
| Sonatina – Bream. | RCA SB 6891 |
| Theme & Variations – Bream. | RCA SB 6876 |

# BENJAMIN BRITTEN

**Born – Lowestoft, England**

**22 November 1913**

**Died – Aldeburgh, England, 4 December 1976**

*Benjamin Britten*

Benjamin Britten started to compose at the age of five. He was taught the piano and the viola. By the time he was fourteen he had shown that he was a talented composer. In 1927 he studied composition with Frank Bridge, and a few years later won an open scholarship in composition to the Royal College of Music.

Britten was soon recognized as a leading composer. In 1963 he composed Nocturnal, having promised Julian Bream some years earlier that he would write a work for the guitar. Based on a 16th century song of John Dowland, it was first performed by Bream at the 1964 Aldeburgh Festival.

Benjamin Britten was admitted to the Order of Merit in 1965, an honour accorded to few. In 1976 he became Lord Benjamin Britten, the first composer to be elevated to the British peerage.

**SELECTED MUSIC**

| | |
|---|---|
| Nocturnal Op.70, ed. Bream. | Faber |
| Songs from the Chinese (guitar & voice) Op.58. | Boosey & Hawkes |

**SELECTED RECORDING**

| | |
|---|---|
| 20th Century Guitar – Julian Bream. | RCA SB 6723 |

**SELECTED READING**

| | |
|---|---|
| Benjamin Britten's Style – | Soundboard, May 1980 |
| Britten's Nocturnal – Donley. | Classical Guitar, May 1987 |

# MARIO CASTELNUOVO-TEDESCO

**Born – Florence, Italy, 3 April 1895**

**Died – Beverley Hills, California, USA, 16 April 1968**

*Mario Castelnuovo-Tedesco*

Mario Castelnuovo-Tedesco was of Spanish/Jewish origin. He began to study the piano with his mother at the age of nine, and almost immediately began to compose. At the age of thirteen he entered the Cherubini Conservatory in Florence, where he studied the piano with Edgar Samuel de Valle. He also studied composition with one of Italy's foremost composers, Ildebrando Pizzetti. Before he reached the age of twenty, the young composer was acclaimed throughout Europe.

In 1925 Castelnuovo-Tedesco won the National Prize for his opera La Mandragola, performed for the first time in Venice. His ballet Bacco in Roscanam was performed in Milan in 1931. At the International Festival of Venice in 1932 he met Andrés Segovia, who asked him to write a piece for the guitar. The result was Variations à Travers les Siècles (Variations across the centuries), Op.71. Over the next few years Castelnuovo-Tedesco continued to write several pieces for the guitar. His Concerto in D Op.99 for guitar and orchestra was written in 1938 at the request of Segovia, and was the last composition Castelnuovo-Tedesco wrote in Italy before the Fascist government's anti-Semitic campaign forced him and his family to leave Italy. They emigrated to the United States in 1939, settling in California. During his early years in Beverley Hills he wrote scores for motion pictures, but later devoted himself mainly to teaching composition and orchestration.

In 1971 Segovia introduced him to the guitar duo of Ida Presti and Alexandre Lagoya. They inspired him to produce a series of works for two guitars: the Sonatina Canonica Op.196, Twenty-Four Preludes and Fugues for 'The Well-Tempered Guitar' Op.199, and Concerto for Two guitar and Orchestra Op.201.

Mario Castelnuovo-Tedesco was a prolific composer. Included among his works are six operas, five oratorios, numerous orchestral pieces (including overtures for eleven Shakespeare plays), over 100 piano works, over 400 songs, over 100 choral pieces, and a great amount of chamber music for various instrumental combinations. For the guitar he composed almost 100 works. One of his last and most beautiful is Platero y Yo Op.190, for narrator and guitar.

**SELECTED MUSIC**

Aranci in Fiore, ed. Segovia. Ricordi
Aria da Chiesa. Bèrben
Balleta, on the name of Christopher Parkening, Op.170/34. Farfisa
Canción Cubana, on the name of Hector Garcia, Op.170/41. Bèrben
Canción Venezolana, on the name of Alirio Diaz, Op.170/40. Bèrben
Canzone Calabrese, on the name of Ernest Calabria, Op.170/48. Bèrben
Canzone Siciliana, on the name of Mario Gangi, Op.170/33. Bèrben
Capriccio Diabolico (Homage to Paganini) Ricordi
Escarraman – A Suite of Spanish Dances from the 16th Century (after Cervantes). Bèrben
Estudio, on the name of Manuel López Ramos, Op.170/2. Bèrben
Homage to Purcell – Fantasia, on the name of Ronald and Henry Purcell, Op.170/46. Bèrben
Japanese Print, on the name of Jiro Matsuda, Op.170/46. Bèrben
Passacaglia, Omaggio a Roncalli, Op.180. Bèrben
Platero y Yo, Op.190. Bèrben
Rondo, Op.129. GA168
Sonata (Omaggio a Boccherini). GA 149
Suite, Op.133. GA 169
Tarantella. Ricordi
Tarantella Campana, on the name of Eugene di Novi, Op.170/50. Bèrben
Tonadilla, Op.170/5. GA 191
Tre Preludi al Circeo, Op.194. Farfisa
24 Caprichos de Goya, Op.195. Bèrben
Variations à Travers les Siècles. GA 137
Variations Plaisantes, ed. Gilardino. Bèrben
Volo D'Angeli, on the name of Angelo Gilardino, Op.170/47. Bèrben.
Concerto for 2 Guitars and Orchestra, Op.210 (piano reduction). Bèrben
Fantasia for Guitar and Piano, Op.145. GA 170
Concerto No.1 for Guitar and Orchestra in D, Op.99 (piano reduction). GA 166
Concerto No.2 in C, Op.160 (piano reduction). GA 240
Sérénade, Op.118 (piano reduction), ed. Behrend. GA 167

**SELECTED RECORDINGS**

Guitar Concerto No.1 – Andrés Segovia. EMI HLM 7134
Concerto for Two Guitars – The Abreu Duo. CBS 61469
Platero and I – Andrés Segovia. Vol.1. MCA MACS 1967
Platero and I – Andrés Segovia. Vol.2. MCA S-26 087
Music of Castelnuovo-Tedesco – Beppe Ficara. C & M PNL 059
Music of Castelnuovo-Tedesco: Fantasia Op.145, Sonatina Canonica Op.196, 4 Preludes & Fugues etc. – David Russell, Raphaëlla Smits, Jos van Immerseel. AGLA AX 850218
Platero und Ich – Sonja Prunnbauer. Harmonia Mundi HM 723 D
The Well-Tempered Guitars: Preludes and Fugues Op.199 complete – Duo Batendo. Etcetera ETC 2009
Sonatina, Op.205 – William Bennett, Simon Wynberg. ASV CD DCA 692

**SELECTED READING**

Mario Castelnuovo-Tedesco. Guitar, February 1978
Mario Castelnuovo-Tedesco. Guitar Review, No.37, 1972
Castelnuovo-Tedesco's 24 Caprichos de Goya and their relation to Goya's etchings – Lily Afshar. Guitar Review No.79, Fall 1989
Mario Castelnuovo-Tedesco: su vida y su obra para guitarra – Corazón Otero. Ediciones Musicales Yolotl, Mexico 1989

*Fine drawing of Castelnuevo Tedesco on music cover*

# PETER MAXWELL DAVIES

**Born –**

**Manchester, England**

**8 September 1934**

*Peter Maxwell Davies*

Peter Maxwell Davies studied music at both the Royal Manchester College of Music (1952-56) and Manchester University. His fellow students included John Ogdon, Alexander Goehr and Harrison Birtwistle. Because of their common interest in presenting music from the European avant-garde, the young musicians became known as the 'Manchester Group'. In 1957 Davies received a grant from the Italian Government and went to Rome to study with Goffredo Petrassi. On his return to England he was appointed music director at Cirencester Grammar School (1959-62). In 1962 he went to the USA on a Harkness Fellowship to study with Roger Sessions at Princeton. After spending some time as composer-in-residence at the University of Adelaide, Australia, he returned to Britain in 1967. He teamed up with Harrison Birtwistle and formed the Pierrot Players, for whom Davies wrote his principal works. It was renamed The Fires of London in 1970, and the guitarist Timothy Walker became a prominent member.

In 1970 Davies moved to Orkney in Northern Scotland. This remote island has become his permanent home, and his compositions often reflect the stark beauty of the Orkney countryside. In 1977 he organized the annual St Magnus Festival there.

Peter Maxwell Davies has written several important works for the guitar, including Hill Runes for Julian Bream in 1981. His Sonata was first performed by Timothy Walker in the St Magnus Festival, 1987. He was knighted as Sir Peter Davies in 1987, and is now generaly known as Sir Peter Maxwell Davies.

**SELECTED MUSIC**

*For solo guitar:*

| | |
|---|---|
| Hill Runes. | Boosey & Hawkes |
| Lullaby for Ilian Rainbow. | Boosey & Hawkes |
| Guitar Sonata | |

*Works including guitar:*

| | |
|---|---|
| Dark Angels. | Boosey & Hawkes |
| Fiddlers at the Wedding. | Boosey & Hawkes |
| From Stone to Thorn. | Boosey & Hawkes |
| Tenebrae Super Gesualdo. | Chester Music |
| The Blind Fiddler. | Boosey & Hawkes |
| The Lighthouse. | Chester Music |
| The Martydom of Saint Magnus. | Boosey & Hawkes |
| Points and Dances from Taverner. | Boosey & Hawkes |
| Psalm 124. | Boosey & Hawkes |
| Renaissance Scottish Dances. | Boosey & Hawkes |
| Shakespeare Music. | Boosey & Hawkes |

# STEPHEN DODGSON

**Born –**

**London, England**

**17 March 1924**

PHOTO: COLIN COOPER

*Stephen Dodgson*

Stephen Dodgson studied at the Royal College of Music, which he left in 1950 after receiving a scholarship to study in Italy.

On his return to England he became active as a composer, teacher, lecturer and broadcaster, and is closely concerned with the work of the Composers' Guild of Great Britain. He has twice been the recipient of Royal Philharmonic Society prizes.

Stephen Dodgson's orchestral works include concertos for harpsichord, viola da gamba, viola, piano, cello and bassoon. He has written a large amount of chamber music, and his compositions for guitar include a trio with flute and cello, two concertos, a set of songs, four partitas and several other solo pieces.

**SELECTED MUSIC**

| | |
|---|---|
| Fantasy-Divisions. | Bèrben |
| Legend for Guitar. | G 123 |
| Partita No.1 for Guitar. | Oxford |
| Partita No.2 for Guitar. | Oxford |
| Partita No.3 for Guitar. | Bèrben |
| Merlin. | Moeck |
| Follow the Star (3 guitars). | B |
| Duo Concertante (guitar & harpsichord). | ESC |
| Capriccio (flute & guitar). | Schott |
| Sonata for Three (guitar, flute, viola). | Orphée |

**SELECTED RECORDINGS**

| | |
|---|---|
| Guitar Concerto No.1 – Williams. | CBS 61841 |
| Duo Concertante – Williams & Puyana. | CBS 61841 |
| Partita No.1 – Williams. | CBS 61841 |
| Fantasy-Divisions – Williams. | CBS 73205 |
| Four Poems of John Clare – Brown, Willliams. | CBS 61126 |

**SELECTED READING**

Interview. Guitar, March 1973

Stephen Dodgson at Prussia Cove. Classical Guitar, November 1985

Stephen Dodgson at Dartington. Classical Guitar, December 1985

The Guitar Works of Stephen Dodgson – Culf. 6 parts Classical Guitar, 1990

# MANUEL DE FALLA

**Born – Cadiz, Spain, 23 November 1876**

**Died – Alta Gracia, Argentina**

**14 November 1946**

*Manuel de Falla*

Manuel de Falla was a pupil of Felipe Pedrell, regarded as the founder of the Modern National Spanish school. Although he wrote only one piece for the guitar, Homenaje pour le Tombeau de Claude Debussy, several other of his compositions have been successfully transcribed for the guitar and have become part of the instrument's standard repertoire.

Falla's opera La Vida Breve won the prize for the best national opera. For eight years Falla lived in Paris, where he counted Debussy, Ravel and Dukas among his friends. Falla was a keen student of native folk song, and many of his compositions had a distinct Andalusian flavour. He arranged several festivals in Spain in order to maintain the cultivation of native folk song.

In 1939, horrified by the events of the Spanish Civil War and also suffering from ill health, Falla settled in Argentina, where he died in 1946 at the age of seventy.

**SELECTED MUSIC**

Homenaje pour le Tombeau de Claude Debussy, ed. Llobet, rev. Duarte. JWC
Omaggio por le Tombeau de Debussy, ed. Llobet. Ric 129390
Miller's Dance and Dance of the Corregidor, ed. Behrend. JWC
Récit du Pêcheur and Chanson du Feu Follet, from El Amor Brujo tr. Pujol. JWC

**SELECTED RECORDINGS**

El Amor Brujo – Finnish Guitar Trio. Chorus CH 8703
El Amor Brujo – Los Angeles Guitar Quartet. GHA CD 126.001
Ritual Fire Dance – Hill/Wiltschinsky. Teldec CD 8.44140
Manuel de Falla – Ernesto Bitetti. Hispavox S60-20
Homenaje/Debussy – Manuel Barrueco. EMI CDC 7 49228 2
El Sombrero de Tres Picos: Night, Miller's Dance, Dance of the Miller's Wife – Manuel Barrueco. EMI CDC 7 49228 2
Suite Populaire Espagnole – Kraft/Hornoy. MMG 1144
Seven Spanish Popular Songs – Christianson/Friebo. Danica DLP 8102

**SELECTED READING**

Manuel de Falla. Guitarra, May 1979
Manuel de Falla. Guitar Review No.41, 1976
Manuel de Falla: On Music and Musicians. Boyars, 1979
Manuel de Falla – Ronald Crichton. Chester, 1976
Article. Guitar Review, Winter 1976
Manuel de Falla – Burnett James. Gollancz, 1981
Falla's 'Homenaje' revisited – Duarte. Guitar, August 1984
El Cante Jondo – Falla, tr. Martinez. Classical Guitar, November 1987

# ALBERTO GINASTERA

**Born – Buenos Aires, Argentina,11 April 1916**

**Died – Geneva, Switzerland**

**25 June 1983**

*Alberto Ginastera*

Alberto Ginastera began his music studies in Buenos Aires, where he remained until 1930. He continued his studies in the USA, returning to Argentina to found a music conservatory in La Plata. A Guggenheim fellowship allowed him to travel to the USA in 1946-47. On his return to Argentina, he was appointed to a teaching post at the National Conservatory in Buenos Aires. He also served as dean of the faculty of arts and sciences at the Argentine Catholic University. From 1969 until his death in 1983, he lived mainly in Geneva, Switzerland.

Ginastera's contribution to the guitar's repertoire is limited to one composition, Sonata para guitarra Opus 47. It was commissioned by Robert Bialek, president of the Discount and Record and Book Shop in Washington, D.C. to celebrate the company's 25th year in business. Its first performance was given in that city by Carlos Barbosa-Lima on 27 November 1976, and received wide critical acclaim. Subsequent opinion has confirmed its reputation as one of the finest works written for the guitar in the twentieth century. It was first recorded by Maria Isabel Siewers.

**SELECTED RECORDINGS**

Music of Argentina – Maria Isabel Siewers:
Sonata op.47. — Guitar Masters GMR 1003
Timo Korhonen: Sonata op.47. — Ondine CD ODE 730-2

**SELECTED MUSIC**

Sonata para guitarra Op.47. — Boosey & Hawkes

**SELECTED READING**

Alberto Ginastera. — Guitar Review, Spring 1985

# RADAMÉS GNATTALI

**Born – Rio de Janeiro, Brazil, 27 January 1906**

**Died – Rio de Janeiro**

**3 February 1988**

*Radamés Gnattali*

Radamés Gnattali, a virtuoso pianist in his youth, became one of Brazil's leading composers, well known for his synthesis of Brazilian popular music, jazz and twentieth century classical composition. He wrote many fine works for the guitar which, although played for many years by Laurindo Almeida and more recently by the Assad Brothers, are only now beginning to gain full recognition.

A popular figure in Brazil, Gnattali was for many years the conductor, composer and arranger for the National Radio Orchestra in Rio. His enormous contribution to modern Brazilian music laid the foundation of Brazilian popular music, including the bossa-nova style, from the 1930s to the 1950s.

**SELECTED RECORDING**

Rafael Rabello plays
Radamés Gnattali. — Visom LPVO-006

**SELECTED MUSIC**

10 Studies for Guitar. — Chanterelle
3 Concert Studies for Guitar. — Chanterelle
Brasiliana No.13. — Eschig
Pequena Suite. — Eschig

**SELECTED READING**

Radames Gnattalli. — Classical Guitar, October 1990

# CARLOS GUASTAVINO

**Born –**

**Santa Fé, Argentina**

**1912**

COURTESY: EDUARDO FALU

*Carlos Guastavino*

Carlos Guastavino began his working career as an engineer. His musical talent was quickly recognied, and he entered the Conservatorio Nacional de Musica y Arte Escenico in Buenos Aires, where he studied under Athos Palma. This he did on a scholarship from the government of the Province of Santa Fé. Guastavino soon established himself as one of Argentina's finest composers and pianists, but became best known for his solo songs and song cycles. At the end of the Second World War he went to London to study with the help of a grant from the British Council.

Although he has concentrated on vocal music, Guastavino has written several important works for the guitar, which have in recent times gained popularity.

**SELECTED MUSIC**

| | |
|---|---|
| Bailecito. | BA 12611 |
| Cantilena No.1. | BA 10893 |
| Cantilena No.4. | BA 11733 |
| La Tempranera (Baez). | LAG 203706 |
| Sonata No.1 (Lara). | BA 12647 |
| Sonata No.2 (Lara). | BA 12763 |
| Sonata No.3 Ceballos). | BA 13020 |
| Tres Cantilenas Argentinas (Lara). | BA 12532 |
| Las Presencias No.6 Jeromita Linares' (string quartet). | BA 12512 |

**SELECTED RECORDINGS**

Music of Argentina:Sonata No.2 – Siewers. Guitar Masters GMR 1003

La Rosa y el Sauce; Viniendo de Chilecito; En los Surcos del Amor – Lendle & Casares. TGF 20-8504

# HANS WERNE HENZE

**Born –**

**Gütersloh, Germany**

**1 July 1926**

*Hans Werner Henze*

Hans Werner Henze began to compose at the age of twelve before he actually received any formal music education. Over the years he has established himself as one of the world's foremost avant-garde composers. His chamber vocal works Kammermusik 1958 and El Cimarrón (1969) contain sections for solo guitar. In 1974 he composed Carillon, Recitatif and Masque for harp, guitar and mandolin. Henze's further interest in the guitar was stimulated by Julian Bream's request for a new major work for the instrument. The collaboration with Bream resulted in the First Sonata on Shakespearian Characters, Royal Winter Music, completed in 1976. The Second Sonata on the same theme was completed in 1979. His guitar concerto, An Eine Aeolsharfe, was first performed in 1987 by David Tanenbaum.

**SELECTED MUSIC**

| | |
|---|---|
| Drei Tentos. | Schott |
| Memorias de El Cimarrón. | Schott |
| Royal Winter Music – First Sonata arr. Bream. | Schott |
| Royal Winter Music – Second Sonata arr. Evers. | Schott |

**SELECTED RECORDINGS**

| | |
|---|---|
| Dedication – Julian Bream. | RCA RL25419 |
| Royal Winter Music – Leif Christensen. | Paula 25 |
| Evers. | EMI Electrola CD MD G1110 |
| Tanenbaum. | Audiofon CD 72029 |
| Drei Tentos – Stefano Grondona. | Dynamic CDS 59 |

**SELECTED READING**

| | |
|---|---|
| Interview. | Guitar, November 1982 |

# VACLAV KUCERA

**Born –**

**Prague, Czechoslovakia**

**29 April 1929**

*Vaclav Kucera*

Václav Kucera studied composition at the Moscow Conservatory of Music under Vissarion Shebalin. He has worked in Czechoslovakian Radio, headed the Cabinet of Contemporary Musical Studies affiliated to the Union of Czechoslovak Composers, and was active at the Institute of Musical Science in the Czechoslovakian Academy of Sciences. From 1969 to 1983 he was secretary of the Union of Czech Composers and Concert Artists. Since 1972 he has taught composition at the Prague Academy of Music and Dramatic Arts, and was appointed Professor there in 1988. In recognition of his achievements, he was in 1979 awarded the state distinction 'For Outstanding Work' and, in 1986, the title of Merited Artist.

Václav Kucera's output is extensive and varied, and includes stage works, symphonies, chamber works, and vocal and electronic works. His interest in the guitar has resulted in works for violin and guitar and for flute and guitar in addition to solo pieces, of which the best-known is Diario, a cycle of pieces based on five days in the life of Che Guevara.

Kucera's compositions have won a number of prizes, including the Italian Radio Prix d'Italia (1972). He is also the author of a number of books and studies, including a monograph on Mussorgsky.

**SELECTED MUSIC**

| | |
|---|---|
| Diario – Homage to Che Guevara. | Panton |
| Capricci for guitar & violin. | Panton |
| Nouvelles. | Edition Moeck |
| Urgestalten – Homage to Hand Arp. | Ricordi |
| Aquarelles for flute & guitar. | Peters |
| Stilistisches bungen. | Hubertus Nogatz |

**SELECTED RECORDING**

| | |
|---|---|
| Diario – Stein-Erik Olsen. | Samt 184 |
| Diario – Vladimir Vectomov. | Panton 01/11 0415 |

# FRANK MARTIN

**Born – Geneva, Switzerland, 15 September 1890**

**Died – Naarden, Holland**

**21 November 1974**

*Frank Martin*

Frank Martin became interested in music at the age of twelve after hearing a performance St Matthew's Passion. After classical studies in Geneva, Zürich and Paris, he performed professionally on both piano and harpsichord. He taught at the Institut Jaques-Dalcroze. Later he became president of the Association of Swiss Musicians. His compositional style went through three distinct changes: from French Impressionism to a more Germanic contrapuntal style, then to the use of twelve-tone procedures. His best-known work is the oratorio In Terra Pax, written to celebrate the end of the Second World War.

In 1946 Martin moved to Holland and taught composition at the Cologne Hochschule für Musik in Germany. Over the years he was very prolific, composing many instrumental and vocal works. His most important work for the guitar, Quatres Pièces Brèves, was composed in 1933 and is one of the earliest guitar works to be written in a truly twentieth century style. Its importance as one of the finest twentieth-century repertoire pieces for the guitar is only now becoming fully recognized.

**SELECTED MUSIC**

| | |
|---|---|
| Quatres Pièces Brèves ed. Scheit. | Universal Edition |
| Quant N'ont Assez Fait Dodo. | G + L 147 |

**SELECTED RECORDINGS**

| | |
|---|---|
| 20th Century Guitar – Julian Bream. | CA Victor SB-6723 |
| Prestige de la Guitare au XX Siècle – Alberto Ponce. | Arion ARN 30 S 150 |

# FEDERICO MORENO TORROBA

**Born – Madrid, Spain, 3 March 1891**

**Died – Madrid, Spain**

**12 September 1982**

*Federico Moreno Torroba*

Federico Moreno Torroba had the distinction of being the first composer to heed Andrés Segovia's request for new guitar music from prominent contemporary composers.

Moreno Torroba's first music teacher was his father, the organist José Lopez Ballesteros. His musical talent was obvious at an early age, and he entered the National Conservatory of Music where he studied extensively with Conrado del Campo, a celebrated musical pedagogue of that period.

Moreno Torroba's compositions are regarded by some critics as milestones in Spanish music in the three creative media into which he chose to direct his talents: the orchestra, the guitar and the zarzuela (the traditional form of Spanish comic opera). The National Orchestra of Madrid has successfully and repeatedly presented such symphonic works of Moreno Torroba's as Capriccio Romantico and the Cuadros Castellanos.

Federico Moreno Torroba wrote many important works for the guitar after meeting Andrés Segovia in the 1920s. They include his Piezas Caracteristicas in two volumes, Sonatina in A Major, Burgalesa in F Sharp and the Castles of Spain Suite. In 1974 Moreno Torroba wrote Dialogos for guitar and orchestra, dedicated to Andrés Segovia, and in 1976 he wrote Concerto Iberica for four guitars and orchestra, dedicated to the Romero Quartet. Moreno Torroba also wrote Concierto en Flamenco for flamenco guitar and orchestra, which was dedicated to and played by Sabicas with the Concert Orchestra of Madrid. These compositions firmly established Moreno Torroba as one of the finest composers for the guitar of the twentieth century.

**SELECTED MUSIC**

| | |
|---|---|
| Aires de la Mancha. | GA 235 |
| Alpujarrena. | BA 10840 |
| Burgalesa | GA 113 |
| Castles of Spain. | Cadencia |
| Characteristic Pieces, Book I. | GA 113 |
| Book 2. | GA 134 |
| Contradanza. | AMP |
| Five Pieces: Zapateado, Capricho, Improvisación, Sevillana, Romancillo. | GA 234 |
| Jaranera. | UME |
| Jota Levantina. | AMP |
| Madrileñas – Suite: Tirana, Copla, Bolero. | Música del Sur |
| Madroños. | AMP |
| Mi Farruca. | BA 10841 |
| Molinera. | AMP |
| Nocturno. | GA 103 |
| Preludio. | GA 114 |
| Punteado y Taconeo Clásico. | ESC |
| Romance de los Pinos, ed. Segovia. | Cadencia |
| Scherzando. | BA 10041 |
| Serenata Burlesca. | GA 115 |
| Sonatina. | BA 10042 |
| Sonatina (New Edition), ed. Segovia. | CO 168 |
| Suite Castellana. | GA 104 |
| Triptico: Pintoresca, Romance, Festiva. | UME |
| Verbenera. | UME |
| Vieja Leyenda. | UME |

**SELECTED RECORDINGS**

| | |
|---|---|
| Concierto Iberico/Dialogos – The Romeros. | Philips 9500 749 |
| Piezas Caracteristicas – Angel Romero. | Angel 37312 |
| Julian Bream plays Torroba/Villa Lobos. | HMV CLP 1763 |
| Moreno Torroba – Pomponio-Zarate Duo. | Erato STV 70549 |
| Two Concertos For Guitar – Sabicas/Tarragó. | Erato EFM 8080 |

**SELECTED READING**

| | |
|---|---|
| Federico Moreno Torroba. | Soundboard, Spring 1983 |

# JANA OBROVSKA

**Born – Prague, Czechoslovakia**

**13 September 1930**

**Died – Prague, 9 April 1987**

COURTESY: MILAN ZELENCA

*Jana Obrovska*

Jana Obrovska was one of Czechoslovakia's most gifted contemporary composers. Although not a guitarist herself, she was married to Milan Zelenka and as a result knew the instrument well.

Jana Obrovska was the first woman to participate in the ORTF Concours International de Guitare composer's competition in Paris. Her composition Hommage à Bela Bartók was selected as a compulsory work for the 18th ORTF Concours. A composer of several chamber and symphonic works, her output of guitar compositions in the years immediately preceding her death was quite prolific, and several of her works have now become standard repertoire pieces. Her early death from cancer at the age of 57 robbed the guitar of one of its finest contemporary composers.

**SELECTED MUSIC**

| | |
|---|---|
| Due Musici. | G & L Publications |
| Hommage à Choral Gothique. | G & L Publications |
| Hommage à Bela Bartók. | Max Eschig |
| Präludien für Gitarre. | Supraphon |
| Album für Gitarre. | Supraphon |
| Studii di Intervalli. | Broekmans & Van Poppel |
| Sonata in modo antiquo. | Van Teeseling |
| Four Images of Japan. | Lemoine |

**SELECTED RECORDINGS**

| | |
|---|---|
| Obrovksa – Concerto for Two Guitars. Zelenka/Brabec. | Panton 8110 0185 |
| Miloslav Matousek. | Panton 8111 0318 |
| Pavel Steidl – Debut. | Panton 8111 0578 |
| Alice Artzt – Musical Tributes. | Hyperion A 66146 |

# MAURICE OHANA

**Born –**

**Gibraltar**

**12 June 1914**

*Maurice Ohana*

Maurice Ohana left Gibraltar for Bayonne, France, as a youth, and it was here he was educated. He went on to study architecture at the Sorbonne in Paris. At the same time he pursued his musical studies with Daniel Lesur, Alfredo Casella and the pianist Lazare-Levy. Ohana also studied in Barcelona with the distinguished pianist Frank Marshall. He in fact began his musical career as a pianist before turning his attention to composing.

In 1947 Ohana started a group called 'Zodiaque' in reaction to the serial intellectualism and academic neo-classicism movements in music. He colours his compositions with the traditions of Andalusia, the land of his birth, and at the same time takes inspiration from North African and medieval music. These influences have led to a most distinctive compositional style.

In 1950 he wrote his concerto for guitar, Trois Graphiques. This work, and subsequent compositions for the guitar, have established Ohana as one of the few important twentieth-century composers who have taken a major interest in the instrument.

**SELECTED MUSIC**

| | |
|---|---|
| Trois Graphiques (1950). | Billaudot |
| Tiento (1955). | Billaudot |
| Si Le Jour Parâit (1963). | Billaudot |

**SELECTED RECORDINGS**

Ohana: Works for Guitar – Alberto Ponce. Arion ARN 38240

Ohana: Guitar Concerto – Narciso Yepes. Deutsche Grammophon DG2530 585

Music of Spain – Julian Bream. RCA RL 45548

# GOFFREDO PETRASSI

**Born –**

**Zagarolo, Italy**

**16 July 1904**

*Goffredo Petrassi*

In his youth Goffredo Petrassi worked as an assistant in a music shop and studied music in his spare time, later having regular lessons in composition with Vincenzo di Donato and Alessandro Bustini. His early compositions were influenced by the work of the neo-classicist Alfredo Casella, but his later work, of which Nunc for solo guitar (written in 1971) is an example, reflects his interest in twelve-tone music.

**SELECTED MUSIC**

Nunc. SZ

**SELECTED RECORDING**

Nunc – Stefano Grondona. Dynamic CDS 59

**SELECTED READING**

Interview. Soundboard, May 1981

# ASTOR PIAZZOLLA

**Born –**

**Mar del Plata, Argentina**

**11 March 1921**

*Astor Piazzolla*

Astor Piazzolla first studied the piano and then composition with Nadia Boulanger. He showed an exceptional talent on the bandoneon, a type of concertina, and also as a composer of music based on traditional tango rhythms. He was encouraged by his musical contemporaries, Boulanger in particular, to explore and develop his unique talent in this field of music. Today he is regarded by many as the most important composer of popular Argentinian music.

Piazzolla has written works for quintet, octet, chamber orchestra, celesta, solo bandoneon and also several film scores. It was after hearing his fellow countryman Roberto Aussel play William Walton's Five Bagatelles that he decided in 1980 to write five original pieces for guitar. These were recorded by Aussel in 1982. Since that time he has written several more important works for guitar, including Tango Suite for the Assad Duo. Some of his more popular tangos have been transcribed for guitar by Baltazar Benitez and others.

Popularly known as the 'King of the Tango', Astor Piazzolla has given the familiar tango style new rhythmic and harmonic qualities which adapt very well to the classical guitar.

**SELECTED MUSIC**

Five Pieces, ed. Aussel. Editions Lemoine
Histoire du Tango. Editions Lemoine
Adios Nonino, arr. Carlevaro.
Guitar Solo
Four Pieces, arr. Benitez. Chanterelle

**SELECTED RECORDINGS**

Baltazar Benitez plays Astor Piazzolla. Nonesuch 979 142-1
Roberto Aussel plays Piazzolla,
Brouwer etc. Disques Circe CIR 822
The Assad Brothers play Piazzolla,
Gnatalli & Rodrigo. GHA 5256001
Concerto for Bandoneon & Guitar,
Histoire du Tango. Carrere CA 681.325
Tango Futur – Astor Piazzolla Orchestra.RCA NL 70-142(2)

**SELECTED READING**

Roberto Aussel & Astor Piazzolla.
Classical Guitar, March/April 1984
Ginastera & Piazzolla. Classical Guitar, November & December 1985

# MANUEL PONCE

**Born – Fresnillo, Mexico**

**8 December 1886**

**Died – Mexico City, 24 April 1948**

*Manuel Ponce*

Manuel Ponce began composing at the age of seven and by the time he was twelve years old was playing a cathedral organ. After studying at the National Conservatoire of Music in Mexico City, he went to Italy and Germany in 1904 to study the piano and composition. On his return to Mexico in 1908 he was appointed professor at the Conservatory of Music. For a few years he had made a special study of the folk music of Mexico, and by 1912 the influence of this music was seen in some of his compositions. In 1925, he returned to Europe and lived in Paris, where he studied composition and orchestration with Paul Dukas. It was during his stay in Paris that he met Andrés Segovia, and his lifelong association with this great guitarist was to be the determining factor for most of his guitar compositions.

In 1931 the Mexican Government arranged for Ponce to make a tour of several South American Republics by aeroplane. It was during this tour that he conducted the first performance of his Concierto del Sur for guitar and small orchestra, on 4 October 1941 in Montevideo, Uruguay, with Segovia as the soloist.

In 1936-37, Manuel Ponce founded and edited the journal 'Cultura Musical' in Mexico City. His impressive guitar works laid the foundation and set standards for future Latin American composers.

**SELECTED MUSIC**

Mazurka, arr. Almeida. No 93
Preludes 1-6. GA 124
Preludes 7-12. GA 125
Preludio. GA 112
Scherzino Mexicano. Southern
Six Short Preludes. Southern
Sonata Clásica. GA 122
Sonata Mexicana (Sonata No.1), ed. López Ramos. Southern
Sonata Romántica. GA 123
Sonata III. GA 110
Sonatina Meridional. GA 151
Suite: Preambule, Courante, Sarabande, Gavotte I and II, Gigue. Southern
Thème, Varié et Finale. GA 109
Three Popular Mexican Songs. GA 111
24 Preludes for Guitar, ed. Alcázar from the original manuscripts. Tecla
Two Pieces: Scherzino Mexicano,Giga Melancólica, ed. Papas. CO 199
Valse. GA 153
Variations on Folia de España, and Fugue. GA 135

**SELECTED RECORDINGS**

John Williams plays Manuel Ponce. CBS 76730
Concierto del Sur – John Williams. CBS 73060
Sonata Meridional – Andrs Segovia. EMI HLM 7134
Sonata Meridional – Andrés Segovia. MCA S-26-087
24 Preludes, Variations and Fugue on 'Las Folias de España' – Galbraith. Watercourse WCRCD1

**SELECTED READING**

Manuel Ponce – A Tribute. Guitar Review No.7, 1948
Manuel Ponce – Corazón Otero. Musical New Services
The Segovia-Ponce Letters. Editions Orphée, 1989

# JOAQUIN RODRIGO

**Born –**

**Sagunto, Province of Valencia, Spain**

**22 November 1902**

*Joaquín Rodrigo*

Joaquín Rodrigo, though blind from early childhood, studied music in Valencia and later went to Paris, as had other famous Spanish musicians including Albéniz, Falla and Turina. In 1927 he entered the Ecole Normale de Musique as a pupil of Paul Dukas. At that time Dukas occupied, as a teacher and composer, a leading position among musicians in Paris, and together with Manuel de Falla and the Spanish pianist Ricardo Vines he exerted a lasting influence on the young composer.

Rodrigo continued to study with Dukas until 1932. In the next four years he travelled extensively, principally in Switzerland, Germany and Austria. On the outbreak of the Spanish Civil War in 1936, he returned permanently to live in his home land. He eventually took up residence in Madrid, and it was there in 1938 that he met the guitarist Regino Sainz de la Maza and the Marqués de Bolarque, a patron of a music. The outcome was his Concierto de Aranjuez, performed for the first time on 9 November 1940 in Barcelona by Regino Sainz de la Maza. The concerto, which was dedicated to Regino Sainz de la Maza, brought Rodrigo immediate world-wide fame, and over the years has become one of the most popular pieces of classical music.

Joaquín Rodrigo continued his association with other guitarists, and was to write some of the most beautiful guitar music of all time. In 1954 he composed another concerto, Fantasía para un Gentilhombre which he dedicated to Andrés Segovia. After this, an association with the Romero family, whom he knew in Madrid before they left for the United States, encouraged him to write in 1967 the Concierto Andaluz for four guitars, in 1968 the Concierto Madrigal for two guitars, and in 1971 Elogio de la Guitarra, which he dedicated to Angel Romero. In 1982 he was commissioned by William and Carol McKay of Fort Worth, Texas, to write a guitar concerto for the social debut of their daughters Alden and Lauri. The result was Concierto para una Fiesta, first performed on 9 March 1983 by Pepe Romero and the Fort Worth Chamber Orchestra conducted by John Giordani.

**SELECTED MUSIC**

Bajando de la Meseta
(Por los Campos de España. SCH 99
Concierto de Aranjuez (Guitar part only). AP 425
Concierto de Aranjuez (Piano reduction): Score. AP 424
Elogio de la Guitarra, ed. Gilardino. Bèrben
Four Easy Pieces from the Album of Cecilia. UME 19440
Invocation et Danse,
Hommage à Manuel de Falla, ed. Díaz. EFM
Junto al Generalife, ed. Behrend. UME 21788
Por Los Campos de España:
En Los Trigales, Entre Olivares. EMM
Sarabande Lointaine. ESC
Sonata à la Española *9* ESC
Sonata Giocosa. JWC
Three Little Pieces. ESC
Three Spanish Pieces: Fandango, Passacaglia, Zapateado. GA 212
Two Preludes for Guitar. ESC

**SELECTED RECORDINGS**

Concierto de Aranjuez, Fantasía para un Gentilhombre – Regino Sainz de la Maza. RCA VICS 1322
Concierto de Aranjuez, Fantasía para un Gentilhombre – John Williams. CBS 37848
Concierto de Aranjuez, Fantasía para un Gentilhombre – Alexandre Lagoya. Philips 6500 454
Concierto de Aranjuez, Fantasía para un Gentilhombre – Eduardo Fernández. Decca 417 199-1
Concierto de Aranjuez – Narciso Yepes. Decca SPA 233
Conciertos Andaluz and Aranjuez – The Romeros. Philips SAL 3677
Concierto Madrigal – Angel and Pepe Romero. Philips 6500 918
Fantasía para un Gentilhombre – Angel Romero. EMI SD 3415
Concierto para una Fiesta – Pepe Romero. Philips 411 133-1
Elogio de la Guitarra – Angel Romero. Angel S 37312
Rodrigo: solo works – Pepe Romero. Philips 9500-915
Music of Spain Vols. 7 & 8 – Julian Bream. RCA RI 45548

**SELECTED READING**

Joaquín Rodrigo – Federico Sopeña. Ministry of Education and Science, Madrid 1973
Joaquín Rodrigo: Su vida y su obra – Vicente Vayá Pla. Real Music, Madrid 1977
Joaquín Rodrigo: Concierto de Aranjuez – Graham Wade. Mayflower Study Guides, Leeds 1985
Rodrigo, Conciero de Aranjuez and Fantasía para un gentil ombre –
Great composers and their music; No. 51. Marshall Cavendish, London 1985

# GUIDO SANTORSOLA

**Born –**

**Candosa di Puglia, Italy**

**18 November 1904**

*Guido Santórsola*

Guido Santórsola was taken to Brazil with his family at the age of five. There he began to study the violin, and by the time he was nine years old he was already performing in public.

He received his early music education in São Paulo, and studied composition with Agostino Cantu and Lamberto Baldi. He later went to Europe to work in Naples and at Trinity College of Music, London.

In 1931 Santórsola moved to Montevideo, Uruguay, where he still lives, and in 1936 he became a Uruguayan citizen. He has performed extensively in string ensembles, both as a soloist with the orchestra and as a conductor. He is the director of the Escuyela Normal de Música in Montevideo. An early interest in the guitar became fully developed when a lasting friendship with Andrés Segovia was made during Segovia's stay in Montevideo during World War II.

Guido Santórsola has written almost two dozen works for the guitar, and a text on the harmonic principles applied to the guitar. His Concerto for Two Guitars and Orchestra (1966) was dedicated to Sergio and Eduardo Abreu.

**SELECTED MUSIC**

| | |
|---|---|
| Chôro No 1 and Valsa Chôro. | CO 245 |
| Giga. | BR 3082 |
| Preludio No 2. | BR 2795 |
| Ringraziamento and Tempo di Minuetto. | CO 242 |
| Sarabanda. | BR 3081 |
| Sonata No 2, Hispanica. | Bèrben |
| Sonoridades 1971: Four Latin American Pieces. | Bèrben |
| Sonoridades 1971: Sonata No 4 (Italiana). | Bèrben |
| Three Airs of Court: Preludio, Aria, Finale (Giga). | CO 219 |
| Concertino for Guitar and Orchestra (Piano reduction). | Southern |

**SELECTED READING**

Guido Santórsola. Guitar International, September 1989

# TORU TAKEMITSU

**Born –**

**Tokyo, Japan**

**8 October 1930**

*Toru Takemitsu*

Toru Takemitsu is a mainly self-taught composer, although at the age of eighteen he did study with the Japanese master Kiyose. His music is often a fusion of European and Japanese elements. Using traditional Japanese instruments alongside European orchestral instruments, he has a distinctive style which has earned him a reputation as Japan's finest living composer.

Takemitsu's first prominent composition for the classical guitar was Folios, written in 1973. Other works for guitar include 12 Songs for Solo Guitar based on the melodies of the Beatles, Gershwin, Arlen and traditional folk songs amongst others. Toward the Sea, a duo for alto flute and guitar, was written in 1981.

Takemitsu has confirmed his admiration for the guitar, and his contribution to the instrument's repertoire is sure to grow in importance in the coming years.

**SELECTED MUSIC**

| | |
|---|---|
| Folios for Guitar: | Salabert |
| Toward the Sea: | Schott (Japan) |
| All in Twilight: 4 pieces ed. Bream. | Schott (Japan) |
| 12 Songs for Guitar. | ZG |
| To the Edge of Dream (with orchestra). | Schott (Japan) |

**SELECTED READING**

The Contemporary Guitar: Schneider. Soundboard, August 1981

# ALEXANDRE TANSMAN

**Born – Lodz, Poland, 12 June 1897**

**Died – Paris, France**

**15 November 1986**

*Alexandre Tansman*

Alexandre Tansman came to prominence following a concert of his music in Paris in 1921. It was during his stay in Paris that he met Andrés Segovia. After that time Tansman wrote a number of important works for the guitar.

Tansman lived and travelled widely in the United States, Europe and Asia. Originally influenced by his fellow countryman Chopin, his compositions reflect the wide experience of his travels together with his own strong lyrical individuality. His works include operas, ballets, orchestral, choral and chamber music as well as concert and solo instrumental music.

In 1952 his composition Cavatina for solo guitar was a prizewinner at the International Music Competition in Siena, Italy.

**SELECTED MUSIC**

| | |
|---|---|
| Cavatina. | GA 165 |
| Danza Pomposa. | GA 206 |
| Mazurka. | GA 116 |
| Pezzo in Modo Antico, ed. Gilardino. | Bèrben |
| Suite in Modo Polonico. | ESC |
| Twelve Easy Pieces. | ESC |
| Variations on a Theme of Scriabin. | ESC |

**SELECTED RECORDINGS**

Tansman and Mompou:
Andrés Segovia. Brunswick AXA 4532
Musique de Cour – for guitar and orchestra:
Sonja Prunnbauer. Schwann VMS 2062E
Musique Française – Alexandre Tansman: Alan Prevost. Cybelia CY 857

# JOAQUIN TURINA

**Born – Seville, Spain, 9 December 1882**

**Died – Madrid, Spain**

**14 December 1949**

*Joaquín Turina*

Joaquín Turina was one of Spain's most outstanding musicians of the twentieth century. He was not only a composer, but also a fine pianist and conductor. He greatly admired the guitar and wrote several pieces for it, which he dedicated to Andrés Segovia. The best known of these are Fandanguillo, Ráfaga, Sonatina, and Hommage à Tárrega. His best-known chamber work, La Oración del Torero was originally written for four guitars.

**SELECTED MUSIC**

| | |
|---|---|
| Fandanguillo, ed. Segovia. | BA 12928 and GA 102 |
| Hommage à Tárrega. | GA 136 |
| Ráfaga. | GA 128 |
| Sacro-Monte, ed. Azpiazu. | Salabert |
| Sevillana: Fantasia, ed. Segovia. | GA 158 |
| Sonatina (Sonata in D). | GA 132 |

# WILLIAM WALTON

**Born – Oldham, England, 20 March 1902**

**Died – Ischia, Italy**

**8 March 1983**

*William Walton*

William Walton was originally a chorister at Christ Church, Oxford. He was mainly self-taught as a composer. His talent was first recognized through a performance of a string quartet at an international festival in Salzburg in 1923. Walton was sometimes called the Hindemith of English music, but most authorities now agree that he is a composer in the English tradition established by Elgar.

It was not until he was sixty-nine that Walton completed his first solo work for guitar, the Five Bagatelles. He had written a song cycle for voice and guitar (Anon in Love) in 1959, but his Bagatelles, written for Julian Bream and dedicated to Malcolm Arnold on the occasion of his fiftieth birthday, are regarded as one of the finest additions to the classical guitar repertory.

**SELECTED RECORDINGS**

Julian Bream '70s. RCA SB 6876
Dedication: Julian Bream. RCA RL 25419
Oeuvres: Walton, Constant,
Berkeley: Roberto Aussel. Adda/Circe CIR 825

**SELECTED READING**

Masterworks – Five Bagatelles: Carlos Bonell. Guitar, June 1983
Behind the Façade: Susana Walton. OUP 1988
Walton's Five Bagatelles: Donley. Classical Guitar, June/July/August 1990

# SOME PROMINENT TWENTIETH CENTURY COMPOSERS WHO ARE NOT GUITARISTS BUT WHO HAVE WRITTEN FOR THE CLASSICAL GUITAR

Ambrosius, Hermann (1897)
Amy, Gilbert (1936)
Angerer, Paul (1927)
Apostel, Hans Erich (1901-1972)
Artner, Norbert (1922-1971)
Auric, Georges (1899-1983)

Bacarisse, Salvador (1898-1963)
Bartolozzi, Bruno (1911-1980)
Baumann, Herbert (1925)
Baur, Jürg (1918)
Berg, Gunnar (1909)
Bettinelli, Bruno (1913)
Bialas, Günther (1907)
Bolcom, William (1938)
Bolling, Claude (1930)
Bondon, Jacques (1927)
Borup-Jørgensen, Axel (1924)
Boulez, Pierre (1925)
Bressen, Cesar (1913)
Burghauser, Jarmil (1921)
Burkhard, Willy (1900-1955)
Burkhart, Franz (1902)
Bussotti, Sylvano (1931)

Cardew, Cornelius (1936-1981)
Carter, Elliott, (1908)
Cerf, Jacques (1932)

David, Johann Nepomuk (1895-1977)
David, Thomas Christian 1925)

Einem, Gottfried von (1918)
Erbse, Heimo (1924)

Farkas, Ferenc (1905)
Feld, Jindrich (1925)
Fheodoroff, Nikolaus (1931)
Fricker, Peter Racine (1920-1990)

Gefors, Hans (1952)
Genzmer, Harald (1909)
Ghedini, Giorgo Federico (1892-1965)
Ginastera, Alberto (1916-1983)
Gowers, Patrick
Gnattali, Radamés (1906-1988)
Guarnieri, Camargo M. (1907)

Halffter, Cristobal (1930)
Halffter, Ernesto (1905)
Hallnias, Hilding (1903)
Harris, Albert (1916)
Hartig, Heinz Friedrich (1907-1969)
Hasenohrl, Franz (1885-1970)
Haubenstock-Ramati, Roman (1919)
Haug, Hans (1900-1967)
Humel, Gerald (1931)

Ibert, Jacques (1890-1962)

Jelinek, Hanns (1901-1969)
Jolivet, André (1905-1974)

Kagel, Mauricio (1931)
Kelterborn, Rudolf (1931)
Klebe, Giselher (1925)
Kont, Paul (1920)
Kotonski, Wlodzimierz (1925)
Kounadis, Arghyris P. (1924)
Kovats, Barna (1920)
Krenek, Ernst (1900)
Kronsteiner, Joseph (1910)
Kubizek, Augustin (1918)
Kucera, Václav (1929)

Lacerda, Osvaldo (1927)
Lampersberg, Gerhard (1928)
Lechthaler, Josef (1891-1948)
Leukauf, Robert (1902)
Linde, Hans-Martin (1930)

Maderna, Bruno (1920-1973)
Malipiero, Gian Francesco (1882-1973)
Martin, Frank (1890-1974)
Migot, Georges (1891-1976)
Milhaud, Darius (1892-1974)
Miroglio, Frances (1924)
Mittergradnegger, Gunther (1923)
Molleda, José Muñoz
Mompou, Federico (1893-1987)
Morancon, Guy (1927)

Nielsen, Tage (1929)

Obrovská, Jana (1930-)

Pfister, Hugo (1914-1969)
Porrino, Ennio (1910-1959)
Poulenc, Francis (1899-1963)
Previn, André (1929)

Rawsthorne, Alan (1905-1971)
Rebay, Ferdinand (1880-1971)
Reitz, Heiner (1925)

Roussel, Albert (1869-1937)
Ruders, Paul (1949)
Ruiz-Pipó, Antonio (1934)

Schibler, Armin (1920)
Schoenberg, Arnold (1874-1951)
Schwertberger, Gerald (1941)
Searle, Humphrey (1915-1982)
Seiber, Mátyás (1905-1960)
Siegl, Otto (1896)
Skorzeny, Fritz (1900-1965)
Sojo, Vicente Emilio (1887-1974)
Sprongl, Norbert (1892)
Stravinsky, Igor (1882-1971)
Surinach, Carlos (1915)
Suter, Robert (1919)

Tippett, Michael (1905)

Uhl, Alfred (1909)
Uray, Ernst Ludwig (1906)

Vlad, Roman (1919)

Walton, William (1902-1983)
Webern, Anton (1883-1945)
Weiss, Harald (1949)
Wissmer, Pierre (1915)

Zbinden, Julien-François (1917)
Zehm, Friedrich (1923)
Zimmermann, Bernd Alois (1918-1970)

COURTESY: DAVID RUSSELL

*David Russell with Spanish composer Vicente Ascencio*

*A selection of Classical Guitar magazines. The world's foremost publication devoted to the instrument*

# THE CLASSICAL GUITAR

## ITS MAKERS

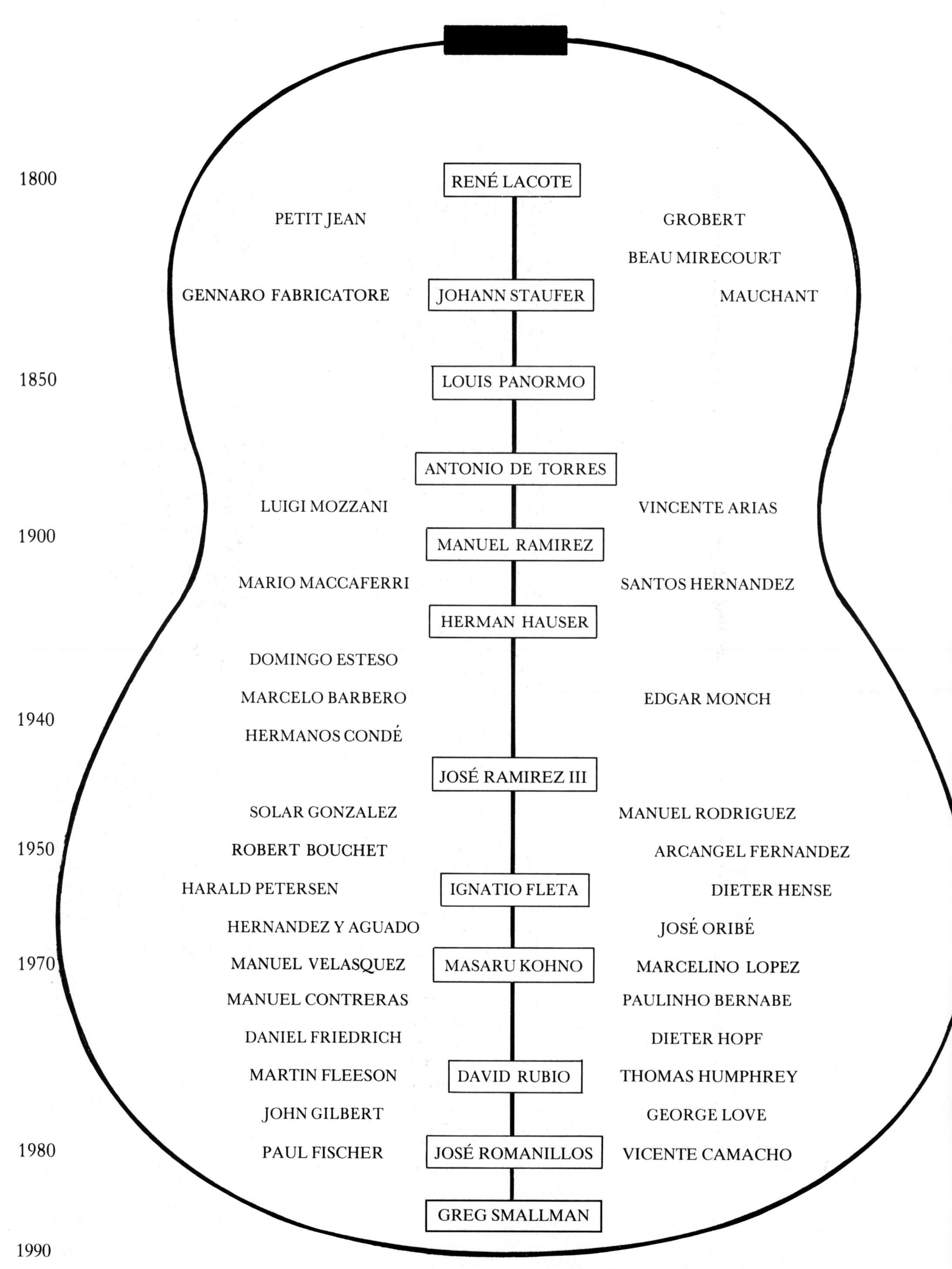


*A general chart showing the finest classical guitar makers since 1800*

# THE CLASSICAL GUITAR SINCE 1800

## ITS GUITAR MAKERS

As has already been pointed out, the evolution of the guitar since 1800 shows a parallel development and growth of the guitarist, guitar repertory and the instrument itself. Historically the luthier and the guitarist have always worked closely together to improve the sound and volume of the guitar.

In the nineteenth century Sor worked with Panormo, Carulli with Lacôte, Legnani with Staufer, Madame Sidney Pratten with Panormo, and Arcas and Tárrega with Torres. It was the joint efforts of these great guitar figures that led to the ideas that contributed to the development of the guitar as we know it today.

In the twentieth century Andrés Segovia, over the years, worked with several important guitar makers, such as the Ramírez family, Hauser and Fleta. In more recent times Julian Bream has encouraged David Rubio and José Romanillos. It was with Andrés Segovia's encouragement and advice that the luthier Albert Augustine was to develop the first nylon guitar string, a vital step forward for the classical guitarist in 1948.

This section of the book spotlights the most innovative guitar makers since 1800.

*Brian Cohen, a prominent English luthier, in his workshop*

# STAUFER

*Staufer guitar*

Johann George Staufer, or Stauffer (26 January 1778 – 24 January 1853), was one of the foremost guitar makers of the nineteenth century. His workshops were in Vienna, and many important guitarists including Regondi, Mertz and Schubert used his guitars. Luigi Legnani also used Staufer's guitars, and suggested several methods of improved construction. Staufer eventually produced large quantities of a guitar bearing the label 'Legnani model'.

Johann Staufer was the inventor of the guitar with a detachable neck, and of the arpeggione. Sometimes called the 'guitare d'amour', the arpeggione (a bowed instrument) was a mixture of the guitar and cello, and first appeared in 1824. Although Schubert was quite taken with the instrument – he wrote a sonata in A minor for it – it did not achieve any further success.

Johann Staufer composed a few pieces for the guitar and was also a publisher of guitar solos.

# LACOTE

*Lacôte guitar*

René-François Lacôte (1785-1855) was born in Mirecourt, France. He made guitars for the most famous players of his day, including Fernando Sor and Carulli.

A writer in the 'Giulianiad' magazine (1833) commented: 'The superiority of Lacôte's guitars consists in their symmetrical proportions; in the quality of the wood; in the mathematical exactness of the frets, neck and head; and in their general workmanship'. On some of his earlier labels Lacôte described himself as a pupil of M.Pone. Later labels read 'Lacôte & Cie' and gave particulars of some of the many medals and decorations that he had won at the great exhibitions.

Lacôte guitars have lute-type fingerboards with top frets let into the table of the guitar. In some, the wood is scalloped out between the frets, and later instruments often have an enclosed machine head. Fine guitars of the Lacôte type are sometimes found without labels; these were probably made by apprentices of Lacôte.

# PANORMO

*Louis Panormo*

Panormo guitars were made by the sons and grandsons of Vincenzo Panormo, who was born at Monreale, Sicily, 30 November 1734.

Vincenzo Panormo was regarded as one of Italy's finest violin makers. He moved to England in 1777 and settled in London with his family. Three of his four sons – Joseph, Louis and George – were to become leading guitar makers.

Joseph Panormo had a workshop in Church Street, Soho. In 1809, Fernando Sor left him his Spanish-made guitar (probably a José Martinez of Málaga) to copy. The result was a blend of Spanish design and Italian craftsmanship. This guitar became the basis of later models to be made by Louis and other members of the Panormo family.

Louis Panormo had a shop at 46 High Street, Bloomsbury, and together with several members of his family developed a prosperous guitar-making business. Louis eventually emigrated to New Zealand, but the business continued under the management of his brother George and nephew George junior. In all, Panormo guitars were made in London for around 70 years. Their output was approximately seven to ten guitars per week for a good portion of this period. The Panormo family offered a selection of good quality instruments, from basic models to high-quality recital instruments. They were used by many of the top players of the day.

**SELECTED READING**

Louis Panormo. Guitar, June 1975

The Panormo Family of Guitar Makers. Classical Guitar, July 1985

Louis Panormo: The Final Years. Classical Guitar, June 1986

*Panormo Guitar*

# TORRES

*Antonio de Torres*

Don Antonio de Torres Jurado was born in San Sebastián de Almería, Spain, on 18 June 1817. He died there on 19 November 1892. He is the man to whom we owe the modern concert guitar.

While Torres was working for the guitar maker José Pernas in Granada that he was approached by one of the foremost classical guitarists of the time, Julián Arcas. For some time Arcas had been unhappy with the sound and volume of his guitar, and put several ideas to Torres about improving the instrument.

With Torres' craftsmanship and ingenuity, the proportions of the classical guitar became enlarged from the original nineteenth century small-bodied guitar to the type of guitar we know today. After Arcas, Torres worked with Francisco Tárrega and developed an instrument which has become the basis of today's classical guitars.

Torres made guitars in two distinct periods. The first period lasted from 1850-1869. Then he retired from guitar making to open a china shop. He returned to guitar making in 1880 and continued to construct many fine instruments until his death in 1892. He never signed the labels of his guitars, and only numbered those of the second period.

**SELECTED READING**


Torres and the First Generation. Guitar, October 1973
Torres. Guitar Review No.16, 1954
Antonio de Torres: José Romanillos. Element Books, 1988

*Torres Guitar*

# RAMIREZ

*Jose Ramirez III*

The Ramírez guitar is one of today's most popular guitars for concert guitarists. Under the management of José Ramírez III and José Ramírez IV, the Ramírez workshops in Madrid employ about seventeen luthiers with several assistants. Their annual production at the moment is about 1,000 concert models, which are exported all over the world, and are in constant demand.

The Ramírez tradition dates back to the second half of the nineteenth century, when José Ramírez I set up a workshop in Madrid. As a child he had been an apprentice guitar builder to Francisco González. In his Madrid workshop José Ramírez I, now recognized as a master luthier, taught his younger brother, Manuel Ramírez, also Julian Gomez and Enrique Garcia.

It was Manuel Ramírez who gave Andrés Segovia one of their finest guitars as a gift, after hearing him play, when the guitarist was still in his teens and unknown. For many years Segovia, on his concert tours throughout the world, played only the Ramírez guitar. Since that time the name Ramírez has been synonymous with the best in classical guitars.

Over the years the Ramírez workshop has had many apprentices who in turn became great guitar makers. Included are Santos Hernández, Domingo Esteso, Marcelo Barbero, Manuel Rodriguez, Manuel Contreras and Paulino Bernabe.

The Ramírez workshops, now managed by third and fourth generation members of the Ramírez family, can be considered a vital part in the development of the classical guitar.

**SELECTED READING**

| | |
|---|---|
| José Ramírez III. | Guitar Player, April 1973 |
| José Ramírez III. | Guitar & Lute, May 1979 |
| Ramírez Guitars. | Frets, January 1982 |

**Workshop address:**
Concepcion Jeronima 2, Madrid 12, Spain.

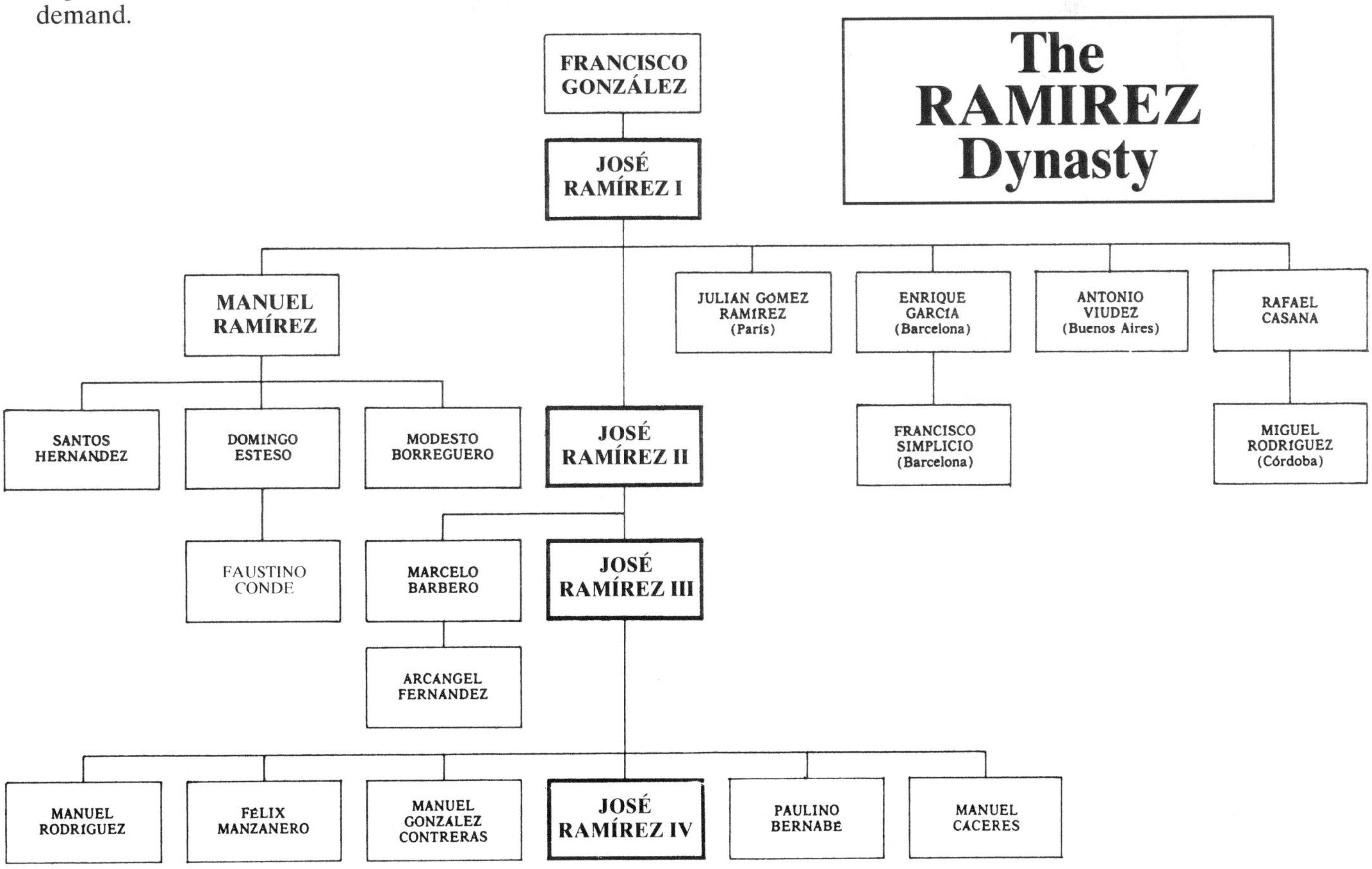

## The RAMIREZ Dynasty

- FRANCISCO GONZÁLEZ
  - JOSÉ RAMÍREZ I
    - MANUEL RAMÍREZ
      - SANTOS HERNANDEZ
      - DOMINGO ESTESO
        - FAUSTINO CONDE
      - MODESTO BORREGUERO
    - JOSÉ RAMÍREZ II
      - MARCELO BARBERO
        - ARCANGEL FERNANDEZ
      - JOSÉ RAMÍREZ III
        - MANUEL RODRIGUEZ
        - FELIX MANZANERO
        - MANUEL GONZALEZ CONTRERAS
        - JOSÉ RAMÍREZ IV
        - PAULINO BERNABE
        - MANUEL CACERES
    - JULIAN GOMEZ RAMIREZ (París)
    - ENRIQUE GARCIA (Barcelona)
      - FRANCISCO SIMPLICIO (Barcelona)
    - ANTONIO VIUDEZ (Buenos Aires)
    - RAFAEL CASANA
      - MIGUEL RODRIGUEZ (Córdoba)

# HAUSER

*Hermann Hauser II, with Hermann Hauser III in the background*

Joseph Hauser, in the late nineteenth century, was the first member of the Hauser family to make musical instruments. He was a talented composer and an accomplished zither player. He won many medals and presentations from the German state for his outstanding achievements in music.

It was his son Hermann Hauser (1882-1952) who extended his father's instrument-making profession. He built a vast selection of string instruments including lutes, viols, zithers, violins and guitars. The first guitars he built were similar to the small-bodied mid-nineteenth century French guitars. In the late 1920s Hermann Hauser was fortunate to have Andrés Segovia as a guest in his house. Much impressed with the workmanship of Hauser's guitars, Segovia suggested that Hauser should make a guitar of the same size as his Ramírez. Within a short period of time Hauser had built a guitar of exceptional sound and quality. Segovia was to use this guitar for many years, establishing Hauser as one of the foremost guitar makers of the twentieth century.

Since Hauser's death, his son Hermann Hauser Junior and grandson Hermann Hauser III have carried on the tradition of guitar making. Hauser guitars remain among the most sought-after in the world.

**SELECTED READING**

Hermann Hauser. Guitar & Lute, May 1978.

**Workshop address:**

Hermann Hauser, 8386 Reisbach an der Vils, Bayern, West Germany.

*Hermann Hauser III, 1991*

PHOTO: MAURICE J. SUMMERFIELD

# FLETA

*Ignacio Fleta*

Ignacio Fleta, regarded by many as the greatest guitar maker of the twentieth century, was born in Huesca, Spain, on 31 July 1897. He died in Barcelona on 11 August 1977. Ignacio Fleta's father was a joiner, and it was from him that Fleta learned many aspects of the craft. As a youth, he was fascinated by music, and at the age of eight he was able to play the bandurria and the guitar. At the age of thirteen he went to Barcelona and learned the basics of guitar construction from a French Luthier. He worked in the luthier's workshop with his two brothers, and studied violin, cello and bass-viol making as well.

In 1927 Ignacio Fleta opened his own workshop in Barcelona. The first instruments he made were cellos, but soon he was making guitars and violins as well. From 1939 to 1945 he reproduced a collection of old instruments for the musical society 'Ars Musica'. The collection included the Gothic harp, fiddle, lute, vihuela, and other instruments right through to the modern guitar. The brilliance of his construction brought Fleta world-wide fame.

In 1955 Ignacio Fleta heard Andrés Segovia for the first time. He was so impressed that he decided from that moment on that he would build only guitars. In 1957 he built the first of three guitars which Segovia would play in his recitals all over the world. Since that time over 700 guitars have been made in the Fleta workshop, many of them owned by today's foremost guitarists.

Since Ignacio Fleta's death in 1977, his two sons, Francisco (born 22 July 1925) and Gabriel (born 21 December 1929), have carried on the business with equal success.

**Workshop address:**
Calle de los Angeles 4, Barcelona, Spain.

*Fleta guitar*

# BOUCHET

*Robert Bouchet*

Robert Bouchet was born on 10 April 1898, and died in 1986. He was trained as a painter in Paris, the city of his birth. Although he played the guitar from 1932, it was not until 1946 that he made his first guitar. After losing his own guitar, he decided to try and make one himself. On his regular visits to the workshop of a friend, a Spanish luthier by the name of Ramírez, Bouchet had observed all the various stages of guitar making. He had always been good at making things, and found that he had no problem in constructing a guitar. Friends were so impressed with his first instrument that Bouchet soon received orders for more. His output was not large, but his reputation grew quickly and many top players came to buy a guitar from him. Included were Ida Presti, Alexandre Lagoya, Emilio Pujol, Oscar Ghiglia, Turibio Santos, Manuel López Ramos and Julian Bream.

After he reached the age of eighty, Robert Bouchet made guitars only rarely. He lived in the countryside on the outskirts of Paris, where he died on 15 August 1986.

**SELECTED READING**

Robert Bouchet. Guitar, February 1973

# MASARU KOHNO

*Masaru Kohno*

Masaru Kohno was born in Mito City, Japan, on 15 August 1926. He graduated from the Tokyo College of Arts and Crafts in 1948, majoring in woodcraft. It was then that he became interested in guitar making, which led him to Spain in 1960. There he spent six months in the Madrid workshops of Arcangel Fernández. On his return to Tokyo, he established his own guitar workshop. Within a short time his exceptional talent was recognized by Japanese guitarists. In 1967, with the award of first prize for guitar making at the Liège Concours National des Guitares, his talent was recognized internationally.

Masaru Kohno has since maintained his reputation as one of the most important of contemporary guitar makers.

**Workshop address:**

Nishiikebukuro 5-27, Toshimaku, Tokyo, Japan.

# RUBIO

**SELECTED READING**


| | |
|---|---|
| David Rubio. | Guitar, October 1972 |
| David Rubio. | Guitar, August 1976 |
| David Rubio. | Guitar & Lute, January 1979 |


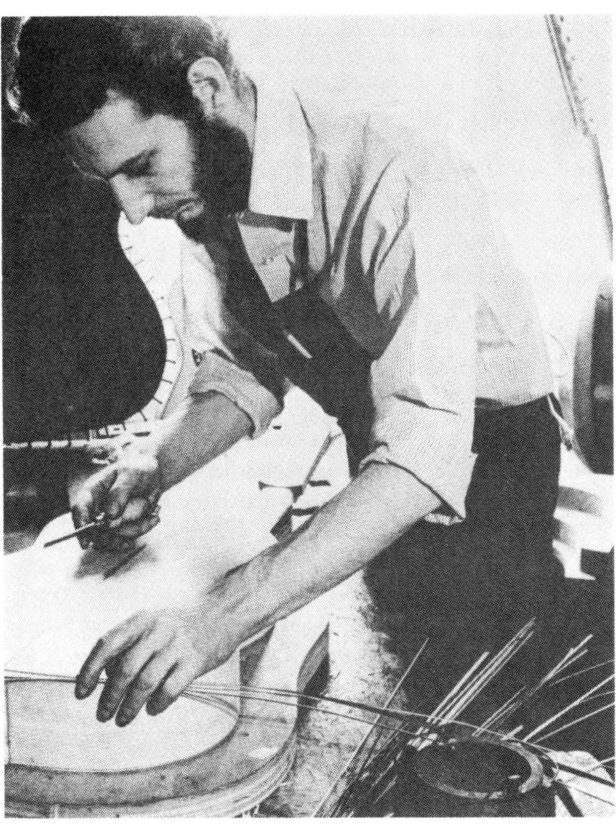

*David Rubio*

David J. Rubio was born in London in 1934. He originally decided to become a doctor, but before he qualified he had already decided that this was not the career for him. He went to Spain to study flamenco guitar, feeling that he would like to be a professional player of the intrument. He settled in Madrid, spending his days practising in the guitar workshop of Sabrinos de Esteso. It was there that he developed an interest in guitar making, and during his three-year stay in Madrid he was able to serve a full apprenticeship as a guitar maker.

In 1961 Rubio moved to New York City and continued to study guitar construction with a maker by the name of Amedeo. In 1963 Amedeo died and Rubio set up his own workshop. He began to build guitars and lutes of exceptional quality, and soon his reputation was such that leading guitarists, including Julian Bream, became his customers.

In 1967 Rubio returned to England and set himself up in Duns Tew, Oxford, as a builder of guitars and lutes. He also began to construct stringed instruments of the Baroque period, including viols, cellos and harpsichords. In recent years he has concentrated on harpsichords, leaving the construction of guitars to other members of his workshop.

*Rubio Guitar*

# BERNABE

*Paulino Bernabe*

Paulino Bernabe was born in Madrid on 2 July 1932. At the age of seventeen he began to study the classical guitar with Daniel Fortea, a pupil of the great Tárrega. It was during the four years he spent with Fortea that he developed an interest in constructing guitars.

In 1954 the young guitarist became an apprentice guitar maker to José Ramírez. By 1969 his skills as a luthier were acknowledged with his promotion to workshop manager for the Ramírez company.

In 1970 Bernabe left Ramírez and opened his own workshop at 8 Cuchilleros Street, Madrid. The change gave him the opportunity to introduce new ideas into the construction of his guitars, and soon the Bernabe guitar became one of the most sought-after classical guitars. In 1973 he completed a 10-string guitar for Narciso Yepes, which the guitarist has used since. In 1974 Bernabe received the Gold Medal at the International Crafts Exhibition held in Munich, Germany, for his craftsmanship.

**Workshop address:**
Cuchilleros 8, Madrid 12, Spain.

# CONTRERAS

*Manuel Contreras*

Born in Madrid on April 21 1928. Manuel Contreras was originally a cabinet-maker. He joined the Ramírez company as a senior journeyman in 1959. In 1962 he left Ramírez and set up his own workshop at Calle Mayor, 80, Madrid.

Since then, Contreras has established himself as one of the finest and most innovative guitar makers in Spain. In 1979 he was awarded the Export Award from the Madrid Chamber of Commerce and Industry. A year later he was given an honourable mention by the same body. Other awards, including the Medal of the City of Salon-de-Provence and the Medal of the City of Digne-les-Bains, were to follow. In 1981 Contreras visited Japan as a guest of the Niibori Guitar Academy as a tribute to his craftsmanship. In 1987 the Isla de la Francia Guitar Circle presented him with the Order of the Good Rosette in recognition of his work in improving the classical guitar's sonority.

Contreras's most famous innovations are his double-top concert guitar (1974), based on an idea of Celedonio Romero, and the Carlevaro model (1983), based on an original idea of the Uruguayan guitarist Abel Carlevaro.

**SELECTED READING**
Interview. Guitar International, December 1987

**Workshop address:**
Calle Mayor 80, Madrid, Spain.

# ROMANILLOS

*José Romanillos*

José Luis Romanillos Vega was born in Madrid on 17 June 1932. Prior to his coming to England, his only real interest in the guitar was as a player. By profession he was a woodworker, and he became interested in the construction of guitars after he had tried to repair some guitars belonging to friends.

In 1956 he came to London. He could not afford to buy a guitar, so he decided to build one. With the help of a guitarist friend, his first guitar was completed in six months. Encouraged by the reaction of his friends to this first effort, he developed his craft by building more guitars. He returned to Spain for three years in 1964, building several more guitars during this time. On his return to England in 1967, he brought two of these guitars with him. He showed them to Carlos Bonell and Gilbert Biberian, who were both most impressed by his craftsmanship and the fine sound. With this encouragement, Romanillos decided to give up his regular job as a cabinet maker to devote his time to guitar making.

In 1970 Romanillos showed one of his new guitars to Julian Bream, who was so impressed that he helped him to set up a workshop near his home in Semley, Wiltshire. For many years the guitarist showed a great interest in the development of Romanillos's new guitars, playing them in concert and on some of his recordings. Bream also used several of the luthier's replicas of old fretted instruments in Channel 4's television series on the history of the guitar in Spain, Guitarra!

José Romanillos has established himself as one of the great twentieth century luthiers. His instruments are prized by guitarists all over the world. In recent years he has given masterclasses on guitar making in many countries. His book, an important biography of the nineteenth century guitar maker Torres, was published in 1987.

**SELECTED READING**

Antonio de Torres, Guitar Maker
His Life & Work (José L. Romanillos) Element Books, 1987

| | |
|---|---|
| Interview. | Guitar, December 1972 |
| Interview. | Guitar, June 1978 |
| Interview. | Guitar, December 1980 |
| Interview. | Guitar, December 1981 |
| Interview. | Classical Guitar, February, 1986 |
| Interview. | Guitar International, March 1987 |
| Interview. | Classical Guitar, January 1991 |

**Workshop address:**
Madrigal, Barker's Hill, Semley, Shaftesbury,
Dorset SP7 9BJ, England.

# HOPF

*Dieter Hopf*

Dieter Hopf was born in Zwote (Klingenthal), East Germany, on 29 May 1936. His family have been violin makers for over three hundred years. In 1949 the family moved to Taunustein/Weben, near Wiesbaden, in West Germany. Here they set up a factory to make cheap guitars, strings and recorders. Dieter Hopf attended a course in violin making at the musical instrument school in Mittenwald. He left there in 1955 and worked for his father for two years. He then went to England to gain experience as an instrument repairer at Selmer's music store in London. In 1958 the young maker returned home with the ambition to make classical guitars which would be accepted internationally as being on the same level as those of Fleta, Ramírez and Kohno.

By 1970. under the direction of Dieter Hopf, the company was well established and successful. Over the years he has achieved his ambition by producing instruments of the highest quality that are now played by many top guitarists throughout the world. His innovations include the 'La Portentosa' model, a large-bodied guitar with a long scale and rosette bridge which help to produce greater volume and clarity of sound.

**SELECTED READING**

Article. Guitar International, May 1984

**Workshop address:**
Platter Strasse 79, D-6204 Taunusstein-Wehen,
West Germany.

# GILBERT

*John M. Gilbert*

John M. Gilbert (born New York, 8 December 1922) started building guitars as a hobby in 1965. At that time he was working as chief tool engineer for the Hewlett-Packard Company. For a period of nine years he perfected his craft as a luthier and guitar repairer while maintaining his engineering career. In 1974 he turned to guitar making as a full-time job.

Gilbert established himself as an innovative luthier within a relatively short period of time, and is now regarded by many as the USA's finest classical guitar maker. His distinctive guitars are used by many prominent guitarists.

Since 1956 Gilbert has been based in Woodside, California, where he has his workshop. He has now been joined by his son William, another fine guitar maker, who will help maintain the tradition of the Gilbert workshop for many years to come.

**Workshop address:**
1485 La Honda Road, Woodside, California 94062, USA.

# FISCHER

*Paul Fischer*

Paul Fischer was born in the Isle of Man, England, on 20 August 1941. His first experience as a musical instrument maker came in 1956-1961 when he had a five-year indentured apprenticeship as a harpsichord, clavichord and spinet maker with Robert Goble in Oxford. He also studied at the Oxford College of Technology and City and Guilds of London Institute. After military service, Fischer became the manager of David Rubio's musical instrument studio at Duns Tew, Oxford. During his six-year stay there, he made guitars, lutes, early fretted instruments and harpsicords.

In 1973 Paul Fischer opened his own studio, specializing in the classical guitar and early fretted instruments. Since then he has established himself internationally as one of the world's foremost luthiers. His instruments are often featured in musical instrument exhibitions, and he lectures regularly in the UK and Europe on the craft of instrument making.

**SELECTED READING**
Interview. Classical Guitar, November & December 1986

**Workshop address:**
West End Studio, West End, Chipping Norton,
Oxfordshire OX7 5EY.

# GREG SMALLMAN

*Greg Smallman*

Greg Smallman was born in Cronulla, New South Wales, Australia, on 19 June 1947. His talents as a guitar maker of unique ability first became known internationally through John Williams, who in recent years has played Smallman's guitars virtually exclusively.

Smallman lives with his family in the rain forest in northern New South Wales, isolated from the world at large as his home and workshop are off the beaten track and he has no telephone. His fine guitars, distinguished by their brilliant sound, volume and ease of playing, are now much sought after by guitarists throughout the world. Smallman's output is very small, usually around four guitars a year, so their exclusivity is guaranteed.

**SELECTED READING**
Interview. Guitar International, August 1988.

**Workshop address:**
c/o P.O. Box 510, Glen Innes 2370, New South Wales, Australia.

# ALBERT AUGUSTINE

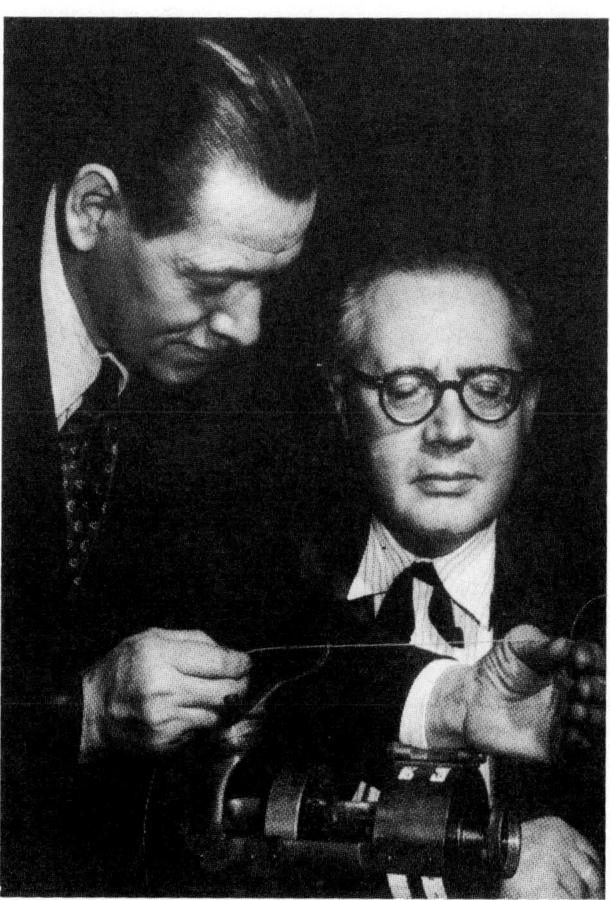
COURTESY: AUGUSTINE STRINGS

*Albert Augustine with Andrés Segovia*

Albert Augustine (1900-1967) was the pioneer of the nylon guitar string. As such he may be regarded as one of the most important figures in the evolution of the classical guitar.

It was with the encouragement of Andrés Segovia that Albert Augustine, luthier and patron of the arts, began to research the possibilities of developing a nylon guitar string. Before 1947 guitarists used gut treble strings and metal wound silk floss basses. They were unreliable, difficult to tune, and soon wore out or broke, even after limited use. During and after World War II the supply situation of good strings for all instruments became very difficult. Segovia, together with Albert Augustine, discussed the matter with an executive of the Du Pont Chemical Company, who made available monofilament nylon originally developed for the manufacture of fishing lines. In 1947 Albert Augustine's workshops in New York produced the first commercially available nylon guitar strings. Since that time, the Augustine brand of guitar strings has remained one of the leaders among the many brands of classical guitar strings available today, including Savarez and Concertiste (produced in France) and D'Addario, Aranjuez and La Bella (produced in the USA).

For much of his life Albert Augustine experimented in the building of guitars, and completed several fine instruments before his death in April 1967. His New York workshop, under the supervision of Frank Haselbacher, continues to this day to produce fine classical guitars. The Augustine string business continues to prosper under the management of his widow Rose Augustine (currently the editor of 'Guitar Review').

## D'ADDARIO

PHOTO: MAURICE J. SUMMERFIELD

*John Jnr, and Jimmy D'Addario*

The D'Addario family business of string making goes back eight generations. They first started making strings in the town of Salle in the province of Pescara, Italy. Charles D'Addario emigrated to the USA in 1909 and continued the family tradition, first by importing and distributing strings and then, in 1916, by making them in a small workshop in Long Island City. At that time the business concentrated on violin strings. John D'Addario joined his father in 1935, and became interested in other aspects of string making. In 1938 they began to make their first steel guitar strings for jazz and western guitars. Their business grew at a rapid rate from then, and after John's son, John Jnr, joined them in the late 1960s they changed their trading name to Darco Music Strings. The company prospered and was bought out by the Martin Guitar Company in 1970. In September 1974 John D'Addario, after leaving the Darco business, was joined by his youngest son James. Together with John Jnr, they began to produce strings again as J. D'Addario & Company Inc. Since that time the D'Addario company has become one of the largest string-making companies in the world, making strings for virtually every stringed instrument. Since 1974 they have maintained a special interest in strings for the classical guitar, working with many of the world's finest players. They have introduced many new manufacturing techniques, including laser technology, which are reflected in their range of Pro Arte classical guitar strings.

The D'Addario family made a further great contribution to the classical guitar in 1981, with the setting up of the D'Addario Foundation. This is a non-profit organization which sponsors an annual concert series in major cities of the USA, giving deserving new classical guitarists a chance to be featured alongside established artists. Janet D'Addario is the Foundation director, and Benjamin Verdery is the artistic director. Now in its ninth year, the D'Addario Foundation's Concert Series has become one of North America's most important events for classical guitarists.

**SELECTED READING**


Meet the D'Addarios. Guitar Player, February 1976

The D'Addario Foundation. Guitar Player, November 1983


## CLASSICAL GUITAR CONSTRUCTION – SELECTED READING


Manual of Guitar Technology: Franz Jahnel. Das Musikinstrument (1981)

Classical Guitar Construction: Irving Sloane. Dutton (1966)

Guitar Repair: Irving Sloane. Dutton (1973)

Classical Guitar, Design and Construction: McLeod & Welford. Dryad (1971)

Make Your Own Spanish Guitar: A. P. Sharpe. Clifford Essex (1957)

Classic Guitar Making: Arthur E. Overholtzer Brock (1974). Williams (1983)

The A-Z of Guitar Construction. Guitar Review No. 28, New York (1965).

Make Your Own Classical Guitar: Stanley Doubtfire. Gollancz (1981)

Making Musical Instruments: The Guitar – José Romanillos. Faber and Faber (1979)

The Fine Guitar: José Oribe. Vel-Or Publishing (1985)

Antonio de Torres: José L. Romanillos. Element Books (1987)

Guitar Making: Tradition and Technology – Cumpiano/Natelson. Rosewood Press (1987)

# MANUEL RODRIGUEZ AND SONS

The pictures below show some of the many stages of the guitar-making process taken in the Madrid workshop of Manuel Rodriguez and Sons.

Manuel Rodriguez was born on October 7, 1926. He began to work in the Ramirez workshop in March, 1939 as an apprentice. After a break of five years to complete his school education the young luthier went back to Ramirez in 1945 and remained there until 1955. Already recognized as one of Madrid's best makers Rodriguez worked from home until 1957 when he established his own workshop in Madrid. In 1959 he decided to emigrate to the USA setting up his workshop in Los Angeles. This was to prove a successful venture and Rodriguez remained there until 1974 when he decided to return to Madrid to once again set up his workshop, with his sons Manuel Junior and Norman, in Madrid at Hortaleza 26 which is still their current Madrid address.

# THE CLASSICAL GUITAR

## ITS SCHOLARS

# THE CLASSICAL GUITAR SINCE 1800 ITS SCHOLARS

Another vital contribution to the evolution of the classical guitar since 1800 has been its numerous scholars, those guitarists who have dedicated themselves to research and education rather than the concert platform.

In the early nineteenth century, François de Fossa, a professional soldier who was also an enthusiastic amateur guitarist and composer, was instrumental in preserving Luigi Boccherini's guitar quintets (written towards the end of the eighteenth century under the patronage of the Marquis de Benavente) for future generations. According to Dionisio Aguado, it was also de Fossa who formulated the rules for the production of artificial harmonics on the guitar.

Since that time there have been many more classical guitarists who have devoted every spare moment to research and to the historical documentation of the classical guitar. The main section of this book has included several classical guitarists and personalities who have made a major contribution to the scholarship of the instrument. Included are Philip Bone, Alexander Bellow, François de Fossa, Domingo Prat and André Verdier. Also included in the main section are contemporary guitarists such as James Tyler and Harvey Hope (early guitar), Simon Wynberg (nineteenth century guitar), all of whom have made and continue to make great contributions in researching the guitar in their particular field.

This section is devoted to some of the other important scholars of recent years. Their enormous contribution to the classical guitar (and that of many other guitar scholars all over the world) is often overlooked by the majority of classical guitar lovers.

## RUGGERO CHIESA

Ruggero Chiesa was born in Camogli, Italy, on 1 August 1933. He first studied the guitar with Carlo Palladino in Genoa. He later attended the Accademia Chigiana di Siena where he studied with both Andrés Segovia and Alirio Díaz. He also studied vihuela with Emilio Pujol at Siena.

*Ruggero Chiesa*

Since 1963 Chiesa has taught at the G.Verdi Conservatory in Milan. Since 1976 he has held an annual course on the transcriptions of tablature, as well as diverse seminars on guitar topics, at the Accademia Chigiana di Siena and also at Gargnano. In 1983 he became the director of the Corsi Accademici di Chitarra held annually at Bassano del Grappa (Vicenza), Italy. Many of Chiesa's pupils have won national and international competitions and now enjoy successful careers as concert guitarists. Amongst these are included Emanuele Segre, Massimo Laura, Elena Casoli and Leopoldo Saracino.

Ruggero Chiesa founded in 1972 'Il Fronimo', a prestigious quarterly guitar and lute magazine of which he is still the editor. He is also prominent as an editor of music. He has edited more than 150 works of various composers and is the author of several didactic works. Among his many publications are the complete works of Luis Milán, Francesco da Milano and Michelangelo Galilei. Chiesa has also edited the complete works for guitar of Nicolò Paganini. Several contemporary composers, including Castelnuovo-Tedesco, Bruno Bettinelli, Franco Donatoni and Aldo Clementi, have dedicated works to him.

**SELECTED READING**


| | |
|---|---|
| Il Fronimo. | Issue 1 (1972) to current issue |
| Interview. | Classical Guitar, July 1985 |
| La Chitarra. | EDT, Torino 1990 |

# JOHN GAVALL

*John Gavall*

John Gavall was born in Liverpool, England on 29 January 1919. He was educated at Malvern and earned his M.A. at Peterhouse.

From the early 1950s he was a frequent performer on radio and television in Great Britain, and it was from that time that he became a very active protagonist of the guitar as an ideal instrument for the dissemination of musical knowledge and education.

In 1954 he became a full-time music teacher. Between 1955 and 1962 he was appointed Music Adviser to the West Riding of Yorkshire Education Authority. In 1962 as a guitarist, in competition with such traditional applicants as organists, pianists and conductors, Gavall took over as Senior Music Adviser for all of the thousand or more schools and colleges of the West Riding Education Authority. In this position, he directed the musical activity and teaching for all schools in one of the largest counties of Great Britain. This was the first time that a guitarist had gained such an important position in musical education in Great Britain.

Over the years John Gavall has been responsible for a large number of publications for the guitar. The most important of these is probably his five-volume set Learning Music Through The Guitar, published by Belwin Mills. Gavall wrote this set of books to prove that the guitar had enormous potential for music education and that it should be a serious part of all teacher training.

In 1972 John Gavall was appointed Lecturer in Music at Moray House College in Edinburgh. From that time Moray House offered tuition and harmony through the guitar, and also the techniques of teaching guitar to large groups of adults or college students. Gavall was also one of the first to use closed circuit television in guitar education.

John Gavall has been one of the most important figures in Great Britain for the promotion of the guitar over the last thirty years. He now lives in London and is a frequent contributor to Classical Guitar Magazine.

# ANGELO GILARDINO

*Angelo Gilardino*

Angelo Gilardino was born in Vercelli, Italy, on 16 November 1941. He studied the guitar, cello and composition with local teachers in Vercelli from an early age. He went on to study harmony and counterpoint with Giuseppe Rosetta at the Viotti Institute in Vercelli. Gilardino also studied musical history, tablature, conducting and accompaniment, and from 1965 was Professor of Guitar at the Viotti Institute. Since 1981 he has been Professor of Guitar at the Vivaldi State Conservatory in Alessandria. He also gives masterclasses and presents seminars for guitar throughout Italy and other parts of Europe.

Now recognised internationally as a musicologist and guitar authority, Gilardino has also had two periods as a concert artist, 1958 to 1968 and 1971 to 1981. His performances were nearly always devoted to twentieth century music, and many well-known composers, including Ascencio, Berkeley, Castelnuovo-Tedesco, Rodrigo, Ruiz-Pipó and Duarte, have dedicated works to him.

In 1968 Gilardino, on the recommendation of Castelnuovo-Tedesco, was appointed editor of modern and contemporary guitar works for the important publishing house Edizioni Musicali Bèrben. He has held that position to the present day. He is a regular contributor to the Italian guitar magazine, il Fronimo. In 1989 his contribution to Bèrben's two-volume Manuale di storia della chitarra volume 2, La chitarra moderna e contemporanea, was published.

Angelo Gilardino is also a prolific composer for guitar, and has had several works published since 1981.

**SELECTED MUSIC**

| | |
|---|---|
| Studi di virtuosita e di trascendenza (5 volumes). | Bèrben |
| Sonata No.1. | Bèrben |
| Sonata No.2. | Bèrben |
| Variazioni sulla Follia. | Bèrben |

**SELECTED READING**

| | |
|---|---|
| Various Articles. | Il Fronimo |
| Manuale di storia della chitarra – Volume 2. | Bèrben |

**SELECTED RECORDING**

| | |
|---|---|
| Gilardino plays Haug, Wissmer, Duarte, Tansman etc. | Bèrben BRMS 0074 |

# FREDERIC V. GRUNFELD

*Frederic Grunfeld*

Frederic Grunfeld was born in Berlin, Germany, on 2 June 1929 and died in 1987. He was trained in both music and art at the University of Chicago, from where he graduated. He began his career as a critic on the radio in the 1950s when he introduced a new programme entitled 'Music Magazine' on WQXR radio station. Grunfeld was involved in several volumes of Time-Life Great Music Series, and wrote several important music books including The Art and Times of the Guitar (Macmillan), one of the finest general histories of the guitar ever written. By 1971 the fourth edition of the work had been printed. In 1974 Collier Books released a paperback edition, and in 1975 Zen-On Publishers of Tokyo published a Japanese edition. The USA specialist publisher, De Capo Press, published a reprint in paperback in 1989.

**SELECTED READING**

The Art and Times of The Guitar. MacMillan, New York 1969

# THOMAS F. HECK

*Thomas F. Heck*

Thomas F. Heck was born in Washington, USA, on 10 July 1943. He began to study the classical guitar in Paris, where he lived while his father was stationed for a number of years with the USA State Department. On returning to the United States, Heck entered Notre Dame, where he received his B.A. degree. He went on to spend a year at the Academy of Music in Vienna, following which he entered the graduate programme at Yale University. In 1970, he earned his Ph.D. degree in Music History there.

In recent years Thomas F. Heck has established himself as a foremost historian, teacher and authority of the guitar. He was an editor and contributor of Soundboard magazine, the quarterly magazine published in California devoted to the classical guitar.

**SELECTED READING**


Interview. Classical Guitar, October 1985
What is a guitar? Soundboard No.3, 1976
Giuliani: Ph.D. Dissertation. Univ. Microfilms 71-76, 249
Articles on Aguado, Carulli, Giuliani, Legnani, Matiegka, Regondi, Tárrega, Ferranti. New Grove, 1980
The role of Italy. Guitar Review No 34, 1971
Article. Classical Guitar, October 1985

# BRIAN HODEL

*Brian Hodel*

Brian Hodel was born in Beckley, West Virginia, on 21 June 1948 Over a period of years he has established himself as a foremost writer, arranger and perfomer in the area of Brazilian music. After several years of music studies in the USA, where he was a guitar teacher at the University of Washington, he went to Brazil to live, and continued his studies there. He returned to the USA in 1989 and settled in Los Angeles, where he received an MA in music from the University of California in 1990.

Hodel has written several outstanding articles on the guitar music of Brazil and other South American countries for Guitar Review. He has also contributed articles to Classical Guitar magazine. He has edited books of Brazilian music for guitar for Macmillan and Big Three publishers in the USA, and has contributed several original pieces to the 'Modern Times' series published by Chanterelle Verlag in West Germany. In recent times he has devoted more of his time to composing, having written a string qauartet, a rhapsody for piano, and a song cycle for three voices and chamber orchestra.

**SELECTED READING**

| | |
|---|---|
| Brazilian Popular Music and The Guitar - Article. | Classical Guitar, May/June 1983. |
| Abel Carlevaro – Article. | Guitar Review, Summer 1985. |
| Egberto Gismonti – Article. | Guitar Review, Fall 1985. |
| Astor Piazzolla – Article. | Guitar Review, Winter 1986. |
| Radamés Gnattali – Article. | Guitar Review, Summer 1986. |
| Ear Training for Guitarists. | Guitar Review, Winter 1987. |
| Grosse Fugue Villa-Lobos. | Guitar Review, Fall 1987. |
| Villa-Lobos and the Guitar. | Guitar Review, Winter 1988. |

# JOHN HUBER

*John Huber*

John Huber was born in Mayport, PA, USA, on 2 March 1940. He played the piano and the violin from the age of six. He changed to guitar at the age of fourteen, at which time his musical interest lay in folk music and the blues. He earned a B.A. in Philosophy at the Marietta College in Ohio. During his time there his interest in classical and flamenco guitar began. A self-taught guitarist, he developed a passionate interest in flamenco which encouraged him to go in 1961 to Seville, Spain, where he lived and played among the leading flamenco guitarists of the day, including Antonio Sanlúcar and Melchor de Marchena. Over the next few years he also developed an interest in guitar construction, and spent time extending his knowledge of this skill with Paco Barba in Seville, Manuel Reyes in Córdoba and Bernabe Ferrer in Granada.

In 1965 Huber moved to Stockholm, Sweden, and joined the Levin guitar company as a guitar maker. In 1967 this company was acquired by the C.F.Martin Company, and Huber returned to the USA to work in the Martin repair department. Within a short period of time he was made Director of Research. Further promotion came with his appointment as Director of Sales in Europe. The combination of Huber's multilingual talents with his güitar playing and construction ability made him the ideal choice for this position. In 1973 Huber left the Martin organization and worked for a while with Juan Orozco in the USA and for Dieter Hopf in Germany. In 1976 his growing interest in the construction of both violins and guitars encouraged him to enrol at the Univerity of Uppsala in Sweden, where he gained a Ph.D. in musicology in 1986. He was then awarded several grants from the Swedish Government to research violin construction at the Academy of Music in Stockholm.

John Huber has written three published books on the violin, and will have his book on modern classical guitars published in 1990. He is well known and respected internationally as a leading authority on the guitar.

**SELECTED READING**
Development of the Modern Classical Guitar.
Gitarre & Laute, 1991

# OLIVER HUNT

*Oliver Hunt*

Oliver Hunt was born on 16 June 1934. He studied the guitar at the Guildhall School of Music in London with Adele Kramer in 1958. He also studied privately with Julian Bream. He continued his musical studies in theory and composition at the Royal Academy of Music with Sir Lennox Berkeley and James Illiff, winning the William Wallace Exhibition for Composition.

Oliver Hunt, who is currently Professor of Guitar at the London College of Music, has composed a wide variety of works including solo works for guitar, piano and organ as well as choral, orchestral and chamber music. A work that attracted considerable attention is his Barber of Baghdad Suite (1976), written for the English guitarist Robert Brightmore. He has also written an excellent text book for guitarists entitled Musicianship and Sight Reading for Guitarists.

**SELECTED MUSIC**

| | |
|---|---|
| The Barber of Baghdad. | Revelo-Cornish Music |
| Leviathan. | Revelo-Cornish Music |
| Garuda. | Musical New Services |
| Two White Doves (duet). | Revelo-Cornish Music |
| Quartet No.1. | Revelo-Cornish Music |
| Quartet No.2 'The Sun'. | Revelo-Cornish Music |

**SELECTED READING**
Oliver Hunt. Guitar, March 1977
Analysis: series of articles.
Classical Guitar, Sep/Oct 1982 to Jan/Feb 1983.
Aural Perception & Training.
Classical Guitar, Jan/Feb 1984 to May/Jun 1984.

# BRIAN JEFFERY

PHOTO: COLIN COOPER

*Brian Jeffery*

Brian Jeffery was born in London on 13 October 1938. He was educated at Oxford, and holds a doctorate in musicology and French. He has been a lecturer in French at the University of St Andrews, and visiting professor in the Department of French at the University of California, at Berkeley and Santa Barbara. He also lectured at the University of Warwick.

At school Brian Jeffery played both the piano and the cello, but it was while he was at Oxford that he started to play the lute and then the guitar. He has published many scholarly articles, books and reviews in the fields of the Renaissance, literature and music. His thesis at Oxford was on the 16th century composer Anthony Holborne. Jeffery's biography of Fernando Sor, and his complete editions of the guitar works of Sor and Giuliani, have been major contributions to the growing library of books and music of classical guitar interest. He published in 1990 a complete reprint of the first editions of all Beethoven's piano sonatas. All these works, and many more, have been published by Jeffery's own publishing firm, Tecla Editions.

Brian Jeffery has appeared as a recitalist and accompanist on both lute and guitar, although today he no longer performs in concert.

**SELECTED MUSIC**

The Complete Works for Guitar of Fernando Sor. — Tecla Editions
The Complete Works of Mauro Giuliani. — Tecla Editions

**SELECTED READING**

Fernando Sor: composer and guitarist. — Tecla Editions 1977
Fernando Sor: concert performer. — Guitar Review, No.39, 1974
Interview. — Guitar Player, July 1979

# MICHAEL MACMEEKEN

*Michael Macmeeken*

Michael Macmeeken was born in Edinburgh on 26 September 1942. He was a pupil of Regino Sainz de la Maza, graduating at the Madrid Royal Conservatory of Music. He went into publishing, becoming a founding director of Editions Chanterelle, a specialist publisher of classical guitar music. Now called Chanterelle Verlag Heidelberg, the company is based in West Germany, where Macmeeken lives. Chanterelle has become one of the most respected and innovating guitar music specialist publishers. The backbone of their catalogue is the collected works of Aguado, Coste, Llobet, Mertz, Paganini, Regondi and Zani de Ferranti.

# FREDERICK NOAD

*Frederick Noad*

Frederick Noad was born in Blankenberg, Belgium, on 8 August 1929. His parents were British. He studied violin and piano at Wellington College under the direction of Maurice Allen. He took up the classical guitar, and this was to become his favourite instrument. After taking his M.A at Oxford, Noad moved to Los Angeles, California, where he opened a Spanish guitar centre modelled on that opened by Len Williams in London.

Joaquín Rodrigo heard him play in 1961, and immediately recommended him for a scholarship to attend Segovia's masterclass in Santiago de Compostela. This Noad attended in 1962, and in the same year completed his first book, 'Playing The Guitar', for Collier Books, New York. It was an instant success, reaching the paperback best-seller lists. After many reprintings, it is now in its third edition.

On his return to the USA, Noad studied composition privately with Mario Castelnuovo-Tedesco. In 1966 he presented the first of what was to be twenty-six programmes of guitar lessons for the KCET television station in Los Angeles. In 1968 he added a further thirteen lessons to the series. In the same year his new method, Solo Guitar Playing, was published by Macmillan of New York; it is now claimed to be the most widely used classical guitar instruction book in schools and colleges in the USA. During the same period, he went to Europe and Scandinavia to undertake research for a new anthology series, subsequently been published by Ariel Music.

Frederick Noad, who is also an accomplished lute player, has taught guitar at various institutions including the University of California and the California Institute of Arts. In 1974 he was one of the original founders of the Guitar Foundation of America, for which he served as chairman in 1975.

In 1981 Noad presented a new series of video lessons for television, 'The Guitar with Frederick Noad'. It was a great success and was seen on television stations throughout the USA and also in many other countries. More recently, he initiated a series of radio broadcasts on National Public Radio for the G. Schirmer publishing house, entitled 'Overtones' and covering aspects of the music of our time.

**SELECTED MUSIC**

| | |
|---|---|
| Solo Guitar Playing Volumes 1 & 2. | Macmillan |
| The Renaissance Guitar. | Ariel |
| The Baroque Guitar. | Ariel |
| The Classical Guitar. | Ariel |
| The Romantic Guitar. | Ariel |

# THEODORE NORMAN

*Theodore Norman*

Born in Montréal, Canada, on 14 March 1912, Theodore Norman first studied violin with Willy Hess and composition with Adolph Weiss. He played first violin in the Los Angeles Philharmonic Orchestra from 1935 to 1942.

Norman became interested in the guitar while composing his ballet Metamorphosis, in which he used a guitar. After concentrated study with the guitarist Aurio Herrero in Madrid, he wrote ten pieces for guitar in the twelve-tone system, the first of their type to be published. In Europe, where he met leading classical and flamenco guitarists, he gave a concert on French radio of his own compositions and works by other composers.

On his return to the United States, Norman played the guitar part in Pierre Boulez's Le Marteau sans Maître and Schoenberg's Serenade, recording both works for Columbia Records.

Theodore Norman has transcribed and had published hundreds of works of the great classical composers for one and two guitars. He has also developed a unique system for notating flamenco music. He is currently Head of the Guitar Department at UCLA in California.

**SELECTED READING**

The Art of Theodore Norman. Guitar Review, Fall 1988

# MATANYA OPHEE

PHOTO: COLIN COOPER

*Matanya Ophee*

Matanya Ophee was born in Jerusalem on 5 June 1932, and began his guitar studies in 1955 with Esther Bromberger, a pupil of Luigi Mozzani. He later studied for two years with Richard Pick in Chicago. Further studies in music theory were taken under Gérard Le Coat at the Conservatoire de Lausanne in Switzerland, and in composition with Eli Yarden in Israel.

Since that time Ophee has lived in the USA, where for many years he has had two succesful parallel careers, one as an airline pilot and the other as a musicologist, guitarist and guitar historian. His many articles have appeared in leading guitar journals throughout the world and in many languages. His research into the repertoire of chamber music with guitar and the history of the guitar in Russia have been notable contributions to public knowledge. He is recognized, among others, for bringing to light the biography and accomplishments of the French nineteenth-century guitarist François de Fossa (1775-1849).

Matanya Ophee established the publishing company Editions Orphée, which is based in Columbus, Ohio, and is recognized internationally as a leading publisher of guitar music and books. In 1989 he retired from aviation, and now devotes his full time to music and the guitar.

**SELECTED READING**
Luigi Boccherini's Guitar Quintets:
New Evidence (with a biography of François de Fossa): Ophee. Editions Orphée, 1981
Article: Chamber Music for Terz-Guitar. Guitar Review No.42
Article: The History of Apoyando:Another View. Guitar Review No.51
Article: The First Guitar Concerto and Legends. Classical Guitar, July 1985
Article: On Primary Sources. Classical Guitar, July 1986
Article: Some Considerations of 19th Century Guitar Music and its Performance Practice Today. Classical Guitar, August 1986

# CORAZON OTERO

*Corazón Otero*

Corazón Otero was born in Mexico City, 8 March 1944. She was interested in music from an early age. She began to study the guitar seriously in 1970. Her teachers have included Mario Beltran de Rio and Manuel López Ramos. She has also taken part in masterclasses with Abel Carlevaro, Leo Brouwer and John Williams.

In recent years she has established herself as a major figure in Mexico's classical guitar world, both as a performer and as a scholar. She is a founder of the 'Concurso Internacional de Guitarra Manuel M. Ponce' in Mexico City. Several composers have dedicated works to her, including Alexandre Tansman, Angelo Gilardino, Guido Santórsola and John W. Duarte.

Corazón Otero has made a major contribution to guitar literature with her books on the lives and guitar works of Manuel Ponce, Alexandre Tansman and Mario Castelnuovo-Tedesco.

**SELECTED READING**
Manuel M. Ponce y la Guitarra. Ediciones Musicales Yolotl, Mexico 1980
(Also available inEnglish and French editions).
Mario Castelnuovo-Tedesco: su vida y su obras para guitarra. Ediciones Musicales Yolotl, Mexico 1987
Alexandre Tansman: su vida y su obras para guitarra. Ediciones Musicales Yolotl, Mexico 1989.

# PETER PAFFGEN

*Peter Päffgen*

Peter Päffgen was born in Düsseldorf, West Germany, on 18 November 1950, and studied music and theatre at university. At the same time he studied lute with Professor Michael Schäffer. He qualified in 1978, earning a Ph.D. with his paper on lute music of the sixteenth century.

In 1979 he began to publish the bi-monthly magazine 'Gitarre & Laute' from Cologne, a well-produced magazine has become the most important German-language publication for classical guitarists in Germany. He has also published several important guitar music works and recordings through his magazine's subsidiary, G & L Publications. In 1988 Päffgen completed his history of the classical guitar, Die Gitarre: Grundzuge ihrer Entwicklung.

**SELECTED READING**

Gitarre & Laute magazine. 1979 to current issue

Laute und Lautenspiel in der ersten Halfte des 16 Jahrhunderts. Beobachtungen zur Bauweise und Spieltechnik. Regensberg 1979

Die Gitarre: Grundzuge ihrer Entwicklung. Schott, Mainz, 1988

# JOZEF POWROZNIAK

*Jozef Powrozniak*

Jozef Powrozniak was born in Staniatki on 4 December 1902. For many years he was Poland's foremost guitar historian and a leading teacher of the instrument. He studied music at the Conservatory of Music in Kraków from 1923 to 1925, and at the Institute of Music in Kraków from 1926 toi 1929. Over the years he wrote many publications for the classical guitar, including transcriptions and methods. It has been estimated that over ninety per cent of Polish classical guitar publications have been written or edited by him.

From 1929 Powrozniak taught at the State Academy in Chorzow. He was the Director of Music at the Music Lyceum in Katowice (1949-1951), and Rector of the State Academy of Music in Katowice from 1951 to 1963, and again from 1972 to 1975. He died in Katowice on 10 July 1989.

**SELECTED READING**

Gitarren-Lexicon (German edition). Verlag Neue Musik, Berlin, DDR

# RONALD C. PURCELL

*Ronald Purcell*

Ronald Charles Purcell was born on 5 October 1932 in San Jose, California, USA. He first began to play the guitar at the age of seven, but it was not until he was in Europe at the age of eighteen that he discovered the classical guitar. He started an intense study of the instrument, and among his teachers over the next few years were several notable guitarists including Andrés Segovia, Emilio Pujol, Alirio D,az and Oscar Ghiglia.

Purcell studied at the Free University of Berlin and the Los Angeles Conservatory of Music, where he received his B.M. degree in composition in 1961. He was a composition student of Mario Castelnuovo-Tedesco for a number of years, and he also studied with the noted musicologist of Hispanic music, Mario Santiago Kastner. Ronald Purcell is the author of a book devoted to Segovia's contribution to the guitar, and of a discography of lute and guitar records. He is a regular contributor of articles to guitar magazines including Soundboard. He was appointed President of the American Guitar Society, and he was also the first President of the Guitar Foundation of America, which was founded in 1973. Since 1975 he has acted as the guitar consultant for the publishers Belwin Mills, and has completed more than thirty-five music publications for guitar.

Ronald Purcell is one of the USA's most highly regarded guitar authorities. He currently teaches guitar, lute, vihuela and other courses at the California State University at Northridge.

# HECTOR QUINE

PHOTO: COLIN COOPER

*Hector Quine*

Hector Quine was born in London on 30 December 1926. He received his general education at Hextable College in Kent. He initially studied music privately with Penelope Englehart. Quine, whose principal instrument is the guitar, was appointed Professor of the Guitar at Trinity College of Music in London in 1958. The following year he was Professor at the Royal Academy of Music in London, and from 1966-1980 he was Professor at the Guildhall School of Music in London. From 1954 he was principal guitarist at the Royal Opera House, London.

Hector Quine is highly regarded in Great Britain as a leading teacher and editor of guitar music. For many years he has edited most of the guitar works for Oxford University Press. His works include some studies and exercises for the guitar composed jointly with Stephen Dodgson, the well-known English composer.

**SELECTED READING**

| | |
|---|---|
| Interview. | Guitar International, |
| Interview. | Classical Guitar, August 1990 |

# AARON SHEARER

*Aaron Shearer*

Aaron Shearer was born in Anatone, Washington, USA, on 6 September 1919. His first musical instrument was the harmonica, which he began to play at the age of six. Three years later he took up the guitar. His first interest was hillbilly music but he eventually developed an interest in both classical and jazz guitar styles.

During the 1940s Shearer gave classical recitals but spent most of his time playing jazz in nightclubs in the north west and Los Angeles. In 1949 he suffered a severe case of tendinitis which virtually ended his hopes of a professional playing career. It was then that he decided to embark upon a teaching career.

On the recommendation of Andrés Segovia, Shearer moved to Washington DC to study with Sophocles Papas. He soon joined, with Papas, the faculty of Washington's American University, founding what is claimed to be the first degree course for guitar in the USA. In the mid-1960s Aaron Shearer became a faculty member of the Peabody Conservatory in Maryland, starting the first guitar degree programme there. Since 1981 he has been director of the guitar programme at the North Carolina School of Arts in Winston-Salem. It was in 1959 that Shearer published his first teaching method, which eventually developed into six volumes. It was highly acclaimed, and has been in publication (Belwin Mills) ever since. He has recently completed a new series of method books (Mel Bay) which he believes are much more comprehensive than the original method. Among his many former pupils are some of the best guitarists of the eighties, including Manuel Barrueco, Ricardo Cobo, David Starobin and David Tanenbaum.

**SELECTED READING**

Interview. — Guitar Player, July 1989

**SELECTED MUSIC**

Classic Guitar Technique. — Belwin Mills

Learning the Classic Guitar. (3 Volumes). — Mel Bay

# RICHARD STOVER

*Richard Stover*

Richard Stover was born in Clinton, Iowa, USA, on 11 September 1945. He has been one of the major figures in the rediscovery of most of the guitar works of Agustín Barrios Mangoré, published and distributed worldwide by Belwin Mills.

Stover was brought up in California. He began to study the guitar when he was an exchange student in Costa Rica. On his return to the United States he studied with Japanese guitarist Ako Ito in San Francisco.

In 1966 he travelled to Spain, where he studied with José Tomás at Santiago de Compostela. In 1966-1967 he studied Spanish literature and poetry at the Faculty of Philosophy and Letters at the University of Madrid. During this time he furthered his guitar studies with Jorge Fresno.

In 1967 he travelled throughout Argentina for over a year. On his return to the United States of America he continued his guitar studies at various guitar courses for a period of a few years. In 1969 he studied with Manuel López Ramos, in 1970 with Rey de la Torre, and in 1978 with Leo Brouwer. In 1975, he earned his Bachelor of Arts degree, with an independent major in Latin American Ethnomusicology, at the University of California in Santa Cruz.

Between 1975-1979 Stover was Associate in Music at the University of California, Santa Cruz. At the same time he was a Visiting Lecturer at the Merrill College, UCSC. He currently resides, performs and teaches in California.

Richard Stover founded his own publishing firm, Gringo Publications, some years ago. Through this he edited a large number of compositions for the guitar by a diversity of composers from both South and North America.

He is also a regular broadcaster, author of many articles for guitar magazines, and has appeared in concert in most parts of the North American continent both as a soloist and with his ensemble Los Gringos. He has recently formed a recording company, El Maestro, which has among its releases several important albums including collections of the original recordings of Barrios and Miguel Llobet.

In 1990 Stover was awarded a Fulbright Fellowship to research the life and music of Agustín Barrios Mangoré.

# GRAHAM WADE

*Graham Wade*

Graham Wade was born in Coventry, England, on 18 January 1940. He began playing the guitar in 1953 after first studying the piano. He was educated at Cambridge University, and is a fellow of Trinity College of Music, London. His first teachers included Jerzy Jezewski and Julian Byzantine.

Wade is known internationally as a writer for the guitar. His books have proved important additions to the growing library of guitar literature. His two-volume Guitar Tutor, with recorded cassettes, published by International Correspondence Schools, has sold in fifty countries since 1974. He has contributed many articles for important music periodicals including Classical Guitar, Guitar Review and Music and Musicians, and he is a contributor to the New Grove Dictionary of Musical Instruments. Wade also provided background research for Julian Bream's important television series Guitarra!, and has written sleeve notes for several leading record companies.

Graham Wade has run his own guitar summer school in Lincolnshire since 1972, and has tutored and lectured at many others throughout the world, including the Segovia Masterclass at USCLA in 1985. He is currently Professor of Guitar at the City of Leeds College of Music, and Guitar Tutor for the University of Leeds.

**SELECTED READING**

Traditions of the Classical Guitar. John Calder, 1980
Segovia: A Celebration of the Man and his Music. Allison & Busby, 1983
The Guitarist's Guide to Bach. Wise Owl, 1985
Rodrigo and the Concierto de Aranjuez. Mayflower, 1985
Villa-Lobos and the Guitar – Turibio Santos (Translation by Graham Wade with Victoria Forde). Wise Owl, 1985
Maestro Segovia. Robson Books, 1986
Interview. Classical Guitar, November 1988

# JOSEF ZUTH

*Josef Zuth*

Josef Zuth was born in Fischern, near Karlsbad, Germany on 24 November 1879. He began to study the guitar and mandolin whilst he was employed as a civil servant in Vienna at the beginning of this century. He first studied under J. Krempl in 1908 and then went on to study with Dr. Richard Batka at the university in Vienna. He made such progress that he was appointed professor of guitar in the Volks-hochule, Urania, Vienna in 1918. Amongst his pupils was the prominent Austrian guitarist, Luise Walker. In 1919 Zuth graduated as a Doctor of Philosophy with his thesis on Simon Molitor (1766-1848), the well known Austrian guitarist.

In 1921 Zuth began to edit the guitar magazine, Zeitschrift fur die Gitarre. This was published by Anton Goll who had also published Zuth's thesis on Simon Molitor. In 1928 Zuth began to make regular contributions to other music journals published in Vienna. In 1928 he began to edit for Anton Goll the series Musik im Haus which included many studies on the guitar and its repertoire. In 1928 Zuth's Handbuch der Laute und Gitarre was published. This book was made up of biographies of well-known guitarists and lutenists. Zuth died in Vienna, 3 August 1932.

**SELECTED READING**

Simon Molitor, Viennese Guitarist and Composer Anton Goll, Vienna 1919
Handbuch der Laute und Gitarre Anton Goll, Vienna 1928

# THE FLAMENCO GUITAR

*La Zambra Gitana, 1890*

# THE FLAMENCO GUITAR

The first edition of this book did not include a chapter on the flamenco guitar. This was a conscious decision, for at the time I felt that flamenco was a separate art form, well dealt with in several books covering all the various aspects of this exciting music. I now respect the opinion that there is a place in this book on the classical guitar for a brief chapter on the great flamenco guitar virtuosos. These virtuosos have over the years borrowed from and extended classical guitar techniques in order to develop their own special art, and in turn they have influenced both the music and technique of the modern classical guitar. This chapter is therefore intended as a guide to interested readers to extend their knowledge and appreciation of flamenco. In particular the selected reading, music and recording lists at the end of this chapter are an excellent guide for further information on the best of flamenco and its guitarists.

Flamenco, as we know it today, is not a particularly old art form. Its origins nevertheless do go back to the time when Southern Spain was occupied by the Moors. After the Moors were expelled from Spain by Ferdinand and Isabella in 1492, nomadic bands of Gypsies were forced by a royal edict to settle in Andalusia . Over the next two hundred years these Gypsies developed their own form of music and dance, absorbing aspects of Arab, Christian, Jewish and Spanish folk music into their own traditions. Many historians agree that the original forms of flamenco were sung without instrumental accompaniment but the guitar, the national and most popular instrument of Spain, became an integral part of flamenco. Flamenco as we know it today originated about two hundred years ago, with the guitar acting as an accompaniment instrument only. Over the years brief solo spots for the guitarists became extended as their virtuosity grew. The first great soloist of which we have recorded examples was Ramón Montoya (1880-1949). He was influenced by Patino (1830-1900), Paco Lucena (1859-1898) and Javier Molina (1868-1956), all virtuosos in their own right. But it is Ramón Montoya who is regarded by most aficionados as the father of the solo flamenco guitar, and it is his virtuosic style that has been a source of inspiration to all flamenco guitarists of the twentieth century.

The guitar used by flamenco guitarists is in general appearance not very different from the classical guitar. The size and shape are similar, but it does have a bright, loud and cutting sound, very different from that of the instrument used by classical guitarists. This unique sound is due to its light construction, with a thin spruce top and back and sides of cypress. The flamenco guitar is also fitted with tapping plates (golpeadores) to protect the spruce top from the vigorous finger tapping of the player. Traditionally the flamenco guitar also had distinctive pegs of ebony or rosewood for tightening the strings, instead of the metal machine heads used on the classical guitar. In recent years several prominent flamenco guitarists have begun to use instruments with the dark coloured palo santo wood, instead of cypress, for the back and sides. Such an instrument, with its distinctive sound, is known as a 'guitarra negra'.

**The origin of the word "Flamenco" has been the cause of much debate over the years. Some authorities claim that it is derived from the Arabic "felagmengu" meaning fugitive peasant. Other authorities believe it is derived from the Arabic "felah men ikum" which means "songs of the labourers". This refers to the menial work given to poor uneducated people.*

*Paco Peña's Flamenco Dance Company*

## RAMON MONTOYA

**Born – RAMON MONTOYA SALAZAR**

**Madrid, Spain, 2 November 1880**

**Died – Madrid, 20 July 1949**

*Ramón Montoya*

Ramón Montoya was an exceptional guitarist. A master of his instrument, he is regarded as being responsible for incorporating the tremolo and arpeggios into flamenco guitar technique. He introduced the Rondeña as a solo guitar work and created many falsetas which are still played by flamenco guitarists. His artistry was equal both as a soloist and as an accompanist. He performed on an international basis with singers Antonio Chacon and Aurelio Selle, and with dancers La Joselito and Antonia Merce ('La Argentinita'). In recognition of his great contribution to flamenco, he was known as Don Ramón Montoya.

**SELECTED RECORDINGS**

Ramón Montoya &Manolo de Huelva. Dial Discos 54 9317-18

Flamenquistas Vol.2. Stinson SLPS 34

Ramón Montoya. Chant du Monde CD LDX 274879

## MANOLO de HUELVA

**Born – MANUEL GOMEZ VELEZ**

**Rio Tinto, Spain, 16 November 1892**

**Died – Seville, Spain, 12 May 1976**

*Manolo de Huelva*

Manolo de Huelva was a contemporary of Ramón Montoya, but unlike Montoya was a somewhat introverted and secretive character. His great artistry was recognized by his contemporaries, but there are only a few recorded examples of his work. Huelva preferred to keep the secrets of his artistry as both soloist and accompanist to himself, so that his impact on flamenco guitar was very limited in comparison to Montoya's. Yet aficionados who heard both players play 'live' regard him as Montoya's equal.

**SELECTED RECORDING**

Ramón Montoya & Manolo de Huelva. Dial Discos 54 9317-18

## NIÑO RICARDO

**Born – MANUEL SERRAPI SANCHEZ**

**Seville, Spain, 1 July 1904**

**Died – Seville, 14 April 1972**

*Niño Ricardo*

Niño Ricardo was taught to play the guitar by his father at an early age. He soon showed great talent, and as a teenager was touring the Spanish bullrings in a flamenco show with Ramón Montoya and La Niña de Los Peines. Ricardo was greatly influenced by his teacher Javier Molina. A great accompanist and soloist, Ricardo introduced new chords and harmonies into the flamenco guitar repertoire, so extending the pioneering work of Ramón Montoya. He also introduced a more aggressive approach to soloing which was emphasized by his re-introduction of the dissonant sounds of the Arabic scales. His style became, and remains today, greatly admired by lovers of flamenco all over the world. Niño Ricardo was also a talented and artistic painter.

**SELECTED RECORDINGS**

| | |
|---|---|
| Flamenquistas Vol.2. | Stinson SLPS 34 |
| Toques Flamencos: | Niño Ricardo. Clave 18-1151 |
| Niño Ricardo. | Chant du Monde LDX 4339 |

## MELCHOR DE MARCHENA

**Born – MELCHOR GIMENEZ TORRES**

**Born – Marchena (Seville), Spain, 6 January 1907**

**Died – Seville, 12 March 1980**

*Melchor de Marchena*

Melchor de Marchena was regarded as one of the greatest accompanists for flamenco singers. Throughout his career he was constantly in demand from the finest singers of the day, including Pepe Pinto, Niña de los Peines and Manolo Caracol.

**SELECTED RECORDING**

| | |
|---|---|
| Melchor de Marchena. | Hispavox 53040 32581 |

# SABICAS

**Born – AGUSTIN CASTELLON CAMPOS**

**Pamplona, Spain, 15 March 1912**

**Died – New York, 14 April 1990**

*Sabicas*

By the time he was thirteen Sabicas had already earned himself a high reputation. His talent was quickly recognised by Ramón Montoya and others. Over the years he was to extend and enrich the new flamenco guitar techniques introduced by Montoya and Ricardo. He became a world-famous artist, accompanying the great flamenco names of the day, including Carmen Amaya. At the same time he established himself as one of the great flamenco soloists of all time, inspiring through his many recordings and live performances generations of guitarists right up to the present day. He lived for many years in New York, where he died in 1990.

**SELECTED MUSIC**

| | |
|---|---|
| The Flamenco Art of Sabicas. | Hansen |

**SELECTED RECORDINGS**

| | |
|---|---|
| Sabicas et Mario Escudero. | Barclay 920 176 |
| Flamenco Concerto/Torroba. | Erato EFM 8080 |
| Day of the Bullfight. | ABC Westminster WG 1009 |
| Sabicas. | Hallmark HM 616 |
| Flamenco Fantasy. | MFP 5174 |
| Sabicas. | Polydor 236 561 |

# CARLOS MONTOYA

**Born –**

**Madrid, Spain**

**1904**

*Carlos Montoya*

Although Carlos Montoya is Ramón Montoya's nephew, his artistry has in the main been ignored by serious flamenco aficionados. This is despite the fact that he has worked with many of the legends of flamenco, including Carmen Amaya, Pilar Lopez and La Argentinita. Over the years he has developed his own brilliant style, but for many flamencologists it smacks of showmanship and lacks authenticity. In 1940 Carlos Montoya married and settled in the USA. Within a few years he had become a major recording artist and an international concert artist. His association in 1955 with the dancer Vicente Escudero was a great success.

Despite any reservations about the authenticity of Carlos Montoya's music, few guitarists have done as much to make people around the world aware of flamenco music.

**SELECTED RECORDINGS**

| | |
|---|---|
| Flamenco Fire. | HMV CLP 1177 |
| Adventures in Flamenco. | HMV CLP 1876 |
| Aires Flamenco. | Musidisc CV 1017 |
| Flamenco Holiday. | Everest 2210 |
| Recital de Guitare Espagnole. | Musidisc CV 901 |
| Malagueña. | RCA Victor LSP 2380 |
| Suite Flamenca. | United Artists SULP 1224 |

## MARIO ESCUDERO

**Born –**

**Alicante, Spain**

**11 October 1928**

*Mario Escudero*

Mario Escudero is of Castilian and Gypsy descent. He made his professional debut in concert with Maurice Chevalier at the Cinema Galia in Bordeaux, France. At the age of fourteen he earned the post of main guitarist with the Vicente Escudero Spanish Dance Company on a European concert tour. He has also toured with Carmen Amaya, Antonio, José Greco and Rosario. In the 1950s he decided to make his home in the USA. He soon became a regular artist on both radio and television and made several recordings. In 1965 he returned to Seville, Spain, to live and work there, although he also continues to teach and play in the USA.

**SELECTED MUSIC**

| | |
|---|---|
| The Flamenco Art of Escudero. | Hansen |

**SELECTED RECORDINGS**

| | |
|---|---|
| Mario Escudero. | ABC 396 |
| Escudero at El Poche. | ABC 492 |
| Classical Flamenco Guitar. | WRC ST 1028 |
| Sabicas et Mario Escudero. | Barclay 920 176 |

## PEPE MARTINEZ

**Born –**

**Macarena, Seville, Spain, 1923**

**Died – Seville,18 September 1985**

*Pepe Martínez*

Pepe Martínez was probably the last direct link with Ramón Montoya. He began his professional career as an accompanist in his teens. It was during this time that he met and played with Montoya. Over the years he accompanied top flamenco artists including Manuel Vallejo, Pepe Marchena, Juanito Valderrama, Niña de los Peines and many others. From his mid-thirties he concentrated on a highly successful solo career. From 1959 he began an annual concert tour every autumn of Great Britain. With the help of Ivor Mairants he made two LP recordings for the Fontana label in London; these were to further his international career.

**SELECTED RECORDINGS**

| | |
|---|---|
| The Lyrical Guitar of Pepe Martínez. | Fontana TL 5207 |
| Pepe Martínez. | Decca SA C7811 |
| Alegrías Flamencas. | Concert Hall SVSC 2456 |

# MANUEL CANO

**Born –**

**Granada, Spain, 23 February 1926**

**Died – Granada, 12 January 1990**

*Manuel Cano*

Manuel Cano began to play the guitar at the age of eight. During his youth in Madrid, he studied flamenco and classical guitar with some of the leading guitarists there. He decided to study the traditions of music and flamenco, and moved to Andalusia. In 1959 he recorded his first LP, called 'Suite Granadina y Flamenco Clásico'. Its success led to his first concert appearance in 1960 in Seville, then another in Granada. In 1961 he appeared in the Curso Internacional de Extranjero in Granada, which was to lead to further concert engagements including several in France. From that time Cano led a successful career as a concert and recording artist, appearing many times on television and radio.

**SELECTED RECORDINGS**

Evocation of Ramón Montoya. Musical Heritage MHS 1154
Manuel Cano: Motivos Andaluces/Semblanzas Flamencas. RCA RPL-8180

# JUAN SERRANO

**Born –**

**Córdoba, Spain**

**1936**

*Juan Serrano*

Juan Serrano learned to play the guitar at the age of nine from his father, Antonio del Lunar, who was a well-known guitarist in Córdoba. In 1952 he moved to Madrid to play in the best flamenco night-clubs.

It was here that he met both Manolo de Huelva and Melchor de Marchena. He was soon recognized as one of the best accompanists of the time, and made several recordings with top singers and dancers. But he decided that he would rather have a career as a soloist and, during a visit to the USA with a dance company in 1962, he realized that there was more opportunity to fulfil his ambition there. He settled in New York in 1963, since when he has led a succesful concert, recording and teaching career.

**SELECTED RECORDINGS**

| | |
|---|---|
| La Virtuosa Guitarra. | Philips BBE 12433 |
| Flamenco Fenómeno. | Polydor 236 569 |

**SELECTED MUSIC**

| | |
|---|---|
| Flamenco Guitar Method. | Mel Bay |
| Flamenco Guitar Solos. | Mel Bay |

# PACO PEÑA

**Born –**

**Córdoba, Spain**

**1 June 1942**

PHOTO: COLIN COOPER

*Paco Peña*

Paco Peña learned to play the guitar from an early age. At the age of twelve he began his professional career as an accompanist with various flamenco companies in Spain. After touring the United Kingdom with one of these companies in 1963, he decided to divide his time between London and Spain. In 1966 he settled in London, embarking on a highly successful career as a concert and recording artist, with many television and radio appearances. Since 1980 he has held an annual international festival of guitar in Córdoba, where he now also has a home. His Spanish Dance Company has for many years enjoyed great popularity, both in the United Kingdom and other countries. Although Peña is a flamenco guitarist following in the traditions of Montoya and Ricardo, he continues to extend the boundaries of the audience for flamenco by his long association with the classical guitarist John Williams, and more recently with the Argentinian guitarist Eduardo Falú, the Chilean group Inti-Illimani and others.

**SELECTED RECORDINGS**

| | |
|---|---|
| Fabulous Flamenco. | Decca PFS 4334 |
| The Art of Flamenco Guitar. | Decca PFS 4270 |
| La Gitarra Flamenco. | Decca PFS 4419 |
| Paco Peña Live in London. | Decca MOR 524 |
| Inti-Illimani: Fragments of a Dream. | CBS CD MK 44574 |
| Music of Montoya & Ricardo. | Nimbus NI 5093 |
| Azahara. | Nimbus NI 5116 |
| Encuentro with Eduardo Falú. | Nimbus NI 5196 |
| Misa Flamenca. | Nimbus NI 5288 |

# ANDRÉS BATISTA

**Born –**

**Barcelona, Spain**

**12 October 1939**

*Andrés Batista*

Andrés Batista studied classical guitar from the age of ten with Antonio Francisco Serra, and flamenco guitar with Miguel Borrull Jnr. Over the years he has accompanied many of the top figures in flamenco including Carmen Amaya, Vicente Escudero and Maria Marquez. Since 1960 he has been a member of the Spanish Society of Authors and has made twelve recordings. He has received many awards, including a gold record from the radio station 'The Voice of Madrid'. He lives in Madrid, combining a career as a composer, guitarist and teacher.

**SELECTED RECORDING**

| | |
|---|---|
| Guitarra Flamenca: Andres Batista. | EMI PCS 7028 |

**SELECTED MUSIC**

| | |
|---|---|
| Flamenco Guitar Method. | UME |

# PACO DE LUCIA

**Born – FRANCISCO SANCHEZ PECINO**

**Algeciras, Spain**

**21 December 1947**

**SELECTED RECORDINGS**

| | |
|---|---|
| Recital de Guitarra Paco de Lucia. | Philips 63 28 036 |
| El Duende Flamenco. | Philips 63 28 061 |
| Almoraima. | Philips 63 28 199 |
| Paco de Lucia interpreta Manuel de Falla. | Philips 91 13 008 |
| Garcia Lorca: Douze Chansons pour 2 Guitares. | Philips 6599 856 |
| Entre Dos Aguas. | Philips CD 814 106-2 |

*Paco de Lucia*

Paco de Lucia is generally regarded as the dominant flamenco figure of the sixties, seventies and eighties. Born into a flamenco family, Lucia began to play the guitar at the age of seven. His father, Antonio Sanchez Pecino, was a semi-professional guitarist who recognized his son's natural talents. He ensured that his son spent all his spare hours practising and developing one of the greatest flamenco guitar techniques the world has yet seen. Lucia began his professional career by appearing in a guitar duo with his brother Ramón. He also appeared with his brother Pepe, a singer, in a duo called Los Chiquitos de Algeciras. This duo entered the Jerez Concurso in 1962 and both young brothers won important awards. Success followed success, and over the years Paco de Lucia has become a major international star with a huge following. He became a major innovator in the world of flamenco by introducing Latin American and jazz harmonies into flamenco, and in so doing influenced a whole new generation of young flamenco guitarists. His television and concert appearances all over the world with jazz/rock guitarists John McLaughlin, Larry Coryell and Al Di Meola have given flamenco a wide international audience. A prolific recording artist, Paco de Lucia is sure to be a major figure in flamenco for many years to come.

# MANOLO SANLUCAR

**Born – MANUEL MUNOZ**

**Sanlúcar de Barrameda, Spain**

**24 November 1943**

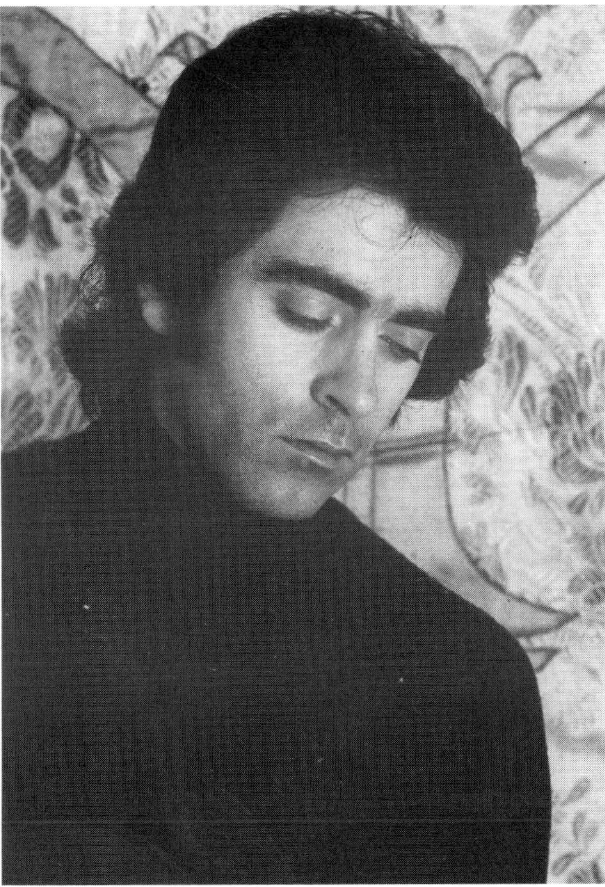

*Manolo Sanlúcar*

Manolo Sanlúcar first learnt the guitar with his father. By the time he was thirteen he was already serving his apprenticeship, accompanying singers that included Pepe Pinto, Antonio Canillas, La Paquera and others. As his career developed, the young guitarist decided to become a soloist. In 1972 he won the prestigious guitar prize of the Jerez Catedra de Flamencologia. He had already made some recordings, but with this competition success he soon earned a recording contract with CBS and later with RCA. Since that time Sanlucar has become established as one of the best of the new breed of flamenco guitarists. Like Paco de Lucia, he has introduced other music forms, including jazz, into his flamenco style.

Sanlúcar has recorded a concerto for flamenco guitar and orchestra on the RCA label. Since 1981 he has recorded for the Philips label.

**SELECTED RECORDINGS**

| | |
|---|---|
| Sentimiento. | CBS NL 35413 |
| Manolo Sanlúcar: Flamenco. | CBS 73488 |
| Fantasía para guitarra y orquesta. | RCA PL 35172 |
| Azahares. | RCA PL 35350 |

# SERRANITO

**Born –**

**VICTOR LUIS MONGE FERNANDEZ**

**Madrid, Spain, 16 July 1942**

*Serranito*

Serranito first studied the guitar with his father. By the age of ten he had already made some public performances, and at eighteen was recognized as a talented guitarist. In 1968 he made his first solo recording, and a successful European concert tour followed in 1970. In 1971 he had two major competition successes, the 'Premio Nacional de Guitarra Flamenca' of the Catedra de Flamencologia de Jerez, and the 'Primer premio Guitarra Flamenca de Concierto'. Serranito won the latter at the fifth Concurso Nacional de Arte Flamenco held in Córdoba. Since these achievements he has enjoyed fame both in Spain and abroad as one of the finest flamenco guitarists of the day.

**SELECTED RECORDINGS**

| | |
|---|---|
| El Flamenco en La Guitarra de Serranito. | Hispavox HH 10-251 |
| Victor Monge: 'Serranito'. | Decca PFS-R 4415 |
| Virtuosismo Flamenco. | Hispavox HH 10-349 |
| Victor Monge: 'Serranito'. | Columbia TXS 3217 |
| Tensión de Sonoridades para dos Guitarras. | Hispavox HH 10-300 |

# THE FLAMENCO GUITAR

## Selected Reading


*Arte y Artistas Flamencos – Fernando el de Triana – Editoriales Andaluzas Unidas SA, 1935*
*Lives & Legends of Flamenco: Donn E.Pohren – Society of Spanish Studies, 1964*
*The Flamenco Guitar: David George – Society of Spanish Studies, 1971*
*The Art of Flamenco: Donn E. Pohren – Society of Spanish Studies, 1972*
*A Way of Life: Donn E. Pohren – Society of Spanish Studies, 1980*
*The Flamencos of Cadiz Bay: Gerald Howson – Hutchinson, 1965*
*Manuel Flamenco: Andrés Batista – UMP, 1985*
*Flamenco, Kunst Zwischen Gestern Und Morgen: Anja Vollhardt – Weingarten, 1988*
*Flamenco, Body and Soul: An Aficionado's Introduction; Serrano/Elgorriaga – Fresno, California, 1990*


## Selected Music


*El Arte Flamenco de la Guitarra: Juan Martín – UMP*
*Metodo de Guitarra Flamenca: Andrés Batista – UME*
*Toques Flamencos: Paco Peña – Music Sales*
*Flamenco Guitar Method: Ivor Mairants – Music Sales*
*Sabicas & Escudero Solos – Hansen*
*Pepe Martínez Guitar Solos – Schott*
*The Exciting Sound of Flamenco: Juan Martín (2 Vols.) – UMP*
*Authentic Flamenco Guitar Transcriptions (3 Vols.) – Gendai Guitar*
*Flamenco Method: Juan Serrano – Mel Bay*
*Flamenco Concert Selections: Juan Serrano – Mel Bay*

# THE CLASSICAL GUITAR

## ITS PLAYERS AND ITS PERSONALITIES SINCE 1800

## INDEX

## ITS DUOS, TRIOS, QUARTETS & MORE



## ITS COMPOSERS



## ITS GUITAR MAKERS



## ITS SCHOLARS



## THE FLAMENCO GUITAR

# SOURCES OF INFORMATION AND SUPPLIES

## GUITAR MAGAZINES

Acoustic Guitar,
412 Red Hill Avenue #15,
San Anselmo,
California 94960,
USA

Australian Guitar Journal,
PO Box 355,
Malvern,
Victoria 3144,
Australia

Classical Guitar,
Olsover House,
43 Sackville Road,
Newcastle upon Tyne,
NE6 5TA,
United Kingdom

Frets,
6-1 Chome,
Umegawacho,
500 Gifu City, Japan

Il Fronimo,
Edizioni Zerboni,
Via M. F. Quintiliano 40,
20138 Milano,
Italy

Gendai Guitar,
1-11 Chihay-cho,
Ikebukuro,
Toshima-ku,
Tokyo,
Japan

Gitarr och Luta,
c/o Erik Mollerström,
Ostermalmsgaten 5,
S-114 4 Stockholm,
Sweden

Gitarre & Laute,
Postfach 410408,
5000 Köln,
W. Germany

Guild of American Luthiers,
8222 S. Park Place,
Tacoma,
WA 98408,
USA

Guitar Extra,
Cherry Lane Music Company,
12 Midland Avenue,
Port Chester,
NY 10573 1490,
USA

Guitar International,
Manor Road,
Mere,
Wiltshire
BA12 6HZ,
United Kingdom

Guitares,
Karel Gilsonstraat 9,
1601 Ruisbroek,
Belgium

Guitar Maker,
Association of String Instrument Artisans,
14 South Broad Street,
Nazareth,
PA 18064,
USA

Guitar Player,
20085 Stevens Creek,
Cupertino,
CA 95014, USA

Guitar Review,
40 W. 25th Street,
New York
NY 10010,
USA

Guitarra,
3145 W. 63rd Street,
Chicago
IL 50629,
USA

Journal of Guitar Acoustics,
146 Lull Road,
New Boston
NH 03070,
USA

Les Cahiers de la Guitarre,
BP83,
94472 Boissy-St-Lèger,
Cedex,
Paris,
France

Musikblatt,
Tannenweg 14,
3400 Göttingen,
W. Germany

Nova Giulianiad,
Lessingstrasse 4,
D-7800 Freiburg-i-Br,
W. Germany

Seicorde,
Via della Commenda, 28 20122,
Milan, Italy

Soundboard (GFA),
Box 1090A,
Garden Grove,
CA 92642,
USA

# RETAIL SUPPLIERS OF CLASSICAL GUITARS, BOOKS, RECORDS, MUSIC

## GREAT BRITAIN

Blackwells Music Shop,
38 Holywell Street,
Oxford
OX1 3SW
*Books/music*

Bristol Spanish Guitar Centre,
2 Elton Road,
Bristol BS7 8DA
*Guitars/music/books/recordings*

Chappells,
New Bond Street,
London WC1
*Guitars/music/books*

English Guitar Centre,
3rd Floor,
St Michael's Chambers,
Spurriergate,
York YO1 1QR
*Guitars/music/books/recordings*

Forsyths,
126 Deansgate,
Manchester M3 2GR
*Guitars/music/books/recordings*

W. & G. Foyle Ltd,
119-125 Charing Cross Road,
London WC2
*Books/music/recordings*

Guitar Record Centre,
9 The Drive,
Kingsley,
Northampton
*Extensive mail order catalogue of recordings*

HMV Record Shop,
150 & 363 Oxford Street,
London WC1
*Specialist recordings*

London Guitar Studio,
16 James Street,
London W1
*Guitars/music/books/recordings*

Ivor Mairants Musicentre,
56 Rathbone Place,
London W1P 1AB
*Guitars/music/books/recordings*

May & May,
Arundell House,
Tisbury,
Salisbury SP3 6QU
*Mail order.*
*New, secondhand and rare books on music.*

Nottingham Spanish Guitar Centre,
44 Nottingham Road,
New Basford,
Nottingham
NG7 7AE
*Guitars/music/books/recordings*

Gordon Simpson Ltd,
6-8 Stratford Place,
Edinburgh EH3 7AY
*Guitars/music/books*

Spanish Guitar Centre,
36 Cranbourn Street,
London WC2 7AD
*Guitars/music/books/recordings*

Tower Records,
1 Piccadilly Circus,
London W1
*Specialist recordings*

J.G.Windows Ltd,
1-7 Central Arcade,
Newcastle upon Tyne
NE1
*Guitars/music/books/recordings*

## UNITED STATES OF AMERICA

Barnes & Noble,
128 5th Avenue,
New York
*Books/music/recordings*

The Bold Strummer,
1 Webb Road,
Westport, CT 06880
*Mail order – books/music*

Jack Cecchini Guitar Studios,
5344 N. Magnolia,
Chicago,
Illinois
*Guitars/music/books*

Guitar Studio,
1433 Clement Street,
San Francisco,
CA 94118
*Guitars/books/music/recordings*

Editions Orphée Inc.,
PO Box 21291,
Columbus,
Ohio 43221
*Mail order – books/music/recordings*

Joseph Patelson Music House,
160 West 56th Street,
New York NY 10019
*Books/music/recordings*

Rose Discount Record Store,
165 West Madison,
Chicago,
Illinois
*Recordings*

Sherry Brener Ltd,
3145 West 63rd Street,
Chicago,
Illinois
*Guitars/music/books*

Tower Records,
at Lincoln Centre and Greenwich
Village, New York
*Recordings*

## CANADA

Eli Kassner Guitar Academy,
19 Belmont Street,
Toronto
*Guitars/music/books*

## FRANCE

FNAC. Several stores in Paris including
Rue de Rennes and Les Halles Forum
Centre
*Recordings/books*

La Guitarreria,
5 Rue d'Edimbourg,
75008 Paris
*Guitars/music/books*

La Libraire Musicale de Paris,
68 bis Rue Réaumur, 75003
Paris
*Books/music*

## BELGIUM

Uni-Sound BVBA,
St Jacobstraat 13,
8000 Bruges
*Books/music/recordings*

## GERMANY

Chanterelle Verlag,
Postfach 103909,
D-6900 Heidelberg
*Mail order – books/music/recordings*

Steinway House,
Colonnaden 29,
2000 Hamburg
*Guitars/music/books/recordings*

Heiner Viertmann,
Beethovenstrasse 27,
Postfach 260128,
5000 Köln 1
*Guitars/music/books/recordings*

## ITALY

Hortus Musicus,
Viale Liegi 7,
Rome 00198
*Music/books/recordings*

G.Ricordi & Co.,
Via Salomone 77,
Milan
*Guitars/music/books/recordings*

## SPAIN

Bowden Music,
Calle Huerto de Torella 13,
Palma de Mallorca
*Guitars/music/books/recordings*

Casa Luthier,
Balmes 77, 08007
Barcelona
*Guitars/music/books/recordings*

Manuel Rodríguez,
Hortaleza 26,
Madrid 28004
*Guitars/music/books/recordings*

## JAPAN

ARP International,
2-24-13 Kamisaginomiya,
Nakano-ku,
Tokyo 165
*Music/books/recordings*

Yamaha Music Store,
Central Ginza, Tokyo
and branches throughout Japan
*Guitars/music/books/recordings*

## MALAYSIA

Mahogany House of Guitars,
43 Jin SS/23/5,
Tamamn S.E.A., 47301,
Petaling Jaya,
Selangor
*Guitars/music/books/recordings*

## NETHERLANDS

Broekmans & Van Poppel,
Baerlestraat, 92-04,
Amsterdam Z
*Books/music*

La Guitarra Buena,
Reestraat 14,
1016 DN Amsterdam
*Guitars/music/books/recordings*

## SWEDEN

Gitarren AB,
Skanstorget 10,
Gothenburg
*Guitars/music/books/recordings*

Musikerma Evert Ahlander,
Box 184,
Bondegatan 20,
S 561 23 Huskvarna

## SWITZERLAND

Aux Gitarres,
Theatrestrasse 7/3,
CH-4051 Basel
*Guitars/music/books*

Music Hug,
Limmatquai 26-28,
8001 Zürich
*Guitars/music/books/recordings*

## AUSTRALIA

Rick Falkiner Guitar Centre
30 Oxford Street,
Paddington,
N.S.W.
*Guitars/music/books/recordings*